POPULATION AND POVERTY IN THE
DEVELOPING WORLD

international union
for the scientific study
of population

The International Union for the Scientific Study of Population Problems was set up in 1928, with Dr Raymond Pearl as President. At that time the Union's main purpose was to promote international scientific co-operation to study the various aspects of population problems, through national committees and through its members themselves. In 1947 the International Union for the Scientific Study of Population (IUSSP) was reconstituted into its present form.

It expanded its activities to:

- stimulate research on population
- develop interest in demographic matters among governments, national and international organizations, scientific bodies, and the general public
- foster relations between people involved in population studies
- disseminate scientific knowledge on population

The principal ways through which the IUSSP currently achieves its aims are:

- organization of worldwide or regional conferences
- operations of Scientific Committees under the auspices of the Council
- organization of training courses
- publication of conference proceedings and committee reports.

Demography can be defined by its field of study and its analytical methods. Accordingly, it can be regarded as the scientific study of human populations primarily with respect to their size, their structure, and their development. For reasons which are related to the history of the discipline, the demographic method is essentially inductive: progress in knowledge results from the improvement of observation, the sophistication of measurement methods, and the search for regularities and stable factors leading to the formulation of explanatory models. In conclusion, the three objectives of demographic analysis are to describe, measure, and analyse.

International Studies in Demography is the outcome of an agreement concluded by the IUSSP and the Oxford University Press. The joint series is expected to reflect the broad range of the Union's activities and, in the first instance, will be based on the seminars organized by the Union. The Editorial Board of the series is comprised of:

John Cleland, UK   Henri Leridon, France
John Hobcraft, UK   Richard Smith, UK
Georges Tapinos, France

Population and Poverty in the Developing World

Edited by

MASSIMO LIVI-BACCI
GUSTAVO DE SANTIS

CLARENDON PRESS • OXFORD
1998

Oxford University Press, Great Clarendon Street, Oxford OX2 6DP

Oxford New York

Athens Auckland Bangkok Bogotá Buenos Aires Calcutta
Cape Town Chennai Dar es Salaam Delhi Florence Hong Kong Istanbul
Karachi Kuala Lumpur Madrid Melbourne Mexico City Mumbai
Nairobi Paris São Paulo Singapore Taipei Tokyo Toronto Warsaw
and associated companies in Berlin Ibadan

Oxford is a registered trade mark of Oxford University Press

Published in the United States
by Oxford University Press Inc., New York

© IUSSP 1999

The moral rights of the author have been asserted

First published 1999

British Library Cataloguing in Publication Data

Data available

Library of Congress Cataloging in Publication Data

Population and poverty in the developing world/edited by Massimo
Livi-Bacci, Gustavo De Santis.
p. cm.—(International studies in demography)
Includes bibliographical references.
1. Developing countries—Population—Congresses. 2. Poor—
Developing countries—Congresses. I. Livi Bacci, Massimo. II. De
Santis, Gustavo. III. Series.
HB884.P66247 1999
363.9'09172'4—DC21 98–28485

0–19–829300–3

1 2 3 4 5 6 7 8 9 10

Typeset in 10/12pt Times
by Cambrian Typesetters, Frimley, Surrey

Printed in Great Britain
on acid-free paper by
Biddles Limited, Guildford and King's Lynn

Contents

List of Contributors

Sudhir Anand	St Catherine's College, Oxford, and Harvard Center for Population and Development Studies
Alaka Malwade Basu	Division of Nutritional Science, Cornell University
F. Branca	National Institute of Nutrition, Rome
Giovanni Andrea Cornia	United Nations University/World Institute for Development Economics Research (UNU/WIDER), Helsinki
Patricia H. David	Population Reference Bureau, Washington, DC
Gustavo De Santis	Department of Statistics, University of Messina
A. Ferro-Luzzi	National Institute of Nutrition, Rome
Anastasia J. Gage	Population Leadership Program, The Public Health Institute
Michael Lipton	Poverty Research Unit, University of Sussex
Massimo Livi-Bacci	Department of Statistics, University of Florence
Cynthia B. Lloyd	The Population Council, New York
Jonathan Morduch	Department of Economics, Harvard University, and Harvard Institute for International Development
Christine Oppong	International Labour Office, Geneva
S. R. Osmani	School of Public Policy, Economics, and Law, University of Ulster
Renato Paniccià	IRPET, Florence
David Satterthwaite	International Institute for Environment and Development, London
Réne Wéry	International Labour Office, Geneva

List of Figures

List of Tables

1 Introduction

GUSTAVO DE SANTIS AND MASSIMO LIVI BACCI

By the end of 1994, much had already been said on poverty. However, it was felt that not all its causes and consequences had been fully analysed, and, also, that the specialized literature—sometimes excessively refined, formalized, and segmented in different disciplines—left perhaps three majors gaps to be filled: one between the various specialized circles concerned with poverty, which only rarely try to exchange views on the subject; another between scholars and the 'public' in the developed world, who, more often than not, feel that poverty, especially in the developing world, is not their concern; and another between what 'experts' say, and what politicians can (or want to) understand.

Demographers, and their leading international organization, IUSSP (the International Union for the Scientific Study of Population), felt that their research could contribute to fill these gaps on poverty: not only in descriptive terms (who, how many, and where the poor are), not only assessing the consequences of destitution on demographic outcomes and behaviours (mortality and health, family and fertility, mobility and migration), but also in trying to assess the mechanisms that generate poverty or provide an escape from it. Having children too early or at too short intervals, becoming an orphan or a widow, losing a supportive member of kin, or experiencing impaired health are all occurrences that do not necessarily depend on the level of wellbeing but certainly may have an impact on it. The reverse is also true: types of family organization, marriage strategies, and decisions to move or settle elsewhere are all demographic factors that may mitigate or overcome situations of destitution.

Demographers are well aware of the intricate causes of life changes and are able to analyse their poverty-generating potential. With these goals in mind, and on the initiative of IUSSP, UNICEF's Child Development Centre, and the University of Florence, a seminar on 'Population and Poverty' was convened in Florence (Italy) in March 1995, where demographers, economists, and, more generally, social scientists, all tried to find a common basis, including a common language, from which to start to make their point clear, first to the rest of the audience, and then, also, to the rest of the world. What transpired from the joint efforts was an apparently successful—or certainly, a potentially fruitful—experiment in striving towards a common end: a deeper understanding of the nature, causes, and consequences of poverty and destitution, with the ultimate goal of its eradication. As is often the case with multi-disciplinary, multi-authored and multi-country books coming out of conferences, this one too has suffered considerable delay before it could be published. This means that the bibliographical references given here may no longer be totally up to date but does not, in our view, undermine the basic ideas offered, which appear to us to be still original and valid.

One of the most striking contradictions that emerge in discussions on poverty is between the clear-cut evidence with which poverty sometimes manifests itself in life and the evasiveness of the concept, once one tries to define it with some degree of precision. The definition is perhaps more complex in the case of relative poverty, when one tries to identify a dividing line between those who have enough resources to be fully part of the community in which they live, and those who don't. But the contradiction is much more striking, and indeed disturbing, when it comes to absolute poverty, concerning those who do not have enough to live on, which is precisely the concept this book tries to focus on.

Most, if not all, authors agree that being poor, even being absolutely poor, is a complex, multidimensional state. But agreement ceases when it comes to defining exactly what dimensions are to be included in the concept and in its measurement, and how to handle the inescapable multicolinearity that results from collapsing several conceptually related variables (say: insufficient income, poor health, illiteracy, and so forth) into just one: poverty.

At the risk of oversimplification, three main lines of thought may perhaps be identified. One is to value especially the range of choices that a 'standard' individual or household may have in a given country at a given moment, and to identify poverty as the prime factor responsible for the restriction of this range. It will be noted, incidentally, that this approach tends to blur the difference between absolute and relative poverty. One problem, here, is that, arguably, the reverse causal order may also work: it is precisely their limited access to social contacts, and their limited capability of tapping such opportunities as job vacancies, health assistance, and the like that keeps poor people in poverty, and puts them at risk (see David, Chapter 7 below). But the main shortcoming of this otherwise intellectually stimulating approach is that it is almost impossible to translate it into sensible empirical indicators: how should one measure a 'range of possible choices'?

So, a second attempt at defining poverty focuses on money (ideally income, in practice often expenditure) and interprets it as a proxy for the potential range of choices referred to above. The basic idea is that (almost) everything can be bought on the market, and that the more money they have, the less likely individuals are to be 'needy': what they need, they can buy.

This vision, which has long been dominant, and is perhaps still so, has many advantages, but it also suffers from several shortcomings. In the first place it ignores the fact that people are not all equal and that the same amount of money may not mean the same once it is related to different initial needs. In principle, one could take these differences into account by using equivalent coefficients (and adjust for, say, different family size, or health conditions), but, in practice, to determine exactly what these coefficients are is extremely difficult and, ultimately, cannot be done objectively; there will always be recourse to value judgements. Unfortunately, these value judgements, and the coefficients that result from them, may vary considerably, and may change dramatically the picture of who is well-off and who is poor (see Anand and Morduch, Chapter 2, and Lipton, Chapter 3, below).

Even more importantly, a great number of the things people need for living, and for living well, are not formally bought on the market, especially in the developing world, where the poverty issue is much more relevant than anywhere else. More often than not, self-consumption, barter, traditions, clan membership, gender, age, and many other non-(formal) market variables determine what an individual can obtain from the local community, and how well off he or she will be. Money is just an instrumental variable, one among many, and quite often not the most important.

So, a third line of reasoning has been suggested: since it is impossible to gauge all of the possible instruments an individual may have at his or her disposal (which is practically the same, and as hard, as measuring his or her range of possibilities), it may well be better to measure results: a poor performance is the best indicator of poverty. Unfortunately, this idea too is fraught with difficulties. The first is that, before results can be observed, sufficient time must pass, so that everybody may express his or her potentialities. When finally there are suffcient elements to allow an answer to the question (was that person poor?), it is generally too late, especially if the aim is to combat poverty, not just observe it.

To put it differently, this approach doesn't generally work at the individual level. So, what one can do is to assume that certain types of individual are homogeneous (say: those who share at least one common characteristic, because they live in the same country or village, or belong to the same ethnic group, and so forth), and measure the outcome of that group as a whole. But what kind of outcome? Several variables may initially be considered appropriate in this respect, but most of them do not work well, because they depend not only on the resources that individuals may or may not have, but also on tastes, traditions, local habits, climate, and so forth. So what is required for this kind of exercise is results that it may safely be assumed everybody would like: for example, longevity, or being healthy, well nourished or well educated. Needless to say, these are not influenced by poverty alone; biology, climate, and a number of other hidden factors also play their part, and blur the picture.

It is often the case that, when two approaches to the study of a problem exist, and neither can be universally claimed as preferable, both are retained. So, in most publications (see, for example, UNDP, 1997; World Bank 1997a,b) income-poverty measures coexist with indicators of other dimensions of poverty, such as low education, insufficient access to safe water, or to food and health services, and high mortality.[1] Some selected figures, which may constitute a useful background to the papers presented in this volume, are reported in Table 1.1. on page 4.

---

[1] Actually, these dimensions combine to form what the UNDP (1997) calls the Human Poverty Index (HPI), conceptually very similar to the Human Development Index (HDI) that the UNDP itself calculates yearly. The main conceptual difference is that the income dimension is excluded from the HPI but included in the HDI.

Table 1.1. Selected economic and demographic indicators for selected regions of the world

	Land Sq. km (,000) 1994 (1)	Arable (%) 1994 (2)	Population (millions) 1980 (3)	1995 (4)	2010 (5)	People per sq km Total 1995 (6)	Arable 1995 (7)	Avg. annual growth rate (%) 1980–95 (8)	1995–2010 (9)	Urban pop. Share (%) 1980 (10)	1995 (11)	Rate of growth 1980–95 (12)	Total fertility rate 1980 (13)	1995 (14)	Life expectancy at birth (Females) 1980 (15)	1995 (16)	Infant mortality rate per 1000 1995 (17)
World	130,314	10	4,430	5,672	6,850	44	435	1.7	1.3	40	45	2.5	3.7	2.9	64	69	55
Low and middle income	99,442	10	3,614	4,770	5,887	48	480	1.9	1.4	32	39	3.2	4.1	3.1	59	66	60
East Asia and Pacific	15,869	10	1,360	1,706	1,974	108	1,075	1.5	1.0	21	31	4.2	3.1	2.2	66	70	40
Europe and Central Asia	24,114	12	437	488	511	20	169	0.7	0.3	58	65	1.5	2.5	2.0	72	73	26
Latin America and the Caribbean	20,064	6	358	478	587	24	397	1.9	1.4	65	74	2.8	4.0	2.8	68	72	37
Middle East and North Africa	10,992	5	175	272	383	25	495	3.0	2.3	48	57	4.2	6.1	4.2	60	68	54
South Asia	4,775	43	903	1,243	1572	260	605	2.2	1.6	22	26	3.3	5.3	3.5	54	62	75
Sub-Saharan Africa	23,628	6	381	583	860	25	411	2.9	2.6	23	31	4.9	6.7	5.7	49	53	92
High income	30,872	12	816	902	963	29	243	0.7	0.4	75	78	0.9	1.9	1.7	77	81	7

	Pop. living on less than US$1 a day (Millions) 1987 (18)	1993 (19)	Share of pop. (%) 1987 (20)	1993 (21)	Estimated illiterate pop. aged 15 and above (millions) 1980 (22)	1995 (23)	Pop. with access to safe water (%) 1994–5 (24)	Adult HIV-1 sero-prevalence (%) 1994 (25)	Malnourished children <5 years (millions) 1990–6 (26)	Commercial energy use (kg. of oil equiv. per capita) 1980 (27)	1994 (28)	GDP per capita (current US$) 1980 (29)	1995 (30)	Avg. annual GDP growth (constant prices) (%) 1980–90 (31)	1990–5 (32)	1980–5 (33)
World	1,227.2	1,313.9	30.1	29.4	847.8	874.3	76	0.6	n.a.	1,419	1,433	2,472	4,915	3.1	2.0	2.7
Low and middle income							56	0.6	158	686	739	883	1,131	2.8	2.1	2.6
East Asia and Pacific	464.0	445.8	28.8	26.0	276.1	209.9	49	0.1	37	378	593	342	786	7.6	10.3	8.5
Europe and Central Asia	2.2	14.5	0.6	3.5	n.a.	n.a.	n.a.	0.0	n.a.	3,105	2,647	2,276	2,261	2.3	-6.5	-0.7
Latin America and the Caribbean	91.2	109.6	22.0	23.5	44.1	42.9	80	0.5	5	888	960	2,119	3,532	1.7	3.2	2.2
Middle East and North Africa	10.3	10.7	4.7	4.1	55.8	65.5	85	0.0	5	825	1,220	2,646	1,928	0.2	2.3	0.9
South Asia	479.9	514.7	45.4	43.1	345.9	415.5	63	0.3	82	123	222	243	353	5.7	4.6	5.3
Sub-Saharan Africa	179.6	218.6	38.5	39.1	125.9	140.5	47	4.3	29	249	237	768	509	1.7	1.4	1.6
High income	n.a.	n.a.	n.a.	n.a.	n.a.	n.a.	94	0.3		4,644	5,066	9,507	24,929	3.2	2.0	2.8

Note: n.a.: Not applicable/not available

Columns (18)–(21): US$1, 1985 prices, PPP used as conversion factor.

Source: World Bank (1997) and own elaborations [(26): UNDP 1997].

While there are still enormous cross-regional (and, obviously, still greater cross-country) differences, there is also a common trend towards overall better living conditions in most parts of the world. Life expectancy is increasing (columns 15 and 16), even in sub-Saharan Africa, where it is by far the lowest in the world (53 years for females). So what are the chances that a new-born infant survives his or her first birthday: infant mortality is nowadays less than 10 per cent in sub-Saharan Africa, and lower still elsewhere in the developing world (column 17).

Gross domestic product (GDP) has generally grown in the last 15 years (columns 31–3), although with exceptions. One of the most remarkable is that of Eastern Europe, where the abrupt transition from state to market economy of the late 1980s and early 1990s has provoked serious social and economic imbalances (discussed by Cornia and Paniccià in Chapter 12 below). However, in some regions, and again notably in sub-Saharan Africa, the annual rate of population growth (columns 8–9) has exceeded that of GDP, thus causing per-capita GDP to decline in real terms, and the number of poor to increase.

While some indicators allow comparisons over a relatively long span of time (notice, for instance, the increase in the use of energy per-capita and the increasing number—but relatively steady proportion—of illiterate people), others are available only for shorter periods, or just at one point in time, and do not reveal trends. Among these are the number of malnourished children (column 26), the share of population having access to safe water (column 24), and the number and proportion of individuals living on less than a dollar a day.[2] As for the latter, there are some indications that their share has been slightly decreasing recently; however, their absolute number is still rising and in 1993 over 1.3 billion people were estimated to live on the verge of starvation.

We have rapidly reviewed the main strands of thought on the definition of poverty, but, how is the issue approached in practice? Here, again, at the risk of oversimplification, it is possible to distinguish four basic approaches, different in principle but mixed in practice. The first is purely descriptive: the purpose is simply to identify the poor and to measure how many and how poor they are, either at the macro or at the micro level. This is a necessary first step before any other operation can be attempted, but, as suggested above, it is so complicated that it defies even the best-equipped research team. The choice of the dimensions in which to operate, the way in which the results are combined, the choice of the equivalent coefficients— or, indeed, of the procedures to estimate them—the definition of the length of time, and many more such difficulties may create formidable obstacles.

As suggested, to overcome most of these problems it is often necessary to resort to subjective choices, which may leave other researchers dissatisfied. Let us mention just one: the size of the household is almost always adjusted for with equivalent coefficients in this kind of study, and we have already mentioned just how difficult it is to estimate them correctly, and how the picture may change according to the results obtained. But what if the characteristics of the households people live

---

[2] 1985 US dollars, using PPP (parity purchasing powers) as conversion factors.

in are (at least partly) chosen by the individuals themselves, and can no longer be considered as reflecting pre-existing needs? Indeed, people have only limited choice as to their families, but they have much more freedom to choose their households, as Lloyd, and Wéry and Oppong very aptly underline (see Chapters 6 and 10 below). Structures and dimensions vary during, and according to, the phases of the life cycle and the business cycle. Households are formed, expanded, reduced, and dissolved, not quite 'at will', but much more so than might ordinarily be assumed. How does one take this into account when studying poverty?

The second approach focuses on the effects of poverty, which are also often the indicators used to identify poverty. Among these rank, as we have seen before, illiteracy, retarded physical and mental growth (see Lipton, and Ferro-Luzzi and Branca, Chapters 3 and 4 below), impaired earning potentials (Lipton, Chapter 3), high fertility and high mortality (Osmani, David, Gage, Basu, Wéry and Oppong, Chapters 5, 8, 9, and 10).

Unfortunately, these factors also rank among the causes of poverty—the third possible approach—and, needless to say, confound the picture. What causes what? And, in both cases, should one privilege the micro or the macro approach? Both run the risk of being interpreted as ideologically biased. By adopting the first, one may be thought to assume that it is the individual or the household level that really matters and even, maybe, that the poor are primarily responsible for their state: they have too many children, they fail to migrate to places where jobs are available, and so forth. By adopting the macro approach, on the other hand, one may be thought to imply that it is some higher aggregation level that actually counts, be it community, society, country, or whatever. To try to combine the two plans seems the obvious answer, but, as in most other cases, this is more easily said than done.

Finally, the fourth approach is that generally adopted by authorities and agencies: they would like to eradicate poverty and destitution, both short- and long-term, and would like scholars to produce simple analyses and effective prescriptions. They are also interested in assessing the links between population change, at the macro level, and poverty, and wish to understand whether a too rapid demographic growth, by impeding economic development, depleting non-renewable resources or otherwise deteriorating the environment, may itself be ranked among the causes of poverty. Can the Malthusian trap be avoided with modern population policies?

Obviously, as mentioned, these approaches may be conceptually distinguishable, but in practice they are strictly interrelated: why combat poverty if one doesn't know its effects (as distinguished from those of, say, tradition, climate, religious practices, and so forth)? How to combat it if one ignores its causes? And how to identify it if one can't even come out with a proper definition of it?

The answer, which has long been known, is to build a complex multidirectional model of causation, with poverty at its centre, and all the related variables properly connected. Often, however, identifying and testing the correct causal chains turns out to be problematic: quality of data, time lags, measurement errors, exceptional events, local peculiarities, all conspire against the identification of a simple, ever-valid model. This is not to say that no progress has been made: single relations have been thoroughly studied, and some clear anti-poverty prescriptions are today little contested[3]: but a completely satisfactory all-encompassing poverty model is still missing.

All the issues referred to above were present in the papers discussed at the 1995 Florence seminar, now collected in this volume. Some contributions have already been cited, in passing; but many others would be worth mentioning. Among these, for instance, is a discussion on the urban poor and the urban environment (Satterthwaite, Chapter 11), a subject which has attracted even greater interest since 1995. Concerns about the sustainability of development are voiced more and more often, and the connections between ecological degradation and poverty are starting to emerge. At the same time, all forecasts indicate that relatively soon more people—and, in particular, more poor people—will be living in an urban than in a rural environment. The possible consequences of such a radical change in the world's future are still largely unknown, but are definitely worth considering in greater detail.

Another major concern is international migratory movements. These have proved scarcely foreseeable in the past, but formidable: over a million people are estimated to migrate annually from the South to the North of the world: both in their official and in their (semi) clandestine segments; both as permanent workers and as hired labourers for fixed periods, both as bread-winners and as dependent members of their families; both as 'ordinary' migrants and as political refugees. All these facets of the problem emerge well in Wéry and Oppong's discussion (Chapter 10).

As we have said, the picture is complex, and new data and research contribute almost daily to an enlargement of our views, and to an enrichment of our understanding. One point is now clear beyond any reasonable doubt: economic backwardness and poverty hit, above all, the most vulnerable groups. Among these rank the aged: in the developed world elderly people are faring better and better, to the point that some analysts, thinking of the pension problem, would say that they may even have progressed too much. However, they are still at risk in many developing countries, where the absence of old-age protection schemes combines with a decrease in the number of children likely to support parents in their old age and, in general, with the dispersion of the traditional family and the attendant reduction in family ties.

Very often, however, vulnerability depends not so much on individual or group characteristics *per se* (such as gender, age or status), as on legal and cultural discrimination. The victims of this are frequently women and children, especially female children, who, in several parts of the developing world, are still exposed to unacceptably high risks of neglect, starvation, retarded physical and mental growth, social exclusion, and so forth.

---

[3] Among these: expanding basic social services (like health and primary education, especially for children and females), improving nutrition, implementing agrarian reforms (aimed at a more equitable distribution of resources), granting credit to all, expanding employment and participation of the poor, ensuring a safety net to catch those excluded by market forces, and pursuing economic growth (see, e.g. UNDP, 1994, 1997; and World Bank, 1997a,b).

Although some things are slowly improving, the consequences of poverty are thus graver than they appear, because they extend far into the future. Poor, ignorant, and sick mothers give birth to (too many) children who, if they survive, are likely to be undernourished, overexploited (if not abused), poorly looked after, little invested in. By the age of four or five, most of their physical and intellectual capabilities, as well as their basic social attitudes, may well be 'fixed'. And today's 'low-quality' children, as some would put it, make tomorrow's low-quality adults, who are likely to generate more low-quality children, thus perpetuating the chain.

It is high time to break the vicious circle of poverty, starting from the youngest generation. This is a morally risk-free operation (children surely can't be blamed for their poor conditions) and, we would argue, a moral obligation. Making parents invest in their children is probably the best way to reduce fertility in the developing world, and to free women from long years of domestic chores. It reduces child mortality and improves children's health and capabilities. It is an economically and ecologically sound investment, requiring only that we are long-sighted enough to see beyond today, and beyond our immediate needs.[4]

Paradoxically, it makes even a demographically and economically stationary society not so appalling as many economists fear: if the (relatively) poor have children while the rich don't, and if being born poor does not prevent the full development of personality and potential, there is ample room for personal upward mobility, with no need for migration or revolutions. Those who were born poor will have the chance of gradually climbing up the social ladder and come to occupy the seats left free by the infertile top classes.

Optimistic and pessimistic points of views constantly confront each other in the debate on poverty, and this happened in the Florence seminar too. While we tend to take an optimistic rather than a pessimistic point of view, we are glad to be able to present a book that reflects both positions and thus allows the reader to gain a balanced insight into a highly complex matter.

---

[4]   In other words, that we value the future, much as we do when we succeed in lengthening our life span, or when we keep real interest rates low (see Lipton, Chapter 3 below).

2 Poverty and the 'Population Problem'

SUDHIR ANAND AND JONATHAN MORDUCH

Introduction

In this chapter, we address three aspects of poverty and the 'population problem' from an economic perspective. First, we investigate the statistical basis for the oft-cited positive correlation between poverty and household size. Second, we re-examine the conflicting economic and demographic interpretations of this correlation. And third, we examine whether restricting attention just to the household level misses an important aspect of the problem. We cite evidence from Bangladesh to suggest that many of the most pressing issues are at the level of individuals, and concern the deprivation of girls and women within households.

Comparative data typically show that larger households are poorer. The relationship also holds at the national level: countries with high fertility rates tend to be poorer as well. Demographers have sometimes taken this correlation to imply causation. According to this view, limiting population growth is seen as an essential first step in reducing poverty, and this has been put forward as the basis of development strategies at numerous international conferences.

Economic theory, however, suggests the opposite causal relationship. The argument rests on the assumption that households have reasonable control over their fertility.[1] If this is so, then to the extent that households do control fertility, can

This is a revised version of a paper presented in March 1995 at the International Union for the Scientific Study of Population seminar on 'Demography and Poverty' in Florence, Italy. We have benefited from discussions with Robert Cassen, Lincoln Chen, Andrew Foster, Paul Gertler, Hitesh Hathi, Allán Hill, John Hoddinott, and the seminar participants. We alone are responsible for all views and errors.

[1] Demographers have tended to argue that parents cannot limit fertility perfectly without family planning programmes. This is supported by historical evidence from country-level and community-level studies on the association between family planning programmes and reductions in family size. Such evidence appears to be at odds with economic models which test hypotheses by focusing on variations in behaviour in cross-sections of households. These models assume that parents can reasonably accurately attain desired family size; thus the introduction or extension of family planning programmes should have only small effects. The relative importance of the claims is an empirical issue. Recent evidence using cross-country comparisons and evidence from the Matlab studies in Bangladesh have been interpreted as indicating that nearly all pregnancies are, in fact, desired, as predicted by the economic model. See Pritchett (1994a) and the ensuing interchange between Knowles, Akin, and Guilkey (1994), Bongaarts (1994), and Pritchett (1994b). T. P. Schultz (1994) provides further evidence from cross-country studies showing limited impacts of family planning programmes on fertility. Gertler and Molyneaux (1994) integrate the two strands of argument in an empirical framework which helps to show the important interactions between economic determinants of fertility change and the availability of contraception.

they really be impoverishing themselves intentionally? Or, to the contrary, might high fertility rates in fact help to reduce poverty? The central reason is that children can help poor families earn extra income and adapt to imperfections in labour and credit markets.[2] Higher fertility may be a way out of poverty, rather than a force which holds poor families down.

We begin by looking at some evidence in order to assess these claims and counter-claims. In Section 2 we present new evidence from Bangladesh that the observed statistical relationship between poverty and household size may largely be due to mismeasurement; this leads us to question the severity of the population problem there, at least at the household level. In Section 3 we turn to the problem at the regional level. We examine the argument that choices made by parents may be rational (as postulated in economic models) but, when taken collectively, the decisions may turn out to be less than optimal for society as a whole. This might be, for example, because parents do not account for their contributions to environmental degradation or to poorer labour market conditions (wages) when making fertility decisions. Thus, high fertility regions may be substantially poorer, even if the evidence is weak that bigger households are poorer than smaller ones in developing countries. Despite much broad discussion along these lines, there is little hard evidence yet that these issues matter empirically.

We turn next to the problem at the individual level, which until recently has not figured prominently in the debate. It is the issue of *who* within families bears the greatest burden of poverty. Increasingly, the evidence suggests that it is girls and women who are most deprived. This is clear in the commonly-observed lower education and health outcomes of girls relative to boys, and in some regions it is manifested in excessively high female mortality and morbidity rates.

Drawing on the two most recent national censuses and two recent household-level data sets from Bangladesh, we document in Section 4 how mortality rates for females are much higher than for males. We also show that fertility rates are greatly influenced by the desire to have boys. The evidence suggests that these two phenomena reinforce each other, and together they push up the high rates of excess female mortality.

This gives us a very different sense in which demographic realities must be confronted in considering poverty, and it turns us towards a broader notion of deprivation that goes beyond simple metrics of wellbeing defined in terms of household income or consumption. The evidence from Bangladesh underscores the importance of considering the poverty of *individuals* and not just poverty at the level of households, families or regions. The evidence also underscores arguments that the notion

---

[2]   Turning to the family is appealing because the repeated nature of family interactions, use of social ties, and low transactions costs, mitigate the sorts of informational and enforcement problems that drive imperfections in formal markets. In addition, the intergenerational links of families and the fact that investments in children can be made in relatively small increments over time make children an attractive social insurance and savings substitute.Thus, high fertility has been shown to provide a partial response to missing insurance markets (Rosenzweig 1988), to missing pensions and credit markets (Cain 1983, Nugent 1985, Hoddinott 1992), and to imperfect labour markets.

of 'wellbeing' should be bound up with the ability of individuals to live full and healthy lives. A central corollary of that concern is freedom from discrimination, particularly discrimination based on gender. The problem is not, then, that fertility rates are too high *per se*. Rather, the problem is that girls and women bear a disproportionate burden associated with the high fertility rates.

1. Concepts of Poverty

Before setting out issues at the intersection of demography and poverty, it is important to discuss what it is we mean by 'poverty'. First we examine issues which matter when poverty is considered in terms of resource deprivation. Then we consider broader notions of poverty. As we describe in later sections, both sets of issues are closely tied to how the links between population and poverty are assessed.

The definition of poverty commonly employed by economists is in terms of income or consumption deprivation relative to a monetary threshold (the so-called poverty line). The criterion specifies the private resources required to purchase a bundle of essential goods (food, clothing, shelter, etc.)—sometimes referred to as 'basic needs'. Clearly, some adjustments to money income or consumption will be necessary to reflect real command over commodities. For example, prices for the same goods vary across regions. Thus, personal incomes must be adjusted by price indices to get a measure of 'real' income.[3]

Adjustments are also needed to account for household composition. Data on income and expenditure are usually collected at the household level, through household income and expenditure surveys. There are, thus, no direct estimates of the command over resources or consumption of *individuals*. The economist's approach to this informational gap is to make assumptions about intra-household allocation of resources. Two assumptions are typically made in the literature about the sharing of household income: either (i) that it is distributed *equally* among all members, or (ii) that it is distributed in proportion to the 'needs' of individual members. In (ii) the variation in personal needs—for example, among children and adults—is recognized, and an 'equivalence scale' is constructed to reflect differential needs according to the age and sex of individuals.[4]

A related issue concerns economies of scale in household consumption. A large household will require more income than a small household to meet the needs of its members. But perhaps the total income that it requires will not be larger *in proportion to* the number of its members (or the number of its equivalent adults). There may be economies of scale in food preparation, in the provision of shelter, and in

---

[3] Deflation of income and expenditure is achieved by dividing income by a given price index, or sometimes through more refined methods (see, for instance, Deaton and Muellbauer 1980).

[4] There are several methods for constructing adult equivalence scales (see Deaton and Muellbauer 1980). Some estimate needs endogenously (Rothbarth, Engel), and some impose them exogenously (by specifying, say, calorie requirements at different ages for each sex; see also Ferro-Luzzi and Branca, Chapter 4 below).

other household (public) goods. Thus we should adjust the number of household members (or the number of equivalent adults) by a size elasticity less than unity.[5]

Another problem with using household income or consumption as the basic metric of economic welfare is that the information obtained through household surveys typically has a short reference period—usually less than one year. Even if the current income of a household is low, its expected future income may not be. If opportunities to smooth income over time are absent, then the household could be 'temporarily' poor but 'permanently' non-poor.[6] If one is interested not just in short-term poverty but in long-run wellbeing, current income—and, to a lesser extent, current consumption—may fail to reflect long-run command over resources.[7]

To see this, consider the neoclassical-economic theory of fertility. It holds that households may rationally choose large families even if they appear to impoverish themselves by doing so. This may hardly seem rational. However, the rationality is more apparent by the time the children are young adults and net contributors to household income. By then, the investments in children will have paid off, and parents can look forward to reaping the returns on their investment in children. That is, in having a large family, a household may make life more difficult for itself in the short term so that in the longer run it has greater resources.

Thus, current income or expenditure per capita is an imperfect indicator of even the economic welfare of the household. If, at the time of procreation, the household was able to borrow against the future income of its children, the household might not have been poor at all—or at least it would have been less poor. However, if households lack such borrowing possibilities, their income and consumption will often move closely together. Short-term impoverishment may be rational if the value of returns to investment is considered. Although, in the short term, keeping household size low may help to maintain income per capita, it will ultimately lead to lower income as households lose out on their chief investment opportunity. This reinforces the argument for improving access to credit for poor households.[8]

Even with all the corrections and adjustments made to household income or consumption, there are some who argue that the notion of economic welfare remains too narrow to reflect individual wellbeing. The most cogent critique has come from Sen (1985a, 1987) who questions the use of both 'opulence' (income, wealth, or

---

[5] A size elasticity between 0 and 1 implies that costs rise with the number of household members (equivalent adults) but at a diminishing rate.

[6] Morduch (1994) describes implications of market imperfections on the extent of poverty. His definition of *stochastic poverty* captures the notion that households may be poor in a given instance due to the absence of means to move income over time by saving or borrowing. In this situation, consumption gives a better indication of deprivation than income. By allowing consumption to be higher than income when income is low, reducing credit market imperfections may help significantly in reducing observed poverty.

[7] See, however, the use made by Anand and Harris (1990) of food expenditure as an ordinal measure of the long-run standard of living.

[8] The effect of market improvements on the demand for children is theoretically ambiguous. On the one hand, families may turn to formal labour and capital markets, leading to a decrease in desired fertility levels. On the other hand, children may become more desirable if their productivity rises with the improvement of markets. The former phenomenon seems to dominate empirically.

commodity possession) and 'utility' (whether interpreted as happiness, desire fulfilment, or simply choice) as measures of wellbeing, arguing that they constitute the wrong space in which to make such assessments. In a direct sense, 'well-being' has to do with *being* well, not with having income—to which it is posterior—or with having utility—to which it is, generally, prior. What is valued intrinsically are a person's achievements—her 'beings' and 'doings'—or her 'capabilities to function'. In the most basic terms wellbeing is about being able to live long, being well nourished, being healthy, being literate, and so on.

Although income, wealth, and commodities do have instrumental importance in enhancing wellbeing, they do not constitute a *direct* measure of the living standard. Likewise, happiness or utility might provide evidence of achievement, but cannot be *equated* with wellbeing. A thoroughly deprived person who sees no way out of her adversity may, as a strategy of living, be reconciled to her condition and take pleasure from small mercies in life.

But why can't income serve as a *proxy* for wellbeing? For some dimensions of wellbeing, such as adequate nourishment, where the instrumental importance of private income is likely to be quite large, the fit with income may be a fairly tight one. But for other dimensions, income is likely to provide only a poor signal. For example, a person's income level does not reveal whether he or she is presently healthy (or suffering from a terminal disease), is disabled and incapable of moving about freely, or is likely to live long.

It is not possible, through income, to account for individual differences in mortality, morbidity, or disability—and these features would seem to deserve priority in any assessment of the living standard. There are also other, non-private, economic goods and services which cannot be reflected adequately through household incomes. These are the standard public or publicly-provided goods—the environment, parks, infrastructure (such as roads), public transport and communication facilities, epidemiological protection, etc. Thus private incomes fail—sometimes miserably—to capture even some very basic instrumental aspects of the standard of living.

As we have argued above, indicators of poverty that are based on income, or on the possession and use of commodities, are also not well suited to examining *individual* deprivation. By contrast, the consequences of individual disadvantage (including gender bias), both within and outside the household, will be reflected most clearly in the achievements of the persons concerned in terms of considerations such as their survival chances, life expectancy, etc. Data on these achievements are collected at the individual level through demographic surveys and population censuses. There is, thus, a strong practical reason—apart from concern for what is intrinsically important—to focus on strictly individual features of wellbeing in examining deprivation and poverty (Anand 1994, Morduch and Ahmad 1996).

Another aspect of welfare that is non-income based concerns people's freedoms and opportunities. People's freedoms can be distinguished as 'negative' or 'positive', after Isaiah Berlin's (1969) two concepts of liberty. The negative view of freedom focuses on the absence of interference or restrictions by others—including the state—in people's 'personal spheres', which embraces the deeply private area of reproductive choice. Restricting a person's freedom to choose within her personal domain will lead to a violation of both her wellbeing and her agency freedom (Sen 1985b).[9]

The positive view of freedom is closely connected to Sen's (1985a, 1987) capabilities approach. In contrast to negative freedom, which focuses on a denial of choices within a person's reach, positive freedom focuses on an *expansion* of choices and opportunities available to her, that is, on what she can succeed in doing or being. From a set of possible 'functionings' available to her, she typically chooses one (described as a vector or an *n*-tuple). In appraising the wellbeing of the person it is important to pay attention to the capability *set*, and not just to the chosen functioning vector.[10] This allows us to assess the overall or positive freedoms that the person has.

Expanding people's capabilities also involves improving women's positive freedoms—especially given the low status of women relative to men. A concern for equity would lead us immediately to try and reduce the sharp inequalities that exist between women and men. A clear manifestation of gender bias in many parts of South Asia (including Bangladesh) has been the lower life expectancy of females compared with males, despite women having a higher maximal biological potential.

Thus, in discussing poverty and population, we shall consider a broad set of issues, including the way that gender biases are manifested in mortality and fertility patterns. This is not only because such gender biases lead to important demographic outcomes, but also because they constitute important elements of the conception of 'poverty' itself.

2. The Positive Correlation between Income Poverty and Household Size: Is it Robust?

We begin, however, by focusing much more narrowly. One common perception of the 'population problem' starts with the observation that poor households tend to be larger than non-poor households. At one level, this may appear to be a tautology. Since poverty is generally measured on the basis of per capita income, increasing

[9]   For example, if population reduction is achieved through compulsion, then the broader notion of wellbeing is compromised by a denial of the negative freedom of people to choose the number of children they wish to have.

[10]   Sen (1985b) provides the example of two persons with identical functioning vectors in terms of undernourishment: one starving out of choice, because of his religious beliefs, and the other because she lacks the means to command food. Even though both persons' achieved level of wellbeing in terms of being undernourished is the same, there is an important difference in their respective capability *sets*. The first person *could have* chosen not to starve, while the second person did not have that choice. In a straightforward sense, the first person's wellbeing freedom, and hence advantage, are greater than the second person's. Note that despite starving to death, the second person's negative freedom may be perfectly intact, if her failure to acquire sufficient food was not the result of interference or restraints imposed by others.

household size while keeping total income constant will make households poorer. Hence, increasing household size is thought to increase poverty. However, in reality total income does not remain unchanged as household size rises. A question which can only be answered through data is: Does total income rise at a faster rate than household size? If so, increasing household size will reduce income poverty. Below we shall examine such correlations using data from Bangladesh.

But if poverty is increased by increasing household size, why do some households appear to impoverish themselves deliberately by having larger families? One answer, of course, is that they do not make a deliberate choice; rather the outcome is the consequence of imperfect fertility control, especially for poorer households. However, the question can also be answered without abandoning the economist's premise that fertility outcomes are voluntary.

While empirical work usually focuses on income as a chief determinant of fertility, much of its role may be as a proxy for the lack of market access faced by poor households. Here, a positive relationship between poverty and household size may emerge because poor households are often those which have the most limited access to formal markets for labour and capital and so, in response, have more children. Population reduction will lower measures of income-focused poverty but make households worse off in terms of broader notions of wellbeing. On the other hand, efforts to redress market imperfections will in general raise the incomes of the poor, reduce household size, and improve economic welfare.

In addition, we may be seeing households which are impoverishing themselves today in order to become less poor in the future—once their children are able to earn a living. Here, the problem is that we see households at a single point in time, and do not see the future consequences of fertility for this cohort. Thus, what is seemingly irrational today could turn out to be wise in twenty years.

Thus, despite there possibly being a positive correlation between income-focused poverty and household size, reducing household numbers will not necessarily improve the welfare of poor households, and in the long-run it may exacerbate poverty—both narrowly and broadly construed.

We now consider the statistical basis of the relationship between income poverty and household size using data from the 1988–9 Household Expenditure Survey of Bangladesh. Bangladesh is of interest because it is among the world's poorest countries, with nearly half of the population below the official poverty line. It is also a country where problems of poverty and population pressure have been closely linked.

The results of most household income or expenditure surveys in developing countries display two features in the cross-section: (i) a positive correlation between household expenditure (income) and household size; and (ii) a negative correlation between *per capita* household expenditure (income) and household size.[11] This negative correlation, however, may be exaggerated because the *per capita* deflation of household expenditure (income) takes no account of economies

---

[11] For these correlations in the case of Malaysia, see Anand (1983).

of scale in household consumption, and it over-corrects for the smaller consumption needs of infants and children relative to adults.

Ranking households by *unadjusted* total expenditure would be a justifiable procedure if all expenditure were a public good; the consumption of such a good by one individual in the household does not affect the amount that can be consumed by another. At the other extreme is the assumption that expenditure is a strictly private good, that there are no economies of scale in consumption, and that each person's needs are the same. This leads to ranking households by total expenditure *per capita*. An intermediate assumption recognizes *some* economies of scale in consumption, while still assuming that household members have similar needs. This is accommodated by dividing household expenditure x_h by the number of its members m_h raised to some non-negative power less than unity.

These alternatives produce rankings of households according to the welfare indicator x_h/m_h^α, where x_h is the total expenditure of household h, m_h is its size, and α is a size-elasticity parameter between 0 and 1. When $\alpha = 0$, households are ranked by total expenditure unadjusted; when $\alpha = 1$, households are ranked by total expenditure *per capita*. For α between 0 and 1, we have more or less strong household economies of scale as α is closer to 0 or to 1, respectively.

Below we report some calculations from the 1988–9 Bangladesh Household Expenditure Survey to illustrate the effects of various assumptions regarding the economies of household size parameter α.[12] We have applied this size-elasticity parameter not only to household size m_h but also to n_h, the number of equivalent adults in the household using an exogenous equivalence scale.[13] Table 2.1 shows the Spearman rank correlation coefficients between household size m_h and the welfare indicators x_h/m_h^α and x_h/n_h^α, respectively, for values of α from 0.0 to 1.0. A positive coefficient indicates that households with more members (or equivalent adults) are better off than smaller households.

We first discuss the correction for the returns to scale parameter α applied to total household size. Later we consider the same correction applied to the number of equivalent adults in the household. The returns to scale correction turns out to be surprisingly important in both cases. Even if there are only very modest returns to scale, adding household members is positively associated with household welfare. The evidence can be seen in the Spearman rank correlation coefficient which is positive for values of α up to $\alpha = 0.8$ and negative only for values of $\alpha \geq 0.9$. In the case of the welfare indicator x_h/m_h^α, the correlation coefficient reverses sign from

---

[12]   The households in the Household Expenditure Survey are drawn from the entirety of Bangladesh, with the exception of reserve forest areas and Chittagong H.T., Khagrachari, and Bandarbhan Districts. Enumeration included 1,871 urban households and 3,804 rural households, comprising 10,496 urban individuals and 21,015 rural individuals. Weights reflect an urban population which is 22 per cent of the total. The survey data were collected over twelve months through random sampling. More details may be found in Bangladesh Bureau of Statistics (1991). The estimates of average household size in the survey closely match those from the 1991 Bangladesh Census of Population (Bangladesh Bureau of Statistics 1992).

[13]   This is a calorie-based equivalence scale for Sri Lanka taken from Anand, Harris, and Linton (1993).

Table 2.1. Spearman rank correlation coefficients between household size m_h and x_h/m_h^α, and between household size m_h and x_h/n_h^α, for α varying from 0.0 to 1.0

α	x_h/m_h^α	x_h/n_h^α
0.0	0.5831	0.5831
0.1	0.5347	0.5371
0.2	0.4801	0.4851
0.3	0.4192	0.4263
0.4	0.3517	0.3604
0.5	0.2777	0.2874
0.6	0.1977	0.2077
0.7	0.1131	0.1223
0.8	0.0253	0.0331
0.9	−0.0632	−0.0581
1.0	−0.1501	−0.1481

Note: The sample size in this table is 5,621 households.
Source: Estimated from 1988–9 Bangladesh Household Expenditure Survey.

positive (+0.0076) for $\alpha = 0.82$ to negative (−0.0013) for $\alpha = 0.83$.[14] This suggests that if the welfare indicator incorporates *no* or *very mild* economies of scale (represented by a value of $\alpha \geq 0.83$), the poor will have a larger average household size than the non-poor. However, if there are stronger economies of scale in household consumption (represented by $\alpha \leq 0.82$), then the poor should have a smaller average household size than the non-poor.

Much the same results are found for the welfare indicator x_h/n_h^α, where n_h is the number of *equivalent adults* in the household. This adjustment corrects both for household economies of scale and for household age-sex composition. The Spearman rank correlation coefficients across households are very similar between household size and the welfare indicators x_h/m_h^α and x_h/n_h^α for values of α between 0.0 and 1.0 (compare columns 2 and 3 of Table 2.1). This suggests that it is economies of scale rather than correction for a differing (larger) proportion of young children to adults among (poorer) households that is responsible for the observed correlations between household size and welfare.

Another way of examining the relationship between household size and poverty is to compare directly the average household size of the poor and non-poor, respectively, where poverty is defined in terms of x_h/m_h^α for different values of α. As the absolute poverty line in Bangladesh (based on an energy intake of 2,122 Kcal per

[14] Atkinson and Micklewright (1992) assumed $\alpha = 0.7$ in their recent study of income distribution of the central European economies. If α were equal to 0.7 for Bangladesh, there would be a *positive* correlation between household size and welfare.

Table 2.2. Average household size for bottom 50 per cent and top 50 per cent of households

Welfare indicator $x_h/m_h{}^\alpha$,	$\alpha =$	Bottom 50%	Top 50%
	0.0	4.3276	6.7762
	0.7	5.2327	5.8708
	0.8	5.4276	5.6758
	0.9	5.6051*	5.4982*
	1.0	5.7830	5.3203
Sample size (number of households)		2,811	2,810

* Difference in average household size not significant at the 0.10 level.
   All other differences in household size are significant at the 0.001 level.
Source: As Table 2.1.

person per day) leads to approximately 50 per cent of the population in poverty, we begin by looking at the bottom 50 per cent of households defined by the welfare indicator $x_h/m_h{}^\alpha$ for different values of α.

Table 2.2 shows the average household size for the bottom and the top 50 per cent of households defined by $x_h/m_h{}^\alpha$ for values of α equal to 0.0, 0.7, 0.8, 0.9, and 1.0. Where households are ranked by total expenditure ($\alpha = 0.0$), the average household size of the bottom 50 per cent is, as expected, much smaller than that of the top 50 per cent. For values of α closer to a reasonable range for the size-elasticity parameter—that is, for α between 0.7 and 1.0—the difference in average household size between the poor and the non-poor is not large. For $\alpha = 0.9$ (very mild economies of scale) there is not a statistically significant difference in average household size; for $\alpha = 0.8$, the poor turn out to have a *smaller* average household size than the non-poor. For the standard *per capita* correction to total expenditure—that is, for $\alpha = 1.0$—the poor do have a larger average household size than the non-poor, which is statistically significant. However, the difference in average household size appears relatively small at 0.46 persons, with average sizes for the poor and the non-poor, respectively, of 5.78 and 5.32 persons.

The evidence on scale economies from Bangladesh suggests that adding children is likely to be much less costly than often thought, and the consequences for income-focused poverty may be considerably over-stated. How then can we speak of a 'population problem'?

3. Poverty, Fertility, and Externalities

If the evidence presented above is correct, the case for a 'population problem' must be found in arguments that go beyond the simple observed relationship between poverty and household size. This takes us to the idea of *negative externalities*—that the actions of a household can have adverse consequences for other households, both in the present and in the future. These consequences will arise even if the household is fully informed and has complete access to family planning services. The problem will be made worse by the above finding that having additional children may not, in fact, be very costly to the household.

The impact of population growth on the degradation of the environmental resource-base provides one nexus of issues here. Other important external effects include the congestion of public services and 'pecuniary' externalities of various types, such as downward pressure on wages. While economists have noted that pecuniary externalities do not affect the efficiency of economic systems, they do affect the *distribution* of wellbeing.

Externalities matter since they lead rational private decisions in respect of fertility levels to diverge from the social optimum. This opens a window for public action beyond that based on assumptions of ignorance or irrationality of households. As pointed out by Ronald Coase, however, government action is not a prerequisite for coordination. In principle, externalities may be dealt with by decentralized negotiation—but in practice, costs of negotiation, information asymmetries, and difficulties in enforcement will limit the efficiency of decentralized solutions (see Dasgupta 1993 and Klibanoff and Morduch 1995 for formal treatments of the problem). Whether or not the solution is decentralized, efficient coordination should be based on the exact source and extent of the externalities, and much progress remains to be made in empirically identifying and quantifying the different externalities.

We consider several cases, beginning with the degradation of the global resource base. The claim is that the planet does not have the resources to maintain the growing number of inhabitants (for example, see Ehrlich and Ehrlich 1990). Proponents of this view point to ozone depletion, natural-resource exhaustion, and other signs of global environmental strain. One way to reduce excessive consumption is to reduce population size, which is an argument often made for stepping up efforts to control population growth in countries such as Kenya or Nigeria. As a matter of reason, however, it would seem that since most consumption takes place in the OECD countries, further population reductions ought to occur *there* (even if population sizes there are already low), rather than in the faster-growing poorer countries. Consistent arguments for reducing population growth in sub-Saharan Africa, Latin America, or South Asia have to be found elsewhere.

An important source of such arguments in some poor economies is the fragility of the local-environmental resource base. This argument has recently been analysed extensively by Dasgupta (1993) and Dasgupta and Mäler (1995).[15] Here, the issue involves the erosion of the local environment as, for example, children must be employed to exploit scarcer and scarcer sources of firewood and fetch water at greater and greater distances. This creates a desire for more children, which then leads to greater degradation, spiralling into a cycle with too many children. Other

---

[15] See Timmer (1994) for policy implications with regard to strengthening the role of agriculture.

local externalities include those associated with information collection and demonstration effects which perpetuate suboptimal social norms (Dasgupta 1993).

Where such negative externalities matter, successful intervention must raise the costs involved in having children through corrective price or tax policies, or via regulation such as compulsory school attendance for children (Dasgupta 1994). These policies force households to 'internalize' the negative externality and reduce their desired family size. The role of education in population policy here takes a very different turn from Malthus's early arguments. Malthus (1803, Vol. 2: 210) had argued that education should be supported because it would help to impress on the public that 'it is not the duty of man simply to propagate his species, but to propagate virtue and happiness'. The essence of Dasgupta's (1994) proposal, on the other hand, is that such propagation is secondary to 'getting the prices right' which makes children a good deal costlier to raise. Ironically, Dasgupta argues that if such costs are imposed on poor households, their welfare can ultimately be improved through mitigating the collective action problem.

In principle, though, it is not clear what would happen to poverty, at least in the short run, as a result of population reduction achieved in this way. The main gains are likely to be reaped by the children of currently poor households or their children's children. Thus, population reduction may help to alleviate poverty in the long run while in the short-term it could be immiserizing. This shows the difficulty of solving such collective action problems.

Another difficulty is that there is little empirical information on the extent of such negative effects (Schultz 1988).[16] The work of Ronald Lee and his associates provides an important exception, and Lee and Miller (1991) review some of the few attempts to quantify externalities. In the United States, for example, they find that externalities associated with a larger population are found to be on the order of +4 to +6 per cent of GDP per capita due to the fact that larger populations lead to a greater spreading of the debt burden and pay-as-you-go social security. In Saudi Arabia these are found to be about −20 per cent, due to the dilution of the value of oil share reserves held by the population. In Bangladesh, Kenya, and Mexico they are negative but small, while in India and Brazil, the congestion of publicly-owned services and facilities and dilution of collectively-held resources lead to negative externalities of about −10 per cent to −12 per cent for Brazil and of +2 per cent to −50 per cent for India.

These estimates are noisy and, while we note the important omission in not accounting for environmental degradation in the estimates, the present numbers give little guidance to support the use of externalities as a justification for a more active family planning policy in Bangladesh, Kenya, and Mexico—three countries in which the 'population problem' has often been thought to be acute.

---

[16] It should be noted that externalities can be both negative and positive. On the positive side, there is an argument that household size is too small. This might be because larger populations can more easily pay for public goods or there exist demand spillovers or increasing returns to scale in production (Lee and Miller 1991).

4. Poverty, Fertility, and Gender Inequality

The possible adverse effects of high fertility considered above will mainly be felt by future generations—through congestion, downward pressure on wages, environmental degradation, and erosion of the local resource base. Here, we consider a very different aspect of high fertility, but one which also involves negative externalities. This aspect of the 'population problem', the differential impact between the genders in mortality and morbidity, is likely to be felt sharply by the current generation— and it has been notable in South Asia.

The problem can be said to involve negative externalities since fertility choices made by parents do not appear to reflect fully the adverse effects on the health of existing children. This is perpetuated as the children have little influence in fertility decisions. That this can be described as an externality with regard to its impact on mothers stems from the observation that household choices may reflect an imbalance in bargaining power between the parents. The best interest of mothers may then not be fully considered in the choice of fertility. These phenomena appear to be intensified by conditions of poverty.

The adverse effects of high fertility on women can be seen in the maternal mortality statistics for Bangladesh.[17] While maternal mortality in Bangladesh has fallen by three-quarters since 1970, it remains at 600 deaths for every 100,000 live childbirths. This is substantially higher than the South Asian average (469 deaths), three times higher than the Latin American average, and more than six times higher than the East Asian rate. To put the number in context, assume that all women in Bangladesh have the same probability of maternal mortality and that they all have a total fertility rate equal to the 1992 average of 4.4 children. Then, roughly 2.5 in every 100 women would die in the process of forming a family. Given the likelihood that poorer women are at much greater risk of maternal mortality (and may have more children), the risk of dying in the process of having children can climb to large numbers for poorer households. Holding all else constant, poor mothers will gain from conditions that reduce the total fertility rate.

Reducing fertility rates can also have important benefits for daughters. This opens up a large literature, and here we only sketch some of the key issues involved. First we consider biases against girls generally, then we consider the role of family size on mortality patterns, and finally we consider the effect of son-preference on the treatment and mortality patterns of females.

Economists often point to female discrimination in the labour market to explain sex discrimination by parents. When the economic returns from investing in the health and education of boys are greater than the returns from investing in girls, sons are often treated better than daughters. These biases can be reinforced by institutional arrangements in which parents live with their sons in old age while daughters

---

[17] The figures reported here on maternal mortality and fertility are drawn from the UNDP *Human Development Report 1995*.

move to their husbands' homes. Through this arrangement, the economic returns to investing in girls are often not recouped fully by the parents themselves—and this can lead to further biases against girls.[18] These tendencies will be reinforced by resource constraints: households are more likely to exhibit discriminatory practices when they are forced through need to make tough decisions about the treatment of sons versus daughters, even if parents do not have inherently biased preferences. It is also possible that preferences change as parents get richer, so that any inherent biases may diminish with higher income and socio-economic status.

In a very simple and powerful way, Amartya Sen has demonstrated just how stark the resulting imbalances can be, employing calculations of 'missing women' (Sen 1992, and elsewhere). While demographers have pointed out the approximate nature of some of these calculations, the numbers have rightly captured the imagination of many who thought the issues were empirically unimportant, and they have set forth a challenge to economists who tend to construct models of the household based on unbiased altruism.

The calculations rest on the fact that populations with significantly more males than females can be explained only by excess female mortality. The implication is that these 'missing women' would not have died had they been treated as well as their male counterparts. Sen's type of calculations, using the sex ratio of sub-Saharan Africa as a benchmark, suggest that roughly 9 per cent of women in Bangladesh were 'missing' in 1981.[19] The 1991 Census reveals that in Bangladesh 105.8 males exist for every 100 females, indicating that about 8 per cent of women are 'missing' by this calculation. If instead of using the male–female ratio from sub-Saharan Africa as the standard, we use a more conservative figure based on Western European historical trends, we still find 3.2 per cent of women missing in 1991. This lower figure remains substantial, reflecting 1.7 million excess deaths.[20]

One aspect of the relationships described above is that biases in female mortality may be conditioned on biases in fertility patterns. This takes us to considering son-preference in fertility behaviour (Ben-Porath and Welch 1976, Leung 1991). To analyse the problem rigorously, the sequential nature of decisions must be modelled since behaviour depends on revelations of the sex of children who are born and who die. In such dynamic models, deriving general, testable rules for fertility behaviour is not simple, and we focus instead on the common assertion that since parents

---

[18]   On the empirical side, see the pioneering work by Chen *et al.* (1981) on rural Bangladesh. A great deal has also been done by economists since the important paper by Rosenzweig and Schultz (1982) on gender-biased mortality patterns in India. Observers point to differences in dowry and inheritance practices as reasons for discrimination, but these are, themselves, the outcomes of more fundamental processes (Haddad, Hoddinott, and Alderman 1994).

[19]   The calculations here draw on Morduch and Ahmad (1996).

[20]   These calculations can only provide rough guides to demographic patterns. Under-reporting of women may explain some of those 'missing', the issue of appropriate benchmarks has been debated, and inference may be complicated by the fact that the results can be skewed by having a younger, growing population (the population of Bangladesh grew by 22 per cent between the 1981 and 1991 censuses). Still, appropriate corrections do not change the general picture: girls fare much worse as measured by mortality.

favour sons over daughters, they are more likely to continue having children if they have not yet had a son (or a desired number of sons). Thus, a stylized implication is that the last children of completed families are more likely to be boys than girls. By the same logic, we would also expect to see that larger families have more girls.

Demographers and economists have estimated hazard models of waiting times as an alternative to this simple proposition, and these have theoretical appeal (Leung 1988, Yamaguchi and Ferguson 1995). But the basic proposition above on stopping rules captures much of the notion. To test the idea, we investigate whether last children are more likely to be boys. The extreme version of the stopping rule would yield that 100 per cent of last children are boys.

We focus on a subset of the national Bangladesh Household Expenditure Survey of 1988–9 where we know if the children are the last children born; these are households surveyed as part of the Child Nutrition Survey of 1988–9. There, however, we have information on children only up to the age of six. If we restrict attention to children aged four and above, we find that 51 per cent of the non-youngest children are boys, while nearly 60 per cent of the youngest are boys. For households in the bottom 50 per cent of the expenditure distribution, 61 per cent of the youngest children are boys versus again 51 per cent of the others. The differences here are statistically significant at the 3 per cent and 11 per cent levels, respectively.[21] This rough evidence indicates that, on average, households systematically consider gender in making fertility decisions.

Given this evidence, we should also expect that larger households have a higher fraction of girls. It turns out that this is not so. In fact, the opposite is found. On average, households with three or four children have 56 per cent boys; with five children, the percentage rises to 57 per cent; with six children it rises to 58 per cent; with seven children it is up to 59 per cent; and with eight children, it is up to 62 per cent.[22]

The results suggest that sex biases in mortality and fertility are associated. The failure to find that larger families have more girls is consistent with the hypothesis that girls in larger families have lower survival chances—and part of this may be that large family size is driven by the attempt to give birth to sons. Two implications follow from these findings. First, improving the 'returns' to females and reducing resource constraints should decrease both excess female mortality and fertility (Rosenzweig and Schultz 1982). More generally, we find that parents'

---

[21] These results are stronger than in the larger data set in which we cannot control for whether the last child in the sample is in fact the last born (another child may have been born and may have died). We find in the larger sample that 54 per cent of the youngest children in families are boys (male:female ratio = 117:100), while just 52 per cent of other children are boys (male:female ratio = 108:100). This difference is statistically significant at the 10 per cent level. The difference is slightly accentuated and is significant at the 2 per cent level for households in the bottom half of the expenditure distribution. (The sample is restricted to children between the ages of 5 and 10 in order to capture completed families and to minimize the effect of out-migration of boys; the sample size is 6,484 children.) Part of the difference may be a biasing upwards of the reported age of boys.

[22] Sample sizes are 1,016, 763, 541, 297, 141, and 58 households with 3, 4, 5, 6, 7, and 8 children, respectively. Even if we restrict attention to children under age 12 to control for out-migration, we do not find the expected monotonic decrease in the fraction male: on average, households with 3 children are 53 per cent male, and households with 5 children are 54 per cent male.

decisions can have a strong influence on the sex composition of their surviving children, and this is likely to be exacerbated by fertility behaviour.

These observations should force us to reconsider how we gauge the 'population problem'. Concern should surely be placed on improving the welfare of the existing population. But the demographic evidence suggests strikingly that concern must also be raised about the population that would exist in the absence of gender bias.

Conclusion

The concept of poverty seems simple enough at first glance. At a basic level it captures the condition of not having the resources to attain minimum consumption of food and other necessities of living. But this simple concept immediately raises issues that are not at all simple. Some of the most difficult of these issues are to be found at the intersection of demography and economics. They hinge on why parents appear to impoverish themselves by having a large number of children, and why parents treat sons much better than daughters.

Consideration of poverty and the 'population problem' can go on at individual, household, and regional levels. We have argued that the logic of the relationships and the empirical bases vary greatly depending on the level being considered. We have examined the statistical bases of claims about population and poverty using data from Bangladesh, one of the poorest and most densely populated countries in the world. And we have examined the logic of arguments concerning demographic outcomes as responses to market failure and market imperfections, to problems of externalities and co-ordination failure, and to the nature of intra-household choices.

The evidence we have presented in this paper suggests three broad conclusions. First, returns to scale in household consumption seem to matter a great deal in the data we have examined from Bangladesh. If even modest returns to scale in household consumption are assumed, the oft-cited positive correlation between income-focused poverty and household size is reversed. Second, arguments based on negative externalities have as yet little empirical foundation generally—at least none that can convincingly support a case for aggressive population-control policies in several densely populated poor countries. Quantifying negative externalities remains an important research priority; in our view, externalities and coordination failure are likely to form the core of the 'population problem'. Third, in considering negative externalities, we turned to an examination of gender inequality. High fertility not only increases the risk of maternal mortality, it also reduces the resources that go to girls. This has contributed to disturbingly high rates of excess female mortality in Bangladesh and other parts of South Asia. While we have argued that high fertility can be an important way that households cope with poverty, we also note that it is mothers and their daughters who often end up paying the highest price. This places an important 'population problem' not at the household level, nor at the community or regional levels, but at the level of the individual.

3 Population and Poverty
How Do They Interact?

MICHAEL LIPTON

1. Correlations and Causes

Owing mainly to better measurement techniques and more and better household surveys, knowledge about poverty has increased more in the past four decades than in the previous two millennia. Also, global poverty incidence has declined more. Sub-Saharan Africa has not shared in this improvement, but in the world's largest low-income countries (China, India, Indonesia, Pakistan), and in 1960–80 in some large middle-income countries (Brazil, Mexico), it has been unprecedented. Most of it happened from the mid-1950s to the early 1980s (World Bank 1990: 40–1); subsequent improvement has been much slower (Chen *et al.* 1995).

Yet the unprecedented poverty reduction of 1955–95 is even more remarkable than it seems, in view of the record demographic growth rates that occurred concurrently. Technical progress responds in part to population growth, but is uncertain and costly. Poverty reduction is also made harder because, within each developing country, population almost certainly grew faster among the 'initially poor'. Suppose we divide the population of a low-income country, around 1955, into two sets of households: R, containing the richer half of persons, and P, containing the poorer half. If national population grows at 2.55 per cent compound from 1955 to 1995—that is, to 2.74 times its initial level—this might plausibly comprise increase at 3 per cent a year in P, and at only 2 per cent a year in R. By 1995, the surviving 'initially poor' and their descendants comprise almost 60 per cent of persons, as against 50 per cent in 1955. These are conservative assumptions; in North-East Brazil—where inequality is admittedly extreme—the population of P (the initially poorer half of the population, plus descendants, minus deaths) rose, for most of 1955–95, over twice as fast as the population of R, the initially richer half (Daly 1985).

Why do initially poorer parts of populations usually grow faster? Persons, especially women, with secondary (or even with completed primary) education will be much better represented in R than in P. So will urban residents, and persons with lower age-specific mortality. Education, low child mortality, and urban residence are all both effects and causes of being in R; of lower total fertility rates (TFRs); and hence of slower natural increase. Independently of education and health, there is a strong negative relationship over most of the range of the variables[1] between real consumption per person, or per-adult equivalent, and both fertility and mortality. However, fertility increases faster with poverty than does mortality. So the populations of the initially poor—with all their special difficulties in becoming richer—grow faster than the populations of the initially non-poor. In these conditions, reduced or even stable poverty incidence is a considerable achievement in arithmetical terms alone.

Nevertheless, the post-1955 combination of unprecedented disimpoverishment and unprecedented population growth has induced extreme caution among analysts. 'The evidence ... does not support across-the-board generalizations about the adverse effects of population growth that once characterized the population debate' (World Bank 1994: 4). This caution is probably excessive; but the evidence is ambiguous.

The reason poorer households are larger is mainly that they experience faster population growth than richer households. But does this indicate that (1) poverty increases population growth, (2) population growth accelerates poverty, (3) some other cause, or set of causes, underlies both poverty and population growth, or (4) both are caused by simultaneous but largely independent events or circumstances? Cause precedes effect; but, as Paul Schultz emphasizes, this fact seldom suffices to sort out the conundrums, since the common causes of population growth and poverty probably include simultaneous, rational decisions about desired family size, expected time-paths of income and security, by the typical poor couple. It may choose high fertility because—while needing income from children's work and, later, security in old age from remittances—it anticipates high child mortality and low child-rearing costs. If ' ... the couple chooses ... family size [alongside] expenditures such as schooling or [child] health [, and] the level of ... consumption ... it is difficult to view [high fertility] as largely a problem of population pressure on family welfare, *causing* adverse effects' (King 1987: 374; her italics).

However, although scepticism about population growth as a cause of poverty is a healthy corrective to causally unstructured correlation-mongering, it has been overdone. As King recognizes, each couple's rational choice to have many children may cause or deepen poverty in other households. Malthus's central observation is correct: population growth among the poor reduces the money-wage relative to the price of food.[2] This does not imply his initial, but later progressively rejected, extreme scepticism that 'schemes of improvement' could reduce poverty at all (1798, 1803, 1824). However, his observation does imply that, other things being equal,

---

[1] At the very lowest levels of real consumption or income per person (or adult-equivalent), poverty may sometimes be correlated negatively with fertility, because the 'supply of babies born alive' is constrained below desired levels by poverty-induced undernutrition and ill-health (Easterlin and Crimmins 1985). Also, at the highest levels—even in a low-income country—there is no reason why incentives should induce lower fertility when real consumption (income) rises further.

[2] Evenson (1993)—showing that, across Indian Districts over a longish period, differences in labour supply growth have substantially affected variations in the growth rates of real unskilled wages—provides one of the first rigorous proofs of the Malthus hypothesis.

population growth among the poor—even if neutral, or even good, for growth—harms the poor themselves. This is perfectly consistent with the fact that population growth creates incentives for technical and institutional adaptation—incentives recognized by Malthus himself, and explored by Boserup (1965), Hayami and Ruttan (1985), Simon (1986), and others. The resulting adapted technology and institutions may be slow or fast in arriving; fully or only partly sufficient to maintain (if population growth threatens it) real output per person; and good or bad at reaching the poor (Lipton 1990).

Poverty—the product of low and/or maldistributed average income—is linked to high birth rates in a number of suggestive, though not firmly proven, causal chains. Cross-national comparisons suggest that high birth rates lead to low growth of real income per person (Kelley and Schmidt 1994). Inequality between rich and poor is increased by prior rapid growth of unskilled-labour households—and in turn may be linked to rapid subsequent population growth (Repetto 1974, 1979; Flegg 1979). There is a statistically robust link between inequality and slower subsequent growth (Persson and Tabellini 1994; Clarke 1995; Birdsall, Ross, and Sabot 1994). Even holding real income per person constant, countries with high birth rates tend to show higher subsequent poverty incidence (Eastwood and Lipton 1997).

All this is suggestive, but not conclusive. To shed light on the question in the title, this chapter explores what 'poverty' is, and which 'population' variables interact with it. I suggest a framework below, but initially we use quite general ideas of 'demographic and poverty variables' and defer precise definitions, while we sort out four questions.

First, to what extent are demographic variables *correlated* with indicators of poverty? The framework in Hajnal (1982) partly explains why larger household size (though correlated with affluence in pre-industrial and early industrial Northern Europe) now tends to accompany poverty in developing countries (Lipton 1983, 1994). Among countries, Kelley and Schmidt (1994) present robust regressions linking rapid economic growth in the 1980s—but not in the 1960s or 1970s—to previous slow population growth; but the links to poverty are explored by Eastwood and Lipton (1997).

The classical models (Malthus 1803, 1824) agree with the moderns (such as Schultz 1981) in implicitly denying that the relationship between population and poverty can usefully be analysed through causally unstructured correlations or regressions. For Malthus, 'schemes of improvement'—if they cause falls in poverty—thereby cause the poor to increase their population; this causes dearer food and cheaper labour; these cause poverty to rise again, unless family size norms decline.

Second, then, how and to what extent does *demographic change cause* changes in poverty? Relatedly, which (if any) policies that affect demographic variables will thereby affect poverty? Neo-Malthusians argue that extra people deplete resources, reduce food output per person, or threaten sustainability, thereby harming the poor in the long term. Optimists claim that exogenous technical progress in food production can prevent this. Both groups concur that the poor are the main losers from population growth, but add (in sharp disagreement with Malthus) that they will benefit if contraception is practised. Sen (1981) criticizes both neo-Malthusians and 'Malthusian optimists' for assuming that poor people's food adequacy depends on changes in food availability rather than food entitlements; Malthus himself (a non-neo-Malthusian) was concerned mainly that extra population depressed entitlements by pushing wage rates down and pushing food prices up.

Others see innovation and invention as endogenous to demographic change. Population increase—even if it initially reduces food supply, or labour income, per person—for that very reason stimulates technical and institutional responses that increase real income per person, especially for the working poor, by raising the food productivity of farming systems (Boserup 1965) or the demand for, and thus income and share of, labour (Hayami and Ruttan 1977, 1985). Malthus did not deny such possibilities, but emphasized their limits, their diminishing returns, and above all their propensity to re-ignite population growth (Malthus 1803, 1824; Lipton 1990).

Third, how and to what extent does *poverty cause* its victims to act in ways that induce demographic change? Repetto (1977) estimates that the elasticity of the fertility rate with respect to the absolute income of the poorest 40 per cent is –0.2, and with respect to their share in total income –0.16. To see how this might work, we need to explore the circumstances under which it is 'rational'—under various assumptions about the aims and process of decisions within the household—for couples, poor or non-poor, to aim at higher, or lower, fertility. Couples, it is claimed, act as if they compare the costs of an extra child (mainly mother's opportunity-costs, plus direct costs, of child-rearing) with the benefits (pleasure, income from working children and adolescents, and remittances in old age). This approach emphasizes the triple role of female education in reducing birth-rates:[3] by delaying marriages, by imparting skills that increase the opportunity-cost of mothers' time, and (as with male education) by enabling parents to 'substitute child quality for quantity' (Becker and Lewis 1973) as a source of parental income and pleasure. Population growth may also be reduced by better child health and nutrition; these, by lowering child mortality, lead parents to reduce fertility by a more than offsetting amount, since fertility is motivated by insurance as well as replacement. Since better health and education normally accompany reduced poverty, so as a rule will reduced family size norms and reduced population growth—a conclusion reached by Malthus (1824) for related reasons.[4]

Fourth, Malthus's question embraced, and to some extent transcended, all three of the above issues. He enquired: can poverty be reduced by 'schemes of

[3]   This effect, especially if educated couples (given age) also have lower total fertility rates per year of marriage, far outweighs the effect of education in reducing breast-feeding.

[4]   The only essential difference is that Malthus saw 'the passion between the sexes' as fixed and as inevitably inducing human (and all other creatures) to breed up to subsistence level; the moderns see the amount of breeding as separable from a (perhaps variable) level of passion, and as determined mainly by perceived costs and benefits of children. Hence, for Malthus, the main demographic role of education was to induce people to raise their expected level of subsistence, to prefer higher consumption-per-person for smaller families, and thus to postpone marriage and to 'abstain' within it.

improvement'?[5] Or must such reduction be temporary, since it induces the poor to have more children, thereby increasing the demand for food and eventually the supply of unskilled labour, so that real wage-rates decline and the poor again get poorer? Early Malthus (especially 1798) replied that only by 'prudential checks', i.e. voluntary population restraint, could the poor become less so. Without it, 'schemes of improvement' would leave them no better off in the long term, and damaged in the medium term as the schemes induced larger populations that were then devastated by 'positive checks'. Late Malthus (especially 1824) argued that some 'schemes of improvement'—especially those that reduced child mortality, or increased and prolonged mass education—would directly encourage poor people to aim at higher living standards for fewer children, thus durably enriching the poor (Lipton 1995).

Malthus's question may involve diverse causal chains that are too complex and interwoven for rigorous statistical proof. Yet it encapsulates the policy issue: can today's schemes of improvement—land reform, modern cereal varieties, public-works employment—help the poor, given their likely demographic response? This fact may justify the use—if it is cautious and largely descriptive—of correlations and regressions, even without proper causal ordering. Though they are the opposite of Malthus's own causally ordered approach, they can establish which data sets might be consistent with that approach. For example, suppose that a set of data reveals strong correlations among household size, poverty, and rapid population growth. This cannot prove Malthus's proposition, but establishes that it may apply to these data.

Malthus's question may lose relevance if, as early J. S. Mill (Hollander 1985: 968–70) believed, contraception is not a vice as Malthus claimed, but a way out of his dilemma about 'schemes of improvement'. Most moderns accept Mill's value judgement, but doubt the empirical claim. Most evidence is that TFRs are much more responsive (elastic) to changes in the family-size norm than to changes in the cost of contraception. If so, Malthus's question remains central. His later (1824) answer partially anticipates the arguments of the new economic demography: that the poor choose rational family-size norms; that, if these have serious negative externalities for other poor people (for example, through the 'isolation paradox' (Sen 1967)), it is mostly incentives to norm formation that need to be changed; and that bad health and low levels of education, especially among women, keep family-size norms high.

Health, education, and rural infrastructure are not pure public goods, but are seldom wholly price-excludable.[6] Private providers therefore supply less than the

---

[5] His examples cover Godwin's and Condorcet's social reforms; Young's land reforms; even Smith's economic reforms.

[6] A pure public good is non-rivalrous (if I use more of the services of a lighthouse, you do not have less) and non-price-excludable (it is not feasible, or not economic, for a provider to charge each user for the benefits). Sometimes it is more socially efficient to supply such goods (collective goods) without State provision, e.g. by an enforceable agreement among the 'public' that benefits from them. Sometimes this is not feasible, and the good is supplied by the State or not at all.

social optimum, and bias provision towards types of customer (and service) where cost recovery is easier. In view of the high costs of group action, State activity is often necessary to remedy this, though of course the possible effect on family-size norms should not be the main reason for enabling the poor to obtain health, education, or the fruits of research. Ruttan (1993) points out a 'time warp': the fiscal crises, and the disillusionment with the State, of the early 1980s impaired public-sector activities such as agricultural research, perhaps for a shortish period, but with long-term results. This reduces the prospect of an improved standard of living if a couple chooses a smaller but better-educated family—a prospect that may be needed to make lower family-size norms attractive for the poor. A similar time warp has harmed children in big, poor households. Such children are especially dependent on public provision to correct their parents' below-average ability to provide them with these semi-public goods. This has been shown for primary education in Ghana (Lloyd and Gage-Brandon 1993: 482) and Malaysia (Shreeniwas 1993: 332), and for nutrition surveillance and preventive health care (Desai 1993: 178) in many countries. The delayed-action effect of undiscriminating anti-statism in the early 1980s, therefore, homes in on big, and often therefore poor, families seeking to maintain or upgrade their children's human capital. That makes it less likely that couples will escape poverty by choosing smaller families with better prospects of survival, health, or education.

However, State expansion of rural infrastructure, farm research, health, and education is not sufficient to provide the poor with services, undersupplied privately, that tend to reduce poverty and birth rates. The 'time warp' of disillusionment with State provision had roots in experience of 'how and why governments misbehave' (Birdsall and James 1993) by steering social services away from the poor. If States are to remedy the ill-effects on children of poor couples' (rational) high family-size norms—and perhaps also to reduce those norms—by expanding as efficient providers of health, education, and small-farm infrastructure, then popular control and overview are usually required.

2. A General Framework

We now 'unpack' population variables, and poverty-related variables, that might be correlated and/or causally connected. Ignoring migration, we have ten sets of relevant *population variables*, comprising four sets of outcomes—population size, density, structure (by age and location), and growth—plus six sets of variables from which the outcomes are deducible: numbers, age distribution, and location of births and deaths.

Available research on population–poverty interactions focuses mainly on four sets of indirect, *poverty-related variables*. These variables are: average levels (and/or growth rates) of (1) real private consumption per person, (2) indicators of its distribution between the poor and the non-poor, (3) other components of real GNP (such as investment, and consumption of collective or State-provided commodities, including health and education), and (4) indicators of their distribution between the poor and the non-poor.[7] The population variables permit direct estimates of the numbers of people, etc., but the poverty-related variables do not directly estimate the extent or depth of poverty. Direct measures of poverty incidence, intensity, and severity[8] are deducible from the indirect variables; their functional relationships (for example, incidence of 'below-poverty-line' consumption-per-person, as a function of nationwide average consumption and its Gini coefficient of inequality) are derived and tested by Datt and Ravallion (1992), but the equations are complex and non-intuitive. Useful discussion of poverty-population links has to go beyond the indirect indicators of some aspects of poverty. We need to ask whether population variables are correlates, causes, or effects of direct poverty indicators—i.e. of inadequate (private) consumption, and of the lack of wellbeing or capability that such inadequacy may bring. What are the direct indicators, and how do they relate to the 'lack'?

Poverty is often defined as existing if, and only if, monthly consumption per person, or per adult equivalent, falls below some norm, associated with the expectation of just meeting some basic need (such as nutrition), and constant across countries and over time.[9] Such private-consumption poverty (PCP) can be measured by incidence, intensity, or severity. Chen *et al.* (1995) report reliable household surveys of PCP for forty-one developing and three East European countries between 1981 and 1992 (there are respectively seventeen and two repeat surveys).

This chapter concentrates on a few of the relationships between the ten demographic variables and four variables bearing indirectly on PCP: average private consumption and 'other GNP', and the shares in them of the potentially poor. This is partly because there is little evidence about the relationship between national-level direct PCP indicators—incidence, intensity and severity—and demographic variables.[10]

---

[7]   To assess the *severity* of poverty (or the links between severity and population variables), we also need to know about distribution among the poor.

[8]   Incidence is the population below the poverty line, divided by total population. Intensity is measured by multiplying each poor person by his or her income gap—the distance between that person and the poverty line, as a proportion of the level of wellbeing (e.g. consumption) per person at that line— before adding the observations and dividing by the total population. Severity also takes into account the distribution among the poor; a convenient measure is to 'multiply' each poor person by the square of his or her income gap, to add the sum, and to divide by total population. For full discussion see Kakwani (1993) and Lipton and Ravallion (1995).

[9]   A commonly used norm is the level of consumption-per-person sufficient, assuming expenditure patterns (e.g. proportion devoted to food) and nutrient needs typical of an Indian at that consumption level, to provide a just-sufficient diet. This assumes, not that we live by bread alone, but that people (especially those at risk of poverty) divide their consumption rationally between food and other basic needs. That consumption is usually measured in US purchasing-power parity dollars of a constant year; US\$ 21.00 per month in 1985 US PPP dollars is in normal use. A somewhat higher absolute poverty line of US\$ 30.42 (1985) US PPP dollars per month is also commonly used, roughly reflecting the level at which a (similarly typical) person might begin to have a surplus for savings, etc. See Chen *et al.* (1995) for data and definitions. Arguments about relative versus absolute poverty are reviewed in Sen (1984), Lipton and Ravallion (1995), etc.

[10]   Eastwood and Lipton (1997) explore cross-national links between population growth (also separated into birth rates and death rates) and subsequent poverty incidence. The links to fertility are positive, strong, and significant.

We also need to know how demographic variables interact with outcomes often *associated* with PCP, such as illiteracy or high mortality. PCP is not the whole of human misery, even economic misery. Access to State or collective commodities may improve the capacity of the potentially poor to convert PCP levels of consumption into adequate outcome indicators of wellbeing—capabilities as well as utilities—such as educational access, low infant and child mortality, etc. This access depends partly on average public and collective outlay on health and education, and its distribution between potentially poor people and others.

High or low population growth, size, or density may be correlate, cause, or effect, not only of PCP or the indirect variables related to it, but also, directly, of 'misery variables' such as mortality or illiteracy (see below). Further, some countries have performed much better than others in transforming high average GNP into low PCP; or in transforming relatively low GNP-per-head and high PCP into low 'misery', such as low death rates and low illiteracy (Lipton 1995a). Such differences in success may have demographic correlates, causes or effects.

The level or change of poverty, in any of these senses, depends upon the level or change of resources[11] per person, of their distribution between poor and non-poor, and (if we seek to measure the severity of poverty) of their distribution among the poor.[12] Population growth may sometimes increase GNP per person (for example, via economies of scale due to higher population size or density), yet so reduce the share of unskilled labour that poverty increases nevertheless (Birdsall and Griffin 1993). Indeed, Malthus agreed with Smith that appropriate reforms—although inducing population growth—could increase GNP per person, but differed from Smith in arguing that such reforms would not in general (in the absence of falling family-size norms) reduce poverty. This underlines the need to review separately the relationships between the various population variables and, first, real consumption, etc., per person and, second, its distribution between rich and (potentially) poor—and, if we are concerned with severity, among the poor.

The framework, then, is as follows. We should consider ten types of population variable for a country or area: birth rates, their timing by age, and perhaps their location; similarly for death rates; and, defined by these (assuming negligible net migration in each age-group), the growth rate, density, absolute size, and age-structure of population. The level or change in each of these ten sets of variables can be a correlate, cause, or consequence of four sets of indirect poverty variables; two sets determine the amount and change of PCP (average per-person private consumption and its distribution); the other two sets ('the rest of GNP per person', viz. the per-person averages of main types of investment and of public and collective consumption; and

---

[11]   These can be measured as private consumption or as income.

[12]   Suppose that countries A and B have the same proportion of persons below the PCP line, and the same average difference between that line and the consumption of the average poor person. If income is more unequally distributed among the poor in A, then A's poverty would be regarded (by almost all observers) as more severe than B's, because A contains a larger proportion of destitute people far below the poverty line.

a set summarizing the distribution of such variables) partly determine the transformation of PCP into outcomes, such as levels of mortality or illiteracy.

The framework thus comprises (a) four sets of indirect poverty variables (each set capable of altering the incidence, intensity or severity of PCP and/or of some composite of 'misery' such as the *Human Poverty Index* [UNDP 1977]) multiplied by (b) ten sets of demographic variables. As discussed in Section 1, most connections between (a) and (b) are possible via (1) zero-order and partial correlations, and simple or multiple but causally unstructured regressions; (2) structures of equations in which changes, or turning-points, in (a) precede those in (b) according to a causal law; and (3) similar structures in which changes in (b) precede changes in (a).[13] This would imply 4 x 10 x 3—that is, 120—possible sequences!

Even this oversimplifies reality. First, just as within demography, so between it and economics, most of the relationships operate via intervening variables. For example, a change in the birth-rate might alter the rate of growth of GNP by changing either the efficiency of labour or capital, or the share of resources devoted to saving, whether to invest in capital or to upgrade labour skills via education. Second, the framework is incomplete. Notably, the efficiency with which people convert a given amount of private consumption into wellbeing does not depend solely on the level, growth and composition of investment and of public or collective consumption. For example, a level of consumption that would mean PCP and undernutrition for A may leave B well fed, though A and B have similar health, education, height, weight, and work (Payne and Lipton 1994; Lipton 1994b).

Fortunately, for many entries in the framework, there is not much research to report! Timing, spacing, and location of deaths, as a cause of the indirect poverty variables, appears almost completely unexplored. I have found little research into the effects of the composition of death rates, for example by age, on poverty—whether via private consumption per person, poor people's share in it, non-private or non-consumption GNP, or poor people's share in that. Not all apparently relevant research is in fact so. For example, the modelling of the age-specific effects of AIDS (see, for example, UN 1993: 53–80) permits projections of the impact on workforce and hence (perhaps) GNP, but is silent about differential effects between poor and non-poor on deaths, work or incomes (see, however, Basu, Chapter 9 below).

It would be impossible to present all 120 framework entries in a chapter of tolerable length, even if all were researched. Nor will it be feasible to keep the distinction between correlations, population-to-poverty causal sequences, and the reverse sequences watertight. The aim is to present some of the more interesting findings in each category, and to point to emerging conclusions and gaps in research.

---

[13]   (2) and (3) can be true of the same data set. Thus Malthus's core argument is that (schemes of improvement leading to) higher average consumption, or a larger share in consumption for the poor, by reducing PCP, leads to rising birth rates or falling death rates among the poor, and that this then lowers consumption among the poor and increases PCP again.

3. Household Size and Poverty

The relationship between demography and poverty has been fairly successfully investigated, at least at household level, by 'unpacking' the simple correlation between poverty and household size. A demographic paradox of poverty in today's developing world is that (1) as per the simple correlation, larger households tend to be poorer (but see Anand and Morduch, Chapter 2 above), (2) household size tends to increase with land ownership and economic status, yet (3) obviously, land and status accompany not poverty but affluence. This paradox has been explored (Lipton 1983; Krishnaji 1984) and partly explained. Hajnal (1982) has analysed the differences between 'two types of household formation'. In Northern European pre-industrial and early industrial household structures, (2) and (3) applied, but not (1), so that no paradox emerged. In today's developing world, (1) applies and—together with (2) and (3)—generates the paradox.[14]

Hundreds of empirical studies confirm that in today's developing countries larger households have higher *incidence* of PCP (Krishnaji 1984; Lloyd 1994; Lipton 1983, 1994: 12–13). For example, in urban Colombia in the 1970s, in the poorest decile of households, 78 per cent contained eight or more persons, as against only 12 per cent for all households (Birdsall 1979). Since the relationship is probabilistic, and even as such is contingent on incentives and other factors, it is not surprising that an occasional localized survey provides an exception. Recent evidence, however, suggests that there are no large regional exceptions, as was sometimes claimed for West Africa, for example; the household surveys in Ghana, the Ivory Coast (Glewwe 1990; Kakwani 1993: 53–4)[15] and Mauritania (Coulombe and Mackay 1994: 48), show a strong positive link between household size and PCP incidence. Probably all, or almost all, the forty-one developing countries with reliable household surveys show this relationship in both urban and rural areas. PCP *intensity* also often increases with household size (see, for example, Bauer and Mason 1993: 34). To say more, we must look at the structure, not just the size, of poor and other households.

First, bigger households tend to be poorer although they contain a larger proportion of children. When the above surveys allow comparison of poverty incidence below a line defined in terms of consumption per equivalent adult, big households usually remain substantially poorer than small, though not as much poorer as when the poverty line is defined in terms of consumption per person.

Second, economies of scale in consumption, for poor households in developing

---

[14]   Strictly it is only a pseudo-paradox. Propositions (1), (2) and (3) are all probabilistic only, so there is no logical contradiction among them. A correct inference from (1), (2) and (3) jointly is that, within a group of households of a given status or level of asset ownership, the tendency for larger households to be poorer must be even stronger than in the population as a whole.

[15]   Kakwani develops significance tests for the Foster-Greer-Thorbecke family of poverty indicators, and shows that both incidence and severity of poverty increase significantly (at 5 per cent) with household size.

countries, do not overcome the greater poverty exposure of large households to any great extent (King 1987, 389). Lazear and Michael (1980) show that in the USA such economies are large for households with average consumption per person, and remain substantial (though smaller) for poorer households. However, such economies of scale—which apply to transportation, meals out, house shelter and security, etc.—are unlikely to count for much in households anywhere near the borderline of food adequacy, i.e. the lower or extreme poverty line, in developing countries. Food, cooking fuel and clothing absorb perhaps 90 per cent of consumption in such households, leaving barely 10 per cent to which economies of scale in consumption might apply. Suppose a household, below the poverty line, doubled in size without changing total consumption (so that real consumption per person would halve, if there were no economies of scale). Now suppose that, for items absorbing 10 per cent of initial consumption, there are huge scale economies, so that a doubling of household size reduces per-person benefit from these items by only 2 per cent. Even then, economies of scale in consumption would mean only that, when household size doubled, real consumption per person would fall to 53 per cent of its initial value (instead of 50 per cent if there had been no scale economies).[16]

Third, the reason why poorer households are bigger than others is not household complexity—three-generation families, polygamy, adult siblings in the parents' house, etc. Complex households are indeed larger than others as a rule (Lipton 1983, 29). However, the nuclear family was the norm in pre-industrial and early industrial Western Europe and in most of the rest of the now-developed world (Laslett 1971; Laslett and Wall [eds.] 1972; Wall, Robin and Laslett [eds.] 1983). Similar results based on village studies, both contemporary and over long periods, are available for India (see, for example Shah 1968, 1973; Lipton 1983, 31) and some other developing countries.

Another reason why complex households cannot explain the linkage of poverty to household size is that these tend to be accompanied by wealth rather than poverty in today's developing countries (ibid; Goody 1972: 122).[17] Poor men can seldom 'afford' more than one wife. Economies of scale in consumption, such as when several married siblings stay under the same roof, are much likelier in better-off households with consumer durables. As for three-generation households, Hoddinott (1993) provides evidence from Western Kenya (and reviews other evidence) that

[16] Lanjouw and Ravallion (1995) present an interesting worked counter-example for Pakistan, suggesting that a household with an income per head at the poverty line—but twice as large as the average-size household at the poverty line—might typically enjoy as much as 1.3 times more consumption than that average-size household. This extreme result suggests that 'local public goods', usable free by all and only household members, loom unusually large. If a household has sole access to, say, a drinking well, supplying at no cost 10 per cent of initial consumption per person and suffering no depletion when the number of users doubles, then the services of that well automatically become 20 per cent of household consumption, if household size doubles and its total consumption of all other goods (i.e. private goods) stays the same. (Note, however, that in urban areas, where rent is a substantial part of consumption even among some very poor households, economies of scale to household size may be more important than in rural areas.)

[17] This was also true in now-developed countries during their pre-industrial period (e.g. Laslett 1971: 95, 181; 1978: 93–4; Ladurie 1979: 4; Klapisch 1972: 277, 279; Wall et al. (eds.) 1983).

poor parents are less likely than others to be able to persuade—in Hoddinott's words, 'manipulate'—their adolescent, or married, children to remain at home and work for their parents in the hope of inheritance (or fear of disinheritance). Family labour is also more forthcoming to better-off parents because their land, or other assets, reduce the transaction cost and risks involved in the informed family worker's seeking and completing work.

Fourth, the link between poverty and household size is not due to a large number of elderly persons in 'big poor' households. On the contrary, the incidence of old people in developing-country households is lower among the poor than among the non-poor (Lipton 1983). The 'old poor' are especially liable to live in a widow-only (Drèze 1990) or two-member household, and to have less chance of persuading their children to help them than wealthier couples do (see previous paragraph).[18]

By 'unpacking' the link between large households and poverty, we see that it weakens only slightly if we measure size in adult equivalents, and allow for economies of scale in consumption. The size–poverty link strengthens if we hold constant the degree of household complexity (extendedness, nuclearity) and/or the proportion of old people; and the link is strongest among households of low status or with few assets. It is children of the nuclear couple, not its siblings, parents or in-laws, who are heavily overrepresented in the big households of the poor. The strong link between poverty and household size therefore reflects an even stronger link, above all for households with few economic or social reserves (that is, respectively, assets or status), between poverty, high child/adult ratios, and relatedly high fertility (outweighing, and responding to risks created by, poor households' higher infant and child mortality). This is not due mainly to replacement fertility—extra births in response to decisions following the death of a child. That compensates for only about one-third of extra mortality; and we do not know whether such compensation is greater in poorer households. About two-thirds of their extra fertility—needed to compensate for their higher mortality, and thus to make them larger than non-poor households—must therefore be due to 'hoarding' of children in anticipation of expected higher child mortality (King 1987).

The special vulnerability of children (see Ferro-Luzzi, Chapter 4 below) means that we can take little comfort from the observation that 20–35 per cent of poverty is transient (Gaiha and Kazmi 1982; Ryan and Walker 1990; World Bank 1990: 35).[19] Most such poverty is a correlate of large household size and high child/adult ratios. The concentration of PCP in large households while they have many children implies that a larger proportion of children than of adults is poor. Where adjustment causes governments to withdraw from providing child-related services, transient poverty 'is likely to increase the vulnerability of children in large families' (Desai 1993, 178–9).[20] At the extreme, many households move out of transient poverty,

---

[18]   Recent data for Mauritania (Coulombe and Mackay 1994: 56) and Mali (Lalou and Mbacké 1993: 216) suggest that size–PCP correlations are stronger in the low-status, low-asset groups of households.

[19]   This is usually for life-cycle reasons. Transient poverty is likeliest when households have a partly housebound mother, one male full-time earner, several young children and, as yet, no inherited assets.

[20]   A commentator (Andrea Cornia) suggests that in Eastern Europe and the former Soviet Union the rapid reduction of State provision may have reduced fertility and 'linked' poverty to *smaller* family size.

and attain smaller size, for the terrible reason that poverty reduces their size by killing their children. Short of this extreme, in large poor households—even if only temporarily so—the consequences for health, nutrition, and primary schooling often hit the most vulnerable: small children. Section 4 explores the causal impact of household size on other poverty-related variables.

4. Fertility and Economic Growth

Most tests of whether changing population variables cause changes in poverty variables are at the household level. This has enabled analysts to separate the impact of different aspects of household demography upon poverty. However, many causal links, by which demographic change is claimed to affect poverty, cannot be captured by comparing households alone. For example, Malthus argued that increased fertility—via increased labour supply and food demand—pushes down the wage rate, increases unemployment, and raises the demand price of food staples. Such effects, if they happen, will affect all workers and food-buyers in a market, not just households with higher fertility. Some household-level studies of fertility and mortality try to capture such things by estimating the impact of community-level variables as fixed effects (Benefo and Schultz 1994) However, only in very remote areas does even 'the community' contain the market, and capture almost all the effects of population change on markets in, say, labour and food.

Only studies at national or cross-national level can capture the full, including external (cross-household, cross-community) and macro, effects of changes in demographic variables upon income, distribution, or direct poverty variables. The effect of population variables on poverty can be divided into two questions. Do they affect aggregates—production, consumption, education spending, etc., or their growth—across countries, or in one country over time? Do they affect distribution of such aggregates between poor and non-poor?[21]

A major study by Kelley and Schmidt (1994) examines how decadal differences between countries, in population growth, size, and density, and in birth rates and death rates, affect the growth of real GDP per person in the decade starting five years later. Effects are examined both directly, and via the possible effect of population on dependency ratios, and hence on the propensity to save and thereby on economic growth. Earlier work by Simon and Gobin (1980) had claimed that high population increase did not affect the growth rate of real income per person. Kelley and Schmidt had access to more powerful statistical tools and far better data. They confirm the Simon-Gobin result for the 1960s and 1970s, but find a strong, robust and highly significant negative relationship between a nation's growth of real GDP per head and of population for the 1980s.

---

[21] Two related causal sequences might be: from population growth, via worsened distribution of income (the Malthus sequence), to slower growth of real income per head (e.g. Clarke 1995); and from population growth, via slower growth of real income per head (this section), to changed income distribution between rich and poor (the alleged Kuznets curve).

If the median developing country's rate of population growth in 1980, *viz.* 2.54 per cent per year, had persisted until 1990, predicted growth of real GDP per person would have been *minus* 0.34 per cent per year. If the growth rate of population had fallen by 0.02 per cent per year to 2.34 per cent in 1990, decadal growth of real GDP per person would have improved by 0.41–0.47 per cent per year, depending on how other demographic and economic variables are incorporated (Kelley and Schmidt 1994: 29, 44–6). The result retains its force if growth in labour force productivity, rather than in real GDP per person, is the dependent variable (Kelley and Schmidt 1994: 48–9). If panel data and time-period dummies are used, the impact of population growth on growth of GDP per person is consistently and significantly negative for developing countries even in the 1960s and 1970s, though the effect remains strongest in the 1980s (Kelley and Schmidt 1994: 52–3).

Importantly, Kelley and Schmidt 'unpack' the impact, upon growth of real GDP per head, of international differences in population growth rates into two components: differences in 'adapted' birth rates and in 'adapted' death rates ('adapted' means excluding infant deaths). In the multiple regression on real GDP per person, the former, adapted fertility, variable is included both contemporaneously with GDP growth (in mid-decade) and lagged 15 years. The authors conclude (p. 59):

Economic growth in the countries with high [population growth] was inhibited in the 1960s and 1970s by high [adapted] birth rates, but spurred by declining [adapted] death rates. . . . [The adapted] death rate for the median [developing country] approached that for the median [developed] country by the mid-1980s. Additional [GDP-]growth-enhancing decreases in the [adapted] death rate will be hard to achieve . . . [T]he growth-inhibiting influence of continued high birth-rates has risen dramatically in the 1980s . . . [helping to] explain the negative influence of [population growth on growth of real GDP per person] in the 1980s.

Thus the findings of Simon and Gobin, that population growth did not appear to affect per-person GDP growth in the 1960s and 1970s, were due to two offsetting effects. Countries with higher (adapted) fertility experienced slower subsequent economic growth; but so did countries with high adapted mortality. After 1980, mortality differences among developing countries were smaller, due to past success in reducing mortality where it had been highest. Hence in the 1980s mortality differences were too small to make as much difference to subsequent growth rates as before. The link between national differences in demography and in subsequent economic growth was dominated by fertility differences. Higher population growth slowed economic growth.

Kelley and Schmidt (pp. 74–6) show how this damage may work. Life-cycle explanations of savings behaviour suggest that high dependency ratios tend to increase savings by stimulating bequests—but to reduce it through diversion of resources to children's consumption, and withdrawal of mothers from the workforce. In developing countries, the bequests effect was much smaller—especially in the 1980s, when differences among countries in death-rates had shrunk. Thus the negative savings impact of higher birth-rates dominated, and the impact of population increase upon the growth of real national product per person became clearly negative. This account is consistent with the fact that in the 1980s a savings constraint came to dominate growth prospects in developing nations, as fiscal pressures on governments tightened.

We must be cautious—as Kelley and Schmidt certainly are—about big inferences from a single study, however persuasive. The debates around the numerous mechanisms allegedly linking high fertility to subsequent economic growth—negatively via resource dilution and depletion, positively via economies of scale and incentives to invent—fill many libraries. Let us suppose, however, that—as I have come to believe—lower fertility in developing countries significantly accelerates subsequent growth of real income per head. What does this tell us about the effect on poverty?

Without considering changes in distribution between poor and non-poor, we cannot conclude that lower fertility—even if it does mean lower growth of GDP per head—must reduce poverty. Trickle-down is by no means automatic (as the experience of Brazil in the 1960s proves). Some critics of structural adjustment claim that, even when it restores economic growth, it may initially harm the poor (or at least the urban poor) through dearer food imports, reduced public-sector job chances, and cuts in public expenditure. However, it is rare for the poor to gain nothing during real long-term growth in output per head, let alone to lose significantly, in developing countries.[22] Where measured in reliable household surveys, the elasticity of poverty incidence to the growth of real income per person ranges from about 0.3 to about 1.5.[23] Hence, if lower fertility does accelerate real output per person, it probably reduces poverty. It not only reduces savings and hence growth via life-cycle effects, but also probably reduces the share of real wages in income by raising labour supply and food prices; this *Malthus effect* is demonstrated across India's districts by Evenson (1993).

Suppose that the national levels of fertility, mortality and household size are given. What is the micro-level and household evidence on how a household's risk of poverty is affected by *its own* demographic patterns?[24] Higher fertility and more children reduce a household's average consumption, increase its risk of poverty, and, apart from this, reduce the ratio of child consumption to adult consumption, especially in poor households. Bauer and Mason (1993: 24, 30) point out that as child numbers increase:

... the increasing budget shares going to children imply declines in consumption [of] 14 to 16 per cent in the Philippines and 17 to 20 per cent in Thailand [but per-child consumption is cut back much more] ... The move from a one-child to a four-child family is associated with ... declines in 'expenditures per child' of 43–48 per cent in urban and rural Philippines and Thailand.

Assumptions about scale economies, and methods of calculating equivalence scales, do not alter the finding of 'very substantial' impact of family size on poverty.

---

[22] As happened to the poorest deciles in Britain and the USA between 1977 and 1994.

[23] Ravallion (personal communication) and others base these estimates on sixteen developing countries with repeated household expenditure surveys since 1980—some with only two or three years between surveys, however—and on long time-series in India. Where elasticity lies, within this range, depends on the labour-intensity of growth, the poverty-orientation of policy, and the concentration of people just below the poverty line.

[24] See also Lipton and Ravallion (1995, Section 4.2) and Lipton (1983).

In Pakistan's 1984–5 household survey, the poorest quintile of households by income-per person averaged 4.3 children, and the least poor 1.5 (Allison *et al.* 1989: 41; compare work by Visaria and others reported in Lipton 1983). Causal links between higher fertility and subsequent higher poverty are estimated by Daly (1985: 331–3).

A review by Mueller (1984: 128-33) confirms that, where there is a significant link between household fertility and subsequent real consumption or income per person, the link is negative.[25] Apparent exceptions arise only where such variables as higher educational level are used, alongside low fertility, to predict higher real income or consumption; fertility then often loses significance, or even reverses sign. However, lack of education (a) is itself made more likely by parents' previous high fertility, and (b) tends both to cause, and to result from, low income per person. Higher fertility induces households to suffer from a bundle of mutually caused attributes—including inability to afford education—clustered around poverty.

Households work their way out of poverty partly by saving and education. In Pakistan, households with higher fertility (just like nations in the Kelley-Schmidt data) are induced, by the consequent high dependency ratios, to reduce (private) saving. Until children reach the age of fifteen years, the saving out of their earnings is much too little to offset the reduction of parental savings to pay for children's consumption (Allison *et al.* 1989). Also, even allowing for differences in real income per person, children in larger households enjoy worse educational prospects; evidence of the causal sequence from high fertility to worse and less education appears for numerous countries in King (1987) and more recently for Thailand in Knodel (1993) and for the Philippines in deGraff *et al.* (1993).[26] The work on twins in rural India by Rosenzweig and Wolpin (1980) shows unambiguously that unplanned, and therefore non-endogenous, increases in fertility cause reductions in the older siblings' access to education. Such relationships, as expected, apply much more strongly to households in the poverty zone than to wealthy households. In most studies, high fertility and large households especially damage the educational prospects of girls (Lloyd and Gage-Brandon 1993, for Ghana; Shreeniwas 1993, for Malaysia; implicitly, Greenhalgh 1985 for Taiwan; see also Lloyd 1994). The educational harm from high fertility, overall and especially for girls, is usually less in rural areas, because there is less to damage. In general, where few people, especially few girls, are educated the effect of sibling numbers on their prospects is smaller or negligible, as in Pakistan (Lloyd 1994; Allison *et al.* 1989, 38–9).

Large household size—apart from reducing children's chance of receiving education—also impairs their prospects of benefiting from a given amount of education. Partly this is because large households tend to be less healthy and worse nourished, and to discriminate more among members; sick children make bad pupils. Larger households provide less care per child, less access to health care, and

---

[25]   Her interpretation of the surveys cited does not fully confirm mine; readers may wish to check for themselves.
[26]   The latter study is unusual in showing the worst effects on older male siblings.

more gender discrimination in food distribution (King 1987; Desai 1993: 179; Mahmud and McIntosh 1980; Lloyd 1994). Much greater risk of undernutrition appears in larger households, for example in the Philippines, Bangladesh, and Mali (King 1987). 'In 12 of 16 countries the addition of a sibling under age 5 has a significant negative impact on children's height-for-age standardized scores' (Desai 1993: 165). In one suggestive study, larger household size (and associated greater poverty risk) brings more damage to nutrition[27] in villages where average consumption is relatively low (Mahmud and Macintosh 1980). As for health, in Mali 'competition between children [and] exhaustion of the mother' are quantified as 'explanatory factors[28] for the same reality: poverty'. Here too, health damage due to large household size is confined to households that own few or no assets (Lalou and Mbacké 1993: 206, 216). Lloyd (1994) presents powerful evidence that the links are subtler than is often claimed—operating not mainly through female exhaustion and sibling crowding, but because larger households tend to be more authoritarian, less equal and less altruistic than smaller households, and more hierarchical by both age and gender.

Child vulnerability in large, poor households declines with effective government action to counter the effects of transient poverty, induced by extra births, on child health and education. That is partly because such action stimulates reduced fertility. Lower infant and child mortality reduces replacement and hoarding fertility; cheaper, better education allows families to substitute child quality for quantity. 'Studies that compared data from the 1970s and early 1990s showed that the decline in fertility in Malaysia was accompanied by a closing of the gap in per-child resources between the lowest and the highest quintiles' of households (World Bank 1994: 39).[29] Fertility reduction, apart from possible effects on PCP, reduces the damage to children from given levels of poverty. If poor families are helped to control fertility, their children benefit even if overall PCP indicators do not improve. In Thailand, children's education improved with falling household size, even with 'household wealth level' (admittedly an imperfect indicator of poverty) held constant (Knodel 1993, 289).[30]

The sibling distribution and timing of the sequence, from high fertility to poverty and from both to bad health, nutrition and education, shows that this is indeed a causal chain. Close spacing of births, not just their total number, links high fertility to both increased health risks to mothers and children, and distribution of consumption

[27] The study is in Bangladesh, where (as in North India and Pakistan) there is evidence of gender discrimination against little girls in food provision or health care. In such circumstances the nutritional damage, associated with larger and poorer families, appears to fall especially on these girls. See Anand and Morduch, Chapter 2 above.

[28] Lloyd (1994) has a more nuanced, socially contextualized account of how large families induce child deprivation.

[29] It is relevant that Malaysia is among many countries where household size and poverty are strongly correlated, and that Malaysian public expenditure redistributes resources towards households with low income per person (a passable indicator of poverty), though not towards those with low income per household (a far inferior indicator) (Datta and Meerman 1980).

[30] More on the fertility–poverty link can be found in David, Chapter 7, and Gage, Chapter 8, below.

poverty and misery towards specific siblings (Lalou and Mbacké 1993, 209).[31] First births substantially raise the risks to mother and child only if they follow early (that is, adolescent) pregnancies. All this is typical of families starting early and poor, and getting larger and thus poorer. So are high-order births, for which risks of death, ill-health, and bad school performance rise sharply. For instance, in Pakistan, 'eliminating all births after the fifth would reduce maternal mortality by half' (Allison *et al.* 1989: 36). At regional level, low average GNP, and hence poor health and hygiene, greatly increase risks from high fertility and large household size. 'In high-fertility areas of West and Central Africa women have a 1-in-20 chance of dying from maternal causes, while in low-fertility East Asia [it is] 1 in 722 and in North Europe . . . 1 in 10,000. . . . Girls who bear a child before age 18 are three times more likely to die in childbirth than [at age] 18–29' (World Bank 1994: 45).

Demographic variables other than population increase, fertility, and mortality can also affect average real income, its distribution, and therefore poverty. Kelley and Schmidt (1994) confirm significant positive effects of a country's population density and absolute size on the growth of GDP per person.[32] The effect of absolute size may be due to economies of scale in government, in research and invention (as emphasized by Simon 1986), or in the provision of rural infrastructure; and/or with gains from being able to trade freely among many different firms, skills, and environments within a nation. Scale economies are likely to give way to diseconomies as rural densities grow—and as a growing proportion of populations comes to live in large cities; the per-person cost of providing and co-ordinating key urban services begins to rise after population reaches a certain (location-specific, and controversial) size. The gains from size as a key to wider-ranging internal trade also diminish as developing countries reduce their restrictions on *international* trade and exchange, as has been a strong trend in the 1980s.

How does higher population density affect the poor? As regards average income, work in Machakos, Kenya (Mortimore and Tiffen 1994) is among several micro-studies suggesting that rural people often find farming methods (such as terracing) that permit sustainable maintenance of real output per person in face of rising population density. The positive cross-national correlation (Kelley and Schmidt 1994) between population density (not population growth) and subsequent growth of real income per person is consistent with a Boserup response of techniques to rising density—not necessarily in the production of subsistence staples, but in the farm and non-farm economy jointly—large and rapid enough that output per person overtakes the effects of an increase in density. However, 'consistent with' does not mean 'causing'; this year's density (and even, probably, the change in density) is positively related to last year's, and the same applies to real output per person. Nevertheless, at local level, people—especially if their numbers are growing

---

[31]   There is some evidence that, if spacing is held constant, children in larger families do not suffer much worse health, nutrition or education. However, there is an almost tautologous link between closer spacing and larger families.

[32]   In the 1980s these effects were dwarfed, in the cross-country regressions, by the negative effects of population growth.

rapidly—are likely to move towards areas of a country able to absorb increases in density while sustaining rapid growth in output.

Nevertheless, many areas—including much of Africa—have in the past been handicapped by low population density in efforts to build cost-effective infrastructures for growth, health and education. That is one source of the widespread reluctance to accept causal links from high fertility, via poverty, to bad health and education. A second source is fear that the links, if accepted, provide an excuse for governments to do nothing about poverty, except blame the poor for having children. A third is justified rejection of simplistic and deterministic accounts of demographic transition. Nevertheless, the facts remain that fertility declines with development; that the better-off find it pays them to reduce fertility sooner—partly because their child mortality falls first, partly because the opportunity cost of their time is more, and partly because it is easier for them to substitute child quality for quantity via education; and that high fertility impedes the escape from poverty in the families in which it occurs.

The main enemy of the 'fertility perpetuates poverty' argument is revulsion from accusing the poor of being irrational. However, no such accusation is implied. High fertility, despite its costs to poor couples as a whole, is usually rational for the individual poor couple. Partly, this is because of a version of Sen's (1967) isolation paradox: while most couples are adding their children to the queue for work, each poor couple is impelled to secure its income by similar action, even though the total effect reduces labour income. The pressure on each couple towards a strategy of high fertility is often fierce—in Bangladesh 'reproductive failure' greatly reduced a couple's survival chances in old age (Cain 1985; cf. Hoddinott 1993: 46)—but if many couples adopt this strategy it helps to perpetuate poverty, for themselves and their children.

But is the effect of high fertility in raising poverty merely a short-run cost—pending a benefit to the poor as invention responds to extra demand for food (Boserup 1965) and to extra supply of labour (Hayami and Ruttan 1985)? Ruttan himself (1993: 128–31), after reviewing the evidence on whether 'advances in indigenous technology . . . induced by rapid population growth would be sufficient to sustain rising levels of per capita income and consumption', concludes that 'a positive response would be excessively romantic'. He reminds us that Lee (1980) demonstrated the negative effects, chiefly via Malthus-style rises in the rent/wage ratio, whenever annual population growth in pre-industrial England rose above 0.4 per cent. Such negative effects could have persisted only if that increasing ratio was neither prevented nor compensated by labour-absorbing technical response.

Ruttan (1993) and others rightly conclude that institutional research response, State-mediated and/or international, to population growth at current high rates (2–4 per cent yearly) is also needed. With such increases, there is little hope that privately induced technical progress alone[33] will be both sufficiently labour-using to prevent

[33] There are problems about private response. First, researchers, resources and savings are largest and most expansible in developed countries where population grows slowly. Second, such researchers do not automatically receive signals to respond to changes in demand (even effective demand) in very poor countries. Third, population growth, especially among persons not of working age, reduces the resources for saving and education required for appropriate research responses.

increasing poverty as per-person entitlements of the unskilled decline (Hayami-Ruttan 1985), and sufficiently productive to enhance the availability of food (or food-exchangeables) (Boserup 1965; Lipton 1990). Even the combination of private, public, international, endogenous, and exogenous technical and institutional responses to population density cannot indefinitely sustain availability, unless it pays the poor to reduce fertility. Moreover, if Ruttan's arguments justify public action, breaking the fertility-to-poverty link by generating more agricultural research than the market provides, do the same arguments not also support public action to induce voluntary fertility reduction? Just as agricultural research has public-goods elements leading to its systematic private undersupply (in response to high fertility or otherwise), so very high fertility is the reverse of a public good: it carries non-reimbursable costs to others, leading to its private oversupply (Sen 1967).

In the past two decades, a new development has made it increasingly unlikely that—without public action to increase the supply of labour-using, food-increasing agricultural invention, and to reduce voluntary fertility—the link between population growth and poverty can be broken. This new development is the emergence of a uniquely prolonged régime of high real interest rates. These signal to all parties—farmers, researchers, scientists, parents—that costs and gains in 20–50 years are of little market value, compared to present costs and gains. Peace-time rates on prime long-term loans ranged between 1.5 per cent and 2.5 per cent for at least a century until 1974. Since the late 1970s they have been 4–6 per cent. This sharp rise in real long-term interest rates has broken the communications between increases in population density and the price signals—the changing incentives—that in the past have induced corrective responses via agricultural invention, conservation or discovery of nutrient and water resources, and reduction of fertility. Very high real rates signal, to farmers, that the income generated by conserving soil and water for production thirty years hence is almost worthless, compared with income from exploitation and depletion now (Lipton 1991). Also, such high rates mean that the (usually long-deferred) benefits of research to governments and nations loom small, and its short-term costs large. Likewise, the long view and delayed gratification, required of parents if they are to 'substitute quantity for quality', giving up income and support from many earning children now in order to educate a few for later, become less affordable and less appealing. It used to be plausible to rely on long-run, endogenous neoclassical responses of research, conservation and fertility to mitigate, or even reverse, the effects of rising rural population density on real output of food and food-exchangeables; on labour income per person in agriculture; and hence on poverty. After two decades of fiscal laxity and tight money in OECD, persistently high real rates of interest make such reliance 'unsafe and unsatisfactory'.

5. Poverty and Demographic Variables

We now look at the opposite causal chain: from poverty variables to demographic variables. There is less evidence here based on fieldwork, mainly because demographic response—for example, if poverty leads to earlier marriage and higher fertility—is both lagged and spread over a long period. Hence few responsive vital events may be observed in a reasonable fieldwork period, such as a year. Cross-sections are more vulnerable, and panels costlier, in testing for poverty-to-demography causation than *vice versa*. If we use national-level comparisons instead of household data, the problem remains: demographic response may lag decades behind changes in poverty.

However, we do expect causal sequences from poverty to fertility, for several reasons. First, the correlations are often closer and stronger than can be explained by causal sequences from fertility to poverty alone. Second, some of the evidence on timing suggests poverty-to-fertility sequences; for example, better-off households normally provide children with longer education than poorer households, delaying marriage and otherwise reducing household size, especially in the case of female education. Third, this sequence typifies the ways in which poverty compels couples to produce many children who are themselves doomed to poverty, or else to risk 'reproductive failure' bringing destitution in old age (Cain 1985). This is a 'cycle of poverty', but not with the usual connotation (to blame the victims and to absolve the rich and the State). In this cycle, inequality and inadequate, or inappropriate, State actions create harsh circumstances in which poor, undernourished and undereducated parents cannot avoid 'rational choices' to produce many children at high risk of being as poor as their parents.

Numerous complicating factors make it extremely difficult to assess how poverty affects fertility, even in the most careful enquiries, such as that of Benefo and Schultz (1994). They find a substantial negative effect of annual household expenditure per person upon fertility in both Ghana and the Ivory Coast when other variables are also included as explanators (women's education, height, age; household assets; townward migration; residence, ethnicity, and religion; community variables such as average child mortality, and the presence or absence of malaria, measles and dysentery, and of latrines, clinic, etc.; and prices of key foodstuffs). However, the authors find that household expenditure per person (and, less decisively, child mortality) is endogenous with regard to fertility—cause as well as effect. When this is allowed for, lower household expenditure per person continues to be associated with higher subsequent fertility in Ghana, but the opposite is true in the Ivory Coast (Benefo and Schultz 1994: 37, 42). Benefo and Schultz conclude, from these and other results, that 'Ghana is at a later stage in the demographic transition than Côte d'Ivoire' (Benefo and Schultz 1994: 47).

However, there are two good reasons to question the implication that early in the 'demographic transition' poverty might result in low rather than high fertility. First, the regressions separate the influence, on fertility, of household expenditure per person from that of education, height, assets, village health, and urban–rural migration. This is analytically useful; but 'holding constant' these latter variables, if they are themselves much affected by poverty, obscures some critical paths along which reduced poverty cuts fertility. For example, higher levels of income or expenditure per household member do not merely proxy, but cause or permit, longer maternal education, and thus enable a couple to reduce fertility. Reduced poverty also reduces child mortality, permitting a couple to plan for fewer children. The structure of the model attributes these effects on fertility to education and reduced child mortality directly—not to the reduced poverty that helped to make these things possible; but reality may be quite different.

Second, the regressions measure the response of fertility to expenditure-per-person at the mean; but this is not the same as response to poverty. The Easterlin model does suggest that fertility initially rises as extreme poverty declines; better health and nutrition, earlier menarche and later menopause, etc., permit births to rise to desired levels (Easterlin and Crimmins 1985). However, the implied inverse-U relationship between household expenditure per person and consequent fertility (Lipton 1983: 19–22) has its turning-point at very low levels of living, where initial poverty is so extreme as to reduce biological fertility well below desired levels. For most developing countries, and perhaps for most poor people in almost all countries, reduced poverty is linked to better prospects of child survival, health and education; to a higher opportunity cost of mothers' child-rearing time; and hence to lower subsequent fertility. Only in extreme poverty would rising income be likely to have fertility-increasing biological effects that outweighed the fertility-decreasing incentive effects. However, the incentive effects are contingent, so there is no automatic fertility transition (Schultz 1981). For instance, where few girls go to school, the causal links from reduced poverty to reduced fertility may be weak or absent.

What can we say about the impact, on the demographic variables, of access to State and collective commodities for the potentially poor? The impact of distinct categories of such expenditure is complementary. This is well understood for impacts on mortality. Ever since the 'Narangwal experiment' in the Indian Punjab (Taylor *et al.* 1978) it has been realized that children's mortality and morbidity decline more if extra public resources are divided between improvements to both health care and nutritional support (assuming both were initially weak), rather than concentrated on just one. Complementarity among types of public and private outlay also applies to the effects in reducing family size norms. It is useful to categorize countries, or smaller areas within them, according to the relative 'backwardness' of provision of different sorts of (partially or totally) public and merit goods that induce poor recipients subsequently to reduce family size norms. A given outlay is normally likelier to reduce poor people's voluntary fertility more (i) if divided between 'social' and 'demographic' interventions to raise their non-private income sources, for example between female education and subsidized distribution of contraceptives; (ii) if the balance is steered towards the part of the 'programme'—social or demographic—that has been relatively neglected in the past, as compared with other developing countries (a useful typology is World Bank 1994: 51–2).

This rule has to be modified to allow for the social acceptability and administrative cost-effectiveness of alternative interventions. However, such modifications should not become an excuse for avoiding difficult but necessary steps, if the goal is to spend usefully on enabling the poor to reduce fertility. For example, though female education and employment in Pakistan are desirable and important, they will be slow in reducing the stubbornly high TFR unless accompanied by 'a very active family planning campaign', because 'average age at marriage for women . . . is already around 20 years', higher than in most South Asian (or Islamic) countries with more female education. 'The future of Pakistan's fertility level seems to rest squarely with the rate of contraceptive use' (Allison *et al.* 1989). A steep fertility decline in Mauritius, without rapid economic growth, 'may be attributed mostly to improved female educational status *and* active family planning programmes' (Lutz and Holm 1993: 98; my italics).

Public provision and poverty reduction, then, appear to be complementary in reducing fertility, and (given initial GNP per person) will both be reflected in reduced inequality. Several studies suggest a direct relationship between inequality of income and subsequent high fertility. Repetto (1979) has established this relationship for Matar Taluk in Gujarat State, India. With a sample of sixty-four countries in the early 1960s, Repetto (1974) regressed a fertility indicator on GNP per person, the Gini coefficient of income inequality, life expectancy, literacy, and population density, obtaining a substantial, significant, and positive elasticity of fertility to the Gini at the mean. Flegg (1979) estimates a smaller, but still significant and positive, link. More significantly for assessing the impact of poverty-related inequality on fertility, Flegg then estimates the relationship across forty-seven developing countries only, replacing the Gini by the Atkinson inequality index (which assigns a greater weight to inequality as it affects the poor). He also includes female illiteracy, the proportion of females economically active, and infant mortality as independent variables, and allows for endogenous fertility. A 10 per cent reduction in the Atkinson index decreases the crude birth rate at the mean by 3.11 per cent, increases female employment leading to a further fall in birth rates, but also reduces female participation, raising birth rates again; nevertheless, the final reduction in the birth rate is 2.2 per cent (for example, from 40 per thousand to 39.1)—well above the reduction following a 10 per-cent fall in female illiteracy (1.2 per cent) or infant mortality (0.7 per cent).

This study, while suggestive, is weakened by its choice of the crude birth rate—unweighted for women's age—as a fertility indicator. Inequality and poverty alter the age structure, not only the crude birth rate and the total fertility rate. Also, both Repetto and Flegg had to rely on the unsatisfactory data available in the 1970s for within-country income distribution. Very few data on poverty, using a standard absolute level of real consumption (or income) and based on reliable household surveys, were then available. Thanks to the contributions of Chen *et al.* (1995) and Kelley and Schmidt (1994), it should prove possible to estimate the relationship between (a) the total fertility rate and (b) reliably measured mean (PPP) GNP, inequality, and poverty (both consumption poverty and the 'misery variables', illiteracy and infant or child mortality), for at least thirty-seven developing countries containing well over 75 per cent of the population of the developing world. Work is in progress on this (Eastwood and Lipton 1997).

Conclusion

There is a long way to go before we have a fully specified model of the main causal links between fertility and poverty. However, we can say with some confidence that, over most of the ranges of the variables in developing countries, households and countries with lower birth rates and low family size norms experience lower levels of poverty, and that these relations embody reciprocal causation. The causal sequences involve both the arithmetical components of poverty. That is, low average real income and expenditure, and unequal distribution between poor and non-poor, are causes and effects of large household size and high fertility in low- and middle-income countries. These sequences operate through rational and adaptive behaviour. In other words, they respond to incentives modified by social norms and institutions. The relationships are therefore defeasible, not universal. However, they hold in most developing countries, most of the time, and over most of the range of the variables.

4 Coping With Poverty
The Biological Impact of Nutrition Insecurity

ANNA FERRO-LUZZI AND FRANCESCO BRANCA

1. Poverty, Food Insecurity, and Malnutrition

About 785 million people have been estimated to have had, in 1989–90, access to amounts of food considered insufficient to meet their biological needs (ACC/SCN 1992). They represent about 20 per cent of the world population. It was also estimated that about 200 million children under five from the developing countries— that is, about 36 per cent of this age group—were underweight. In certain areas of the world, such as Southern Asia, this proportion was reported to be even higher, about 60 per cent (de Onis *et al.* 1993). Also adult malnutrition, a problem recently recognized as being of growing concern, is highly prevalent in Southern Asia: 12 per cent of adults in China are malnourished and almost 50 per cent in India (Shetty and James 1994). These staggering figures justify the intense concern expressed in the opening statement of the final report of the International Conference of Nutrition: 'Hunger and malnutrition remain the most devastating problems facing the majority of the world's poor' (FAO/WHO 1992).

For the sake of clarity, before addressing the nature of the links between poverty and malnutrition, we define the terms used in this chapter. We have adopted the definition of poverty used in the UN system, that is, the insufficient availability, control and management of natural, financial, organizational or human resources. Food insecurity is defined as the physical and economic incapacity of individuals or communities to secure a stable and sustainable basket of foods that is adequate in quantity, quality and safety (United Nations 1990). Finally, malnutrition is a biological concept and applies to the deterioration of the body's integrity and functions, directly or indirectly caused by a deficiency of energy, nutrients or both.

Food insecurity is conventionally expressed as the number of people whose energy intake does not sustain normally active life. For convenience, the energy needs are currently expressed as multiples of the basal metabolic rate (BMR). A value of 1.54 times the BMR has recently been adopted as an acceptable level, thought to provide energy sufficient to maintain health, functional integrity and also

We gratefully acknowledge the help of Ms. Stefania Sette in analysing data and elaborating the table, of Mr Bruno Rossi and Ms Elisabetta Toti in preparing the figures, and of Ms. Patrizia Ferranti in providing secretarial assistance.

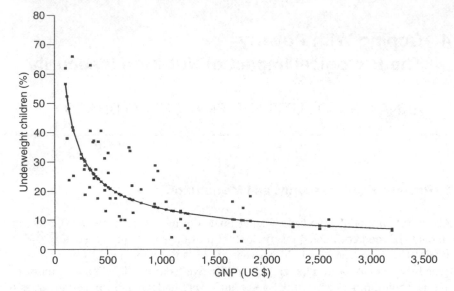

Fig. 4.1. Relationship between the prevalence of underweight (weight-for-age below –2 *z* score) in children under five and the Gross National Product in Third World countries in the 1980s
Source: ACC/SCN (1992).

to allow at least a light level of physical labour (ACC/SCN 1990). The measurement of food insecurity remains a reasonably reliable indicator of the risk of malnutrition. The most widely used indicator of malnutrition is the proportion of children with weight-for-age below –2 *z* score.[1] Adult malnutrition is classified on the body mass index (BMI), a particularly suitable combination of weight and height (kg/m^2). A BMI below 16 classifies the person as severely malnourished or in Chronic Energy Deficiency (CED III), a BMI between 16 and 17 is a grade II CED. Between 17 and 18.5, the deficiency is mild (James *et al.* 1988; Ferro-Luzzi *et al.* 1992).

Poverty, food insecurity, and malnutrition are interlinked. An example of the association between malnutrition and poverty is given in Figure 4.1, showing the exponential rise of malnutrition prevalence in children as Gross National Product (GNP) drops below the threshold of US\$ 1000 (ACC/SCN 1992). Although it can be stated with a certain confidence that the basic causes of malnutrition lie in scarcity of resources, the nature of the links between the two is complex and still incompletely understood. In the most credited model, poverty is thought to gener-

---

[1] The *z* score (or sd score) of weight-for-age indicates the position of a child's weight in the distribution of weights of children of the same age in the reference population (WHO 1983). By definition, in a healthy population, only 2.3 per cent of the individuals should be below the –2 *z* score cut-off point; any greater prevalence indicates the presence of malnutrition. Furthermore, a weight-for-age below –2 *z* score carries an increased risk of morbidity and mortality (Pelletier 1994).

ate malnutrition through food insecurity as well as through inadequate access to health services, sanitation or care. In this model, food security is shown to be a necessary but insufficient condition to prevent malnutrition. Diseases can cause loss of appetite and thus a decreased dietary intake that might be compounded by impaired intestinal absorption, an increased metabolic demand and a loss of nutrients from the body. A vicious circle is therefore soon generated, leading to the progressive deterioration of bodily functions and a propensity for infectious diseases of longer duration and higher lethality.

Given the extent of the malnutrition problem in the world, it is not surprising that much attention has been paid to the mechanisms and strategies used by man and society to avoid, respond to, or adapt to stress generated by food insecurity. The most exhaustive review of the topic is the excellent book by Payne and Lipton (1994) which provides a conceptual framework for the study of adaptation to dietary energy stress. They developed a model showing how external factors affect the individual or the household, progressing from the appearance of an external agent—causing the level of energy requirements to increase relative to energy intake—to energy imbalance (the stress itself), then to the bodily signs of reaction to stress (the strain), and finally to the negative or undesirable consequences. At any of these levels, individuals or households may respond in various ways, from avoidance of the stress, to redirecting it towards less vulnerable times or tissues, to resistance, to tolerance—that is, the acceptance of some level of damage. One way to look at this model is to imagine a spiral, going from left to right and from the first row to the next. The individual—or the community—would go through the spiral, each step denoting increasing degrees and duration of stress and decreasing ability to respond. When the individual has reached the last stages of tolerance and has endured irreversible damage, he no longer has recourse to the prior levels, unless substantial external aid is provided in terms of physical rehabilitation, donation of assets, or food aid. Such a scenario has been described as the *energy trap* (Longhurst 1984).

2. Biological Strategies for Coping with Food Insecurity

2.1. Adults

The approach proposed by Payne and Lipton merges socio-economic and behavioural responses with those of a purely biological nature. While links and interactions undoubtedly exist between the two categories of responses, there is a clear-cut initial dichotomy, not only in their nature but also in their timing. Thus, while the former are triggered earlier and respond to food insecurity, the latter come into play only when food insecurity has evolved into energy stress—that is, when the body has entered a state of negative energy balance. When this happens, the individual has three options: to mobilize the energy stored in the body; to decrease energy output as much as possible; or to increase the efficiency with which the cells handle the limited energy resources (Ferro-Luzzi 1990).

Table 4.1. Theoretical energy saving resulting from a 10-kg weight loss in an adult, based only on size reduction

		Normal	Adapted for size
Weight	kg	70	60
Height	cm	175	175
Body mass index	kg/m^2	23	19.6
Expenditure at 1.86 PAL	kcal/d	3255	2970
Net energy saving over normal	kcal/d	–	285
Net energy available for work	kcal/d	1505	1373
	kcal/kg	21	23

The first option, which is also the earliest, and without which the other two are not activated, consists of a loss of body weight. This is in itself a fully physiological process that uses the body energy stored for this purpose in the adipose tissue. However, it can only be considered as a form of first aid, the body storing only finite amounts of energy that need to be replenished. Once weight loss has begun, a phased combination of diverse processes and mechanisms is primed, aimed at reducing energy output through saving and sparing.

The saving occurs through the reduction of the cost of maintenance of the diminishing body mass, and the attendant decreased cost of mechanical work. Table 4.1 shows the theoretical saving achievable through these means. The first column describes normality; the second column shows the kind of saving that can be attained by a body mass that is 10 kg lighter (60–70 kg). The global saving in this case has been calculated to be about 285 kcal/day. This is an appreciable amount, corresponding to about two hours of moderately intense physical work, and allows the maintenance of a normal daily PAL (Physical Activity Level) of 1.86.[2] A weight loss of 10 kg, although exceptional, has been observed at times of drought, famine or war. If the starting body mass index (BMI) is 23, the final BMI is just below the normal range, and thus might be compatible with good health and functions.

The sparing of energy is achieved through the deliberate or subconscious curtailment of physical activity. Physical activity, in fact, represents the main component of total energy expenditure and is under voluntary control. It thus offers the simplest way to reduce energy output and could become, if needed, the main means of adapting to energy stress. A drastic fall in physical activity was seen in a semi-starvation experiment in Minnesota when the volunteers had lost 25 per cent of their body weight and were profoundly apathetic and drowsy (Keys *et al.* 1950). The situation under real life circumstances is much less clear-cut; a meta-analysis of selected studies on energy expenditure was unable to show that, once the effect of smaller body size had been accounted for, Third World adults spend less energy

---

[2] The Physical Activity Level (PAL) of an individual is the average multiplier of the Basal Metabolic Rate of the various activities carried out during the day (weighted for the time spent on each) required to calculate total energy expenditure.

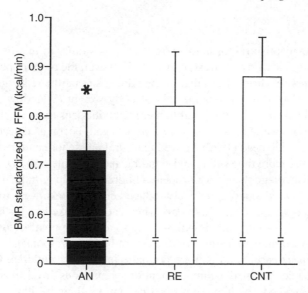

Fig. 4.2. Basal metabolic rate corrected for fat-free mass in patients affected by anorexia nervosa, compared to nutritionally rehabilitated patients and to normal controls
Notes: BMR = basal metabolic rate; AN = anorexia nervosa (N=20); RE = rehabilitated (N=9); CNT = controls (N=10); * p<0.01 vs. RE and CNT
Source: Polito *et al.*, unpublished data.

than well-fed adults of industralized societies (Ferro-Luzzi 1988). On the other hand, time–budget data obtained in a nationwide study conducted in Rwanda before the civil war show a BMI-associated gradient in the level of physical activity, such that those individuals with a lower BMI tend to spend less time in physically demanding work and increase the amount of time spent resting or in sedentary work (Shetty and James 1994).

The last possible form of adaptive response to energy stress is the metabolic one, involving improved energy utilization at the cellular level. The biological plausibility of this mechanism has been well established on an experimental basis in man. Under the rather extreme conditions of the Minnesota experiment (Keys *et al.* 1950), a fall of about 40 per cent in basal metabolic rate (BMR) was recorded, only partially explained by the 25 per cent body weight loss; a 15 per-cent reduction in the BMR persisted after accounting for the concomitant loss of fat-free mass (FFM). A 17 per-cent reduction in FFM-standardized metabolic rate has also been observed in anorexic women with a BMI of 15, compared to well-nourished controls (Figure 4.2). According to Shetty and Kurpad (1990), the decrease of BMR in semi-starvation may be at least partially attributed to a reduced metabolic activity of the tissues, mediated by altered circulating levels and turnover of catecholamines and by changes in hormone-receptor interactions.

2.2. Children

In children, the adaptive response to energy stress is similar to that of adults, and also encompasses the delay or arrest of growth. However, the order of occurrence of the various responses differs from that of the adults, so that the reduction in physical activity is believed to precede the loss of body weight (Waterlow 1990). This might be explained on the basis of their higher metabolic sensitivity and by the time-lag required before weight loss or arrest of weight gain becomes detectable. Thus, Rutishauser and Whitehead (1972) showed that rural pre-school children in Uganda spent significantly more time sitting and standing and less time walking and running than well-nourished age-matched European children. In a longitudinal study, pre-school children placed at a progressively reduced energy intake were found first to reduce their energy expenditure, and, only when energy intake was further reduced, to decrease the rate of their weight gain—height gain being unaffected (Torun and Viteri 1981). According to Torun (1990), the reduction of spontaneous physical activity takes place earlier and is more dramatic in younger children. Chavez and Martinez (1979) documented the impairment of spontaneous physical activity of 2-year-old malnourished children, showing that, unlike their healthy counterparts, they had lost their exploratory drive, and responded to environmental stimulation only by seeking shelter close to their mothers.

The arrest of weight and length (or height) growth becomes measurable at a later stage of energy stress. Evidence comes from natural experiments of seasonal energy stress, such as in studies conducted in Southern Ethiopia, where a delay, if not a complete arrest of growth in children of all ages was recorded during the lean months of the year (Branca *et al.* 1993). Growth failure allows short-term economy, as the energy required to synthesize new tissues, as well as the energy stored as tissue, are spared. In most cases, growth retardation suffered during childhood persists throughout adult life, particularly if the growth defect has persisted during school-age or adolescence (Martorell *et al.* 1994). The slight delay in maturation experienced by malnourished children, whose growth continues until the age of 20–25 years, allows only partial catch-up, so that small children tend to become short adults. Poor growth also leads to long-term economy, as the smaller body size of the stunted individual requires less energy for maintenance. Indeed, this appears to be particularly advantageous, as short stature allows a small size to be achieved with a normal body mass index. In the example shown in Table 4.1, if the adult weighing 60 kg has a stature of 165 cm, his BMI is 23, rather than 19.6, and there is a net sparing of 285 kcal per day without any substantial depletion of the fat stores. Stunting is a widespread phenomenon in the world. Most of the large number of children classified as malnourished on the basis of low weight-for-age are stunted, while only a relatively small proportion have low weight-for-height (de Onis *et al.* 1993).

Finally, as in adults, the energy turnover rate of active tissues in children can respond to energy stress by decreasing. A reduction in metabolic rate per kg of body weight has been observed in marasmic children (Parra *et al.* 1973). This was confirmed by Waterlow, Golden, and Patrick (1978) after careful data standardization. In order to control for the gross alterations in body composition, typical of marasmic children, they expressed the children's BMR with reference to total body potassium, an indicator of cell mass, and found a 15 per cent reduction. Such reduction occurs both in muscle and in visceral organs, but the latter seem to be more dramatically affected: Brooke and Cocks (1974) calculated that when the whole-body metabolic rate was reduced by 13 per cent, the non-muscle metabolic rate, standardized by non-muscle potassium, was reduced by 34 per cent .

3. Biological Cost of the Adaptation to Energy Stress

According to Waterlow (1985), adaptation should be a sustainable steady state, conservative of functions under threat, and sometimes, though not necessarily, reversible. Long-term sustainability is the key issue. According to Payne and Lipton (1994), sustained exposure to energy stress causes a progressive shift from the low- or no-cost adaptive biological responses to the area of strain (coping) and damage. Modest or reversible degrees of damage might still belong to the area of adaptation; however, the precise boundaries where or when the transition from adaptation to coping occurs are largely unknown.

The following section describes the functional consequences of the responses illustrated above, for adults first and then for children, attempting to evaluate the overall biological cost to the individual.

3.1. Adults

As has already been said, the initial response to energy stress in adults is the loss of body weight. Body-weight loss is a commonly observed strategy and, in principle, largely physiological. Most rural communities of the Third World experience modest weight loss during the pre-harvest period when food energy is short and the agricultural calendar requires intense physical labour (Ferro-Luzzi *et al.* 1988). In these circumstances, the weight loss seldom exceeds 3 kg, a level that is normally free of any adverse effects. However, under Third World circumstances, even such modest declines in body mass may involve biological damage. All losses of body fat are in fact accompanied by loss of lean tissue, and it is known that the proportion of lean tissue lost is inversely related to the amount of fat present in the body (Forbes 1987). Thus, a well-fed healthy adult with a BMI of 23 losing 3 kg, corresponding to less than 5 per cent of his body weight, would also have a concomitant loss of about 3 per cent of his lean body mass. A great proportion of Third World rural adults, however, have small body fat stores and a precarious nutritional status. We calculated that a 3 kg body weight loss in an emaciated person with a BMI of 16 would involve the loss of almost 1200 gram of highly valuable lean tissue (Ferro-Luzzi *et al.* 1994; Figure 4.3). The loss of lean body mass concerns mostly muscles, but vital organs are eventually affected, as it has been demonstrated by several

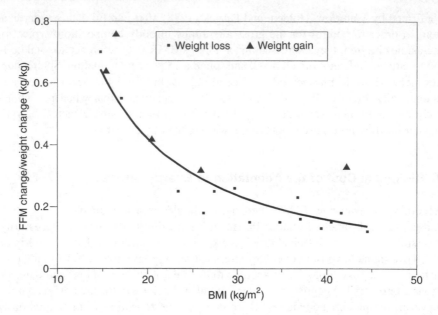

Fig. 4.3. Proportion of weight loss (or gain) represented by fat-free mass (FFM), according to the body mass index value at the beginning of the weight loss (or gain) period
Source: Modified from Forbes (1987). For references of additional studies, see Ferro-Luzzi *et al.* (1994).

autopsy studies performed among famine victims (for review, see Keys *et al.* 1950). In adults of 20–60 years who had lost 30–50 per cent of their initial body weight due to prolonged starvation, the liver and spleen weighed only about 50 per cent of those of comparable persons in a normal state of nutrition, and the kidneys and the heart weighed 75–80 per cent, only the brain remaining unaffected (Stein and Fenigstein 1946). Thus, while in well-nourished individuals a modest weight loss can be tolerated without any measurable consequence, the same might entail, under Third World circumstances, a disproportionately high cost.

A large body of evidence is available on the adverse effects associated with the erosion of lean tissues and the deterioration of the associated functions that occur in low-BMI adults. Recent data collected in India show that adults with low BMI (<16.9 kg/m^2) have markedly impaired immune functions, as documented by lower white cell and total lymphocyte counts, lower natural killer and helper cells, a marked depression of the capacity of the lymphocytes to respond to proliferation tests and a lower response to skin testing (Ferro-Luzzi, unpublished observations). This might contribute towards explaining the higher morbidity and mortality observed among Third World people with low BMI. The National Food Consumption and Household Budget Survey conducted in Rwanda in 1982 showed that malnourished adult women (with BMI below 17.5) were reported to be sick in bed four times as often as those with an adequate

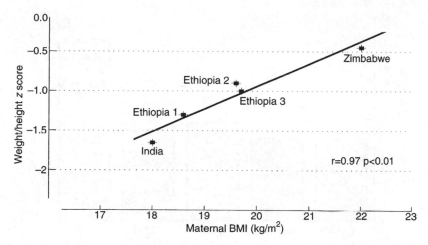

Fig. 4.4. Relationship between the nutritional status of mothers (expressed as body mass index) and that of their own children (expressed as weight-for-height *z* score) in selected studies from Third World countries
Source: Ferro-Luzzi, unpublished data.

nutritional intake (Shetty and James 1994). Similar findings were obtained in Brazilian women (de Vasconcellos 1994) and in Bangladeshi men (Pryer 1993). It should not therefore appear surprising that mortality also increases at low BMI levels. Indian data, where malnutrition is highly prevalent among the adults, show that the mortality rate increases at BMI below 18.5, and that at BMI below 16 mortality is almost threefold that in normally nourished individuals (Naidu and Rao 1994).

Another negative impact of low BMI is that exerted on the reproductive capacity of women. Elaboration of national statistics in India shows a steep increase in average birth weight and a rapid drop in the relative risk of delivering a small baby with increasing maternal BMI, such that at BMI 16 the risk of delivering a low birth weight baby is almost twice that at BMI 20 (Naidu and Rao 1994). Similar data have been obtained in East Java, where the proportion of low birth weight among women with BMI <16 was 21 per cent—that is, four times that of women above 18.5 (Kusin *et al.* 1993). Low maternal BMI and low birth weight might be regarded as the first stage in an intergenerational cycle entrapping Third World populations. Figure 4.4 shows the strong correlation observed in Ethiopia, India, and Zimbabwe between mean maternal BMI and the prevalence of wasting in children. Also at the world level, statistics elaborated by the ACC/SCN (1992) show that the prevalence of underweight children in the 1970s is correlated to the prevalence of underweight women (weighing less than 45 kg) ten years later. They also show that in the 1980s the latter was related to low birth weight, and low birth weight to growth retardation a few years later.

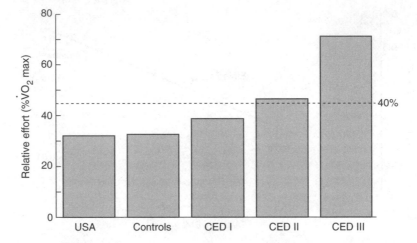

Fig. 4.5. Relative effort (estimated as a proportion of VO_2 max) required to carry a 20-kg load in normal North American (USA) and Colombian men (Controls) and in three groups of Colombian men with mild (CED I), moderate (CED II) and severe (CED III) malnutrition *Source*: Modified from Spurr (1988).

While stunted adults with normal BMI show no evidence of increased morbidity and mortality, this condition should not be regarded as a truly adaptive condition, given the above-mentioned lower birth weight of children born to small mothers. The 'small but healthy' concept is also contradicted by the observation that a small body size may affect the physical work capacity—that is, the ability to carry out highly demanding physical activities. Measured in terms of the body's maximal capacity to consume oxygen (VO_2 max) and expressed as litres of oxygen, the reduction in work capacity observed in stunted healthy individuals seems to be entirely explained by their smaller lean body mass, while there is no demonstrable deficit of muscle function (Barac-Nieto 1978). This reduced VO_2 max impinges on the individual's work productivity, as shown by several studies (Spurr 1988, for review). For example, Davies (1973) showed that a relationship existed between VO_2 max, the rate of sugar cane cutting (kg/minute) and daily productivity in Sudanese labourers. The decline in productivity might be explained by the fact that long work shifts are sustainable only if the level of the effort is maintained within 35–40 per cent of maximum capacity. Thus, given the lower maximum capacity of a shorter and lighter individual, he will have to operate at a higher proportional level of his aerobic capacity than a normal counterpart to perform the same job (Spurr 1988). In Figure 4.5 the worker labelled as CED III—that is, affected by severe Chronic Energy Deficiency (BMI <16 kg/m²)—is seen to be working well above 40 per cent of his maximum aerobic power, to do the same job that the better fed counterparts do at a much lower—and thus sustainable—level. He will therefore become fatigued earlier and will be unable to perform the required task.

Adapting to energy stress might also entail, as discussed before, a reduction in physical activity. This response is potentially capable of powerfully contributing to energy sparing, since total inactivity would halve the energy needs. However, even to a much lesser extent than total inactivity, this form of adaptation would be most disturbing because it can significantly affect productivity and, through its progressive deterioration, jeopardize the likelihood of future recovery of the individual or the community (Longhurst 1984). Even if productive activities are spared, social and discretional activities may be affected. An example comes from rural women in Ethiopia, who spent an extra 500 kcal per day on productive work during the season of peak agricultural labour, at the expense of social and leisure activities (Branca *et al.* 1992).

3.2. Children

In children, the same considerations apply as in adults, but additional costs related to the dynamic processes of growth and development should be taken into account. Curtailment of physical activity is the front-line response in children. The long-term consequences of the early depression of exploratory activities and interactive behaviour have been the object of research and have been found to reduce maternal responsiveness, to cause impairment of the child's social-emotional and cognitive development, and of his learning capacity (Grantham-Mc Gregor *et al.* 1990). While it is as yet uncertain whether these early functional deficits are reversible, the continuation of the stress is highly likely to lead to an adult with underdeveloped intellectual potential.

Growth retardation comes as a second response, involving impaired musculo-skeletal development, and manifesting itself as low height-for-age (stunting) and low weight-for-height (wasting). A reduction in physical fitness has been observed in growth-retarded children. Spurr *et al.* (1983) showed that differences existed in maximal oxygen consumption between stunted and normal children. Already at seven years of age, growth-retarded and wasted Colombian boys have a significantly lower capacity to engage in energy-demanding activities than normal peers. As in adults, there is no basic defect in muscle function, and the deficit is fully explained by a smaller muscle mass. Thus, as well as in adults, the effect of nutritional status disappears when work capacity is expressed per unit body weight or lean body mass. Even in childhood, under Third World circumstances, a deterioration in work capacity may result in economic handicap, as countries rely on children's labour, despite their young age.

As with adults, small body size in a child is associated with increased morbidity and mortality. Several studies have recorded an increase in the prospective risk of death in growth-retarded children, with a curvilinear relationship that varies slightly in the various regions of the world. Kielmann and McCord (1978) found that 1–36 month-old Punjabi children with weight-for-age between 70 and 80 per cent of the standard had a fourfold higher risk of death than children with weight-for-age at or above 80 per cent. In Bangladesh, Chen *et al.* (1980) showed that, at the age of

13–23 months, children with height-for-age below 85 per cent of the reference or with weight-for-age below 65 per cent of the reference had a mortality between three and seven times higher than normal children living in the same rural area.

Conclusions

In this chapter, we have shown that the biological response to energy stress can take several forms, according to the degree and duration of the stress. The theory of adaptation at zero cost (Sukhatme and Margen 1982) does not stand up in the light of fairly ample evidence of the measurable damages inflicted by graded energy stress. From an individual perspective, practically all the responses have some functional consequences. Only body-weight loss, provided sufficient energy stores are available, can be regarded as an entirely cost-free form of adaptation.

Size reduction, whether with normal or low body mass index, impairs the capacity of the individual to conduct an active life and to maintain health and well-being. Low BMI may have an unacceptably high cost, affecting the very capacity of the individual to survive. In children, the responses described have a biological and social cost, and they are only partially reversible. The reduction in work capacity and productivity that results from small body size provides a strong argument against those who maintain that stunting is a successful form of adaptation. Under real-life conditions, low productivity would affect the salary of the worker, as well as his likelihood of being hired. If we reckon that the majority of the actively employed population of Third World countries are likely to be engaged in moderate to heavy physical work, the long-term cost of this form of adaptation to energy stress may be exceedingly high.

From the perspective of a community, or a species, the sacrifice of the individual may be required for the survival of the group. However, short-term societal survival may have long-term negative implications for, for example, the viability and functional performance of the next generation, or the overall economic capacity of the group, and therefore is not cost-free.

The conclusion is that nutritional insecurity always has profound biological effects. When avoidance, repartitioning or resistance strategies of a socio-economic nature fail, then some stress has to be suffered, whose immediate or later consequences on the biological functions of the individual or the community represent the cost.

5 Famine, Demography, and Endemic Poverty

SIDDIQUR R. OSMANI

Introduction

Studies on the connections between famine and poverty have usually been concerned with the causality running from long-term processes of poverty to periodic famines. But the reverse causation—from famine to endemic poverty, or more generally from 'conjunctural' to 'structural' poverty in the words of Iliffe (1987)—has remained relatively unexplored. I shall attempt in this paper to clarify some of the issues involved in understanding this reverse causation and to identify some of the possible channels of causation, citing along the way whatever little empirical evidence there is.

In order to study the consequences of famine for endemic poverty, one would ideally require longitudinal investigations tracing the socio-economic circumstances of those afflicted by famine, covering a long period of time and possibly spanning more than one generation. In the absence of these ideal conditions, one can still make certain inferences, however, by drawing upon certain strands of famine literature, of which two are most important. One of them is the growing literature on the demographic responses to famine. These responses—as reflected in the crucial demographic variables such as fertility, mortality, nuptiality, and migration—have usually been studied from the demographer's perspective: that is, with the objective of assessing the impact of famine on the size, composition, and growth of population (see, for example, Bongaarts and Cain 1982; Dyson 1993; Hugo 1984; Watkins and Menken 1985). But these demographic responses also have direct and indirect implications for the economic viability of the poor in the post-famine period. It will be one of the aims of this chapter to try and draw out some of these implications.

The second strand of famine literature that is relevant for the present purpose is the growing set of economic and sociological studies on 'coping strategies'. It is increasingly being recognized that when the poor are afflicted by famine, they do

The author is grateful to Tim Dyson and Frank Geary for many helpful comments on an earlier draft of the paper forming the basis of this chapter. Comments from participants in the seminar on 'Demography and Poverty' organized by the IUSSP in Florence and in the annual conference of the Development Studies Association held in Dublin were also very helpful. However, all remaining errors and inadequacies are entirely his responsibility. A previous version of this chapter appeared in the *Journal of International Development*, Volume 8, Number 5.

not simply resign themselves to a passive acceptance of their fate, but try actively to protect themselves from present and future destitution by adopting various strategies (see, for example, Corbett 1988; Campbell 1990; Davies 1993). These so-called coping strategies also affect the processes that have a bearing on endemic poverty.

By drawing out the implications of these coping responses as well as demographic responses to famine, and by combining them with general insights gleaned from demographic and economic theories, it is possible to generate certain hypotheses about how famines might, or might not, affect long-term endemic poverty. Let us start from where all studies of famine and demography have to start—the Reverend Thomas Malthus.

From the Malthusian perspective, famines are not seen as a cause of poverty, but rather as an adjustment mechanism that brings temporary relief to the survivors. We may call it the hypothesis of 'famine as an escape valve'. Our ideas of both famines and demography have of course changed quite radically since the time of Malthus. But the new ideas that have emerged are not all in agreement with each other. There are significant differences in contemporary views on both the importance of famines in shaping the demography of a society and on the nature of interactions between demographic and economic variables. Different sets of views on these matters lead to different hypotheses about the impact of famine on endemic poverty. I am not suggesting that these hypotheses were explicitly derived by those who happened to hold the views from which they follow; only that certain hypotheses follow as logical implications of the views held. I shall distinguish three hypotheses that follow from different strands of post-Malthusian views.

The first of these I shall call the hypothesis of 'famine as the principal perpetuator of poverty'. The views from which this hypothesis follows share the Malthusian idea of famine being a major regulator of population in pre-industrial societies but imply the non-Malthusian idea that far from being an escape valve for the surviving poor the occurrence of famine is the principal mechanism through which poverty was perpetuated in the long run. The next hypothesis is a complete antithesis of the preceding one. It is fundamentally non-Malthusian in the sense that it does not regard famine as a major influence on long-term population trends or on the long-term processes of poverty. I shall describe this hypothesis as 'famine does not matter—in the long run'. The final hypothesis can be seen as a cross between the preceding two. It shares some of the premises of the second post-Malthusian hypothesis, but nonetheless maintains that famine can have very important effects on the processes of endemic poverty, without however going as far as the first hypothesis does to depict it as the villain of the piece. I shall describe this hypothesis as 'famine matters—even in the long run'. In the remainder of this chapter I shall elaborate on the four hypotheses, one Malthusian and three post-Malthusian ones, arguing in the end that there is a strong case in favour of the final hypothesis.

1. The Malthusian Hypothesis of 'Famine as an Escape Valve'[1]

In the Malthusian scheme, famine was assigned the role of an adjustment mechanism that brought the size of population into rough balance with nature's ability to provide food. However, despite some popular misconceptions to the contrary, Malthus did not see famine as an inevitable outcome of the unequal contest between population and food. There were several other adjustment mechanisms at work, and famine was supposed to strike only as the last resort. The one adjustment mechanism that he failed to foresee—namely, sustained improvement in the productivity of agriculture—was of course the one that was eventually to put the spectre of famine to rest in the Western world. But he did visualize several other mechanisms that could in principle keep famines at bay. Some of these were malign—such as war and pestilence, which together with famine were described as positive checks. But there was also a benign mechanism, the so-called preventive check, whereby people adjusted their fertility so as to a maintain a conventional standard of living. Famines would occur only if preventive checks and all other positive checks failed to restore balance: 'Should success still be incomplete, gigantic inevitable famine stalks the rear, and with one mighty blow, levels the population with the food of the world.' (Malthus 1798: 139 40)

1.1. Famine as Nature's Substitute for Preventive Checks

The significance of preventive check in Malthus's schema is not just that it had the potential to keep famines at bay, but also that it enabled a population to enjoy a level of living above that of bare biological survival despite the constraints on food supply imposed by a niggardly nature. It is indeed this ability to transcend the survival frontier that in Malthus's view distinguished the human species from all other animals. Of course not all human societies were equally successful in this regard. Where the preventive check was weak, the ability to transcend the survival frontier was correspondingly poor, and there famine had to intervene to push the community above the frontier.

Malthus believed that the English were better off than the Europeans because they were more successful in applying preventive checks, and the Europeans in turn were better off than the rest of the 'old' world where preventive checks were virtually non-existent. The reason for these differences in the prevalence of preventive checks—or of fertility regulation in modern parlance—lay, in his view, not in any intrinsic differences among races but in the nature of human institutions.

It is now generally agreed that almost all pre-modern societies were characterized by a regime of natural fertility: that is, a regime in which there was very little conscious control of marital fertility. So fertility regulation could only occur through

---

[1] It should be stressed that this hypothesis follows more clearly from the Malthus of the *First Essay*. His later views were much more nuanced than is allowed for by the hypothesis as presented here.

variation in nuptiality, in the rate and duration of marriage. There is strong evidence that European and non-European societies did differ significantly in this regard. In much of the non-Western world, where extended families were a predominant institution, universal marriage linked fairly rigidly to the age at menarche was a common phenomenon. The decision to marry was not constrained by a couple's ability to support themselves because the extended family could be expected to tide them over until they could pay for themselves. By contrast, in England and in the Western world generally, newly married couples were expected to establish their own homes and to support themselves from their own earnings. This convention meant that marriage was linked more to a man's perceived ability to support a family than to the age at menarche. The resultant delinking of marriage from the age at menarche and its dependence on the ability to earn a livelihood ensured that nuptiality could function as an adjustment mechanism in response to variations in food supply: people would marry late or not marry at all in times of scarcity and conversely in times of plenty. It has been confirmed by recent research that the rate of nuptiality did indeed respond strongly to variations in food supply in pre-modern England (Schofield 1983).

It is thus clear that the institutions governing family formation had a significant impact on the scope of fertility regulation. In Malthus's own view, there were also other institutions that were no less important. In modern terminology, his arguments boil down to the question of property rights. Where people are denied the right to the fruits of their labour by institutions—as in a despotic society— they would of necessity be myopic and discount any future gain in consumption that might arise from the limitation of fertility. The guarantee of property rights was therefore a necessary condition for preventive checks to prevail.

That, in Malthus's view, was an important reason why preventive checks were applied so successfully in England, where liberal political institutions ensuring private property rights were more firmly established. Leaving aside for the present the contentious issue of whether Malthus was right in his claim about the absence of property rights in non-Western societies, the point that needs to be emphasized here is the importance he attached to institutions in determining whether preventive checks will prevail and thereby allow a population to live a reasonably decent life.

In view of this link between institutions and preventive checks on the one hand, and the obvious link between preventive check and the level of living on the other, one can conclude that extreme poverty was caused not so much by the niggardliness of nature as by the failure of human institutions—at the levels of both society and family. If the institutions are right, preventive checks will prevail and this will enable the population to escape from extreme misery. If institutions fail, preventive checks will no longer operate and it is then that famine will appear so as to provide an alternative escape route. From this perspective, then, famine can be seen as nature's way of trying to achieve what human institutions failed to do: that is, to transform the intolerable misery of the numerous into the tolerable living situation of the many.

To put it differently, famine tends to function as a substitute for preventive checks in providing an escape valve from extreme misery and raising the level of living above the floor of survival—albeit in a particularly cruel manner. It is in this sense that the Malthusian perspective can be said to regard famine as having a beneficial effect on the survivors in the long run.[2]

Apart from wiping out a part of the population, there are a couple of other ways in which famine can be seen to raise the level of living of those who survive. These mechanisms were not suggested by Malthus himself, but I include them here under the rubric of Malthusian hypothesis since they reinforce the argument that famine may entail a long-run beneficial effect. One of these mechanisms operates through famine's effect on fertility, and the other through the process of natural selection.

1.2. Short-term Effects of Famine on Fertility

In such diverse societies as England, Russia, Holland, Ireland, and Bangladesh, famines have almost invariably resulted in a reduction of fertility (Schofield 1983; Antonov 1947; Stein *et al.* 1975; Boyle and O'Grada 1986; Chen and Chowdhury 1977). This effect is most conspicuous in societies where variation in nuptiality provides a flexible mechanism for adjustment. Thus, while commenting on the social and demographic consequences of the great Irish famine, Connell (1955: 82) observed that 'Of all the casualties of Irish social life in the decades after the Famine, one of the most significant was marriage. . . .' But even in societies where this adjustment mechanism is either non-existent or weak (as in Bangladesh), total fertility still declines owing to a reduction in marital fertility.

There are several behavioural and biological reasons why this happens. Perhaps the most important reason is the separation of couples that frequently occurs as the male partner migrates in search of work and food, or as the wife is sent to her parents' home or even divorced so as to save on food. Besides, extreme undernutrition can reduce the fecundity as well as libido of both men and women. It is also possible that as lactating mothers tend to prolong breast-feeding as much as possible in order to save on outside food for the children, the resulting prolongation of post-partum amennorhea brings down the rate of conception. Whatever the reasons may be, the effects are not in doubt.[3]

It has to be noted though that this reduction in fertility is somewhat offset by a subsequent rebound that takes fertility above the normal level. This rebound is explained by the fact that the post-famine population contains an unusually high proportion of women susceptible to conception, for a couple of reasons. First, excessive infant mortality during famine leaves an unusually high proportion of women

---

[2] In the same sense that preventive checks are supposed to have a beneficial effect, the only difference being that while preventive checks operate by standing in the way of more people being born, famine operates by eliminating some of those already born. Whatever may be the ethical or emotional differences between the two modes of operation, their effects on the size of the population and hence on the balance between people and resources are essentially similar.

[3] In both the Irish famine of the 1840s and the Bangladesh famine of 1974, birth rates dropped by nearly one-third (Boyle and O'Grada 1986; Chen and Chowdhury 1977).

who are non-lactating and are thus unprotected by post-partum amennorhea, and secondly, the immediate decline in the rate of conception following the onset of famine raises the proportion of non-pregnant women above the normal level in the post-famine period. It has been estimated, however, that the rebound does not completely offset the initial decline in fertility, so that a net depressive effect still remains (Schofield 1983; Hugo 1984; Watkins and Menken 1985). To that extent, famine eases the pressure on resources, to the benefit of future generations. [4]

1.3. The Selection Effect

Those who survive the mayhem caused by famine are on average likely to be better endowed genetically to withstand the vicissitudes of life than the pre-famine population. Bongaarts and Cain (1982) invoked this hypothesis as one of the explanations for the commonly observed phenomenon that mortality tends to fall below the normal level in the immediate post-famine period. The quantitative significance of such a selection process is not known, but to the extent that it does operate it would imply not just reduced mortality in the short term but also less morbidity and greater work capacity of the surviving population in the long term and hence a potentially better standard of living.

A related effect operates through the impact of famine on the surviving population's age structure. After most famines the population age structure is found to be characterized by a significantly higher fraction of prime age adults (say, 15–50 years), as famine takes a heavier toll of the very young and the very old. The resulting increase in labour force participation ratio and the corresponding decline in dependency ratio should aid the process of post-famine economic reconstruction.[5]

Through the combined effects on mortality, fertility, and natural selection discussed above, famines may thus entail a beneficial effect on the level of living in the long run. This is the basis of the notion that famine may be viewed as a potential escape valve from extreme poverty for those who survive.

2. The Hypothesis of 'Famine as the Principal Perpetuator of Poverty'

The hypothesis that, far from acting as an escape valve from poverty, famine may actually perpetuate it follows from the combination of two sets of ideas. One of them relates to a specific historical view of pre-modern societies in which famines and other periodic crises are assigned a primary role in shaping mortality behaviour, and the other is embodied in what I shall call the classical version of demographic transition theory in which mortality behaviour is accorded a primary role in shaping fertility behaviour. The combination of these two sets of ideas gives rise to a chain

---

[4]   This conclusion pertains to the short-term effect of famine on fertility. The long-term effect can be quite different; its discussion is postponed until Section 4.

[5]   Michelle McAlpin (1983a) has advanced this hypothesis in the context of South Asian famines of the colonial era.

of causation flowing from famines to mortality, from mortality to fertility, and finally from fertility to poverty. In order to see how this chain of causation leads to the hypothesis of famine being the principal perpetuator of poverty, it will be instructive to begin by considering the logically converse question of how poverty was conquered and growth perpetuated in parts of the modern world.

In his panoramic study of world economic growth, Jones (1988) has observed that while the so-called 'modern economic growth' is a comparatively recent phenomenon, there were many instances in the earlier history of the world when the seeds of growth seemed to have germinated. In each instance, however, the momentum was lost resulting in renewed stagnation or even decline. It was only in the early modern Europe that for the first time in the history of the world the incipient growth process did not lose its momentum, giving rise eventually to the modern phenomenon of sustained economic growth.

Why was the momentum lost so invariably in the past, and what happened in Europe in the last couple of centuries that made sustained growth possible? One possible answer can be constructed in terms of the chain of causation referred to above in which the recurrence of famine and other mortality crises assumes a critical role.

2.1. The European Escape from Hunger

How did Europe finally escape from endemic hunger? At the most proximate level of analysis, the escape from hunger came about through an unprecedented rise in agricultural production coupled with improvements in transportation and marketing networks that allowed enough food to be made available wherever it was in demand, while demand itself was kept expanding by increased purchasing power generated by the industrial revolution. There were of course more fundamental causes underlying each of these developments, and much incompleteness still remains in understanding these fundamental causes. One thing is certain, however. Whatever may have caused increased food availability on the one hand, and enhanced purchasing power on the other, none of these would have had a lasting impact on living standards if something else had not happened. That something else was the unprecedented decline in fertility that began to occur in the late nineteenth century—the so-called demographic transition.

The classical economic theory—of Smith, Ricardo, and Malthus—had not prepared the world for what happened in the nineteenth century. According to their theory, population would respond systematically to the availability of resources (capital in the case of Smith and Ricardo, land in the case of Malthus), rising when resources expanded and falling when resources declined, making long-term living standards fluctuate around what was called the natural wage rate. This theory did not envisage any possibility of permanently breaking away from the conventional standard of living because an expanding population would stand in the way. As the standard of living improved, both mortality would fall and fertility would rise, thus depressing it back to the old level. A permanent improvement was only possible if somehow fertility failed to rise in response to rising living standards. This could not happen in the popular version of classical economic theory, which earned it the epithet of a dismal science. But it did happen in Europe in the late nineteenth century (and somewhat earlier in France), and that is what made the permanent break possible.[6]

2.2. The Classical Version of Demographic Transition Theory

The earliest version of the demographic transition theory suggested that the mortality decline that had occurred in the early nineteenth century was primarily responsible for precipitating fertility decline after a lag. There were several mechanisms that could possibly have brought this about. Until recently, the most popular among them was the 'replacement hypothesis' which stated that so long as mortality remained high, fertility also remained high, since parents needed to have more children in order to maintain their desired family size (Notestein 1945; Heer and Smith 1967). As mortality declined, the motivation for replacement declined as well.

From the perspective of this hypothesis what was wrong with classical economic theory was the implicit assumption that mortality and fertility were somehow independent of each other. As resources expanded and living standards rose, according to the classical economic theory, there would simultaneously occur a decline in mortality and a rise in fertility which would reinforce each other to swell the population. But the classical theory of demographic transition argued that this mutually reinforcing effect could only be short-lived. Sooner or later, the very fact of a sustained mortality decline would bring fertility down nullifying the reinforcing effect, so much so that the rate of population growth would eventually fall. This is what, many believe, happened in nineteenth century Europe.

2.3. Famines and the Secular Decline in Mortality

If this view of fertility decline is accepted, then the search for the clue to the European escape from hunger has to be pushed back one step more. One must ask: what led to the sustained decline in mortality that preceded fertility decline? This is where famine enters the picture. In the 1960s, a consensus emerged that the high average mortality of pre-modern Europe was attributable to periodic famines and other mortality crises which raised normal mortality rates by 50 to 100 per cent or more. It was argued that it was the elimination of these peaks rather than lowering the plateau of normal mortality that was primarily responsible for overall mortality decline in the nineteenth century (see, for example, Flinn 1970, 1974; Helleiner 1967; Wrigley 1969).

These mortality crises were precipitated by either acute harvest failure or the outbreak of epidemics. The two of course might have been related, either through

---

[6]   Schofield (1983) has shown that the classical theory did indeed hold in England up to about the middle of the eighteenth century but not thereafter.

the undernutrition-infection nexus or otherwise (for example, beggars spreading diseases at times of food crises; Meuvret 1965). It was thus agreed that most of the mortality crises were brought about directly or indirectly by famines and near-famine situations. Accordingly, it was supposed that it was primarily the conquest of famines that had stopped the recurrence of crisis mortality and thereby brought about the decline in overall mortality that was observed in the nineteenth century.

By combining this particular theory of mortality decline with the classical version of the demographic transition theory, one may now postulate the following relationship between famine and endemic poverty. The recurrence of famine kept average mortality high in pre-modern Europe, which in turn kept fertility high, and that in turn was responsible for perpetuating hunger by dissipating any gains made in food production. Conversely, when famines were eventually conquered, the average level of mortality came down, which in turn brought about the demographic transition towards a low fertility regime, and that in turn allowed productivity gains to be consolidated instead of being dissipated away as before. It was then that the incipient growth process of modern Europe finally turned into a self-sustaining one.

From this perspective, then, it was the regular occurrence of famine that was ultimately responsible for keeping the pre-modern society entrapped in a state of endemic poverty. There was no escape from hunger because fertility was not sufficiently regulated so as to consolidate the gains in production furthermore, fertility was not regulated because mortality was high; and mortality was high because of recurrent famines. It is this chain of reasoning that leads to the hypothesis that famine was the principal perpetuator of poverty.

3. The Hypothesis that 'Famine Does Not Matter—in the Long Run'

The next hypothesis to be considered is at the polar opposite of the preceding one; it says that famine leaves very little lasting impact. The logical basis of this hypothesis consists of two planks: one involves a critique of the premises on which the preceding hypothesis is based and the other draws on some recent evidence on the long-term demographic effects of famine. I shall elaborate on each of these below.

As we have seen, the preceding hypothesis was based on two premises: a particular version of the demographic transition theory that made mortality decline the triggering mechanism for fertility decline, and a particular explanation of mortality decline which rested heavily on the conquest of famines. During the last couple of decades, however, new ideas have emerged and new evidence has come to light which render both these premises highly questionable. In consequence, the plausibility of the hypothesis itself would now seem to be in considerable doubt.

3.1. Reformulation of Demographic Transition Theory

It is by now well known that there are several problems with the classical version of the transition theory. The 'replacement hypothesis' which underlies this theory assumes that parents have a notion of a desired family size which they wish to maintain. It is because they are assumed to aim for a desired size that they are supposed to have high fertility in response to high mortality—in order to replace the children that are expected to die. But this assumption flies in the face of accumulated evidence which shows that marital fertility happens to be close to natural fertility level in almost all pre-industrial societies. The idea of having a desired family size and the corresponding notion of replacement are relevant only after a society has made the transition from a natural fertility regime to a regime of controlled fertility. In other words, the replacement hypothesis wrongly transports the logic of a post-transition society to a pre-transition one (Caldwell 1976).

There is also a good deal of empirical evidence that is inconsistent with the replacement hypothesis. Knodel (1975), for example, has shown that this hypothesis is evidently false in a sample of pre-industrial European parish populations. Furthermore, Lee's (1980) analysis of English data for the period from 1550 to 1724 showed that the rates of population growth (over units of twenty-five year periods) had a strong positive relationship with life expectancy, which implied the absence of any significant positive relationship between mortality and fertility over the long term. In the short term, the relationship in fact turned out to be negative.

Such conceptual and empirical anomalies have resulted in significant reformulations of the demographic transition theory. In an influential contribution, Caldwell (1976, 1982), for example, has suggested that fertility begins to decline when social and economic circumstances change in such a way that the direction of intergenerational resource flow is reversed—that is, when resources, instead of flowing from the young to the old, as happens in most pre-modern societies, begin to flow from the old to the young. This requires fundamental changes in both economic organization of production and intra-familial relationships. An additional, but related, factor is the degree of women's autonomy in making decisions regarding their labour use pattern as well as reproductive behaviour. The decline in mortality is neither a necessary nor a sufficient condition for all this to happen, although in some cases it may hasten the process.

3.2. The Unimportance of Famine for Secular Mortality Decline

While such reformulation of transition theory serves to undermine one of the two premises of the 'famine as the perpetuator of poverty' hypothesis, the other premise has also come under increasing attack. The view that famines were responsible for the generally high level of mortality in Europe in the pre-industrial era is now increasingly being questioned. Some striking evidence has emerged from Wrigley and Schofield's (1981) reconstruction of English demographic history covering over three centuries from 1541 to 1871.

In order to test the short-run relationship between food crises and mortality, they took food price as an indicator of scarcity and used it to explain variation in mortality. Not surprisingly, they found a positive association between the two variables, indicating that food crises did lead to heightened mortality—in the same year at times of extreme scarcity, and delayed for one or two years otherwise. However, two aspects of this relationship are of particular interest. First, the correlation was very weak—only 16 per cent of the variation in mortality was explained by price fluctuations. Secondly, there was a negative feedback echo later on, which depressed mortality below normal levels, so that over a five-year period the effect on mortality almost disappeared. In other words, food crises left no lasting effect on mortality. Furthermore, as far as the long-term trends are concerned, not even a weak association was found between mortality and food supply (Schofield 1983).

Using the same basic data, Fogel (1992) has adduced further evidence to cast doubt on the significance of famine mortality. He considered all mortality crises, not just those associated with famines, and estimated crisis mortality as a proportion of total mortality for units of quarter centuries as well as centuries. The following findings emerged from those estimates. First, for none of the quarter-centuries did crisis mortality account for as much as 10 per cent of total mortality. Secondly, the 'normal' mortality rate of the eighteenth century was as high as the total mortality rate of each of the preceding two centuries, despite the fact that the eighteenth century experienced far fewer crises. Finally, nearly three-quarters of the decline of mortality between 1726–50 and 1851–71 was due to reduction in normal mortality, despite the relatively high level of crisis mortality at the beginning of this period and its negligible level at the end of it. The conclusion is thus inescapable that '. . . dramatic as they were, mortality crises, whether caused by famine or not, were too scattered in time and space to have been the principal factor in the secular decline in mortality after 1540.' (Fogel 1992: 247)

It would thus appear that neither was famine responsible for keeping mortality high in the pre-industrial world nor was mortality responsible for keeping fertility high and thereby keeping livings standards down. Therefore, contrary to the preceding hypothesis, famines cannot be held responsible for perpetuating endemic poverty. Indeed, in addition to this re-interpretation of European history, much new evidence is also emerging around the world which might tempt one to draw the very opposite conclusion, namely that perhaps famines do not matter all that much in the long run. This evidence comes mostly from studies on the demographic responses to famine in Asia and Africa.

3.3. Demographic Responses to Famine: the New View

To most people in the world the recent famines of Africa evoke a picture of millions of emaciated people dying on the roadside or in refugee camps. Many serious researchers are now claiming that this picture is fundamentally flawed. In particular, the numbers of famine deaths that are often quoted in the media are now believed to be widely exaggerated. Caldwell (1975) was one of the first to point this out in the context of the Sahel famine of the early 1970s. For the entire period 1970–4, he roughly estimated excess mortality to be no more than a quarter of a million despite newspaper headlines about six million people facing starvation death. The reason for this discrepancy between popular perception and what is now believed to be the real picture is not difficult to find.

Demographic records of Africa are notoriously poor and they become even more so during famine periods. Many casual commentators rely on pure guesswork or generalize from unrepresentative small samples. By contrast, careful researchers such as Faulkingham and Thorbahn (1975) who were engaged in a detailed study of a village in Niger both before and during the famine, did not find any exceptional increase in mortality. The villagers were certainly in great distress during the drought, but through various coping strategies such as migration and eating of 'famine foods' picked up from the wild, they managed to avoid any serious excess mortality. Similar findings have been reported in various other studies in other parts of Africa (Seaman 1993).[7]

According to this new view, what the rest of the world sees on their television screen at times of famine is not very different from the situation that faces the poorest in Africa even in normal times. Since the awfulness of this normal situation is beyond the conception of Western people, they take it to be an exceptional calamity wrought by famine. Of course what they see is not normal for the average African, but it is normal for the most disadvantaged groups. In a careful recent study of a region in Mali, Hill (1989) has shown that it is these disadvantaged groups that become most visible during famines because they are the ones that take to the road or assemble in refugee camps and on the outskirts of towns in search of food and thus represent the face of Africa to the television cameras.

Hill and his colleagues compared the demographic characteristics of the long-term residents in two central towns of Mali—Mopti and Sevare—with those of new immigrants who had arrived in the wake of the droughts of the mid-1980s. Child mortality was found to be significantly higher for the immigrant group. This might have indicated to the casual observer that drought had raised the level of child mortality, but careful analysis showed otherwise. When the probabilities of dying of the new immigrants were calculated for earlier periods, no substantial change in childhood mortality was found for the preceding thirty years. None of the earlier droughts, not even the great Sahelian drought of 1973–4, had apparently left a mark on the history of childhood mortality of the migrant group. Hill therefore concludes: 'The data from Mopti-Sevare suggest that the low-income, low-status groups bring their already high mortality patterns with them rather than suffering from short-term mortality crises. Some of the large increases in mortality reported by other researchers from sites where the destitute congregate may be simply due to the importation of the previously unrecognized very high mortality of the rural poor rather than due to any short-term worsening of mortality.' (Hill 1989: 178)

There are of course a few studies that show otherwise; for example, in the study area of Beilik and Henderson (1981) there was a genuine increase in mortality in the wake of drought. But their area was somewhat exceptional in that it suffered from a complete breakdown of civil order. Leaving aside these exceptional cases, Hugo

---

[7] For other coping strategies, see also Ferro-Luzzi and Branca, Chapter 4 above.

(1984: 16) thus generalized the experience of Africa as follows: 'Modern famines do not appear to have taken the massive toll of lives that they did prior to World War II and in general they have had little discernible impact on mortality levels at the national level.'

Hugo further commented that the situation may be different in Asia where excess mortality due to famines appeared to be genuinely high. While this judgement still remains generally valid, recent research has unearthed some notable exceptions even there, especially in the Indian subcontinent (Dyson 1991a, 1991b, 1993; Dyson and Maharatna 1991, 1992; Maharatna 1992). Dyson explains these exceptions in terms of some special epidemiological features that obtained in British India. Most famines were precipitated by droughts, and the hot and dry conditions that accompanied drought were especially inhospitable for mosquitoes and fleas. As a result, the incidence of malaria and plague, which were normally among the biggest killer diseases, often declined below normal levels in the first few months of famine. Of course, later, as the monsoon returned, malaria would turn particularly vicious and that is what accounted for most of the famine deaths in the nineteenth century. Occasionally, however, the timing of the monsoon was such that malaria could not spread in the usual manner; in such cases total famine mortality, counting the initial decline, could turn out to be negligible. In some cases, mortality could even decline, as it did in parts of the Bombay Presidency in the famine of 1905–6 (Maharatna 1992).

India's epidemiology has changed greatly since then; so what was true in the nineteenth and early twentieth century probably no longer applies there. There were, after all, high numbers of excess deaths both during the Bengal famine of 1943 and the Bangladesh famine of 1974. But it is interesting to note that Dyson and Maharatna (1992) did not find any significant increase in infant mortality during the Bihar famine of 1966–7 even though the authorities are known to have failed singularly to organize sufficient relief and public works on this occasion unlike in times of other crisis in the post-Independence period. On the basis of these experiences, Dyson (1993: 25) concludes that even for south Asia, 'excess mortality is not an inevitable component of famine'.

It is nonetheless true that famine mortality was generally significant enough in British India to have had a discernible effect on long-term population growth. This is particularly true for the half century between 1871 and 1921. Population growth was particularly depressed during this period—averaging just about 0.37 per cent as against 1 per cent in the following three decades. In trying to explain the reason for this difference, McAlpin (1983b) considered many alternative hypotheses, including possible improvement in living standards and public health measures in the later period; but she eventually came to the conclusion that the only plausible explanation was that an unusually frequent occurrence of famines and epidemics during this period was responsible for depressing population growth below the normal level.

India's experience in this regard is rather unusual when one recalls how little impact famines have had on long-term population growth in both pre-industrial Europe and contemporary Africa. It could be argued though that what made this experience unique was the unusually close succession of many disasters that occurred in the shape of either famine or epidemic in the late nineteenth and early twentieth centuries. The question then arises: considering the more usual frequency of famines, what can one say about the demographic impact of famines in general? Watkins and Menken (1985) have recently provided an answer to this question through a simulation exercise.

After collating a huge amount of material on historical and contemporary famines, they developed some stylized facts about the frequency, duration, intensity, age-sex specific mortality and fertility effects of famine. Then under some alternative specifications of these parameters, they calculated short- and long-run effects of famine on population growth for a closed society with zero net migration. In one of the specifications it was found that following a severe famine (one that raises crude death rate by 110 per cent over a two-year period), a population that was initially growing at 0.5 per cent regains its initial size in only 11 years, and after 90 years total population size remains only 7 per cent below what it otherwise would have been. It would thus appear that a one-shot famine, even a rather severe one, would have negligible effect on long-term population growth.

Of course, whether in practice the population recovers or not would depend on how frequently it is subjected to these shocks. In order to bring this dimension into analysis, Watkins and Menken estimated the frequency that would be required to nullify the recuperation of population. They then noted that this 'required' frequency is much higher than the typical frequency of famines observed in the real world. So they conclude: '. . . the only way famines and other mortality crises could have been a major deterrent to long-term population growth when the underlying normal mortality and fertility rates would have led to even moderate growth is if they occurred with a frequency and severity far beyond that recorded for famines in history.' (Watkins and Menken 1985: 665).

This conclusion would apply even more strongly to contemporary developing countries where the 'normal' rates of population growth are much higher than those assumed in the simulations, because the higher rate of normal growth would make recovery that much quicker. It would thus appear that in so far as endemic poverty is affected by long-term population change, famine does not matter for long-term poverty, whatever immediate hardship it may cause.

It must be remembered however that the simulations referred to above applied to closed societies with zero net migration. In an open society, famines would generally induce migration; and to the extent that it constitutes permanent migration, famines would clearly affect population growth as well as living standards in the long run. It has long been believed that the great Irish famine of the 1840s provides an archetypal example of this kind of effect. The conventional account of this famine has seen it as a classical Malthusian phenomenon of too many people trying to live off the limited capacity of land. In the wake of the famine, a quarter of the Irish population was lost, nearly half of it in the form of permanent migration to Britain and America. The long-term reduction in population that followed is believed to have been the dominant influence on the subsequent evolution of all aspects of Irish social life, including the role it played in improving living standards over time (see. for example, O'Brien 1921).

But this conventional wisdom began to be questioned in the 1960s. A revisionist view emerged which was tantamount to the claim that famine did not matter. In particular, it was argued that the famine had very little to do with the migration that ensued. Following a trail of argument first advanced by Marx and Cairns, the revisionist historians argued that the migration that had happened would have happened anyway because of certain changes that were taking place in relative prices of commodities in the international market. The price of potato, the principal crop of Ireland, was falling relative to that of livestock products, which induced a massive shift in the use of land from tillage to pasture. But since livestock farming was much less labour-intensive relative to potato cultivation, there was a huge reduction in the demand for labour, which is what was really responsible, according to this view, for inducing the migration. (Cullen 1960, Crotty 1966)

As we shall see in the next section, this revisionist view of the Irish famine has itself come under attack in recent years. The point we wish to stress here is that the revisionist view does complement quite neatly Watkins and Menken's analysis for closed populations by showing that even when migration is allowed famine may not matter in respect of long-term population trends, and therefore may not affect living standards in the long run—in so far as these are affected by population growth.

4. The Hypothesis that 'Famine Matters—Even in the Long Run'

We shall now present the case for the view that famines can have profoundly adverse effects on long-term living standards. It should be clarified, however, that by arguing for this case we do not intend to revive the extreme view represented by the first post-Malthusian hypothesis which saw famine as the principal perpetuator of poverty. As we have seen in section 3, there are very good reasons for rejecting this hypothesis, especially since recent research has shown that two of its principal premises are based on rather shaky grounds. However, its rejection does not necessarily warrant the acceptance of the second post-Malthusian hypothesis that famine doesn't matter in the long run. That proposition was based primarily on the recent evidence on demographic effects of famine. It was seen that the short-run effects were actually much less pronounced than previously thought and were in any case transitory in nature, as the long-term effects seemed to be extremely small, if they existed at all. I shall nevertheless argue that there are sound reasons for believing that famines leave a trail of adverse consequences even far into the future.

First, even if we believe that the demographic effects are only transitory in nature, we have to allow for the possibility that short-run non-demographic effects can have lasting consequences for economic well-being. We shall in fact identify three channels—involving economic assets, nutritional status, and institutions respectively—through which the non-demographic effects may operate.

Secondly, we must also allow for the possibility that even the short run demographic effects themselves may have long-term economic consequences. The point here is simply that even when the impact on a particular demographic variable is reversed over time, this may leave an irreversible impact on some other variable that may be of significance. We shall illustrate this point by considering the impact of famine on sex differentials in the mortality rate.

Both these lines of argument rely on the concept of irreversibility, that is, the idea that short run effects of both demographic and non-demographic nature may leave some irreversible impact on the individual, the family, and the society, which will have long-term implications for living standards.

Finally, we shall suggest that perhaps the new view of long-term demographic responses to famine discussed in the preceding section is not so watertight after all. Specifically, it will be argued that the new view does not allow for certain mechanisms through which famines may affect long-term fertility behaviour and through it long-term living standards.

In short, we shall consider five different channels through which famine may entail adverse consequences for long-term living standards. Three of these are non-demographic in nature—involving assets, nutrition, and institutions; and two are demographic—involving sex differentials in mortality rate and long-term fertility behaviour.

4.1. Irreversible Effects via Non-demographic Routes: Shrinkage of the Endowment Set

A useful way of classifying the coping strategies is to note the sequence in which they are usually adopted. Corbett (1988) has identified a three-stage sequence in which people try to cope. In the first stage, they try to augment current income, draw upon the conventional insurance mechanisms of the 'moral economy', and sell off unproductive assets that have primarily been kept as store of value. If all these actions fail to maintain conventional levels of consumption, people 'choose to starve' and allow themselves to become undernourished rather than sell off their productive assets. However, when the state of undernourishment has become too severe, they begin to sell productive assets—this is the second stage. The third stage comes when a household becomes totally destitute and cannot survive even after selling off whatever assets it had. Migration and congregation at refugee camps then remain the final option.

The major distinction between the strategies in the first and the second stages is that the first-stage strategies purport to maintain the subsistence basis of the household by protecting the productive assets for as long as possible, while the second-stage strategies destroy it. In the revealing terminology of de Waal (1989), these are called 'non-erosive' and 'erosive' strategies respectively. I shall argue a little later that the first-stage strategy of letting oneself become undernourished is not necessarily 'non-erosive'. However, the distinction is still a useful one and so is the sequential analysis. Households do try to avoid the second stage for as long as possible; but many of them eventually fail. It has been observed, for example, that distress sales of land went up sharply during the Bangladesh famine of 1974. A survey of eight villages showed that the number of land transactions in 1974 was double the level of 1972 and almost two-thirds higher in 1973 (Alamgir 1980). National-level data also confirmed the heightened level of land transactions in the famine year (Khan 1977).

Similar phenomena have also been observed frequently in Africa. After reviewing a number of cases, Corbett (1988: 1106) concludes: 'Each of these African studies confirms a finding that has been discussed in the South Asian context, that households respond to food crisis and famine by selective and sequential disposal of assets.' Indeed, the loss of productive resources at times of distress is not just a contemporary phenomenon; it also happened, for example, in early modern France (Le Roy Ladurie 1974).

If assets lost in bad times could be recovered in good times, then of course such loss would be of no great consequence for the long term; for, after all, good times do usually come again. In a world of perfect markets one would indeed expect such recovery to take place. But markets are not perfect; of particular significance here are the imperfections of credit markets. For well-known reasons, the poor have unequal access to credit markets as compared with the rich; and such unequal access can prevent recovery of assets in at least two ways.

First, the productive assets are usually of such high value relative to the current income of the poor that the only way they can acquire the necessary finance is either by a prolonged process of saving in small amounts or by borrowing. The savings option is an exceedingly difficult one, not only because of the pressing consumption needs of the poor but also because inflation of asset value can render this option infeasible by presenting an ever-receding target. So if the borrowing option is ruled out by the imperfect credit market, it becomes impossible to recover the assets.

The second way in which credit constraints can prevent recovery is by driving a wedge between the supply price and the demand price of assets. By virtue of their superior access to the credit market, the rich may be able to use their assets more profitably than the poor by using better and more expensive technology and complementary inputs. If this is so, the economic value of the same asset will be higher for the rich than for the poor, with the result that the price at which the rich would be willing to sell back the asset will be higher than what the poor will find it worthwhile to pay. In consequence, the reverse transaction will never take place.

This is why, most of the land transactions that take place in Bangladesh even in normal times are seen to flow from the poor to the rich, and precious little the other way round, leading to increasing concentration of land (Khan 1988). Much the same is true of the sale of livestock by the pastoralists of Africa. In a study of the Wodaabe pastoralists of Niger, White (1987: 482) has noted that while the national stock of livestock recovered from the shock of the 1973 drought by about 1980, the ownership of livestock had been redistributed away from the Wodaabe households, leaving only 10 per cent of them with enough animals even for bare subsistence. White of course rightly emphasizes that not all of this redistribution is attributable to drought, just as not all the redistribution of land in Bangladesh can be attributed to distress sales in times of crisis, but in both cases crisis sales no doubt played a part.

Thus both theory and evidence suggest that the sale of assets that occurs during famines and other crises is usually an irreversible process. As such, these sales represent an irreversible shrinkage of the endowment set of the poor, which reduces their future entitlements even long after the famine is over and good times have returned.

4.2. Irreversible Effects via Non-demographic Routes: Long-term Nutritional Status

The irreversible nature of asset disposal is of course recognized by the poor themselves; this is after all precisely the reason why they try to postpone it for as long as possible. But there are also other irreversibilities that may not be so easily recognized. Recall the point made earlier that the strategy of 'choosing to starve'—that is, allowing oneself to become undernourished in order to save productive assets— is usually considered to be 'non-erosive' in the coping strategy literature. But this line of thinking ignores the fact that acute undernutrition can cause irreversible damage to one's physical and mental development which can do nothing but harm to the viability of a household. A considerable body of evidence exists by now to support this contention.[8]

The long-term effects of undernutrition are more serious the earlier in life it is experienced. The problem can begin in the mother's womb. Women who suffer serious undernutrition during pregnancy tend to produce children who carry a life-long disadvantage in terms of both physical and mental health. The proportion of low-birthweight babies tends to be higher among undernourished mothers; such babies are more likely to die sooner than babies of normal weight, and even if they survive their growth tends to be stunted. Even normal-weight babies can become stunted if they are subjected to serious undernutrition early in life. Better nutrition in subsequent years may repair some of the damage, but a degree of permanent growth retardation cannot generally be avoided.

Severe stunting can cause a variety of problems throughout life. During childhood, the severely stunted children will be more susceptible to recurrent infections and will also be more likely to suffer retardation in cognitive development. In adult life, they will have lower physical capacity to work, and greater susceptibility to morbidity and premature mortality in comparison with adults of normal height. Thus episodes of serious undernutrition during childhood (including the foetal stage) can have deleterious consequences for both physical well-being and earning capacity in adult life.

It should be noted that there is usually a threshold effect in all the consequences of undernutrition mentioned above. That is to say, these consequences generally

---

[8]   See, for example, Srinivasan 1983; Dasgupta and Ray 1990; Gopalan 1992; Osmani 1992; James and Shetty 1994; Fogel 1994; and Steckel 1995. See also Ferro-Luzzi and Branca, Chapter 4 above.

follow only when the degree of undernutrition becomes severe, falling below what is called mild-to-moderate undernutrition. But that is precisely what is most likely to happen at times of famine. The poorest segment of the population already survive at a level of mild-to-moderate undernutrition; further loss of nutrition during crisis periods is very likely to push them quickly below the threshold. Thus even a modest degree of further undernutrition among young children and pregnant mothers can make all the difference in setting in motion an irreversible process of life-long disadvantage for the coming generation.

This way of looking at things suggests that the usual analysis of famine mortality may be deficient in a fundamental way. When a population is subjected to recurrent crises, the cumulative long-term effects of the resulting undernutrition will be reflected in the so-called 'normal' levels of morbidity and mortality. The estimation of crisis mortality as a deviation from normal mortality will then underestimate the true extent of the damage.[9] Equally, it will be a mistake in any long-term analysis to make too strong a dichotomy between changes in the incidence of crisis mortality and secular changes in 'normal' mortality.

This argument has obvious implications for the continuing debate over the European escape from hunger. We have noted earlier that most historians are now convinced that since crisis mortality constituted only a small proportion of total mortality in pre-industrial Europe, it was the reduction in normal mortality rather than elimination of crisis mortality that must have brought mortality down permanently in the nineteenth century. As an explanation of the reduction in normal mortality, it has been suggested that the crucial part was played by secular improvement in the nutritional status of the population, which gave them greater immunity against infectious and other diseases (see, for example, McKeown 1983; Fogel 1992, 1994). Some doubts still exist regarding the validity of this explanation based on the nutrition–infection nexus[10]; but the point we are making here is that even if one accepts this explanation it may not be right to play down the importance of the conquest of famines. If, as we have argued, the cumulative effect of recurrent famines is to depress the so-called 'normal' level of nutritional status, then the conquest of famines may well have played a role in bringing about the observed secular improvement. How important that role was is an empirical matter on which judgement must be withheld at the moment, but the possibility that it might have been very significant cannot be ruled out. At the very least, it needs to be acknowledged that through its irreversible impact on long-term nutritional status famine can have hitherto unsuspected implications for secular changes in living standards.

---

[9] In a recent re-examination of the Bengal famine of 1943, Dyson and Maharatna (1991) have claimed that Sen's (1981) earlier analysis may have exaggerated mortality by showing a tail of elevated mortality for several years after the famine whereas their own, presumably superior, data do not show any such tail. However, an implication of the argument regarding the long-term effect of undernutrition is that the non-existence of the tail does not necessarily ensure that a delayed mortality effect did not exist.

[10] Livi-Bacci (1983) argues, for instance, that since the life expectancy of British aristocrats was not much different from that of the general public before the eighteenth century, it is not clear that undernutrition was the principal factor behind excessive death due to infections and epidemics.

4.3. Irreversible Effects via Non-demographic Routes: Breakdown of the Moral Economy

While the preceding discussion was concerned with irreversibilities specific to the individual, famine may also bring about irreversible changes in social institutions that may have long-term implications for living standards. Social anthropologists have shown that in most traditional societies there exists some form of moral economy through which people manage to tide themselves over temporary crises and the weaker members of the society are protected from extreme suffering. The emerging literature on coping strategies has confirmed how this moral economy has come to the rescue during the recent crises in Africa. But it has also been found that the institutional basis of the moral economy can rupture under severe strain, and this is likely to be an irreversible change endangering the livelihood of vulnerable groups.

One instance of such change has recently been noted among the Wodaabe pastoralists in central Niger (White 1987; Hill 1989). This community practises a system of pre-inheritance whereby the herd is held in a kind of collective trust for the next generation; a heifer would be assigned to a child at birth which would form the core of the offspring's own herd when he or she grows into an adult. One consequence of this system of pre-inheritance is that the weaker members cannot be forced out of the pastoral economy. Furthermore, since there is a certain shame involved in having poor relations in the administrative fraction, a redistributive mechanism works in the form of gifts, loans of dairy cows, and *habba nai* loans (the temporary gift of a cow until she has produced three calves).

The foundations of this moral economy have been severely damaged, however, in the wake of the recent droughts. As a result of livestock reductions by both death and forced sale, the pre-inheritance system can no longer ensure that every adult is able to start his or her own herd. Some people migrate out of the pastoral economy, thus losing the traditional support base. Others become contract herders, in which case, too, the traditional support system no longer operates. In particular, they cease to have access to loans of animals under the traditional *habba nai* sharing system since lenders fear infection from animals belonging to outsiders. There are also other ways in which their livelihood security is endangered. For example, the new owners of herds restrict their mobility so as to maintain contact with their stock; as a result, the herder can no longer seek out the best grazing lands.

4.4. Long-term Effects on Fertility Behaviour

We have noted earlier that famine does have a short-term effect on fertility—it almost invariably reduces fertility at a very early date, but often this is partially offset by excess fertility after the famine, and the net effect turns out to be fairly negligible. The long-term effect has not been so well documented, however; the best one can do is to speculate. Thus Cain (1981) and Bongaarts and Cain (1982) speculate that since children are viewed by parents as old-age insurance in a society where formal mechanisms of social insurance do not exist, an event such as famine that raises the risk of child mortality will discourage parents from exercising fertility control. To that extent the task of moving the society from a regime of natural fertility to one of controlled fertility would be that much harder in a famine-prone society than in a famine-free one.

The Bongaarts–Cain argument about the long-term effect on fertility can be generalized in a couple of ways. First, the insurance motive need not be the only relevant consideration. In a regime of natural fertility resources flow from the young to the old in a variety of ways, of which old-age insurance is only one. Even when the parents are in their prime, children play a crucial role in the household economy by augmenting household resources in a number of ways (Caldwell 1983). Therefore, anything that elevates the risk of child mortality is a potential threat to the livelihood security of the household. Famine is precisely such a threat; that is why the transition to a regime of fertility control would be harder to achieve in a famine-prone society.

Second, it is not simply the increased risk of child mortality that matters here; the risk of adult mortality is also a relevant consideration. We have argued earlier that through the long-term effect of childhood undernutrition, the recurrence of famine results in a generation of adults that has a lower physical capacity to work and is more susceptible to morbidity and mortality than would otherwise be the case. In a society in which adults are so handicapped, the need for resources flowing from the younger to the older generation cannot but assume greater significance—to cover the contingency of premature death or serious disability of the adult breadwinner. That too will make it harder to effect the transition to a regime of controlled fertility.

All these arguments imply that a famine-prone society is also very likely to be a high-fertility society. An example of how famines may strengthen the support for high fertility can be seen from Hill's (1989) analysis of the Bambara community of the western Sahel. For sound economic reasons the Bambara community tends to prefer very large residential units. But, as Hill notes, this institution inevitably implies strong social support for high fertility; and since this institution has been found to become more deeply entrenched at times of crisis (Toulmin 1986), it follows that famines and other crises would help perpetuate the regime of high fertility. So far, an open land-frontier has spared the Bambara people from any adverse effect of high fertility, but the eventual closing of the frontier is bound to make the effect felt sooner or later.

4.5. The Irish Famine: A Case of Benign Irreversibility?

The irreversibilities I have considered so far are all of the malignant kind—they all tend to depress the long-term living standards of one group or another. For the sake of completeness, we ought to consider whether there can exist any benign irreversibility. Some very recent re-examination of the Irish famine seems to suggest that there might be one. In the preceding section, I referred to the revisionist view that the Irish famine did not matter all that much at least as far as mass migration was concerned. In a counter-revisionist analysis, O'Rourke (1991) has recently concluded that the famine did matter after all. He used a computable general equilibrium model to test the revisionist hypothesis that by reducing domestic demand for labour the ongoing changes in relative commodity prices would have induced migration anyway even in the absence of famine. His estimates show that while the change in relative prices would have shifted production from highly labour-intensive cereal to less labour-intensive livestock, the production of labour-intensive potato crop would have increased due to various inter-sectoral linkages between livestock and potato. As a result, total demand for labour would not have declined much—at any rate not enough to induce the massive migration that followed.

O'Rourke goes on to conclude that the famine acted as a crucial catalyst for the migration, by shocking the Irish labour market into a beneficial integration with the international labour market. Since the international wage rates—especially those in Britain and America—were considerably higher than those in Ireland, once the shock integration occurred it set in motion an irreversible trend of outmigration. In the process, not only did the migrants find a better life abroad, those staying at home also enjoyed higher real wages as migration brought the domestic wage level closer to the international one.

While this case of benign irreversibility is a matter of considerable historical interest, it can give little comfort to the contemporary developing world for whom the scope for mass international migration is utterly restricted. The malignant irreversibilities discussed earlier are much more relevant for them, which means that the effect of famines on the long-term evolution of their living standards can hardly be anything other than harmful.

Conclusion

We have attempted in this paper to gain an understanding of the possible long-term effects of famine on endemic poverty. As an expositional device, we have classified these effects under four hypotheses—one Malthusian and three post-Malthusian. In the Malthusian perspective, famine is seen to provide the survivors with an escape valve from extreme poverty, giving them an opportunity to raise their living standards beyond the level of bare biological survival. This perspective however does not take sufficient cognizance of the long-term effects of famine that operate through various economic and demographic channels. These long-term issues are considered more fully by the post-Malthusian hypotheses.

One such hypothesis would see famine as the principal perpetuator of poverty in the long run, rather than as an escape from it. This notion is based on two specific views on the economic and demographic history of the Western world. One of them holds that famines were chiefly responsible for the high level of mortality in pre-industrial Europe; and the other—the so-called classical version of the demographic transition theory—suggests that it was the high level of mortality that accounted for the high level of fertility that obtained. The combination of these two views implies that famines were ultimately responsible for keeping fertility high and thus dissipating any productivity gains; hence the notion that the long-term effect of famine was to condemn a society to secular stagnation.

Recent research has shown, however, that there are serious problems with both the propositions on which the preceding hypothesis is based. Neither is famine now seen to be responsible for keeping mortality high in the pre-industrial world, nor is high mortality seen to be the main factor behind high fertility. These revisionist views, coupled with newly emerging evidence on the demographic impacts of past and contemporary famines, would seem to entail the very opposite hypothesis—that famine does not matter much in the long run.

But this rather comforting view is based mainly on the direct demographic consequences of famine. A deeper analysis shows that short-run demographic and non-demographic effects of famine may have some irreversible consequences for the individual, the family, and the society. These irreversibilities pertain to the endowment set of the household, the long-term nutritional status of the individual, the structure of the family, and the structure of the moral economy. Most of these irreversibilities are seen to exert a deleterious influence on the long-term living standards of the people. This tendency is likely to be further aggravated by the long-term effect of famine on fertility behaviour, since a famine-prone society is also likely to be a high-fertility society.

6 Household Structure and Poverty: What Are the Connections?

CYNTHIA B. LLOYD

Introduction

Improved living standards have usually been associated with a tendency towards smaller and less complex households. Yet, growing numbers of female-headed households, which also tend to be smaller and less complex, have often been associated with increasing rates of poverty among women and children. In the first instance, economic trends are viewed as the determinants of household structure while, in the second case, changes in household structure are seen as the cause of increasing poverty. These trends appear contradictory but are not. The problem is that the household unit is used as the basis for measuring living standards, poverty, and inequality, despite our fundamental interest in the fate of individuals. Indeed, given the way data are collected, we have no way of knowing how individual women and children have fared within different types of households but only that, when they are observed separately in their own households, women and children in female-headed households often appear disadvantaged (particularly when assessed on the basis of income) relative to those in male-headed households.

This chapter assesses *household structure* and *function* as factors in the well-being or poverty of individuals. In the literature, the term 'household structure' can include dimensions such as complexity (nuclear versus extended), dependency (consumers relative to producers), and the locus of responsibility and authority (the sex and marital status of the head) but does not usually include household size, despite obvious interconnections between size and structure.[1] Collectively, these dimensions help in the conceptualizing of the internal cohesiveness of the co-residential unit as it relates

This paper has benefited from the helpful comments of John Bongaarts, Judith Bruce, John Casterline, Elizabeth Durbin, Lawrence Haddad, and Barbara Ibrahim and the computer programming assistance of Jin Wei. This is a revised version of a paper by the same title presented at an IUSSP seminar on Demography and Poverty, Florence, 2–4 March 1995, and at the Annual Meeting of the Population Association of America, San Francisco, 6-8 April 1995.

[1] In a recent review of the literature on the consequences for children of high fertility, I conclude that children from large families, particularly in societies undergoing rapid development, are increasingly disadvantaged. In large families, parental time and resources are more constrained, limiting the resources available for investment in each child and limiting parents' ability to assist their children in taking advantage of new opportunities. In addition, there is likely to be greater inequality among siblings, with girls suffering particular disadvantage (Lloyd 1994).

to the scope of its responsibilities. This contrasts with the term 'household function', which I define here as the extent to which individual members' caring and sharing relationships are subsumed within their residential household or extend in important ways beyond it. Because welfare is essentially experienced individually, this review assesses the structure and function of the household from the point of view of its returns to individual members and contrasts this approach with a more corporate view in which its collective resources are assumed to be fully shared by all members. While households can be units of production (in the case of family farms)[2] as well as units of consumption and redistribution, my focus here is on the element that all households have in common: co-residence of their members.

The challenge of such a topic is that the data available for analysis are organized around a particular view of the household that this chapter questions. Like an archeologist constructing an image of pot-making from the exploration of fragments collected in the shifting sands, the researcher exploring the relationship between household structure and poverty is forced to construct a map of sharing relationships among family members, wherever they reside, from information on co-residential households. Furthermore, an individual's household affiliation is neither *life-long*, as with family ties, nor necessarily *long-term*, as in the case of marriage, but *relatively easy to adjust* over the short term in response to changing economic and social conditions. Thus, household structure may be as much a response to economic and demographic constraints and opportunities as a factor explaining them.

A full understanding of the links between household structure and the poverty of its members requires knowledge of (1) the relationship between poverty and the process of household formation or affiliation, (2) the patterns and extent of inter-household economic exchanges and their implications for resource-pooling within the household, and (3) the internal distribution of responsibilities and resources in different types of households. While there has been growing attention to the issue of intra-household resource distribution, relatively little attention has been given to the determinants of household formation or affiliation or the economic relations that exist between individuals residing in different households.

The chapter begins with a discussion of the economics of the household and its potential implications for the measurement of poverty. This is followed by some data illustrating the variety of patterns that appear when comparing the economic well-being of different types of households using household-based measures of living standards. The third section discusses household-family links and their implications for the relationship between household structure and the distribution of poverty among individuals. The final section reviews the key points emerging from a growing literature on the internal distribution of household resources as it relates to household structure and individual poverty. The chapter concludes with some

---

[2] An extensive literature (not reviewed here) on the relationship between the size and structure of peasant households and their economic performance dates back to the work of the Russian economist Chayanov in the 1920s (see Shapiro 1990).

thoughts about the appropriateness of the household as our demographic and economic unit of measure and some suggestions for alternative approaches.

1. The Economics of the Household and its Implications for the Measurement of Poverty

For practical reasons, statisticians group people by residence rather than by relationship. The resulting household unit is typically viewed as the most appropriate unit of measure for assessing poverty (Blackwood and Lynch 1994).[3] This is because of the resource-sharing that is assumed to occur within households. As described by Hammel (1980), the household is 'the smallest grouping with the maximum corporate function'. Any individual's economic circumstances depend not only on his or her own production and earnings but also on support from and responsibilities to other family members. This means that when low-earning individuals are members of higher-earning households, they are not separately classified as poor (Fields 1994). Typically, the only adjustment that is made to convert collective measures of household income or consumption to individual measures is to divide household income by the number of members or the number of 'equivalent adults'.[4] Using this approach, an assessment of the distribution of poverty by sex involves comparing the proportion of all women who live in households defined as poor with the proportion of all men living in these same households (Casper, McLanahan, and Garfinkel 1994).

There are several problems with the use of the household unit as the basis for assessing the welfare of a particular individual: (1) it assumes that each individual is a member of only one household (Greeley 1994); (2) it assumes that an individual's current household affiliation is given rather than chosen (or forced) in response to economic circumstances; and (3) it assumes that the resources of all household members are fully pooled and then distributed 'equitably' among all members.

1.1. Household and Family

In the economic literature, household economics is usually synonymous with family economics. The words 'household' and 'family' are typically used interchangeably and sometimes combined into the term 'family household' (Kuznets 1978). However, in the parlance of demographers, 'household' refers to a co-residential

---

[3] In the United States, poverty lines or family income needs are based on the cost of a nutritionally adequate diet for households of a given size and composition multiplied by three. The multiplier is based on a 1955 survey showing that families of three or more spend 35 per cent of their after-tax income on food on average. It is assumed that the poor should not earmark a larger proportion of their income for food than the non-poor (Sawhill 1988).

[4] Because of economies of scale in large households as well as differences in consumption needs of children and adults, adjustments are required to convert the number of household members into an estimated number of equivalent adults (see Anand and Morduch, Chapter 2 above).

unit,[5] whereas 'family' refers to a group of individuals related by blood, marriage, or adoption. The economic theory of the household relies on the assumption that cohesive family units reside together within households, sharing resources among themselves but not with other households. Its usefulness depends on 'the degree to which co-residence is consistently associated with other family transactions' (Ben-Porath 1980).

The economic theory of the household fits reality better in some situations than others but is likely to have become less and less descriptive of reality. In addition to social practices such as exogamy, polygamy, and child fostering that have tradition-ally separated family members into different household units in some societies, declining household size and complexity and greater mobility in marriage, work, and residential location make it increasingly likely that individuals will be linked economically (and emotionally) to family members with whom they do not currently or exclusively reside. Furthermore, the diversification of economies makes it less likely, even in rural traditional settings, that the residential household repre-sents a cohesive family production unit. Indeed, growing residential mobility—a product of a global economy—suggests that theories of family formation and disso-lution may be inadequate for understanding individual decisions about forming a household or joining or remaining with an existing household.

These distinctions between household and family have implications for the signif-icance of the household as the 'economic decision and recipient unit' (Kuznets 1978) and thus for the measurement of poverty. The link between the economic position of an individual and the economic position of the household in which that person resides will be attenuated to the extent that the individual is economically linked to family members who reside in other households and carries economic entitlements or responsibilities that are not shared by other members of his/her residential house-hold. While poverty measures are typically based on an estimation of the collective value of household consumption (including the value of home-produced consump-tion), the household head will have difficulty accounting fully for the consumption of each member when some members engage in production, consumption, and exchange away from the household and with family members who are affiliated with different residential households.[6] Blended family households in which children co-reside who do not collectively share the same parents are a particularly good exam-ple of this problem. In these households, the head is not in a position to fully report on or redistribute resources among children within the household because some chil-dren have specific economic entitlements that derive from parents and other relatives who live outside the household and whom they regularly visit and spend time with.

---

[5] The current United Nations definition of households combines the housing unit concept (a unit occupying all or part of a dwelling) with the housekeeping unit concept (a unit sharing resources to provide members with food and other essentials).

[6] Here, I am thinking particularly of the World Bank Living Standard Measurement Surveys, conducted over the last ten years in a number of less-developed countries. These surveys assess house-hold living standards on the basis of consumption, relying on one respondent to report on the full consumption of all household members.

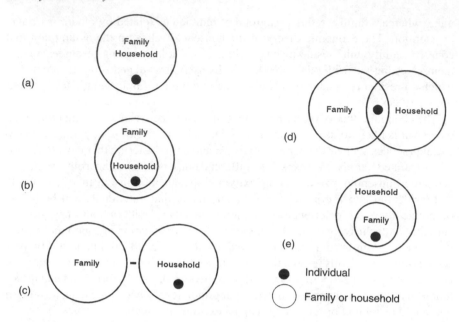

Fig. 6.1. Possible relationships between an individual's residential household and primary family unit

To illustrate the implications of different units of analysis for measures of income distribution, Greenhalgh (1982) compared income distribution in Taiwan using two income units: the household and the 'chai', or corporate kin group. Larger and longer-lasting than the individual household, the 'chai' is organized around the joint ownership of property among males. She found that distributions of 'chai' income were more unequal than distributions of household income. The implications of this finding for income inequality among individuals will depend on how income is shared within households and among households within larger kin groups.

Figure 6.1 illustrates the possible relationships between an individual's primary residential household and his or her collective family, which, for the purposes of this illustration, encompasses the individual's primary caring and sharing relationships. Figure 6.1a illustrates the 'family household' described above, which forms the basis of the economic model of the household. Figure 6.1b shows a more typical case of an individual who lives exclusively with family but also has economic links with other family members who reside outside the household. This could include the child of a divorced mother or migrant father, a child fostered to relatives, or a polygamous husband. In this case, only if all resources flowing into and out of the household are controlled by the head, fully pooled, and distributed equitably can collective household consumption be used to assess the economic standing of a particular individual within the household. Figure 6.1c includes individuals who live apart from family and have important economic links with family members who reside elsewhere. This would include migrant husbands or wives who have left home in search of work, who may be living alone or with people to whom they are not closely linked in terms of family ties. Figures 6.1d and 6.1e are further variants, illustrating the possibility of sharing residential space with unrelated individuals while retaining family connections. Here the assumption of full resource-pooling within the household is particularly problematic.

Each of these illustrations allows individuals to be formally a member of only one household. Obviously, if individuals move between households, producing and consuming resources in each, as they often do in cases of temporary migration, shared custody, polygamy, or child-fostering, then the possible range of scenarios would multiply further. More fundamentally, if poverty is viewed as the absence of certain 'entitlements' and/or 'capabilities' (Sen 1983) rather than the lack of certain basic needs (such as food, health care, education, shelter), then the ability to leave a household, form a new one, or join a different one should be seen as an important dimension of those capabilities. As noted by Livi-Bacci (1994), while 'the absence of mobility is not by itself correlated with poverty, . . . we may easily posit that absence of mobility impairs the optimal allocation of human resources and precludes one of the most efficient routes of escape from poverty'. When mobility results in the separation of family members who remain linked economically, then the economic standing of their respective residential households may give only a partial picture of the extent to which their basic needs are met or their 'capabilities' have been fulfilled.

Mobility is highly diffentiated by gender, with men much more able to move in response to economic opportunities than women. Indeed, 'the growth of labor markets and geographic mobility lowers the cost of defaulting on the implicit contracts of family life' (Folbre 1994). As a result, women may be disadvantaged relative to men, who are often able to improve their economic situation by setting up a new household while leaving major care-giving and economic responsibilities in the hands of women who are left behind.

1.2. Intra-household Resource Allocation

The traditional model of the household and the measurement of poverty on which it is based further assume that household resources are equally or 'fairly' distributed among members by an altruistic head (Becker 1991). 'Fairly' is sometimes interpreted as equally and sometimes as according to need. These two approaches have different implications for the measurement of poverty. Per-capita income measures are based on the assumption of an equal level of resources per person. However, because children, particularly when young, are known to need fewer calories per day than adults to remain healthy, they are sometimes counted as only a fraction of an 'equivalent adult' from the point of view of consumption and the measurement of poverty. Thus, when families of the same size and income but with different ratios of children to adults are compared, those with the highest child/adult ratio

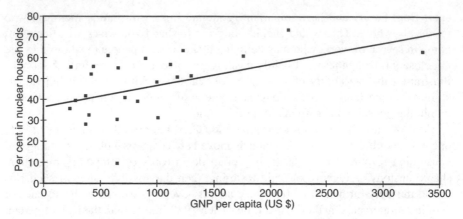

Fig 6.2. Relationship between GNP per capita and percentage of women living in nuclear households
Source: GNP per capita (1988 US$), World Bank; percentage living in nuclear households, United Nations (forthcoming).

would be deemed to be best off because, after feeding the children, they would presumably have more resources to spare for other needs.

However, there is increasing evidence that resources (including leisure) are often distributed unequally or unfairly among household members. For example, using illustrative data on food consumption from the Philippines, Haddad and Kanbur (1990) show that, if one ignores intra-household inequality, measures of the levels of inequality and poverty could be understated by 30 per cent or more. Women and children are the most vulnerable to differential treatment because of their lack of power and/or relative youth.

2. The Empirical Association between Household Structure and Poverty

Historical studies of household structure have found that the nuclear household has always been relatively common. The larger extended households tended to be wealthier, particularly in rural areas where land ownership was important (Burch 1982). Furthermore, female headship was primarily associated with widowhood and occurred relatively late in life. These facts coexist with the conventional wisdom that the extended household is a more traditional form that has been declining in prevalence with lower household size as economies develop. While we cannot re-explore the historical record, we can look at some contemporary patterns to learn how household forms currently correlate with income and rates of poverty across countries.

Comparable data on various dimensions of household structure are a recent development. Figure 6.2 shows the relationship between real GNP per capita and the

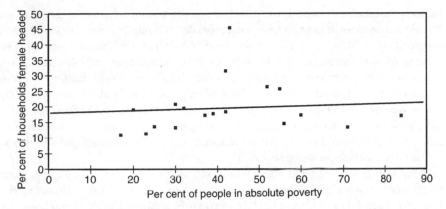

Fig. 6.3. Relationship between percentage of people in absolute poverty and percentage of households headed by females
Source: Percentage in absolute poverty, UNDP (1994); percentage of female-headed households, Ayad *et al.* (1994).

percentage of reproductive-age women living in nuclear households for a diverse group of twenty-four less-developed countries.[7] Each US$100 increase in real GNP per capita is associated with an increase of one percentage point in the proportion living in nuclear households, and the coefficient is statistically significant. Thus, this sample of countries appears to lend some truth to the notion that rising living standards are associated with a greater proportion of nuclear households.

At the same time, female-headed households have been linked with poverty. Figure 6.3 examines the relationship between the percentage of people in absolute poverty (as defined by the World Bank) in per capita terms and the percentage of households that are female-headed for eighteen less-developed countries. Here there is no correlation between female headship and poverty, at least when the incidence of female headship across a diverse set of less-developed countries is examined.

Increasing concern for gender inequality and poverty among children has led to growing attention being given to the economic circumstances of female-headed households—typically the only households in which the economic situation of women and children can be examined in the absence of men. A large number of country studies have looked at the incidence of poverty among female-headed households in less-developed countries. The most recent review (Quisumbing, Haddad, and Peña 1995) of the literature found female-headed households to be poorer than male-headed households on average in most but not all cases.[8] Per-adult-equivalent

---

[7] Unfortunately, data are not available on the proportion of all households that are nuclear. However, for cross-country comparisons the percentage of reproductive-age women living in nuclear households is a reasonable proxy.

[8] Nine out of eleven studies from South and Southeast Asia and sub-Saharan Africa with complete and comparable data on household per capita income found female-headed households to be poorer on average than male-headed households.

income measures showed an even stronger relationship between poverty and female-headedness in cases where female-headed households were poorer. A more comprehensive but less rigorous review based on sixty-seven studies from all world regions showed female-headed households to be poorer than male-headed households in three-quarters of the cases (Buvinic and Gupta 1994). Factors likely to explain these overall differentials include inferior access to land (not just use rights but ownership) and other assets, higher dependency burdens, lower earnings, lower education, and fewer earners (often only one earner) in female- than male-headed households (Kossoudji and Mueller 1983; Agarwal 1994; DeGraff and Bilsborrow 1993; Lloyd and Gage-Brandon 1993).

None of the studies cited above has assessed the joint effects of headship and household complexity on average income or poverty. It is often assumed that female-headed households are nuclear—primarily mothers and their children—but extended structures are also common in a variety of forms, including three-generation households formally headed by a grandmother, a grandmother and her grandchildren alone, or two sisters and their families. One reason extended households have more resources than nuclear households in rural agricultural societies is that land ownership, an important factor in wealth, is usually in the hands of the family patriarch, who is the oldest male member. Extended female-headed households, which are more likely to be headed by older women (typically widows), may be better off than nuclear female-headed households if the head has inherited the family land or other property, but may be worse off if the property is passed on exclusively through the male line (Agarwal 1994).

To illustrate the differences that can emerge when assessments of both aspects of household structure are combined, I have chosen three countries from the Demographic and Health Survey (Cameroon, Egypt, Philippines) to explore the relationship between household complexity, headship, and average household living standards. The analysis is confined to households with children. Nuclear households include the head, the spouse of the head, and their children. Extended households include one or more regular members who are not members of the nuclear family of the head. The household standard of living is assessed using an index of household amenities that is comparable across countries and varies in value from 0 to 10. It includes various dimensions of healthy living (access to clean water, modern toilet, and non-dirt floors), time-saving technologies (electricity and nearby water), possession of modern goods (radio, bike, television, refrigerator, car, or motorcycle), and privacy for sleeping (measured as number of people per rooms for sleeping). Because this index captures dimensions of a household's living standards that can be shared with varying numbers of members without being in any way diminished, this construction of the index does not depend on household size or composition.

The results presented in Table 6.1 show mean household amenities scores according to household structure. Among these three countries, Egypt is the most developed and Cameroon the least developed. Not surprisingly Cameroon has the highest percentage of extended households and Egypt the lowest. Female-headed

Table 6.1. Household amenities score (HAS)[a], by household structure (illustrative countries)

	Nuclear		Extended	
	Male head	Female head	Male head	Female head
Cameroon				
Unadjusted HAS	3.9	4.2	4.8	4.5
Adjusted HAS[b]	4.2	4.0	4.6	4.4
%	36	3	49	12
N	916	83	1250	308
Egypt				
Unadjusted HAS	6.7	5.8	6.0	6.4
Adjusted HAS[b]	6.5	5.8	6.6	6.2
%	68	3	25	3
N	5493	281	2039	246
Philippines				
Unadjusted HAS	4.9	5.5	6.0	6.1
Adjusted HAS[b]	5.0	5.5	5.8	5.9
%	61	3	29	7
N	6053	341	2863	724

[a] each household gets a score of 1 for (1) clean water, (2) water less than 30 minutes away from the house, (3) toilet (traditional or modern), (4) modern flush toilet, (5) possession of a car and/or motorcycle, (6) possession of a television and/or refrigerator, (7) possession of a radio and/or bicycle, (8) nondirt floor, (9) electricity in the household, (10) a ratio of number of sleeping rooms to household members of 0.3 or more. The total score can range from 0 to 10.
[b] Using MCA, adjusted for dependency ratio, household size, and urban/rural residence.
Source: DHS Household Data.

households are more common among extended than among nuclear households, representing between 11 and 20 per cent of the former and 5 and 8 per cent of the latter. Interestingly, female-headed nuclear households represent 3 per cent of households in all three countries. Thus variations between countries in the prevalence of female-headed households are entirely explained by variations in the prevalence of female-headed extended households.

When differences between household types in the mean household amenities scores are adjusted for household size, household dependency ratio, and urban/rural residence, extended households are better off than nuclear households in all three countries, and this is true for both female- and male-headed households. Male-headed households are better off than female-headed households in Cameroon and Egypt but not in the Philippines, where female-headed extended households are the best off and male-headed nuclear households are the worst off. Similar results are found when using the percentage of households with a score of 3 or lower as a measure of poverty.

The following observations emerge from these illustrative cases: (1) while female-headed households are often poorer, there appears to be no automatic relationship between female headship and poverty; (2) mothers and children living alone are more likely to be disadvantaged than those living in extended female-headed households; (3) if extended households are wealthier than nuclear households yet become less prevalent as societies develop, it must be because they are seen to have disadvantages that increasing numbers of people can afford to avoid by forming nuclear households as incomes rise.

3. Changing Household–Family Links and Implications for the Relationship between Household Structure and Poverty

Despite increasing attention to the distribution of resources within households, there has been little study of the factors affecting an individual's decision to form a household or to remain with, join, or leave an existing household. Household affiliation is usually taken as given—part of an individual's background and context that is fixed, at least in the short run. In some ways this is surprising given the central focus on individual choice in economic theory. The explanation for this neglect, alluded to earlier, is that economists implicitly assume that the concepts of 'family' and 'household' are synonymous. Thus the determinants of family formation and dissolution are seen as synonymous with determinants of household formation and dissolution. Households, however, can encompass several families, and sometimes close family members (even husbands and wives, or parents and children) live in different households. Therefore, the determinants of household formation and composition involve not only factors affecting marriage and marital dissolution but also factors affecting residency.

3.1. The Formation of Extended versus Nuclear Households

In response to this gap in the literature on households, Ermisch and Overton (1985) have developed a theory of household formation based on 'minimal household units' (MHUs)—the smallest divisible familial elements within households. These units comprise single individuals and various parent-child combinations. They are seen as effective decision-making units that group together, for purposes of description and analysis, individuals according to their intensity of sharing resources and time. MHUs make choices about their optimal household grouping based on some combination of component goods associated with household type and composition. Burch and Matthews (1987) have suggested a fairly comprehensive list of these component goods, including privacy, companionship, domestic services, and consumption economies of scale. The value ascribed to each of these is likely to vary in different cultures, with some cultures giving greater emphasis to collective values and others to individual values.

The attainment of a particular bundle of these component goods associated with household living arrangements would be subject to constraints of budget and the availability of housing and of kin. Individuals with greater economic means and/or more kin would have greater residential choices, including the choice of forming an independent household apart from kin. Using data from the General Household Survey of British households, Ermisch and Overton (1985) found that single-parent families are increasingly likely to form separate households as income rises rather than affiliating with extended households, probably because rising income allows greater privacy.[9] Similar findings from the United States (Ellwood and Bane 1984, cited in Sawhill 1988) show that each additional US$ 100 per month in welfare benefits leads to an increase of 15 per cent in the number of young single mothers able to establish independent households separate from their parents. Thus, household structure, in particular female headship, should be seen as a function of income and is likely to rise in prevalence as standards of living improve, even if rates of marital dissolution remain unchanged.

I suggest that another dimension of the value associated with separate residence is personal autonomy and household authority over the allocation of resources. If income permits, wouldn't a mother-child unit prefer to form a separate household with its own decision-making autonomy rather than join a more complex household under other (most likely male or older female) authority? This tendency could be linked to rising female wages and rising female economic autonomy—forces associated with the 'second demographic transition' in developed countries that has included later age at marriage, a reduced propensity to marry, and continuing declines in fertility (Lesthaeghe 1992).

A positive income elasticity of demand for privacy and autonomy means that, as incomes rise, growing numbers of primary family units (or MHUs)—in particular, single-parent families—encompassed within larger households form separate households. Because these family units are likely to have been previously disadvantaged in the allocation of household resources, rising income may appear to be associated with greater inequality between households, when, in fact, actual inequality between MHUs (whose income was previously unmeasured within larger households) may not have changed to the same extent or may even have declined.

Even when the percentage living in poverty has increased along with a rise in the proportion of female-headed households, as it did in the United States during the 1980s (Eggebeen and Lichter 1991), welfare may have improved for some if individuals are willing to trade privacy, which is part of their standard of living, for income. This point was noted by Sawhill (1988) in her discussion of the dramatic post-war shifts in US household composition that have reduced the level of resource-sharing between those with adequate earnings (prime-age males) and those without (women, children, and the elderly).

The same forces that lead MHUs to form separate households may also produce increasing numbers of these units as changes in the sexual division of labour with rising female wages and declining male employment lead to declining gains to

---

[9] Earlier household data for thirteen countries gathered by the United Nations (1973) showed a moderately strong positive relationship between income and headship rates, suggesting that poor adults are less apt to head their own households and thus more apt to live with someone else.

marriage for women and men and rising rates of marital dissolution (Becker 1991). A recent empirical study in the United Kingdom suggests that women in poorer economic circumstances (due in part to earlier age of marriage and premarital child-bearing) are at greater risk of marital dissolution, thus compounding their economic plight (Ermisch and Wright 1994).

While rising incomes may lead to smaller and less complex households, poverty may lead families to group together into extended households as a survival strategy. Neupert (1992) provides a variety of examples from Latin America in which vulnerable MHUs have joined other adult relatives in order to reduce dependency burdens and share expenses.

3.2. Family Ties between Households

Further complications in the study of household structure and poverty include the fact that members of some primary family units do not live together regularly even though they continue to view themselves as a unit, at least for some shared purposes. For example, a detailed study of social transactions (including production, consumption, sexual union, and socialization of children) among and within households in Ghana found that at least 50 per cent of them occurred between rather than within households (Sanjek 1982). Despite ongoing emotional and/or economic ties, parents and dependent children and even spouses sometimes live in separate households for reasons of job location, marital status, children's schooling, or kin solidarity. In such circumstances, the relevant economic unit may be a 'multi-local household' (Caces *et al.* 1985).

When these inter-household exchanges are important, the economic resources produced and consumed within an individual's primary residential household will surely be less than fully descriptive of that individual's economic position or welfare. Evidence of the potential importance of inter-household economic flows comes from studies on the variation among female-headed households in their economic circumstances, the flows of economic support to elderly parents, migrant remittances, and child-fostering.

A variety of in-depth studies reveal that female-headed households are a heterogeneous lot; they include economically viable mother-child units without male support, women whose husbands have migrated in search of work either as a result of poverty or in response to better economic opportunities (and may or may not be sending remittances), widows who are raising grandchildren with or without their mother's presence and/or their parents' support, and women alone. Not all are single-parent households; many are extended family households (see Table 6.1 and De Vos 1987). In some cases poverty has led families to separate in search of work, despite a preference to remain together; in other cases women choose to be alone because of a desire for personal autonomy and privacy, despite the availability of kin to live with.

Several recent studies have compared the economic circumstances of different types of female-headed households according to head's marital status and husband's migrant status. For example, in Ghana, where 29 per cent of households are female-headed, their household income per equivalent adult was shown to be higher than that of male-headed households on average for the group of households headed by prime-age married women, lower for those who were divorced or separated, and lowest for the widowed group of female-headed households (Lloyd and Gage-Brandon 1993). This was interpreted to be a function of the head's access to support from her children's father, which was most likely in the case of married heads (who are typically not co-resident), less steady in the case of women who were divorced, and least likely in the case of widows because of discriminatory inheritance practices within customary law. 'The wealth or poverty of mothers and their children is determined to an important degree by whether fathers, regardless of marital or residential arrangements, contribute economically to their children, not by the family's normatively ascribed headship or household type' (Bruce and Lloyd 1997).

On the other hand, in Ecuador, households headed by married females are among the poorest, poorer than those headed by divorced and widowed women even after remittances have been taken into account (DeGraff and Bilsborrow 1993). This was interpreted by the authors as a response to poor economic conditions, in particular suboptimal landholdings. In other words, the poverty of these families led to male outmigration and female headship; consequently these households may be less poor as female-headed households than they would have been had the couples remained together within male-headed households. Nonetheless, they remain poor. Similar results were found when comparing the average expenditure levels of de facto (where the self-declared male head is absent at least 50 per cent of the time) and de jure female-headed households in Kenya and Malawi (Kennedy and Peters 1992). In each case, women with part-time husbands were worse off, except in the case of women in Malawi whose husbands had migrated to South Africa at a time when male earnings were sufficiently high to make these households by far the best off. Finally in Jamaica, where many households are declared female-headed even when the head's spouse is in residence, female-headed households with a partner were worse off than those without, suggesting that residence in and of itself does not imply anything about the extent of support provided by the husband to the wife (Handa 1994).

Internal and international migration as well as occupational diversification has increasingly separated adult children from their aging parents in terms of residence. Rising levels of income have also allowed separate residences even when parents and children live nearby. In cultures that maintain a strong tradition of family support for the elderly and where government systems of social security have limited reach, non-residential children remain an important source of economic support. In Thailand, despite declines in family size, children no longer co-residing continue to support their parents (Knodel, Chayovan, and Siriboon 1992). In Vietnam, extended family households are in the minority, and even when children establish separate households they maintain regular contact with older parents (Hirschman 1994). A detailed analysis of informal transactions (in cash, in kind, and in time) through inter-household exchange in Malaysia found them to be significant relative to household income and to be particularly important for nuclear households whose elderly parents lived separately (Butz and Stan 1982). In Kenya, where family size remains large, aging parents in rural areas are best off when both resident and non-resident children provide support, with non-resident children providing more support in cash and resident children providing more support in kind in the form of food and direct assistance with household tasks (Hoddinott 1993).

Migration can separate spouses and children temporarily or intermittently. Migration may be a response to poverty, a strategy for diversifying family risk (Massey 1990), or a means of achieving a relative improvement in standard of living within the community of origin (Stark and Taylor 1989). During a spouse's absence, the rest of the family may live as a single-parent household or as part of a more extended household, depending on economic circumstances and availability of kin. Remittances can be an important source of family income, helping to finance housing and business investments back home as well as underwriting regular consumption expenditures. In Mexico, the vast majority of 'migradollars' go directly to households at the lower end of the income distribution (Massey and Parrado 1994).

Just as with migration, the impetus for child fostering may be a family crisis or the desire of parents to secure educational and training opportunities for their children. Regardless of its cause, parent-child separation is likely to lead to an increase in inter-household transfers as parents who are absent continue to contribute to their children's support. Parent-child separation does not necessarily lead to poverty but may well be a response to poverty (Lloyd and Desai 1992).

The difficulties in finding systematic links between household structure and poverty stem from the many reasons that lead to the separation of family members into different households: (1) poverty, (2) relative deprivation, or (3) the demand for privacy and autonomy that can accompany rising income. In the first case, members of a minimal household unit who would otherwise prefer to live together are forced to separate, whereas in the third case members of a MHU who would prefer to live with one another but not with members of their extended family are able to form a separate household while maintaining strong economic and emotional ties to the extended family.

4. Household Structure and the Internal Distribution of Resources

The distribution of resources within the household depends on the total resources within the household (property, other assets, labour power), the degree of co-operation among members in the pursuit of common goals, the bargaining power of individual members with respect to work obligations and resource entitlements, and the obligations and entitlements of individual members to/from other households. In exploring the implications of household structure for the internal distribution of resources, in particular the division of resources between men and women and between parents and young children, I focus on three dimensions of household structure as discussed above: complexity, dependency, and the locus of responsibility and authority.

4.1. Household Complexity

Sen (1990) has proposed a model of the household centred around the competing forces of co-operation and conflict. 'Social arrangements regarding who does what, who gets to consume what and who takes what decision can be seen as responses to this combined problem of co-operation and conflict.' Households that encompass more than one MHU or primary family unit are defined in the literature as extended households. The extension can be vertical (involving more than two generations), horizontal (involving more than two families), or both. The need for co-operation and the potential for conflict and inequality are greatest in these types of households because of competing loyalties and authority structures. A woman may be simultaneously responsible to her husband and to her mother-in-law or father-in-law (one of whom is probably the head of the household). A man may be simultaneously responsible for several wives and their respective children. A child may have multiple 'mothers' and 'fathers', each responsible for different aspects of their care. Discord among women or men within extended households in Bangladesh has been reported as a proximate cause of household partition (Foster 1993).

Reviews of the historical record (Hajnal 1982; Burch 1982) have concluded that extended household structures have never been the predominant household form among today's industrialized countries. In less developed countries, while they form a minority of all households even in rural areas (De Vos 1987; Hirschman 1994), extended households nonetheless represent an important residential phase in the lifecycle of many individuals—particularly during the early years of marriage and in later life. Extended household structures are more common where the older generation disproportionately controls economic wealth, such as land, livestock, and other physical assets, and where the younger generation has limited resources in the form of human capital (Parsons 1984).

Women's economic disadvantage relative to men is likely to be most acute in extended households when the sexual division of labour is most fully elaborated along traditional lines. Because a larger percentage of their work is likely to be unpaid, women are perceived to produce less (Sen 1990) and are therefore expected to work more and consume less. Where women are perceived to make a contribution by bringing food or cash from the outside, sex disparities in treatment are less pronounced (Boserup 1970; Sen 1990).

4.2. Dependency

If resources are fully shared, an increase in the ratio of dependents to prime-age adults in the household should have no effect on the division of resources between dependents and producers. However, children have little bargaining power and must rely on their parents to be their agents in the distribution of resources. Bauer and Mason (1993) use household expenditure data and estimates of the costs of children in Thailand and the Philippines to estimate the reduction in expenditures per adult and per child as the number of children in the household rises from one to four. They conclude that children with more siblings suffer differentially a loss in resources relative to adults even after accounting for children's lower consumption 'needs'. Thus larger families mean greater inequity between the generations in terms of resource distribution. Further evidence reviewed in Lloyd (1994) suggests that there is also greater inequality among children in terms of both birth order and sex in large families relative to small families.

Furthermore, the implications of a high dependency burden are not gender-neutral. Larger families are the direct result of women spending a significant proportion of their lives in childbearing, with its attendant risks and responsibilities (Lloyd 1994). With increasing numbers of children, mothers' work burdens increase more than fathers' without any apparent increase in their economic contribution to the family—indeed there may even be a decline in earnings during the childbearing years (Bruce, Lloyd, and Leonard 1995).

4.3. Locus of Responsibility and Authority

Much recent research has focused on household headship, in particular the sex of the head, as a potential factor in intra-household resource allocation. The designation of a 'head' is used by censuses and household surveys to identify a 'reference person' to whom all other members of the household can be linked for accounting purposes. Because household members are free to name the head without reference to definitional requirements (except certain aspects of residency), the headship designation has no inherent content but is subject to various externally imposed interpretations. Some common attributes ascribed to the head include primary economic responsibility, primary decision-making authority, and most-respected person (Bruce and Lloyd 1997).

Because female heads are more likely to embody all these attributes than male heads, members of female-headed households are expected to engage in more co-operation and less conflict (Bruce and Lloyd 1997). For example, female heads are more likely to be the sole earner and to have full knowledge of all household production and consumption, whereas in male-headed households the wife may be an important secondary earner and, in some domains of household activity, she may be more knowledgeable than the husband (Lloyd and Gage-Brandon 1993). At the same time, however, female-headed households are more likely to be poor in most settings, unless they retain strong links to family members within other households. These two considerations combine to suggest that, while female-headed households may have fewer resources, they allocate them more efficiently.

Furthermore, evidence is emerging that women spend their income differently from men, allocating a larger share to their children, particularly for food.[10] This may explain why female-headed households with lower income often display expenditure patterns that are more favorable to children (Horton and Miller 1989; Louat, van der Gaag, and Grosh 1992) in terms of nutrition or education as

---

[10] See Haddad, Peña, and Slack (1994) for a review of this rapidly growing literature.

compared with expenditures by male-headed households, which are otherwise better endowed in terms of resources (Kennedy and Peters 1992; Kossoudji and Mueller 1983; Lloyd and Blanc 1996). However, it is not headship per se that makes the difference but women's access to and control over income and their greater ability, in female-headed households, to implement their spending preferences. For example, children in Jamaica were found to fare best in terms of health, school enrolment, and workload in households where the woman was the main provider, whether or not she was reported to be the head (Handa 1994).

Conclusion

The poor who lack food, good health, education, marketable skills, and basic household amenities are found in households of every structure. The poorest of the poor—more often women than men—are those who are immobile in terms of household affiliation and unable to access resources from outside the household. Yet, there is nothing inherent in a household's structure that predicts poverty or, alternatively, promises resource adequacy.[11] Household structure is likely to adapt to economic circumstances and, in many cases, to be a dimension of individual welfare. Individuals differ in the value they associate with such attributes of living arrangements as privacy, companionship, and personal autonomy. When people are poor, their economic circumstances dictate their living arrangements. For those with greater resources, various desirable attributes of different living arrangements may become more salient in their choice of household structure. The value attached to these attributes is likely to vary across cultures and to be reflected in differences in the propensity to live alone at different phases of the life cycle, the propensity to live with non-relatives, and the propensity of married couples to maintain separate residences for work-related reasons.

Taking into consideration the changeability of individual household affiliation, the permeability of households in terms of resource flows, and the frequent inequality among household members in their work responsibilities and resource entitlements, it would seem advisable to assess poverty directly at the individual level rather than at the household level. As stated recently in a leading economic journal, 'household economics . . . has not taken individualism seriously enough' (Browning *et al*. 1994). Important differences between men and women and between adults and children, which bear fundamentally on issues of equity in society, are obscured using the household approach.

An individual approach to poverty assessment may be less difficult than it would appear. Household surveys can still be used to gain access to individuals, but instead of asking the head or one knowledgeable person to report on all members of the

---

[11] A recent cross-national study of family structure and child health in less-developed countries found no evidence that children in extended household are worse off than those in nuclear households (Gage, Sommerfelt, and Piani 1995).

household, particular groups such as women or children could be targeted for attention. In the case of children, the resident biological or social parent could provide the entry point for an inquiry into the well-being of children, linking them with all other biological and social parents and siblings that live elsewhere. In the case of women, they could be interviewed separately. In each case, we would want to construct a picture of an individual's resource networks both inside and outside the household (Blanc and Lloyd 1994).

There is already increasing attention in the literature to nutritional status (see Ferro-Luzzi and Branca, Chapter 4 above) which is assessed at the individual level with particular attention to children. We need to broaden that focus to assess other dimensions of individual 'capabilities' and 'entitlements' such as age-appropriate educational attainment for children or the proportion of children receiving economic support from both parents. For adults, we can look at individual earnings, levels of health and education, access to amenities, ownership of assets, access to information, legal rights, and mobility.

Furthermore, if we want an accurate picture of the distribution of resources among individuals, we need to shift from household economics to family economics. Each individual's family is unique to that person and should be defined to include those who care about and share with that individual. An individual's capabilities can be supplemented by support from family members; this support represents an additional and critical dimension of his or her wealth or poverty. An assessment of poverty needs to combine information about individual capabilities and entitlements with information about family networks of support. This represents a challenge to both demography and economics, each of which continues to focus on the household as the primary unit of analysis.

7 High Fertility and Short Birth Spacing: The Poverty Consequences of Family-building Patterns

PATRICIA H. DAVID

Introduction

Is high fertility a strategy or a mechanism that can enable families to escape from poverty, or does it perpetuate or lead to a descent into poverty in the long term? This question has been the subject of debate and public interest since the time of Malthus. The answer is fundamental to our understanding of the determinants of fertility behaviour and the causes of persistent poverty, but posing the question presumes that we can disentangle cause from effect. That task is not straightforward. It may require us to go beyond attempts to model very complex relationships, using alternative methods of data collection to supplement quantitative survey analysis.

Different disciplines have framed the question in various ways, and relevant research is widely dispersed across economics, demography, health and nutrition, education, sociology and anthropology, and development studies. The costs and benefits of high fertility may depend on the unit of analysis: the outcome for a family may be quite different from the outcome for one of its members. And, although income and economic security are important measures of impoverishment, our conception of what constitutes poverty has widened to encompass other aspects of the lives people lead. This includes the ability to function productively over a reasonable span of healthy life. An important measure of well-being is the achievement of a reasonable expectation of life, escaping premature death, preventable illness or undernourishment (World Bank 1990; Anand 1994; see also Lipton, Ferro-Luzzi and Branca, and Osmani, Chapters 3, 4, and 5, above). Good health is fundamental to an individual's ability to exploit opportunities and fulfil his or her own potential, and health determines and reflects economic success or failure (Sen 1995).

This chapter examines the effects of family size and birth spacing on the chances of family members being able to participate fully in society and to have a reasonable expectation of a healthy and productive life.

Most effects of high fertility on individuals are hypothesized to be adverse ones. More children may provide additional labour for a family, but while child labour may

I am grateful to John Cleland, Carine Ronsmans, Sarah Salway, and Heather Joshi for their helpful comments on an earlier draft of this chapter.

benefit family fortunes, it usually precludes further education and the chance for children to realize their full capacities. Many children born in rapid succession may also mean that a mother must limit her participation in the labour market. This can reduce a woman's autonomy and her potential contribution to the family economy. The need to spend more on food, health care, education, and other necessities dilutes the amount available for each member and may lessen a family's ability to acquire material goods and savings, until the children become net contributors to the family economy. Nevertheless, the security children can provide parents in later life may balance or outweigh these negative consequences. The first section of this chapter reviews and summarizes the evidence that large families restrict the opportunities available to their members.

It is now conventional wisdom that children born into large or closely-spaced families are at greater risk of mortality, morbidity, and malnutrition than children in smaller families. This is thought to result from increased competition for scarce material resources, time, and the mother's physiological and nutritional reserves. Some aspects of the research designs that have provided much of this evidence have received insufficient attention and their implications for determining causality have not been critically assessed. The second section of this chapter examines the empirical evidence that mortality risks increase for children born into large or closely-spaced families.

Unobserved heterogeneity in models that have produced much of this evidence is an unresolved problem. One difficulty stems from the fact that studies focus almost exclusively on outcomes to individual children and do not sufficiently allow for risks that may affect *all* children in the family—risks shared by the whole family. Neglecting to evaluate experiences early in the course of family life, the 'feedback' effects of prior events on fertility behaviour, and unmeasured causes of risks common to all children in a family can lead to mis-specification of models used to investigate the health consequences of family-building behaviour. High fertility may not increase risks to individual family members, but instead reflect prior deficits in available resources which lead poor families into particular patterns of reproduction.

The findings from several micro-level studies of families in poverty are also discussed. These give examples of the insights that might be obtained from a multidisciplinary approach to research on the consequences of fertility behaviour. Focusing on processes operating in families may be one way to increase our understanding of the factors that determine an individual's life chances in large and closely-spaced families.

1. Consequences of High Fertility for Individual Well-being

1.1. Labour Force Participation

Fertility behaviour that results in large or closely-spaced families can adversely affect the welfare of individual members. High fertility may increase the family's demand for child labour, either as waged labour, contributions to subsistence farming, or other family-based economic activity. Children may also substitute for the home work time of the mother or other adults. This is likely to limit opportunities for education and increase the potential for injury or poor health, reducing the likelihood that a child will escape from poverty.

The extent of child labour activity outside the home will depend on opportunities in the labour market, and therefore is likely to vary considerably from one setting to another. While evidence is scarce that children in large families work more in formal waged labour (Cochrane *et al.* 1990; Tan and Haines 1984, cited in Cochrane 1990), a recent Brazilian study found that older children from large families were more likely to be economically active than those from smaller families (Levison 1989, cited in Lloyd 1994).

Examining how work time is allocated among household members may be more fruitful for evaluating the consequences of family size on child labour. A recent study in rural Maharashtra suggests that children from small families are more likely than children from larger ones to work at all, while the time contribution of working children is greater in large families. Elder daughters bear the major work responsibility irrespective of family size. They substitute for their brothers (who are at school) in farm and waged labour in small families. In large families, their labour reduces the need for brothers and younger sisters to work (Jeejebhoy 1993). These findings suggest that earlier-born siblings in large families are more disadvantaged than later-born children, but such findings are not universal.[1]

Where agricultural production is the dominant occupation, large families are beneficial because children provide a guaranteed source of labour during crucial harvest periods. For poor farmers, family labour reduces the need to borrow capital to hire in workers (King 1987). Thus, children in large families may work more, but only sporadically. Their labour may serve as a coping mechanism for poor families in times of crisis.

A mother's domestic work increases with numbers of children disproportionately to other adults in the household (King and Evenson 1983). Mothers of large families spend more time pregnant, breast-feeding, and caring for children, especially early in the family life cycle. The burden of household work and child care for older children also increases, especially when the mother engages in market employment (Basu 1993; DeGraff *et al.* 1993; Lloyd 1994). Among poor families in Uttar Pradesh and Tamil Nadu, more 10–12 year-olds in large families were involved in child care than in smaller families. School participation rates for girls of this age were lowest in large families with working mothers (Basu 1993).

High fertility can also limit the ability of women to work outside the home, reducing potential family income and a woman's future earnings. The opportunity costs of childbearing are affected by the expected wages a woman can command,

---

[1] Studies of educational attainment and family size have shown that first-borns are more likely to be educated than younger siblings, until they are themselves net contributors. Their remittances can then be used to pay for the education of the youngest children. It is middle children who are most disadvantaged (Gomes 1984, cited in King 1987).

the presence and cost of mother-substitutes for child care and the compatibility of jobs with child care (Mason and Palin 1983). All are factors that may simultaneously influence family decisions about childbearing *and* women's employment, but are likely to vary over the life cycle.

Studies in developed countries have shown that women's weak economic position relative to men is due in part to the earning power lost during childbearing. A woman's potential earning power is reduced by childbearing, restricting her potential lifetime earnings. Women are also poorly remunerated for the time spent rearing children compared with what their participation in the labour force would yield (Joshi 1990). Where children promise large economic benefits in future, such a conflict between individual interests and family size is less important, although this can eventually increase a woman's dependence on others (Folbre 1994).

Large and closely-spaced families increase the workload for both parents, with a concomitant decrease in leisure time, and may increase levels of stress and poor health. It appears that at least temporary increases in the number of hours worked by fathers of large families occur when the family is young (King and Evenson 1983). Fathers may be under more economic pressure to increase working time in urban areas. Where the opportunity to intensify labour is limited, high fertility may result in greater participation in marginal activities under poorer working conditions (Rodgers 1984). Stress is an important mechanism that may mediate the relationship between poverty and health in more developed countries (Williams 1990; House and Mortimer 1990). Studies of stress and health have not specifically addressed the effects of family size on stress, but this deserves closer attention.

1.2. Family Expenditures and Investment in Children

Large families also lead to increased expenditure on necessities. This may reduce the amount saved or assets accumulated, placing families at greater risk in times of crisis. The assumption is that a fixed pool of family resources is diluted by additional children. The evidence for this effect is mixed, some arguing that children who survive to adulthood can replace savings, acting as insurance against risk (Cain 1986). With more family labour, larger families may be better able to acquire larger landholdings than small families, which can also act as risk insurance (DeLancey 1990; see also Anand and Morduch, Chapter 2, and Lipton, Chapter 3, above).

One reason that the evidence is not clear-cut is that empirical research has employed different measures of the independent variable. Some studies measure high fertility as family size or number of living children. Others use the number of children under age five or the number of people in a household or compound, really measuring 'crowding' rather than fertility. For individuals, a high birth order or birth shortly after a sibling is often employed.

Moreover, expenditures are difficult to quantify, since some are fixed whatever the size of the family, and intra-household allocation of resources is not necessarily equitable. Evidence from the Philippines and Thailand shows greater declines in per child expenditure than per adult with increasing household size, suggesting that children are more disadvantaged than adults in large families (Bauer and Mason 1993). Per capita food consumption is also negatively related to family size. This relationship is more pronounced in poorer settings (King 1987). An increase in the proportion of total income spent on food and a decrease in the quality of food consumed is also related to family size (DeLancey 1990; Mahmud and McIntosh 1980). Examining outcome measures such as nutritional status and educational attainment may be necessary to understand the impact of family size or other fertility-related factors on the investments made in children in large families.

Competition between siblings for household resources such as food and care is one mechanism that may increase risks to a child, especially to higher order children in large families. This mechanism has also been proposed to explain gender disparities in nutrition or educational attainment for children, which may be exacerbated when more children are present. An anthropologist was one of the first to alert us to the consequences of high fertility for how children are cared for. Scrimshaw suggested that high fertility combined with scarce resources and overcrowding can lead to the most severe form of underinvestment—selective neglect sometimes resulting in death (Scrimshaw 1978; see also Scheper-Hughes 1987).

Evidence for the competition hypothesis can be obtained by examining the relationship between high fertility and child nutrition. Some authors have suggested that severe malnutrition can indicate neglect. A child brought to the health services with severe malnutrition has suffered from lack of care in the earlier stages, whether undernourishment was due to lack of knowledge, lack of food, or the interaction of infection and nutrition (Echeverria *et al.* 1986). They suggest that care would be sought earlier unless the child were the victim of neglect or discrimination.

Empirical evidence shows that children with more, closely-spaced, siblings are at greater risk of long-term undernutrition—stunting—and underweight (Sommerfelt and Stewart 1994; Desai 1993; Wolfe and Behrman 1982). In twenty-six out of twenty-eight DHS surveys, bivariate tabulations show that level of underweight (low weight for age) was higher among children born shortly after a sibling. Stunting (low height for age) was most prevalent among children born less than two years after a previous child, and among children of birth order 6 or more, and less common among first-borns. This pattern was not found in sub-Saharan African countries.

A factor that may affect parental investments in feeding and care of particular children is their expected probability of survival (King 1987). This is an important consideration if parents make decisions about 'child quality', since the returns on investment are greater if a child has a high probability of surviving. The prior 'health endowment' of a child is rarely measured, however.[2]

Given the empirical evidence of inequality among siblings (such as gender disparities in mortality and nutritional status), more information is needed about the

---

[2] Some exceptions include studies by economists, including Behrman and Wolfe (1987), and by groups that include economists, such as the Cebu Study Group (1991). Epidemiological studies rarely consider such factors.

endowments of particular children, including but not limited to, birth order and gender. Much of the empirical work on intra-family resource distribution does not estimate the effect of other endowments on the distribution of resources to individual children; nor does it examine how mortality risks influence parents' decisions (King 1987). For example, breast-feeding decisions may depend on the infant's demands, conditioned by prematurity or low birth weight and weak suckling behaviour (Lunn 1985). These endowments may be well perceived by the parents, and may include the expected earnings or the intellectual ability of the child. Traditional ideas about gender roles and the extent of sex discrimination in society are also likely to condition parents' perceptions of a child's endowments, leading to a persistence of gender inequality.

Studies of child nutrition are usually small-scale ones, where the influences beyond the household context are homogeneous. For example, Tekçe (1990) examined health behaviour in a slum community in Cairo, employing quantitative measures of current nutritional status and qualitative observations of processes families used to cope with scarce resources. She found that families manage the available resources in different ways, and that the health consequences of specific behaviours depended on the material resources families assembled. Even when severely constrained by the general level of resources in the community, the consequences for child health are different among those families better able to mobilize and manage those resources.

In this Cairo slum, the effect of feeding patterns on child growth depended on the household environment in which they took place. Poor growth among children not breast-fed was found only in homes without piped water and sewer connections. Breast-feeding patterns only made a difference to a child's weight for age when the household income fell below the sample median. Only under conditions of severe material scarcity did differential allocation of resources (care during diarrhoeal illness and food) have serious consequences for a girl's growth in this community.

Similarly, in a slum community in Khulna, Bangladesh, Pryer found that girls suffered from poorer nutrition more than boys only in the two lowest income groups (Pryer 1993). In households where severely malnourished children were found, all other household members also showed signs of malnourishment, suggesting severe food shortage. Household sizes in each income group were not significantly different, but household structure varied considerably. The lowest income groups were composed of female-headed families or those where the male head was ill or disabled. Severely malnourished children also had a higher incidence of disease, the synergy between the two possibly more important than food availability.

These two small-scale studies suggest that only the most vulnerable families are likely to use differential allocation of food resources as a coping mechanism. In larger-scale studies, differences between families like these, who are all at the bottom of the socio-economic scale, may be lost. Note, however, that neither study considered fertility factors at all or give any indication of the duration of such strategies.

Despite the evidence that chronic malnutrition is more prevalent in large families, the causes of malnutrition are complex and cannot be explained simply by lack of food. Nutrition differentials that do exist may result from the dilution of a mother's time and care, or diminished quality of care when older siblings take on caring roles (Ahlburg 1994). The differences may also result from the interaction of infection and nutritional status, especially if closely-spaced children are at increased risk of infection (see next section). Whatever the cause, poor nutrition in early life can also condition a child's subsequent opportunities, since good nutrition and health are important prerequisites of success in school (Lloyd 1994; Ferro-Luzzi and Branca, Chapter 4 above).

1.3. Feedback Effects

Studies of how fertility patterns affect the health and welfare of family members are found wanting when viewed in a framework of decision-making within the household. This framework starts with the assumption that causes go in both directions. Household decisions regarding fertility, health and education expenditures, labour participation and savings are better thought of as simultaneous tradeoffs than as one-way consequences (Cochrane *et al.* 1990). Investments in child quality (expenditures on food, education and medical care) are made with some knowledge of a given child's expected contribution to family welfare and some knowledge of his or her endowments (either through sex or ability). Many studies of health and welfare outcomes associated with high fertility have treated fertility as a *determinant* of these outcomes. These have led to conclusions that the negative association between family size or spacing and a child's health or educational attainment is evidence of causality (King 1987). This may be justified if couples do not exert some degree of control over their fertility. But even in so-called 'natural fertility' populations, evidence is accumulating that couples make decisions about their family-building pattern, the timing and number of their births.[3]

A recent micro-level study (Axinn 1993) of one community in Nepal illustrates why the simultaneous nature of decisions about fertility and investments in children must be allowed for. The study examines fertility as an outcome, but considers the influence of children's schooling on parental fertility decisions. The results indicate that the schooling of children in the household affects subsequent fertility behaviour in the family more than parents' own education, positively influencing use of contraception and reducing their desire for more children: '. . .parents perceive that they obtain sufficient benefits from educating their children to invest in the children they have, and reduce their total childrearing expenses by limiting their fertility' (Axinn 1993: 493). Most empirical studies of educational attainment treat family size or birth spacing as exogenous factors that influence a child's educational opportunities. They do not consider the inhibiting effect educating children may have on fertility.

The societal context, the joint nature of fertility decisions and resource allocation,

---

[3]   See Bledsoe *et al.* (1994) for further treatment of decision-making and high fertility in Africa.

and the often-unobserved differences in the strategies families use to cope with poverty all affect the consequences of high fertility for the family as a whole, as well as its individual members. Yet studies that have linked high fertility to the health of children have not sufficiently addressed these difficult issues. Let us look more closely at the evidence that high fertility is causally related to one of the most important indicators of poverty—premature mortality—in light of these conclusions.

2. The Conventional Wisdom: Consequences of High Fertility and Short Birth Spacing for Life Chances of Children

The idea that high fertility and close spacing of births can have direct and indirect health consequences for children has now become part of conventional wisdom. The adverse consequences of fertility behaviour for maternal and child health have largely been adopted as important justifications for promoting family planning as an intervention to reduce both fertility and mortality, although the issue is still debated by demographers (Bongaarts 1987; Hobcraft 1987; Bongaarts, Potter, and Trussell 1988; UN 1994).

The belief, arising from comparative analyses of World Fertility Survey and other large-scale survey data, is that family planning can bring about benefits to families through reductions in the number of 'high risk' births that occur, especially where children and mothers are already at risk due to limited financial resources, riskier living environments, and limited opportunities to improve these. In other words, the poor should be the most important beneficiaries of changes in their family-building patterns.

Children born into large or closely-spaced families are assumed to be at greater risk of mortality, morbidity and malnutrition, and to have fewer chances to acquire an education. Lloyd (1994: 5) summarizes the argument: 'This is considered to be the result of family resource constraints that cause each child to get a smaller share of family resources, including family income, parental time and a mother's physiological and nutritional resources, all of which are important to infant and child development'. This view is pervasive. For example:

Family planning would prevent, predominantly, those births which are known to be 'high risk'—the births which are within two years of a previous birth, or to mothers who are under 18 or over 35 or who already have three or four or more children. Because a great majority of child deaths are associated with these risk factors, the well-informed timing and spacing of births would result in a far more than proportionate reduction in child deaths (UNICEF 1992, 58–9).

And:

The length of time between two births in a family greatly influences child survival . . . birth intervals less than 2 years long are too short—the shorter, the more hazardous . . . taking premature births into account reduces the effect of short-interval births only slightly. . . . On average 1 of 5 infant deaths would be averted through good birth spacing (Maine and McNamara 1985, 7–17).

Hobcraft sounded a more cautious note, one which evidently went unheeded:

We have deliberately avoided this issue [the consequences of child-spacing for child mortality], not because it is unimportant, but because we do not believe there is adequate information available to permit useful assessment (Hobcraft 1987, 47).

Despite this caution, the World Bank recently joined this chorus:

Short birth intervals pose substantial risks to child health throughout the first 5 years of life. ... [Studies show that many of these closely-spaced births are] unwanted, so if they were delayed, child mortality might be reduced by more than 20% (World Bank 1993: 83).

Close spacing of births and resultant large families were seen in the past primarily as evidence of unregulated fertility, the result of poverty and ignorance (Rainwater 1956). Now it is widely-accepted that most couples exercise considerable control over their family-building, even in populations where large families are still the norm and child mortality remains high (Rahman and DaVanzo 1993; Bledsoe and Hill 1994). It is particularly instructive to examine the relationship between short birth intervals—one aspect of high fertility measured at the family level—and adverse child health outcomes. The relationship reflects the dynamic but often unobserved processes operating within families, and is the product of both biology and behaviour. The societal and household context can play an important mediating role affecting financial and time constraints for large families, but the evidence that other resources—primarily the mother's own physiological and nutritional ones—can be spread as evenly across large numbers of children remains an unresolved issue.

2.1. The Empirical Evidence

2.1.1. Birth Order and Family Size

Tabulations of both World Fertility Survey data and more recent Demographic and Health Survey data reveal a clear excess mortality for first births, compared with birth orders two and three, but only during infancy. For birth orders four to six no excess mortality is found during infancy, but risks rise slightly in later childhood, becoming unimportant when mother's age and other factors are controlled. For higher birth orders, risks are elevated for children in both infancy and later childhood compared with birth orders two and three, but when age of mother and other factors are allowed for, high order births to older mothers are at only marginally higher risk. The elevated risks for high-order births to younger mothers suggests that a spacing, rather than order, effect predominates (Hobcraft 1991).

A number of studies have found that even first-born in large completed families are at increased risk of dying in infancy. This could not have been caused by the subsequent attained family size or pace of childbearing in the family (Gardiner and Yerushalmy 1939; Magaud and Henry 1968). A selection process resulting from previous deaths can cause large families to have apparently higher mortality rates than smaller families. This process has been demonstrated to affect the apparent increased risks of higher-parity women experiencing a foetal death (Roman 1984; see also Santow and Bracher 1989). The combination of selectivity—women with a higher risk of experiencing a death going on to higher parities—and the heterogeneous distribution of risk among women results in a spurious association between parity and risk to the child. There is little evidence that either high birth order or family size has any effect at all on survival chances.

2.1.2. Birth Interval Effects

Studies based on diverse data from both historical and contemporary populations have found a consistent negative association between short birth intervals and a child's chances of survival. When birth histories were obtained in the World Fertility Surveys, enabling analysis of data for individual births, strong evidence that this relationship was nearly universal was obtained (Hobcraft, McDonald, and Rutstein 1983).

The risks are highest in infancy, especially in the neonatal period, decreasing by about half for ages one to four. The risk appears strongest when a child is born less than two years after a preceding birth and the child who begins the interval dies before the succeeding birth. A less consistent increase in risk has been found for the child whose birth *starts* a short subsequent interval (Hobcraft 1987).

Tabulations of recent data suggests that this pattern persists, with risks doubling for those born within eighteen months of the previous birth, but there is a good deal of variability across countries, with only small excess risks in a number of sub-Saharan African countries and especially high ones in a number of others (Hobcraft 1991).

The question, of course, is are these widely-observed relationships evidence of cause and effect? While the evidence for the correlation between short birth intervals and health is strong, the evidence for a causal association is lacking.

Three mechanisms have been hypothesized to explain the relationship. One hypothesis is that crowding of children in space and time may result in increased rates of infectious disease. Two others deal with the idea that some kind of 'competition' exists for the limited pool of resources available to families. This may take the form of competition between siblings for limited resources (food and care) after birth, discussed in the previous section. Or, it may emerge before birth as pre-natal competition between the foetus and earlier-born siblings for the mother's physiological and nutritional resources.

Another mechanism that may explain the association is selection. Large, closely-spaced families may have higher risks, but these are not causally related to their family-building pattern. Unobserved heterogeneity in the risks experienced by all children in a family—what some have called 'death clustering'—is an important alternative explanation for the association between all the fertility factors and risk of dying.

Those investigating effects of fertility factors on health outcomes have only recently tried to evaluate the importance of heterogeneity at the family level. Only a handful of studies have attempted to do so, still finding an increased risk associated with short birth intervals (Curtis, Diamond, and McDonald 1993; Zenger 1993; Guo 1993; Miller *et al.* 1992). Family risks are now of demonstrated importance, and deserve closer consideration.

2.2. Intervening Mechanisms

Increased risk of infection in large and closely-spaced families has been proposed as an indirect mechanism by which short birth intervals affect mortality risk. More children closer in age comprise a larger pool of 'susceptibles', more likely to acquire and transmit infection (Reves 1985). When several young siblings are present, inadequate methods for sanitary disposal of excreta may exacerbate risk of infection (Haaga 1989).

Children in large families or with closely spaced siblings, especially girls, may be more vulnerable to risk of severe infection and higher case fatality rates, due to crowding and increased probability of contracting infections as 'secondary' cases (Aaby 1988; 1992; Aaby *et al.* 1993). These effects, however, have been found for only one disease—measles—which is not an important cause of death in early infancy, when birth interval effects are strongest. Measles mortality becomes important in the second year of life, when the association between short intervals and risk weakens. Moreover, the studies that provide the strongest evidence for such a mechanism have been carried out only in West Africa and have not yet been replicated elsewhere in the contemporary developing world.

Children born after a short interval may already be at increased risk of infection due to prematurity or intra-uterine growth retardation. There is evidence that low birth weight, in addition to increasing risk at time of birth, and low weight-for-age after birth, is associated with a depressed immune system and increased risk of infectious disease in later childhood (Victora *et al.* 1988; Ferguson 1978; Read, Clemens, and Klebanoff 1994).

If short intervals are related to increased susceptibility to infection because they are also associated with prematurity or retarded intra-uterine growth, they may play an indirect role, rather different than suggested by the 'crowding' hypothesis. But if short intervals do not *cause* prematurity or retarded foetal growth, this increased susceptibility is not related directly to close spacing.

Competition between siblings after infancy for household resources such as food and care is another mechanism by which short intervals may increase risks to a child, especially to later-born children in large families.

Addressing this hypothesis as a cause of undernutrition, Boerma and Bicego (1992) found only a weak relationship between short intervals and undernutrition when breast-feeding, sex, survival of the previous child, and socio-economic factors were controlled. They also found no evidence that short intervals were associated with increased prevalence of diarrhoea, child immunization, or medical service use, suggesting that pre-natal competition may be a more likely cause of the relationship.

The third causal mechanism hypothesized to explain the increased risks to children born after a short birth interval is *maternal depletion*—mothers who bear more children in a short period of time may suffer deleterious effects to their own health because they have insufficient time to recover from the physiological demands of the previous pregnancy and breast-feeding. The maternal depletion hypothesis is based on the idea that a mother has a fixed reserve of physical resources that is not spread evenly among her children, but depleted by a number of births in rapid succession. This physical depletion may affect subsequent births if it results in low birth weight, prematurity or breast-feeding failure, but there is no evidence that a mother's cumulative fertility causes such outcomes. Diet and nutrition may play the deciding role (Winkvist *et al.* 1992). Psychological depletion may also contribute to the short-interval–risk relationship. A tired mother, worn out by the demands of caring for several small children, may not provide optimal care unless she has the support of others.

Although the data are inadequate to establish the existence of a depletion syndrome caused by reproductive patterning, the hypothesis cannot be dismissed (Merchant and Martorell 1989). Longitudinal studies are necessary to determine if cumulative maternal depletion results from a woman's reproductive pattern. Where poor nutritional status is common, poor weight gain during pregnancy may account for much of the incidence of low birth weight, and hence may be indirectly responsible for the interval–risk relationship (Kramer 1987; Winikoff 1987). Prematurity—associated with low birth weight—has been found to explain much of the association between short intervals and risk of dying (Miller 1989a; Koenig *et al.* 1991; Miller *et al.* 1992).

Epidemiological studies strongly suggest that women who are malnourished before pregnancy and have insufficient energy intake during pregnancy are at higher risk of delivering a growth-retarded infant (Institute of Medicine 1992). The longer-term effects of maternal nutrition on mortality and morbidity after birth, and on maternal lactation, are difficult to evaluate with the available evidence. There is as yet no convincing evidence that a woman's health suffers from repeated childbearing when she is well nourished.

2.2.1. Does a Short Interval Contribute to the Probability of a Premature or Growth-retarded Birth?

Miller explored the maternal depletion hypothesis by examining the relationship between very short birth-to-conception intervals (less than eighteen months) and retarded intra-uterine growth using Swedish data (Miller 1989b). She found that lower average birth weights of infants born after a short interval could not be completely attributed to shorter gestations. But she found no dose–response relationship between length of interval and risk of intra-uterine growth retardation. This study was unable to control for confounding social factors, so selection of women for short conception intervals could not be ruled out.

The evidence to date, based primarily on high-quality data from developed countries, suggests that women who have short birth intervals *are* a selected group of women. These women were at higher risk *a priori* of giving birth to a small infant (Klebanoff *et al.* 1988; Erickson and Bjerkedal 1978). The tendency to experience repeated losses, intra-uterine growth retardation and low birth-weight births by women with short intervals suggests that heterogeneity in these often unobserved factors may play an important role in the relationship between pace of childbearing and increased risk to children. The association between short intervals and these outcomes is mediated through maternal weight, lower socio-economic status, and 'more adverse living conditions and lifestyle habits' and possibly genetic factors (Klebanoff *et al.* 1988; Bakketieg *et al.* 1986; Ferraz *et al.* 1988; Mavalankar *et al.* 1994; Ounsted 1986; Magnus, Berg, and Bjerkedal 1986). Authors of the prospective studies conclude that short inter-pregnancy intervals are primarily markers for women who are otherwise at high risk (Klebanoff *et al.* 1988; Erickson and Bjerkedal 1978). As yet there is no evidence that short intervals themselves *cause* these birth outcomes.

These findings, however, cannot be extrapolated to nutritionally-deprived populations. In poorly-nourished populations, further study of a woman's propensity to have repeated poor birth outcomes, and the effects of pre-pregnancy weight and weight gain during pregnancy, is needed to establish a definitive link between reproductive patterning and risk of retarded growth, prematurity, or subsequent mortality.

2.2.2. Unobserved Heterogeneity—Why Family-specific Factors Matter

The studies of short birth interval and risk have clearly demonstrated the importance of family risk dependence, both length of interval and survival of the preceding birth are strong predictors of risk. Survival status of nearest siblings has often been used to control for factors specific to the mother as well as for the physiological effects of a child's death on the succeeding interval (Knodel and Hermalin 1984). However, few studies of the relationship between fertility and childhood mortality risk have employed an adequate statistical allowance for the lack of independence in risk to births of the same mother. Those that do have demonstrated the importance of family-specific factors, still finding an excess risk associated with short birth or inter-pregnancy interval (Miller *et al.* 1992; Curtis, Diamond, and McDonald 1993; Guo 1993; Zenger 1993). These do not, however, tell us anything about the factors that contribute to family risk variability.

Studies of historical populations also provide evidence for the importance of family risk heterogeneity (Lynch and Greenhouse 1994; Nault, Desjardins, and Legare 1990). Lynch and Greenhouse found that risks to children at higher birth orders were significantly raised by mortality of first- and second-born siblings, not just by that of the immediately preceding child. Their analysis of risks to all children in completed families allowed them to fully allow for the familial dimension in modelling risks to children of a given order. Siblings of all birth orders experienced similar risks, and they found no evidence of discrimination among higher-order births resulting in excess mortality risk. Neither length of the interval nor mother's age at the time of birth were significantly associated with risk of infant mortality. Such a finding among completed families in an historical population is especially troublesome for imputing a causal link between close spacing and child survival in contemporary populations, but no contemporary data present the same analytical opportunity.

Extensive analysis of data from the World Fertility Surveys suggests that there is also a considerable correlation between successive birth intervals within families, and that some women have a propensity to repeat long or short birth intervals (Trussell *et al.* 1985; Rodriguez *et al.* 1984). Length of the previous interval is an important predictor of the length of the next.

The persistence of this relationship may reflect poor measurement of other family-level factors that affect birth spacing. These may be factors related to unobserved variability in omitted proximate determinants such as fecundability, coital frequency, and health-related infecundity which are captured by a control for length of the previous interval. Emerging evidence suggests that prior nutritional status and diet may have important effects on proximate biological determinants of interval length (Popkin *et al.* 1993). Differences in maternal nutritional status, diet, and workload may be another source of unobserved heterogeneity in both fertility and birth outcomes (Institute of Medicine 1992; Panter-Brick 1993). The relationship may also reflect poor measurement of socio-economic factors, especially those measured concurrent with the interval of interest (Rindfuss *et al.* 1989; Guilkey *et al.* 1988).

The effect of deaths early in the family-building cycle on a couple's subsequent reproductive pattern has not been fully explored. An early start to childbearing and loss of the first child have both been shown to influence the average pace of subsequent childbearing (David 1994). Simulations based on data from Bangladesh demonstrate that a selection effect can operate to produce a heterogeneous distribution of birth intervals in families, those with more prior deaths going on more quickly to higher parities and hence having a series of short intervals (Zenger 1992).

Adolescent health status, maternal health at the start of childbearing and other circumstances in early life are usually unmeasured, but could affect a woman's entire series of births. Familial factors associated with differences in the parental family of upbringing have been shown to play an important role in the relationship between young maternal age (Geronimus and Korenman 1993), maternal education (Behrman and Wolfe 1987), and child health and survival.

In demographic studies the unit of analysis is usually births, and data come from cross-sectional surveys. When data are collected about health outcomes, factors affecting risks to all children in a family, especially those that arise early in the family's life cycle, are usually unobserved. The evidence that unmeasured family factors are important sources of variability suggests that they cannot be ignored, especially if analyses of reproductive factors and risk aim to provide guidance to policy-makers on effective points of intervention. The findings about family risk variability are important because they suggest that we might learn more about causes of health and mortality outcomes by analysing differences between *families* than by looking for differences between births.

2.2.3. In-depth Studies

The persistent association between socio-economic status and health, even in developed countries, implies the need to identify which circumstances underlying deprivation are most strongly linked to health outcomes. Some may be related to family-building patterns and some family-specific factors may be unobservable, at least in surveys. Micro-level studies can reveal where unobserved heterogeneity in family fertility behaviour and family risks can be reduced. Small-scale studies of particularly vulnerable groups are useful, because many factors are controlled by focusing on a more or less homogenous group. These can highlight important differences between families in the way they cope with their poor environment and suggest reasons why health and welfare outcomes vary. While none of the following studies provide direct evidence regarding fertility and health outcomes at the household level, the information they provide can be particularly useful for understanding what influences family coping strategies.

Tekçe's study discussed earlier described differences in the ability of families to manipulate an environment already severely constrained by the low level of community resources available (Tekçe 1990). Several other studies suggest that a mother's ability to cope with such an environment depends to some extent on her personal characteristics (Myntti 1993; Scrimshaw and Scrimshaw 1990).

Contrasting extreme cases (case-control studies of 'positive and negative deviants') can point to sources of these differing abilities. The role models poor women see in adolescence and before they begin their families may enable them to become more 'proactive' when caring for their own families (Scrimshaw and Scrimshaw 1990). The apparent incompetence of mothers noted by some studies may be partially rooted in early life experiences, as well as in the support networks they are able to call upon (Myntti 1993). 'Women whose children experienced greatest risks were socially isolated, without supportive spouses or regular, cordial relations with kin and neighbors. ... The women with the healthiest children were not only better integrated socially, but were able to mobilize help for child care and other household tasks' (Myntti 1993: 8). Such support is rarely operationalized and measured in large health surveys, and life histories of parents are rarely available, but these factors may be sources of variability in both reproductive behaviour and child health outcomes.

Family coping strategies are the subject of many studies in the development literature, where their importance is widely recognized (see Chambers 1989). But these primarily focus on socio-economic outcomes and often fail to examine health and other aspects of well-being. Household size or dependency ratios are usually measured, but not direct information about fertility patterns. As well as relying on in-depth interviews and observation, some have made progress in developing survey instruments to examine coping strategies, but much more work is needed (see, for example, Moser and Sollis 1991).

Several studies that do examine health outcomes provide evidence of considerable heterogeneity of economic activities within slum settlements, and identify a complex of factors that differentiate the urban poor into those who are relatively better off and more vulnerable groups (Pryer 1989; Evans 1989). Identifying particularly vulnerable households and comparing outcomes among them may explain why some families are more successful in coping with extreme poverty and whether family size or fertility behaviour plays a role in their success.

Often, small samples preclude quantitative examination of intra-family differentials, but these in-depth studies show that a better understanding of the processes operating within households—how families use and are affected by the social institutions that surround them—can inform the collection and analysis of quantitative data.

Conclusion

Both economic and anthropological studies show the importance of examining dynamic processes that take place within families and between families and their environment that affect a myriad of behaviours. Studies that take a life-course perspective could be particularly useful for understanding how reproductive patterns influence the health and welfare of family members.

Few studies have dealt with the difficult estimation problems that are necessary to establish causal links, and data for a number of health outcomes, especially birth weight, childhood nutritional status, and adult health are particularly deficient. We still know too little about how a child's endowment—his or her ability, prior health status, and risk of dying—is perceived and used by parents when decisions are made to invest in the health and well-being of children (Schultz 1984; Cebu Study Team 1991). A sickly child, or a dull child, may not be given an equal share of resources, if decisions must be made that are meant to enhance the welfare of the whole family. Too little is known about how parents weigh up the decision to allocate scarce resources to family members, including the breadwinner. A decision to increase the number of children may be made to ensure the continued survival or the possible upward mobility of the family as a unit (Elondou-Engueye 1994).

These considerations present considerable difficulties, both for data collection and analysis. Such two-way relationships cannot usually be modelled with current data sets, which contain much information about either fertility and health (such as the World Fertility Surveys and Demographic and Health Surveys) or household economic status (for example, the World Bank Living Standards Measurement Surveys), but not enough about both (Cochrane *et al.* 1990). Although fertility surveys obtain massive amounts of data, socio-economic information about the family is sparse and pertains only to the time of interview. A great deal of behavioural and biodemographic data is obtained on individual birth intervals, but pertains to relatively few intervals, and can mitigate the explanatory power of current socio-economic status (Guilkey *et al.* 1988).

The Cebu Study Team's recent work demonstrates the advantages of a multidisciplinary approach. They have developed structural models to examine the effects of both parental behaviour and prior child health status on specific health outcomes. These models also estimate family-specific effects, but have not addressed the short-interval–risk relationship (Guilkey, Popkin, Akin, and Wong 1989; Popkin *et al.* 1993b; Cebu Study Team 1991 1992).

The full effect of fertility on the welfare of family members may be too complex to model. The household and societal context will also influence this relationship (Lloyd 1994; Desai 1993). Networks of social support also vary among families, and those with more social resources to call upon are better able to cope with adverse circumstances. One feature of families or individuals living in poverty is a reduction in the number of supportive contacts and a smaller social network than those economically better off, and this may be a cause, rather than a consequence, of poor health (Williams 1990; Syme and Berkman 1976; House *et al.* 1988).

The economic context and the position of the family in it are also important, but highly variable, factors influencing both fertility behaviour and its consequences (Rodgers 1984; Mueller and Short 1984; Eloundou-Enyegue 1994). The level of development, the level of public services and provision by society to share the burden of child-rearing will all affect the well-being of members of large families (Lloyd 1994; Desai 1993; Folbre 1994). Lloyd's survey of the education literature showed that measures of children's school participation, progression, and parental expenditures on schooling were often negatively related to family size, but the size and significance of these effects varied substantially, both within and between countries. She emphasizes the importance of allowing for differences in the context in which large families cope with resource constraints, challenging the assumption that family resources are always fixed, diluted with each additional child. The practice of child fosterage in sub-Saharan Africa, active participation of children in household tasks, the extent to which older siblings can contribute to the family income and hence support for successive siblings, and settings where the extended family can provide care, ' . . . breaks down household economic boundaries and spreads the impact of additional children on family resources across a wider kin network. . . . The family circle within which resources are shared can extend both laterally as well as vertically' (Lloyd 1994, 11–12).

Studies of small homogeneous groups living in poor conditions may help to clarify the mediating processes that families use to cope with limited resources, and the factors that enable them to cope. The study of high-risk families compared with so-called 'positive deviants' may provide further clues to the underlying differences between families.

Averages hide much diversity, as both quantitative and qualitative studies of family risk variability show. Focusing on families, rather than on individual members may provide us with further information on factors that affect all household members. The welfare of family members is linked, and more information on family units will help us to understand better the relationship of fertility in the family to the outcomes for individual members.

8 The Social Implications of Adolescent Fertility

ANASTASIA J. GAGE

Introduction

Adolescent pregnancy and childbearing have emerged as a source of social and policy concern in a number of countries during the last two decades. However, the cultural and social circumstances surrounding adolescent fertility are so diverse that they defy generalization. In many countries of sub-Saharan Africa, adolescent child-bearing is the norm: teenage childbearing exceeds 150 per thousand, and births to women under the age of twenty comprise about 15–20 per cent of total births (Demographic and Health Surveys (DHS) 1990). On average, more than 50 per cent of young women give birth before the age of twenty, and in some countries, as many as 40 per cent of women have their first child before the age of eighteen. The low age at first marriage means that most adolescent childbearing occurs within marriage, although in some countries, the proportion of children born before marriage is not trivial, and is of increased visibility, particularly in urban areas (Bledsoe and Cohen 1993; Gage-Brandon and Meekers 1993). In the United States, on the other hand, adolescent childbearing is relatively uncommon. It occurs largely out of wedlock and is selective of particular groups of women (Geronimus 1987).

The potentially negative consequences of teenage childbearing are well documented. For example, a panel established by the National Research Council concluded: 'Women who become parents as teenagers are at greater risk of social and economic disadvantage throughout their lives than those who delay childbearing until their twenties. They are less likely to complete their education, be employed, to earn high wages, and to be happily married: and they are more likely to have larger families and to receive welfare' (Hayes 1987: 138).

These concerns are not altogether specific to the United States. Among unmarried teenage women in sub-Saharan Africa, untimely pregnancies are viewed as a barrier to achievement and social mobility, being associated with forced school expulsion or high rates of school drop-out (Boohene et al. 1991; Dynowski-Smith 1989; Ferguson et al. 1988; Khasiani 1985). Most research also highlights the negative medical outcomes of teenage pregnancy—unsafe, sometimes fatal, abortions in many African countries where abortion is illegal or restricted; increased risk of HIV infection due to the association between premarital sexual activity and a potential cumulative increase in the number of sexual partners, and health disadvantages of infants born to teenage mothers. Even though boys are more likely than girls to have sexual intercourse at an early age (Agyei *et al.* 1992; Ajayi *et al.* 1991; Kane *et al.* 1993; Orubuloye *et al.* 1992), except where girls enter arranged marriages at or before puberty (Dixon-Mueller 1993), the vast literature on adolescent childbearing focuses for the most part on the effects of early childbearing on the mother, and to a lesser extent on the adolescent father.

The aim of this chapter is to consider the implications of adolescent pregnancy and childbearing for women and children. I will concentrate on topics that are relatively rich in empirical research—such as educational attainment, timing of marriage and its stability, health, and the economic and social situation of children. The first section of the chapter highlights the varying social contexts of adolescent sexual activity, pregnancy and childbearing. This serves as a prelude for considering how the timing of fertility and the social environment may shape the consequences of early childbearing for women and children. The following sections discuss some of the evidence linking the timing of fertility to various socioeconomic and health outcomes.

It is to be noted that since the late 1980s, most of the demographic literature has centred on sub-Saharan Africa and discusses how adolescent sexuality and contraceptive use are related to out-of-wedlock pregnancy and childbearing, and to a lesser extent, transmission of sexually transmitted diseases (STDs). Articles drawing on surveys in the United States deal with the sexual behaviour of unmarried adolescents and the long-term implications of adolescent fertility for the economic and social situation of women and children. The literature reviewed in this chapter is drawn primarily from these two regions.

1. The Social Context of Teenage Childbearing

The social context and level of adolescent fertility vary widely across countries. In sub-Saharan Africa, birth rates among women aged 15–19 range from a low of 52 per 1000 in Burundi and 56 per 1000 in Rwanda to a high of more than 200 per 1000 in Niger and Mali (see Table 8.1). In North Africa and Asia, teenage birth rates are generally lower than 100 per 1000, and three countries (Morocco, Sri Lanka, and Tunisia) have teenage birth rates of less than 50 per 1000. Teenage birth rates are generally higher in Latin America than in the North Africa/Asia region. Guatemala and El Salvador have the highest adolescent fertility rates, and Peru the lowest. By comparison, teenage birth rates in the United States are around 50 per 1000 and are twice as high as in Canada (Singh and Wulf 1990). In Europe, early childbearing is more prevalent in the central and eastern parts of the region than in the western Europe, partly a reflection of later marriage patterns, greater use of contraception, and a greater preference for terminating pregnancies among adolescents in Scandinavian countries (David 1992). In Bulgaria, at least 20 per cent of live births occur to women under age 20 compared with less than 5 per cent in Belgium, Finland, Luxembourg, Netherlands, Switzerland, Ireland, and Germany (David 1992).

Early marriage is one factor contributing to high levels of teenage fertility in many African countries. As Table 8.1 indicates, the proportion of women aged 15–19 who have ever been married exceeds 30 per cent in eight out of the twenty countries examined and is as high as 75 per cent in Mali. With the exception of a few countries, notably Botswana and Namibia, most adolescent childbearing occurs within marriage. In this context, early parenthood is normative and also highly desirable, for social reasons that confer value on women through childbearing (Bledsoe and Cohen 1993). While the society does not consider marriage and child-bearing among young uneducated rural women as a social problem, early child-bearing among school girls is often subject to social criticism, largely because it inhibits women from exploiting new economic opportunities.

It is worth noting that although adolescent fertility is increasingly perceived as a source of social and policy concern, this does not necessarily mean that fertility rates among teenagers have increased over time. In the United States, it has been observed that teenagers bear relatively fewer children now than they did in the 1950s (Hayes 1987). In sub-Saharan Africa, empirical analysis of DHS data for six countries reveal that the proportion of women having first intercourse before the age of twenty has changed little over time. Although much of the evidence is based on cross-sectional data, and while cohort trends may reflect the relative displacement of dates of vital events or difficulties in determining the exact date of first marriage given the protracted nature of the marriage process and great diversity in marriage patterns, there is strong evidence in many countries of a significant decline in the propensity of teenage marriage over time (Gage and Meekers 1994a). Thus, a study by the National Research Council concludes that 'in Africa, as well [as in the United States], teenage childbearing is coming to be defined as a problem only as the age at marriage is rising and overall fertility rates among young women are declining' (Bledsoe and Cohen 1993: 35).

While teenage childbearing is not more common in the United States or in Africa, unmarried parenthood among teenagers is. Several studies in sub-Saharan Africa note that the decline in the propensity of teenage marriage has been accom-panied by an increasing tendency for women to engage in premarital sexual activity and premarital childbearing (Feyisitan and Pebley 1989; Gage and Meekers 1994a). However, levels of teenage premarital fertility vary widely. More than 20 per cent of unmarried teenagers in Botswana and Liberia have had a baby compared to less than 1 per cent in Mali. In Latin America, the percentage of unmarried teenagers who have had at least one live birth is less than 2 per cent in all the countries exam-ined, except Bolivia, where it is about 5 per cent.

In the United States, nonmarital childbearing has increased dramatically in all sub-populations during the past several decades, despite a steady and sharp decline in marital fertility in the general population. The proportion of all children born out of wedlock was 23 per cent in 1985 compared to 5 per cent in 1960 (Furstenberg 1990). From 1985 to 1990, the percentage of births to unmarried women rose from 12 to 17 per cent among whites, from 51 to 56 per cent among Puerto Ricans, and from 61 to 67 per cent among African-Americans (Manning and Landale 1994). The

Table 8.1. Selected indicators of adolescent fertility (women aged 15–19)

Country	Year of survey	Births per 1000 women	% who have given birth	% ever married
Sub-Saharan Africa				
Botswana [a]	1988	125	23.5	6.1
Burkina Faso [a]	1993	154	24.2	44.6
Burundi [a]	1987	52	3.2	17.7
Cameroon [c]	1991	164	29.7	44.2
Kenya [b]	1993	118	16.8	16.2
Liberia [a]	1986	184	37.2	36.0
Madagascar [b]	1992	156	24.6	26.7
Mali [a]	1987	201	44.5	75.4
Namibia [c]	1992	109	17.7	7.7
Niger [a]	1992	219	31.1	58.6
Nigeria [b]	1990	144	23.5	38.6
Rwanda [b]	1992	56	8.2	9.8
Senegal [b]	1992/3	132	20.1	43.5
Sudan (North) [a]	1989/0	69	8.7	15.9
Tanzania [b]	1991/2	139	23.2	28.3
Togo [a]	1988	127	21.4	17.2
Zambia [a]	1992	152	27.2	29.6
Zimbabwe [a]	1988	109	16.3	19.8
Uganda [a]	1988/9	187	30.3	40.8
North Africa/Asia				
Egypt [a]	1992	69	7.5	13.9
Indonesia [b]	1991	70	9.1	19.8
Jordan[a]	1990	52	5.3	10.6
Latin America/Caribbean				
Northeast Brazil [a]	1991	85	11.0	16.1
Colombia [a]	1990	70	9.7	13.3
Dominican Republic [a]	1991	91	13.4	17.6
Peru [a]	1991/2	68	9.0	11.7
Paraguay [a]	1990	98	14.1	15.4
Trinidad and Tobago [a]	1987	84	11.0	24.6

[a] Fertility rate refers to the period 0–4 years before the survey.
[b] Fertility rate refers to the period 0–3 years before the survey.
[c] Fertility rate refers to the period 0–2 years before the survey.
[d] Fertility rate refers to the period 0–5 years before the survey.
Source: Demographic and Health Surveys

increase in nonmarital childbearing is also noted among adolescents. For instance, in 1985, 13 per cent of all babies were born to teenagers of whom about three-fifths were unmarried. These changes are accompanied by a growing acceptability of premarital sexuality during adolescence, a trend that Furstenberg (1990) links to the widespread availability of contraceptives.

In sub-Saharan Africa, the increase in premarital sexual activity among teenagers is perceived to be a consequence of the erosion of fundamental values and norms in African society (Armstrong 1987; Gage and Meekers 1994a; Lema 1990). However, the exact degree of change between traditional and modern society is sometimes difficult to establish. A review of the literature by Caldwell *et al.* (1989) reveals that in traditional African societies, high levels of polygyny and a large age gap between spouses meant that men frequently did not marry until they were in their mid-twenties; this created a long period of exposure to premarital sexual activity during which few societies imposed restrictions of premarital sexual relations for men. Tolerance of female premarital sexual activity varied greatly in patrilineal societies, while in matrilineal societies, children were often regarded as welcome additions to a woman's lineage regardless of marital status at the birth of the child.

The ambiguities concerning the perception of adolescent fertility as a social problem in sub-Saharan Africa may be linked to the high value ascribed to children and the tenacity of pronatalist pressures. In contemporary African societies, women's roles are still largely defined in terms of childbearing and infertility is considered to be the worst fate that can befall a woman (Fortes 1959; Kershaw 1973; Ngubane 1977). Many studies note that with an extension of the period between menarche and marriage, and increasing emphasis on monogamy, it is increasingly important for a man to know if his future bride will be able to have children. Consequently, proof of pregnancy is becoming a prerequisite for marriage (Barker and Rich 1992; Gage and Bledsoe 1994; Karanja 1987). Societies in sub-Saharan Africa are therefore perceived to send mixed or conflicting messages to adolescents regarding the appropriateness and desirability of early childbearing.

In the United States where adolescent sexual behaviour and childbearing occur largely outside marriage, explanations for teenage fertility are rooted in theories of social behaviour (socialization theory, social control theory, problem behaviour theory, and rational choice/opportunity cost theory), and generally identify attitudes and related personality variables, and family statuses and events that influence adolescent sexual activity, the likelihood of pregnancy, and its resolution. Models that derive from problem behaviour theory maintain that adolescent behaviours, including premarital childbearing, are a function of individuals' personality system and their perceived environment (Jessor and Jessor 1977). Thus, sexual activity, childbearing, and unmarried motherhood among adolescents are perceived to be a reflection of low self-esteem and internal locus of control, and low aspirations and expectations regarding the attainment of salient goals (Rosenberg 1990; Plotnick 1992).

The socialization and social control perspectives view adolescence as a trouble-prone period during which children need to be constrained by parents. These perspectives relate adolescent behaviour to family statuses and events. The socialization perspective hypothesizes that women who grow up in a mother-only family during childhood are socialized in ways that produce a high risk of premarital childbearing while the social control perspective hypothesizes that the numbers and types of adults present during the adolescent years are important predictors of the likelihood of premarital childbearing (Wu and Martinson 1993). Another perspective is the instability and change hypothesis which views adolescent fertility as a response by some women to the stresses and strains that accompany family change such as a divorce or remarriage. However, empirical support for these theories is inconsistent (see Plotnick 1992; Wu and Martinson 1993 for a detailed discussion).

One school of thought that has emerged in recent years is that teenage childbearing may not be deviant or mistimed in certain populations, but is rather a response to underlying sociostructural constraints and opportunities (see for example, Geronimus 1987; Geronimus and Korenman 1993; Geronimus *et al.* 1994). Among poor African-Americans in the United States, for instance, early childbearing has been viewed as a rite of passage to adulthood (Stack 1974). It is also viewed as a strategically planned lifecycle event that enables socially disadvantaged women—who may not be able to afford to pay for childcare while employed or withdraw from full-time employment at the birth of the first child—to take care of their infants under the care and protection of their families of origin before becoming gainfully employed (Geronimus 1987). Ladner (1971) notes that in these communities, those teenagers who are believed to have the academic potential to overcome the social and economic barriers to upward mobility are actively discouraged from bearing children during their teenage years. Thus, it is argued that due to their social environment, some African-Americans who become teenage mothers are 'in some sense, motivated to do so and are not "accident" victims' (Geronimus, 1987: 257).

2. Educational Attainment

It is fairly well established that teenage childbearing reduces educational attainment and economic status. In Kenya, it is estimated that over 10 per cent of female students (Eshiwani 1985)—between 8,000 and 10,000 girls (Ferguson *et al.* 1988) are lost to the school system each year as a result of pregnancy. In Botswana, it is estimated that in 1986, the secondary school dropout rate for pregnancy was 56 per cent (National Institute of Development Research, and Documentation (NIR), 1988). In many countries of sub-Saharan Africa, the consequences of teenage childbearing for educational attainment are exacerbated by policies that expel pregnant girls from school (Armstrong 1987; Eshiwani 1985). High pregnancy-related school dropout rates undermine women's status and prospects for advancement, in view of the fact that girls normally have lower enrolment rates and higher attrition rates than boys at every level of schooling. In countries where pregnant girls are legally allowed to return to school, schools do not generally admit girls who have given birth for fear that they may be a bad influence on other female students (Bledsoe 1990).

Although United States policy does allow teenage mothers to return to school, the literature documents that on average non-teenage mothers are more likely than teenage mothers to finish school and attend college (see for example, Hoffman *et al.* 1993). However, the extent to which teenage childbearing contributes causally to low levels of educational attainment is subject to controversy. Some studies have found that prior to pregnancy, teenagers who become mothers are more likely to do poorly academically and to score poorly on standardized tests than teenagers who postpone childbearing, even within fairly homogeneous populations (Abrahamse *et al.* 1988; Moore and Snyder 1991; Zabin *et al.* 1989). Other studies note that non-teenage mothers have higher socioeconomic status and are more likely to be middle class, and less likely to receive public assistance (Hoffman *et al.* 1993; Geronimus 1987 and 1992). Although many studies control for differences in socioeconomic status between women who have first births in their teens and those who have first births at older ages, most socioeconomic controls are considered inadequate because they are based on measures of current socioeconomic status, and do not capture socioeconomic status of the maternal family of origin which may be related to both achievement and the risk of teenage childbearing.

In order to clarify the causal association between teenage childbearing and selected outcomes, some investigators have controlled for women's family background characteristics by comparing teenage mothers with their sisters (Hoffman *et al.* 1993; Geronimus and Korenman 1993). Even after controlling for family background, through sister comparisons, Hoffman *et al.* (1993) found that teenage parenthood significantly reduces educational attainment and general social wellbeing. However, the extent to which the results of this study reflects differences in academic abilities and opportunities between sisters from the same family is unknown (Geronimus *et al.* 1994). Furthermore, families may distribute resources differentially among siblings or alter their socioeconomic environment in ways that may exacerbate or mitigate differences between them (see for example, Bledsoe and Isuigo-Abanihe 1989; Bledsoe 1994 of sub-Saharan Africa).

There are no known studies of sub-Saharan Africa that have attempted to sort out the causal relationship between family background, educational attainment, and adolescent pregnancy. One study of unplanned pregnancies among urban Zulu schoolchildren in the Republic of South Africa by Craig and Richter-Strydom (1983) found stark differences in socioeconomic background between the 212 pregnant schoolgirls and a group of 1,311 schoolchildren of both sexes, which suggests that socioeconomic disadvantages may select women into untimely teenage parenthood. The pregnant schoolgirls were more likely to be rated as 'coming from lower socioeconomic classes'. They were more likely to reside in households where the head was an unskilled worker or menial labourer (61 per cent of cases compared to 8 per cent of the general school sample). They were also more likely to live in one-parent households. Mothers were reported as head of the household in 38 per cent of cases compared to 13 per cent in the school sample. Only 38 per cent of pregnant girls lived with both parents compared to 81 per cent of the rest of the school sample.

Pregnancy itself may not automatically end a schoolgirl's career. Many girls may choose to terminate their pregnancies, although this may entail considerable health risks in countries where abortion is illegal or restricted. Teenage mothers, particularly schoolgirls, and their children often receive considerable support through multigenerational shared parenting arrangements which may mitigate some of the negative consequences of teenage childbearing for girls' education and subsequent life chances (for the United States, see Burton 1990; Stack and Burton 1993; for sub-Saharan Africa, see Du Toit 1987; Gage and Meekers 1994b). Even where pregnant girls are expelled from school, they may enrol in another town where they are not known and where they can avoid the embarrassment of being an unmarried mother (Bledsoe 1990).

However, the difficulties of combining motherhood and childbearing, particularly the time and money investments required to care for a baby, may not allow a young mother to continue with her education. In Burkina Faso, Görgen *et al.* (1993) observed that young female students with children were often tired, had high repetition rates, and were likely to drop out of school about two years after the birth. They may also face additional difficulties if they consider relocating to another town to continue their education. Potential guardians may be reluctant to take them in, fearing blame if the girls continue their past behaviour (Bledsoe 1990). If the adolescent mother does return to school, her educational career is often terminated by additional pregnancies. In a study of adolescent mothers in Baltimore, Furstenberg (1981) found that among women who had three or more subsequent pregnancies, 85 per cent had left school before obtaining a high school diploma. In contrast, only one third of young mothers who did not become pregnant again after returning to school failed to complete high school.

In some settings in sub-Saharan Africa, subsequent pregnancies among unmarried adolescent mothers who return to school are linked to the withdrawal of parental support or economic constraints associated with raising a child. There is evidence from a number of countries that female students facing adverse circumstances often turn towards sexual relationships with older men for much needed economic and personal support to complete their education (Schoepf 1988; Ulin 1992; see also Basu, Chapter 9 below). Far from being opposed to their daughters starting these sexual relationships, families may actually encourage such relations with older men who fit their concept of desirable partners due to their social position or wealth (Akuffo 1987: 161; Bledsoe 1990; Görgen *et al.* 1993). Although there are no reliable data to estimate the prevalence of this practice, it is undoubtedly linked to the risk of additional pregnancies and school drop out among female students.

Although the extensive literature on the economic consequences of early childbearing focuses on the adolescent mother, a few studies have given some attention to the adolescent father. In general, young fathers are less adversely affected by early childbearing than young mothers (Card and Wise 1981). However, studies based in the United States have found that teenage parenthood negatively affect men's educational careers as well. Teenage fathers are more likely to drop out of high school than other youth, even if they do not marry their pregnant partner (Furstenberg *et al.* 1989; Marsiglio 1986). However, research on the economic consequences of teenage childbearing for fathers is limited by the lower levels of reported parenthood among teenage fathers than teenage mothers (Furstenberg *et al.*

1990). This is undoubtedly partly due to the reluctance of some teenage fathers to acknowledge parenthood and to the fact that a substantial proportion of children born to teenage mothers are fathered by men over age 20 (Furstenberg *et al.* 1990; Barker and Rich 1992).

3. Marriage Timing and Stability

Besides terminating a girl's school career, premarital pregnancy may reduce her chances of marriage or precipitate entry into marriage with negative consequences for union stability due to the increased likelihood of a conjugal mismatch. Studies in the United States have found that non-teenage mothers are more likely than teenage mothers to be ever married, currently married, and married at first birth (Hoffman *et al.* 1993). Trends in marriage in the United States further indicate that there has been a decline in the probability of marriage and a corresponding increase in the likelihood of cohabitation. In the early 1970s, for example, 45 per cent of women who became pregnant while unmarried, and who bore the child, married before the birth, compared with only 27 per cent of women in the late 1980s (United States Bureau of the Census 1991).

In much of sub-Saharan Africa, on the other hand, the question as to the effect of adolescent fertility on girls' chances of marriage is largely irrelevant because of early marriage patterns. However, it is recognized that a premarital pregnancy may ruin a girl's chances of contracting a desirable marriage or lower the amount of bridewealth payments. Hence, among some ethnic groups in Botswana, seduction damages are available to the father of a girl who becomes pregnant out of wedlock as compensation for the reduction in his daughter's marriage prospects should the man not intend to marry her (Molokomme 1990). In other instances, fear of an untimely pregnancy is a principal reason why many rural parents do not send their daughters to school and for the few who do so, it is a principal reason for withdrawing them from school around puberty and marrying them off before they have completed their education (Bledsoe 1990, on the Mende of Sierra Leone; Pilon 1994, on the Moba Gourma of Togo).

Furthermore, the relationship between adolescent fertility and girls' marriage chances is complex in the African setting where marriage is rarely a single definitive effect but a process extending over a period of months or even years. In an insightful analysis of the quest for education and the marriage process among Mende girls of Sierra Leone, Bledsoe (1990) shows how adolescent sexuality is integrated into conjugal negotiations and rural girls' efforts to obtain an education. She observes that families may obtain assistance for their daughter's education from a prospective suitor and treat this as a marriage payment. Although there is overt disapproval of schoolgirl pregnancy, the families concerned often allow the girl to commence sexual relationships with the suitor who is providing school fees, and may even insist on it, a phenomenon that some link to economic hardship. In the event of pregnancy, parents simply withdraw the girl from school and send her to live with the man who paid her school fees. Hence, for some adolescent girls, the relationship between education, childbearing, and marriage reflects the extent to which power and resource imbalances impinge on their ability to determine their own sexual and reproductive lives (see also Dixon-Mueller 1993; Basu, Chapter 9 below).

In demographic surveys, the connection between adolescent sexual activity, marriage, and childbearing is rendered more problematic by difficulties of dating the beginning of marriage and defining which stage of the marriage process should define the start of the union (Bledsoe 1990; Bledsoe and Cohen 1993; van de Walle and Meekers 1994). Furthermore, evidence from a number of anthropological studies suggests that in the indigenous marriage model, sex and reproduction are not conditional on the final marriage ceremony or the completion of bridewealth payments (see for example, Schapera 1941, on the Tswana). Some societies require proof of fertility before marriage (Karanja 1987, on Nigeria; Makinwa-Adebusoye 1991, on Nigeria; Harrell-Bond 1975, on Sierra Leone; Obbo 1987, on Uganda; Du Toit 1987, on Africans in Pretoria, South Africa) while in others, cohabitation may not take place until several children have been born (van de Walle and Meekers 1994, on Côte d'Ivoire). Among these groups, unions and their offspring are recognized as legitimate well before cohabitation begins (van de Walle and Meekers 1994). Ironically, many large-scale surveys use the date of cohabitation as a proxy for the marriage date. Hence, births are defined as premarital if they occur or were conceived before the date of cohabitation rather than the time the union received the requisite social sanctions from the kin and community.

Empirical evidence on the relationship between teenage childbearing and marital disruption is largely indirect and stems from studies which examine the effect of early marriage or a premarital birth or conception on marital stability. These studies are rarely restricted to adolescent women but do control for age in multivariate analyses. Some that have examined the relationship between age at first marriage and separation or divorce have found that women who first marry as teenagers are more likely than those who marry later to experience marital disruption. In the United States, for example, 48 per cent of teenage marriages, compared with 35 per cent of non-teenage marriages, end by the time women are in their thirties (Singh and Wulf 1990). In Colombia, the difference in the likelihood of marital disruption between teenage and older brides is about 12 percentage points. Singh and Wulf (1990) note that in Latin America, the negative relationship between age at first marriage and marital dissolution is intensified by the greater tendency for teenagers to enter consensual rather than legal unions. Consensual unions are often associated with a higher probability of dissolution than legal marriages (Singh and Wulf 1990; Gage-Brandon 1993).

Many studies find an increased likelihood of marital separation or divorce for women with either a premarital birth or premarital pregnancy (Becker *et al.* 1977; O'Connel and Rogers 1984). Where a distinction is made between a premarital birth and a premarital pregnancy, it has generally been found that premarital births are more strongly related to marital dissolution than premarital pregnancies (Teachman

1983; Morgan and Rindfuss 1985; Billy *et al.* 1986). However, the destabilizing effect of a premarital birth may be partially counteracted by an older age at first marriage.

Women who have premarital pregnancies have often been found to experience rates of marital disruption that are similar to those of women who had not been pregnant or mothers at the time of first marriage (Teachman 1983; Billy *et al.* 1986). This similarity has sometimes been linked to the significance for marital stability of marrying the biological father of the child. However, the effects of marriage–birth sequencing on marriage stability have been found to vary by race and over time. Data examined by O'Connel and Rogers (1984) show that the effect of premarital births on union stability has declined over time for whites but that the relationship was inconsistent across marriage cohorts for blacks. Similarly, an analysis by Billy *et al.* (1986) of the long- and short-term effects of marriage–first birth sequencing confirms that in the past, having a premarital first birth increased the risk of marital stability but that this effect has declined over time for whites. The effect of a premarital birth on marriage stability has also been found to decline with an increase in the duration of marriage among white women in the United States (Morgan and Rindfuss 1985).

4. Health Risks and Outcomes

4.1. Mothers

The prevalence of poor health outcomes among teenagers is difficult to study. First there is little data on the context in which pregnancy occurs. In most countries, information on maternal morbidity and mortality is derived from hospital facilities which do not provide an accurate or complete picture of the health status of the general population (AbouZahr and Royston 1991). Health records are biased toward complicated cases, and higher socioeconomic classes who can afford to pay hospital fees. Furthermore, in areas with poor health facilities, a substantial proportion of births may not occur in hospitals and health centres, and even severely complicated cases may not reach the hospital. A second problem has to deal with poor vital registration or cause of death statistics. In many developing countries, there is a low level of completeness of vital registration and the classification of the cause of death is often inadequate (United Nations 1989). In most developed countries, on the other hand, the quality of vital registration is satisfactory but teenage mothers are a rare occurrence. Consequently, the data may be limited by small samples which render estimates of maternal mortality and prevalence rates unreliable. Research on the relationship between teenage fertility and health outcomes for mothers may also be limited by the level of aggregation of years of age. Published data may not aggregate women's age in sufficient detail to permit a separate evaluation of teenage health outcomes, thus limiting statistical comparability across countries (United Nations 1989).

Pregnancy complications are one of the most frequently cited consequences of teenage pregnancy, and in some countries, are the leading cause of death among teenagers (United Nations 1989). In Bangladesh, about 40 per cent of deaths among teenage mothers can be attributed to maternal causes (Koenig *et al.* 1988) compared to most developed countries where teenage fertility is low and complications of pregnancy and delivery usually account for less than 1 per cent of deaths to teenage girls (United Nations 1989). Data for several countries also show that, with the exception of high parity women in the age group 40–49, there is a higher risk of maternal deaths among teenage girls than among older women. For example, a 1982 study of 35,650 deliveries in five hospitals in Ibadan city, Nigeria revealed a maternal mortality rate of 526 per 100,000 live births among women aged 15–19 compared to 144 among those aged 20–24 (Adewunmi 1986).

The causes of death among teenagers are often very different from those of older women. A study of all health institutions in Oran, Algeria during the period 1971–88 revealed that in general, two-thirds of maternal deaths were from direct obstetric causes of which haemorrhage was the most important, followed by sepsis and hypertensive disorders of pregnancy. However, women below twenty were more likely to suffer from hypertensive disorders of pregnancy while those aged 30–45 were found to be most at risk of haemorrhage (Abouzahr and Royston 1991). A similar pattern was observed in Brazil in a study of 121,039 admissions in thirty-seven hospitals during the period 1979–81 (Vieira Matos *et al.* 1985 cited in Abouzahr and Royston 1991). Some studies have also found that teenagers are more likely to die of abortion complications than older women. One study in Nigeria found that during the period 1985, induced abortion accounted for at least 70 per cent of all maternal deaths in the 15–19 year age group and for all deaths among girls aged 15 years or less, compared to 8 per cent of all maternal deaths among women aged 20–24 (Unuigbe 1988). A similar observation was made by Kwast *et al.* (1986) for Addis Ababa, Ethiopia.

Induced abortion is also a leading cause of maternal morbidity among teenagers in some developing countries. However, it is difficult to assess the prevalence of induced abortion and related complications among adolescent mothers. Retrospective surveys tend to produce gross underestimates, undoubtedly a reflection of the sensitive nature of the subject, and in some settings, the illegal or restricted nature of induced abortion (Barreto *et al.* 1992; Paxman *et al.* 1993). In Nigeria, for example, abortion is a criminal act punishable by a maximum of fourteen years imprisonment (Okagbue, 1990). However, a large number of clandestine abortions continue to be performed, particularly in situations where schools do not allow pregnant girls to continue their studies; in these circumstances, the decision to terminate a pregnancy is often necessary for those who want to continue their education.

The prevalence of induced abortion among teenagers is documented in a few studies based on retrospective reports or hospital data. A study of 950 randomly selected secondary school girls in Nigeria revealed that 24 per cent of sexually active girls reported ever having an induced abortion (Odujirin 1991). Another study of young persons aged 12–24 in five rapidly growing cities of Nigeria revealed that 23 per cent of ever pregnant girls had at least one induced abortion and that teenage girls accounted for 28 per cent of pregnancy terminations (Makinwa-Adebusoye 1991). In Liberia, Nichols *et al.* (1987) observed that among adolescents currently enrolled, nearly two-thirds of those aged 14–17 and half of those aged 18–21 who have been pregnant elected to terminate their first pregnancy by means of induced abortion.

Hospital-based studies of admission for complications from illegal abortions in African countries generally show that teenagers, especially those who are unmarried and childless, make up a large proportion of women suffering from abortion complications. For example, a survey of five hospitals in Nigeria in 1984 found that 55 per cent of abortion patients were under twenty and only 10 per cent were over thirty-five. About 85 per cent were single women (Okagbue 1990). In comparison, the percentage of all abortions performed on women under twenty ranges from 20 per cent to 25 per cent in England and Wales, Norway and the United States, to less than 10 per cent in Czechoslovakia and the Federal Republic of Germany (David 1992). In Latin America, induced abortions are most frequent among older, urban women who are married and have several children. However, there is some indication of a gradual change in the age and marital status of women seeking abortions. A study conducted in Mexico revealed that almost half of the women seeking abortions were single women and more than 61 per cent were nulliparous (David and Pick de Weiss 1992). Similarly, it has been observed in Indonesia, that young unmarried women are increasingly represented among those seeking induced abortions, a phenomenon that has been attributed to changing mores in a rapidly modernizing society (Hull *et al.* 1993).

The complications of induced abortion are more severe among younger women for several reasons. Many teenagers fail to obtain early abortions, a factor that has been attributed to their relative inexperience in recognizing the symptoms of pregnancy, an unwillingness to accept the reality of their situation, ignorance about where to seek advice and help, and their hesitation to confide in adults (Tietze and Henshaw 1986). In addition, few teenagers may have the cash needed to procure abortion from a licensed practitioner. For example, in Nigeria, Konje *et al.* (1992) note that the average cost of treating an illegal septic abortion in Ibadan is about US\$ 200, whereas the typical monthly salary is around US\$ 45. Hence, teenagers may resort to self-induced abortions or to untrained practitioners using unsafe procedures.

Abortifacients, herbs, and abdominal massage are among the most widely used traditional methods of inducing abortions (Hull *et al.* 1993). Inserting rubber catheters and sticks of various sorts into the uterus is also a common practice (Paxman *et al.* 1993). In sub-Saharan Africa, more dangerous methods such as an overdose of chloroquine tablets, swallowing beer bottle glass ground in a mortar, and ingesting detergent and gasoline have been reported in surveys (Castle *et al.* 1990; Görgen *et al.* 1993). In Latin America, abortifacients include various pharmaceuticals such as hormonal preparations, uterine contractors, and medicines meant to cure other diseases. In Brazil, for example, Cytotec, an anti-ulcer drug that initiates labour, has been directly associated with the practice of illegal abortions (Barbosa and Ariltrio 1993; Costa and Vesey 1993; Schonhofer 1991).

The health consequences of improperly performed induced abortions can be severe. Some complications include post-abortive infertility, perforation, cervical injury, ectopic pregnancy, sepsis, haemorrhage, and trauma. These complications are often worsened by shortage of medical supplies and the lack of skill of the provider. Where abortion is illegal, complications are aggravated not only by the use of unsafe methods but also by the unsanitary environment in which abortion is performed (Odujinrin 1991; Okagbue 1990). These costs and risks of induced abortion stem less from abortion itself than from the legal, social, and economic conditions which make safe abortion impossible (Bledsoe and Cohen 1993).

In addition to the dangers of teenage childbearing, early sexual activity can carry other long-term health implications. For example, Barron (1986) observed that the risk of developing carcinoma of the cervix is found to be double in women who began sexual activity before age of seventeen. Early marriage and childbearing are most commonly associated with vesicovaginal fistulas and cephalopelvic disproportion which commonly occurs when first pregnancy occurs too soon after menarche before the growth of the pelvis is complete. Vesicovaginal fistulae are a common occurrence in Northern Nigerian societies where it is commonly believed that a woman should be married and living with her husband at the time of her first menses. In Zaria, Northern Nigeria, the average age of patients with vesicovaginal fistula is sixteen years (Lister 1984). In general, the risk of vesicovaginal fistulae is highest among teenage primigravidae aged sixteen years and younger than among other women (Harrison 1989). Higher rates of toxaemia of pregnancy and anaemia have also been found among adolescents aged 15–19 than among older women (Adedoyin and Adetoro 1989).

In recent years, the relationship between young maternal age and adverse health outcomes has become a subject of great debate. Several studies emphasize the role of antenatal care as a factor responsible for the poor health outcomes in pregnant teenagers. One study in Harare found that pregnant teenagers aged fourteen years and younger were more likely not to have attended antenatal care, and if they did, had fewer visits and booked for antenatal care later, but that these differences were not significant (Mahomed *et al.* 1989). Similarly, LeGrand and Mbacké (1993) found in a regression analysis using data for urban centres in the Sahel that teenagers, especially those under the age of eighteen were significantly less likely to seek early prenatal care than mothers aged 25–39 at the birth of their children. The adverse effects of young maternal age on the occurrence and timing of prenatal care is considerably more pronounced among unmarried schoolgirls, a phenomenon that the authors attribute to the high rate of unwantedness among these women. Young unmarried women who become pregnant may also delay prenatal care for fear of social sanction, and because of the negative attitudes of health care providers in some countries towards young single women who are sexually active (Huntington *et al.*, 1990).

Aside from inadequate utilization of health services, other social and environmental factors are implicated in poor obstetric or neonatal outcomes. Poverty, malnutrition, and famine may compound pregnancy complications such as cephalopelvic disproportion and its attendant sequelae such as obstructed labour and vesicovaginal fistulae. In Bangladesh, for example, social factors related to the unequitable division of food among household members in rural areas contribute to anaemia and related pregnancy complications in rural areas, women and girls being more disadvantaged than men and boys in intrahousehold food allocations (Carloni 1981). Social constraints on women such as limited mobility and preference of home delivery for the first birth, the extreme shortage of female doctors and the acceptance of illness and death related to childbearing are also important determinants of maternal morbidity and mortality in some societies (Blanchet 1988 cited by AbouZahr and Royston 1991).[1]

4.2. Children

It is well documented that infants of teenagers suffer from excessive mortality rates when compared with infants of mothers who had their first birth at the age of twenty or older. Recent data from the Demographic and Health Surveys indicate that in twenty-two out of twenty-eight developing countries, children born to young mothers under twenty have a 10–50 per cent greater chance of dying before the age of five than those born to mothers aged 25–34 (see Table 8.2). Young maternal age at birth was more strongly linked with child mortality than old maternal age at birth (thirty-five years or more). For all countries combined, the median excess under-five risk associated with young maternal age is 31 per cent. The excess mortality risk associated with young maternal age at birth declines with the increasing age of the child. In the Latin American/Caribbean region, for example, the increased risk of dying in the neonatal, post-neonatal and 1–4 year age segments were 17, 46, and 4 per cent, respectively. In sub-Saharan Africa, the corresponding median estimates are 45, 23, and 34 per cent (Sullivan *et al.* 1990).

Risk factors associated with excessive mortality and morbidity among infants of teenage mothers include low birth weight, history of sexually transmitted diseases, maternal weight during pregnancy, gestation age, length of interval between pregnancies, and low socioeconomic status. LeGrand and Mbacké (1993) note that in some urban centres of the Sahel, children of teenage mothers weigh significantly less at birth than children of older mothers, even after controlling for birth order, sex of the child, multiple births, and socioeconomic status. In the United States, pregnant teenagers, especially those under fifteen have higher rates of premature and/or low birthweight babies than older mothers (Strobino 1987). Most births to teenagers are first births, and regardless of maternal age, first births are of a higher risk than birth order 2–6 (United Nations 1989). But second or higher-order births to teenage

---

[1]   For the implications of sexual activity, and condom use, on the spread of STDs, notably HIV, see Basu, Chapter 9.

Table 8.2. Relative risks of dying of children born to teenage mothers compared with children born to mothers aged 25–34, Demographic and Health Surveys 1985–90

Country	Relative risk of dying				
	Neonatal mortality (0–29 days)	Post-neonatal mortality (30–364 days)	Infant mortality (0–364 days)	Child mortality (1–4 years)	Under-five mortality (0–4 years)
Sub-Saharan Africa					
Botswana	0.82	1.22	0.98	1.23	1.06
Burundi	2.14	1.45	1.73	1.29	1.45
Ghana	1.48	1.11	1.31	1.37	1.32
Kenya	1.67	1.14	1.34	1.62	1.43
Liberia	1.41	1.26	1.32	1.34	1.31
Mali	1.50	1.73	1.61	1.24	1.35
Ondo State (Nigeria)	2.12	1.36	1.69	1.35	1.27
Senegal	1.69	1.25	1.45	1.01	1.16
Sudan (North)	1.31	1.13	1.23	1.35	1.27
Togo	1.17	1.02	1.10	1.17	1.13
Uganda	1.39	1.07	1.21	1.49	1.31
Zimbabwe	1.42	1.40	1.41	1.62	1.46
North Africa/Asia					
Egypt [a]	1.44	1.69	1.56	1.63	1.56
Indonesia [a]	1.94	1.18	1.51	0.88	1.27
Morocco [a]	1.62	1.48	1.56	1.06	1.38
Sri Lanka [a]	1.09	1.06	1.08	1.40	1.15
Thailand [a]	1.67	0.79	1.25	1.68	1.33
Tunisia [a]	1.28	1.36	1.32	0.27	1.02
Latin America/Caribbean					
Bolivia	1.14	1.29	1.22	1.12	1.18
Brazil	1.29	1.25	1.27	0.84	1.20
Colombia	0.88	1.75	1.25	1.18	1.23
Dominican Republic	1.20	1.78	1.44	1.17	1.36
Ecuador	0.85	1.08	0.94	0.79	0.91
El Salvador	1.67	1.65	1.66	0.96	1.49
Guatemala	1.49	1.24	1.35	1.52	1.39
Mexico	0.89	1.48	1.15	0.93	1.10
Peru	1.25	1.44	1.35	0.87	1.19
Trinidad and Tobago	0.95	5.89	1.46	5.59	1.61

[a] Refers to ever-married women
Source: Sullivan *et al.* (1994), Table 3.4, pp. 21–3.

women represent an especially high risk group because of short birth spacing (see David, Chapter 7 above). In a small study of adolescent girls attending a postnatal clinic in Cameroon, Lovel (1988) found that, out of 259 pregnant women aged 13–19, 61 per cent were having their second or third pregnancy and a third of current pregnancies had ended in foetal death.

Research in developed countries indicates certain adolescent developmental characteristics that may impair the health of adolescent mothers and their children. Studies in the United States have demonstrated that teenage mothers are more likely than older mothers to smoke or drink during pregnancy (Dryfoos 1990). They are also less likely to breastfeed (Martinez and Krieger 1984), use adequate prenatal care or seek routine paediatric check-ups and immunizations for their children (Ventura 1984). In 1982, only 32 per cent of pregnant women under fifteen years of age initiated prenatal care in the first trimester compared with 79 per cent of women aged 25–29 (Prada *et al.* 1988). Teenagers in the United States are also noted to have poor eating habits (Hayes 1987) which may contribute to some of the adverse health conditions that are commonly associated with teenage pregnancy and childbearing, such as premature births and low birth weight.

Recently, some studies have concluded that the excessive mortality associated with teenage pregnancy and childbearing may be more a consequence of socioeconomic factors than of early fertility *per se*, and that earlier research failed to control adequately for socioeconomic background (Geronimus 1987; Geronimus and Korenman 1993; Makinson 1985). In the United States, teenage mothers come disproportionately from socioeconomically disadvantaged populations and these groups are more likely to have excessive risks of infant mortality and morbidity and are less likely to seek adequate prenatal care, routine paediatric care and childhood immunizations (Gould and LeRoy 1988; Taffel 1989). Once these confounding socioeconomic factors are controlled, the effects of maternal age on pregnancy-related health and child mortality are often diminished or eliminated (Moore and Burt 1982; Geronimus and Korenman 1993). For example, Geronimus and Korenman (1993) examined the relationship between maternal age and a number of health-related factors such as smoking or drinking alcohol during pregnancy, prenatal care, and breastfeeding, using sisters who delayed childbearing as a natural control for teenage mothers. With the exception of smoking among whites, Geronimus and Korenman (1993) found that within family, teenage mothers appeared no more likely than non-teenage mothers to engage in unhealthy behaviours during pregnancy and no less likely to bring in their infants for routine paediatric care and immunizations. Family background, race, and ethnicity were more important determinants of pregnancy-related health outcomes than maternal age at birth.

Some authors have suggested that children born outside marriage may have higher levels of mortality than children born within marriage (Adegbola 1987; Guèye and van de Walle 1988; Meekers 1994). This differential has been attributed to their varying degrees of social acceptance and the different support systems available to these categories of children (Guèye and van de Walle 1988). However, empirical evidence of the relationship between premarital childbearing and infant mortality is limited and inconsistent. Analyses of data from Benin, Cameroon, Côte d'Ivoire, Ghana and Lesotho reveal that infants born before marriage had a higher probability of dying than those born afterwards (Adegbola 1987; Lesthaeghe *et al.* 1989). In Senegal, northern Nigeria, and Kenya, on the other hand, there is little difference in children's mortality risk by parent's marital status at the birth of the child. While it has been suggested that higher mortality levels among children born before marriage may be largely attributed to their lower birth order, Guèye and van de Walle (1988) note in an analysis of data from Bobo-Dioulasso (Burkina Faso) that the effect of parents' marital status remained significant even after controlling for birth order and maternal education.

Recognizing that the progressive nature of African marriage and the way in which marriage is defined may influence the categorization of births as marital or premarital, Meekers (1994) identified discrete components of the marriage process which may be important for children's chances of survival using data for Côte d'Ivoire. The results of his analysis indicate that children born before a woman begins cohabiting with a man suffer higher mortality risks than children born after a more stable union is in place. Hence, parents' marital status *per se* appeared to be less important for child survival than the presence of a stable partner, whether or not he is the biological father of the child.

5. Economic Status

The economic consequences of teenage childbearing are a matter of great policy concern. Studies in the United States have shown that teenagers who become mothers are disproportionately represented among the poor and among those dependent on public assistance. Data on welfare expenditures in 1975 indicated that approximately 50–56 per cent of Aid to Families With Dependent Children (AFDC) budget in that year was directed to households in which the mother was a teenager at first birth (Hayes 1987). The disparity in welfare dependency between teenage and nonteenage mothers is more visible when premarital pregnancy is considered. Fustenberg (1981) found that, among women in a Baltimore study, one-third of teenage mothers were receiving at least one-fifth of their income from welfare compared to only 4 per cent of their classmates who had not conceived premaritally. Moreover, 70 per cent of the classmates who had not had a prenuptial conception contributed to their own support through employment, compared to 45 per cent of teenage mothers.

One of the factors predisposing teenage mothers to needing welfare receipts is the difficulty they experience in finding renumerative employment. This stems in part from their lower levels of education. Furstenberg (1981) found in the Baltimore study that on average, teenage mothers had had approximately two fewer years of schooling than their classmates by the five-year follow-up. Although US policy allows teenage mothers to continue their education, they are more likely to drop out of school than non-teenage mothers, especially if the first birth is followed by a subsequent pregnancy. As mothers on welfare generally had large families and young children, the difficulties and expenses of arranging childcare may preclude teenage mothers from becoming economically self-supporting (Furstenberg 1981; Hayes 1987).

However, some studies indicate that chronic welfare dependency is the exception rather than the rule, and that the majority of teenage mothers use the welfare system to cope with their economic constraints only in the early stages of parenthood. For example, Furstenberg and Brooks-Gunn (1985) found that among women in Baltimore, the probability of being a welfare recipient rose sharply during the five years following the birth of a first child. After five years, the probability of going off welfare increased sharply and within the five years preceding the seventeen-year follow-up, two-thirds of women in the sample did not receive any welfare assistance.

Recent research supports the notion that the relationship between early childbearing and women's socioeconomic wellbeing operates largely thorough the structure of the women's family of origin. Geronimus et al. (1994) found that although teenage mothers have lower incomes than non-teenage mothers (US$ 16,000 compared to US$ 27,000 on the average), the difference narrowed considerably after controlling for pre-pregnancy family background through sister comparisons (US$ 17,000 for teenage mothers versus US$ 20,000 for non-teenage mothers). Nonetheless, most studies indicate that women who give birth as teenagers will not achieve complete economic parity with those who postpone childbearing. In a comparison of sisters who were aged 21–33 in 1987, Hoffman et al. (1993) found that a teenage birth reduces significantly a woman's economic wellbeing. The results of a regression analysis showed that a teenage birth lowers a woman's income–needs ratio by more than 30 per cent, nearly doubles the probability that she is poor, and reduces the probability that she is at least middle class by more than half.[2]

The poorer economic situation of teenage mothers is also a reflection of their lower levels of partner support, more specifically, of the low levels of paternal commitment to children born out of wedlock and to children of dissolved marriages. In the United States, levels of enforcement of child support payments are low and the likelihood of support drops sharply over time as relations frequently deteriorate between the child's parents. The follow-ups to the Baltimore study of teenage mothers conducted in the 1960s indicate that while 63 per cent of fathers were still maintaining relations with their children five years after the birth, only one-fifth were actually living with their children. Father–child contact was more limited if the mother had married a man other than the child's biological father (Furstenberg 1981). Seventeen years after the birth of the child, only 11 per cent of never-married

---

[2]   The income–needs ratio was defined as the natural log of average income–needs ratio for 1986 and 1987. Needs were set equal to the official poverty standard for a family of a given size. Middle class was defined as an income–needs ratio > 3.0 (Hoffman et al. 1993).

and 23 per cent of formerly married fathers were helping to support their children compared with 43 per cent of unmarried fathers the year after delivery (Furstenberg *et al.* 1989). Furstenberg (1990: 168) also observes that, in the United States, 'the amount of child support paid by non-custodial fathers is abysmally small', and that compared to fathers in other Western nations, American fathers contribute little income to their children.

The question remains as to why some men who father children out of wedlock assume more economic responsibility for their children than others. Studies note that some teenage fathers never acknowledge paternity and that in some cases, women may conceal the pregnancy from the father of the child, especially in cases involving incest, rape, or casual sex (Barker and Rich 1992; Furstenberg 1981). Yet in other cases, the weak economic position of males who father children out of wedlock may impede their ability to provide stable economic support. This factor has been linked to the reduced motivation to marry of teenage mothers from disadvantaged minority populations in the United States, and to their increased likelihood of marital disruption (Furstenberg 1981; Manning and Landale 1994). Sometimes, teenage mothers are actively discouraged by their families from seeking paternal support for fear that the father's participation may exert a negative influence on the child (Furstenberg 1981).

Few studies of sub-Saharan Africa have examined the economic implications of adolescent childbearing for mothers and children. This is probably due to the fact that adolescent childbearing occurs largely within marriage and that there are few or no social welfare programmes designed to address income and social inequities. However, it is generally recognized that the woman's family often bears the responsibility of maintaining and rearing children born out of wedlock. For example, Gage-Brandon and Meekers (1993) observe that in Botswana, only 46 per cent of teenage mothers who were not currently married were receiving some source of support from the child's father whereas 91 per cent were being supported by their own mother. Unfortunately, no distinction was made between support of a monetary or nonmonetary nature. Another study found that in Namibia and Zambia, fewer than one out of ten children of never-married mothers were currently residing with their fathers (Gage and Meekers 1994b).

In the context of sub-Saharan Africa, levels of father–child co-residence and partner support for out-of-wedlock births may reflect not only the acknowledgement of paternity but customary laws regarding child maintenance. A number of studies in Southern Africa have found that under strict customary rules, the responsibility for maintaining a child born out of wedlock rests primarily on its mother's family group, and that women could not claim maintenance directly from the child's father (Armstrong 1992a and 1992b; Garey 1992; Molokomme 1991). This affects women's perceptions of their rights to claim maintenance in civil courts. In addition, teenage mothers and their families often avoid taking legal action against the father in the hope that the couple may eventually get married. In this light, legal maintenance claims for children born out of wedlock are perceived to deter the father from initiating the complex negotiations necessary for the establishment of a valid customary marriage (Armstrong 1992b: 126). Studies of maintenance law and practice in six countries of Southern Africa have also revealed that men generally tend to equate maintenance payments with rights to sexual relations with the mother; women who were reluctant to continue sexual relations often decided to forgo their rights to maintenance (Armstrong 1992b:48).

6. Child Development and Social Wellbeing

Early childbearing is often perceived to be detrimental to child development. Studies in the United States document that children of teenage mothers score poorly on standardized tests and have considerably poorer cognitive performance and lower levels of school achievement than children of older mothers (see Hofferth and Hayes 1987 for a detailed review). The academic disadvantage of children of teenage mothers persist through adolescence. For example, Brooks-Gunn and Furstenberg (1986) found that among African-Americans in the Baltimore Study and the National Survey of Children, half of the adolescents born to teenage mothers had failed a grade compared to only 20 per cent of adolescents born to later childbearers. They also observed that problem behaviour in school, an indication of lack of interest and learning problems, were twice as prevalent among those adolescents whose mothers were teenagers at their birth than in those whose mothers were older (Brooks-Gunn and Furstenberg 1986).

However, the causal linkages between early childbearing and children's cognitive development have not been well delineated. In the United States, for example, women who give birth as teenagers differ from women who delay parenthood in a number of ways. Teenage mothers are more likely to have grown up in disadvantaged families and are less likely to have completed high school by the time the child is born. They also tend to have lower scores on tests of cognitive attainment. Maternal academic ability has been found to be a significant predictor of young children's cognitive attainment (Moore and Synder 1991). In addition, teenage mothers are more likely to reside in disadvantaged neighbourhoods and their children are more likely to attend low quality schools and experience high rates of family instability (Furstenberg *et al.* 1989). Thus, children of teenage mothers are perceived to grow up in environments which are less intellectually stimulating (Hofferth and Hayes 1987). Some studies also suggest that teenage parents may have less adequate parenting skills than older mothers (Furstenberg *et al.* 1989), which may adversely affect child development. However, results of empirical research on teenage parenting abilities are conflicting (see Hayes 1987 for a review).

Most studies have found that, after controlling for socioeconomic status, the effect of teenage childbearing on children's academic achievement diminishes considerably, but nonetheless persists. However, the question remains as to whether research examining the link between teenage childbearing and child development has adequately and appropriately controlled for differences in socioeconomic status between women who first give birth as teenagers and those who do so at older ages. Geronimus *et al.* (1994) note that in most of the research, measures of socioeconomic status are based on current maternal characteristics, that is, after the event (teenage childbearing) has occurred. They argue that children of teenage mothers may fare worse than children of non-teenage mothers because the same social disadvantage that selects women into early parenthood may contribute to impaired child development. By comparing first cousins whose mothers were sisters, thereby controlling for mothers' pre-pregnancy socioeconomic background, they find little support for an adverse effect of teenage childbearing on early child development.

It is unclear whether the associations between early parenthood and children's development and social behaviour in the United States are applicable to other cultures, particularly those in developing countries. Where teenage childbearing is the norm rather than the exception, the impact of selectivity into teenage motherhood is probably more limited than in the United States. In addition, the greater involvement of the extended family in sharing parenting responsibilities may mitigate some of the adverse consequences of teenage marital and premarital childbearing in some cultures. Even in the United States, it has been found that the offspring of teenage mothers fared better in their own teenage years if their mothers had received family support during the early stages of parenthood (Furstenberg 1990, on the Baltimore Study).

Another question of interest in the United States is whether children of adolescent mothers go on to become teenage parents themselves, leading to the intergenerational transmission of the cycle of poverty with which teenage childbearing is associated. Furstenberg *et al.* (1992) found that while adolescent children of teenage mothers in the Baltimore Study were more socioeconomically disadvantaged than the children of women who delayed childbearing, the majority were experiencing successful transitions to adulthood. Two-thirds of adolescents whose mothers gave birth as teenagers had completed high school or got a GED (General Education Development) certificate; 85 per cent of the males and 64 per cent of the females had not become parents before the age of nineteen. However, adolescent children of teenage mothers were more likely to have given birth to a live baby before the age of nineteen than were children of older mothers. Thus, the evidence suggests that today's teenage parents may be more vulnerable than their mothers to economic dependency and poverty and less likely to overcome some of the handicaps of early childbearing. Comparing daughters who became adolescent mothers with their own mothers at a comparable age in the twenty-year follow-up of the Baltimore Study, Furstenberg *et al.* (1990) found that the daughters have bleaker educational and financial prospects than their mothers had and are less likely ever to have married. The daughters were almost twice as likely as their mothers to have failed one or more grades in school and were more likely to be receiving public assistance (60 per cent as against 31 per cent) even after taking into account differences in marital status between the two generations.

Conclusions

This review highlights that teenage pregnancy has important social and economic outcomes. One important outcome is the loss of educational opportunities when women drop out of school as a result of pregnancy. In sub-Saharan Africa, this is identified as the major problem associated with adolescent fertility. But even where teenage childbearing is viewed as normal or traditional, early childbearing imposes considerable health risks on mother and child. Teenage women suffer from higher rates of pregnancy complications than older women and their babies also suffer from low birth weight and heightened risks of mortality. Teenage women who bear children out of wedlock are likely to be poor and to be the primary support of children for a substantial proportion of their lives due to their lower marital prospects, higher rates of marital disruption, and lower paternal commitment to children of dissolved unions. Their children may also suffer from restricted kinship networks with adverse consequences for access to property and inheritance, particularly in rural patrilineal communities in sub-Saharan Africa, where property ownership is vested in males.

The assessment of the consequences of adolescent fertility is rendered problematic by issues of selectivity. The problems associated with adolescent fertility may stem not only from maternal age but also from other factors. For example, the pregnancy complications and elevated child mortality risks associated with adolescent childbearing may be due to low socioeconomic status, concentration of first order births among teenage women, poor nutrition, and inadequate prenatal care.

The review indicates that the social context may shape the impact of early childbearing on the life chances of the mother and child in profound ways. For sub-Saharan Africa, Bledsoe and Cohen (1993: 144) conclude that 'for very young married women living in rural areas, where society may define early childbearing as normal and even desirable, the social and economic risks of *not* bearing children probably outweigh the physical risks of bearing children'.

Where laws stipulate that pregnant girls be expelled from the school system, differences in the ability of social classes to pay for safe abortion may determine whether the adolescent girl continues her education. Moreover, the educational and employment opportunities available to adolescent parents may influence the society's attitudes towards early pregnancy. The social context of adolescent fertility and the support networks that are available to women who bear children at an early age may in turn determine not only the economic costs but also the psychological costs to women of early pregnancy.

This review has not discussed the costs of teenage pregnancy to the state but it is recognized that, in countries with well-established social programmes that provide aid, medical care, and food and housing subsidies to poor families (such as the United States), teenage pregnancy can create a huge public burden. In countries where it is difficult to procure legal and safe abortions, teenage unwanted pregnancy may exact enormous economic and social costs. Jacobson (1990) notes that about half of the Brazilian health system's obstetric budget is directed toward treating complications from induced abortion, even though such cases represent only 12 per cent of obstetric admissions. For countries trying to reduce their rates of population growth, the larger family size usually found among women who start childbearing at an early age is of additional economic and social concern.

9 Poverty and AIDS
The Vicious Circle

ALAKA MALWADE BASU

Introduction

The connection between poverty and HIV/AIDS is not, at first sight, as obvious as that between poverty and poor health in general. When the epidemic first hit the world, it seemed to be the case that the better-off groups in a population were more susceptible to getting the infection. In the industrialized world, for example, it was perceived as an illness of the rich and famous, as a number of individuals from the world of the arts and entertainment succumbed to it. In other regions, too, a similar pattern prevailed—the better-off seemed also better able to afford the lifestyle that first seemed to be the chief transmitter of the infection. For instance, among 5,900 male employees of a textile factory in Zaire, the seroprevalence rate rose with the status of the job from 2.8 per cent among workers to 4.5 per cent among foremen and 5.3 per cent among executives (Ainsworth and Over 1994).

However, this initial picture leads to a false sense of complacency about the AIDS prospects in poor countries and poor households. All the evidence shows that the profile of AIDS sufferers is changing rapidly and in the direction of increasing cases of infection among those nations and individuals least able to prevent or deal with the spread. By the late 1980s there seems to have been a stark reversal of geographical advantage in the matter of the spread of the infection (WHO 1992), with a proportionate decrease in the number of total cases and new cases in the affluent, industrialized regions of North America and Western Europe, and sub-Saharan Africa now taking the lead in the cumulative number of cases—between 6 and 7 million according to most estimates. While this temporal pattern may partly reflect a later detection and counting of cases in Africa, it does also seem to be true that the more developed countries are seeing a slowdown in the spread of the infection and in the pattern of its spread—from being a problem of homosexual communities to now being spread more by heterosexual contact for example.

Other parts of the developing world are also increasing their relative ranks in this respect. Latin America and the Caribbean are estimated to have more than a million cumulative cases of the infection, with South and Southeast Asia not far behind. In

This is a revised version of the paper prepared for the IUSSP/UNICEF/University of Florence Seminar on Demography and Poverty, Florence, 2–4 March 1995.

particular, the big worry now is that India and Thailand will soon between them account for the largest proportion of and increase in HIV/AIDS infections in the world.

The World Health Organization estimated that by 1990, 80 per cent of HIV-infected people lived in the developing world. Worse, it projects that by the year 2000, this will increase to 95 per cent. According to the World Development Report 1993 (World Bank 1993), by 1993, in Thailand one in fifty adults was infected, in sub-Saharan Africa one in forty, and in some cities in Africa, the figure was as high as one in three.

Similar variations exist in the extent of the infection *within* these underdeveloped regions. Certain areas or groups are much more at risk than others and very often these areas and groups can be recognized by their relative poverty, social disadvantage, and often political or ethnic strife. The situation of the indigenous peoples of many countries may be similarly vulnerable because they tend to be so often marginalized; very often a deterioration in their health conditions is not even noticed until large proportions of the population are affected (McKenna 1993).

Two factors seem to be changing this pattern of interregional and intraregional prevalence. First, the higher socioeconomic groups are quicker to receive and respond to information which changes high-risk behaviour. At the same time, current expenditure on AIDS prevention is skewed in exactly the opposite direction. In 1993, of the US$ 1.5 billion being spent on AIDS prevention globally, the developing world accounted for a mere US$ 200 million (World Bank 1993). And second, the higher socioeconomic groups are transmitting the infection to the poor, especially women, who are often in a relatively powerless position in matters of rich–poor interactions, as later paragraphs discuss.

This chapter sets out some of the major evidence that supports the assertion that the poverty–AIDS nexus is a vicious circle which can only get worse unless there is a new commitment to dealing with it by simultaneous interventions at several points. The interrelations between HIV/AIDS and poverty can operate at several levels and call for action to alleviate poverty itself as much as for interventions to be disproportionately targeted towards the poor, the weak, and the marginalized. The contrast seems to exist at the level of *exposure* to the infection, at the level of *acquiring* the infection once exposure occurs, and at the level of the *impact* of the infection once it occurs. In the following paragraphs, each of these levels of disadvantage is elaborated to identify some of the ways in which AIDS is increasingly a disease of poverty and underdevelopment. The chapter places a new emphasis on transmission factors, the health care system in particular, which are outside the control of individuals. It also stresses some of the poverty-related consequences of HIV/AIDS. An important conclusion is that we need much more evidence on such consequences and societal and household coping strategies, so that the limited resources available to alleviate the impact of the infection can be targeted more effectively.

But first, what does one mean by the poor? As mentioned a little earlier, this term should rightly include the weak and the marginalized together with those on low income (these categories do not necessarily completely overlap) and therefore refer to those disadvantaged on any measure that goes to make up the quality of life rather than only to those who earn an inadequate income. And *among* those with inadequate income, some sub-groups may be defined as relatively more disadvantaged than others. Thus from the point of view of the AIDS epidemic, within the ranks of the 'poor' as defined by income, certain sub-groups—migrants, women, commercial sex workers, children, and occupationally mobile groups such as truck-drivers—need to be separated out as being more vulnerable than the poor in general.

1. Poverty and the Risk of Exposure to HIV

In the case of sexual transmission of the infection, the 'risk of exposure' refers to the probability that the index person, that is, the person whose risk is being measured, will be exposed to sexual relations with an infected person. This probability depends on two factors—the number of sexual partners that the index person has and the nature of these sexual partners; the latter factor determines the probability that this sexual partner carries an HIV infection. Unfortunately, we do not have much data on sexual behaviour in the developing countries. The surveys sponsored by the Global Program on AIDS of the WHO suggest that there is great variability in sexual practices and that strict monogamy over the entire lifetime is the rule in only a very few cultures even if it is the stated norm. Both premarital and extramarital sexual activity are much more prevalent than the norm would suggest and when the norm is particularly strict, the unfortunate outcome is for this multi-partner activity to be of a more 'unsafe' kind than is the case where individuals have more sexual licence.

For example, norms about female chastity before marriage in the absence of similarly strict controls on young men (a situation that characterizes much of the Asian region) means that young men are more exposed to commercial sex with strangers. As ages at marriage rise, as they are in most of Asia, this recourse to commercial sex by young men is reported to be increasing over time in many studies. The commercial sex partners of these young men are in turn more likely to be infected themselves if they belong to the poorest groups—because, as compared to higher-priced sex workers, these need many more partners to earn a decent wage and because they are less able to enforce preventive measures such as condom use (see, for example, Ford, Fajans, and Wirawan 1994). Since it is the poorer men who frequent the lower-priced prostitutes, they are thus more likely to become infected themselves and to pass on the infection to other sexual partners including their wives.

Single male or female migration into the cities of the developing world is similarly weighted in favour of the poor. Most of this migration is driven by economic factors and can increase the risk of exposure to infection because it tends to be accompanied by a loosening of sexual constraints in the anonymity of the town or the city, by a greater control over income, and by the absence of stable sexual partners at least to begin with. The unprecedented rates of migration and urbanization in most of the developing world are therefore a major contributor to the spread of the infection among the poor.

The probability of exposure to an HIV-infected partner also rises with the prevalence of the infection in a society. Given the current situation of HIV infection in the developing world, including Asia (for example, one in fifty adults may be currently infected in Thailand), the index person in many parts of the developing world is naturally at greater risk of exposure to the infection. This situation can only get worse if the projected rise in cases in the developing countries is realized.

The other major mode of transmission, intravenous drug use, is also associated with poverty in the contemporary world. For example, Ford and Koetsawang (1991) document the heroin addiction which plagues much of northern Thailand and which may be attributed to the poverty of the surrounding regions and the civil turmoil which make heroin production a major commercial activity. Myanmar, and those parts of India—and, increasingly, China—that border it, represent another major pocket of drug use, poverty, and civil unrest.

The prevalence of HIV infection in intravenous drug users has also risen by leaps and bounds in all parts of the developing world. For example, about 71 per cent of intravenous drug users were found to be HIV-positive in Myanmar in 1991; the figure was 45 per cent for those in northeast India (UNDP 1992). These figures are attributed largely to the sharing of infected needles, but are also certainly fuelled by the question of overlapping categories—after all, drug users are also sexually active. While an important part of this sharing is certainly associated with the culture of drug use, a large part is also the result of poverty—new, disposable needles come at a price and a price which cannot be easily met for three reasons. First, intravenous drug users are more likely to belong to the poorer sections of society. Second, addictive drug use itself impoverishes the user as it closes off avenues of employment. And third, the prohibitive cost of drugs leave little money for the addicted user to buy clean needles.

Poor children represent yet another important and growing category of high-risk individuals. This group consists largely of the floating urban population of young boys and girls that make up the slum or street life of the cities in most developing and many developed countries. The anarchy and imposed self-sufficiency of this group often mean that they are easy prey to two of the common routes to HIV infection—drug use and commercial or non-transactional multi-partner sex (see, for example, Connolly and Franchet 1993; Miguez-Burbano *et al.* 1993).

Finally, the maternal mode of transmission needs a special mention in the context of poverty, if only to illustrate how otherwise health-promoting behaviours like prolonged breastfeeding can become risky in the new world of HIV and AIDS. It is unfortunately ironical that with the spread of the epidemic to the poorer parts of the world, precisely those practices which are more common among the poor and which protect their health in an otherwise high-risk health environment may now contribute to the spread of HIV infection. The policy implications of this development are unclear to say the least; but as pointed out by Latham (1993), one does need to weigh the relatively small risks of HIV transmission through breastfeeding against the tremendous risks of gastrointestinal and other infections through not breast-feeding.

2. Poverty and the Risk of HIV Transmission

Once an index person has sexual intercourse with an infected person, it does not follow that he or she will get the infection. Several mediating factors seem to determine the probability that sex with an infected partner will lead to infection. Most of these mediating factors are currently more intense among the poor. To begin with, the poor are at greater risk of getting the infection once they enter sexual relations with infected partners because they are less likely to be practising safe sex in the sense of using condoms. While ignorance about the value of condoms is certainly a factor in this situation, the more practical issue of access to condoms is also an important constraint on use by the poor. Defining access as the knowledge of a source of supply within thirty minutes, the World Health Organization's Global Programme on AIDS (GPA) surveys in Africa found that only 15–38 per cent of men had effective access to condoms (Cleland and Way 1994). While the situation in Asia on this score may be less disastrous because of a history of national family planning programmes, many of these programmes have over time reduced their emphasis on condoms and concentrated on what appear to be more effective contra-ceptive methods like the pill and sterilization.

Then there is the important role of existing sexually transmitted disease in either the infected person or his/her non-infected partner in increasing the chance of trans-mission of the HIV virus. From all accounts, all over the developing world, the prevalence and intensity of STDs is high and much greater among the poor. For example, intensive studies of women in India, Bangladesh, and Egypt have found reproductive tract infection rates ranging from 52 per cent to 92 per cent, less than half of which were recognized by the women as abnormal. This level of infection and, especially, the inability even to recognize a health problem are attributable to several factors, some of them cultural, but a large number related to household poverty and poor access to information and services for care. Chancroid is similarly highly endemic in many tropical regions, especially in Southeast Asia, where high levels of commercial sexual activity only make the problem worse.

Where poor women are concerned, the risk of exposure leading to infection is even greater than it is for poor men. The evidence thus far is that the vast majority of women infected with AIDS have received the infection through heterosexual intercourse. Two groups of vulnerable women may be identified—women as wives or partners in stable unions, and women as sexual partners in casual or temporary unions, whether or not such relationships have a transactional element to them. In both cases one or more of two attributes contribute to their special vulnerability—their low economic status and the gender inequalities that characterize their relationships.

The special disadvantage of poverty is easy to see. It is also easy to see why such economic dependency is influenced by and in turn breeds gender inequalities. In the specific context of increasing the risk of getting an HIV infection, the main culprit is the fact that the conditions under which sexual relations take place are not in the control of women (see also Gage, Chapter 8 above).

Within marriage or stable unions, women are exposed to the risk of infection when their partners are infected and they do not have the means or authority to impose safe sexual behaviour. The AIDS prevention lesson of strict monogamy is irrelevant to such women because all accounts indicate that the large majority of HIV-positive women are in fact monogamous (Reid 1993). What they lack is monogamous partners. But the light on the horizon is the emerging evidence, at least from Africa, that thanks to the new knowledge about AIDS, sexually transmitted infection in a husband is slowly becoming a legitimate reason for the wife's refusal to have sex with him, or at least refusal to have unprotected sex with him (see, for example, Orubuloye, Caldwell, and Caldwell 1991; Awusabo-Asare *et al.* 1993). But this is still a very new consciousness, and community recognition about female rights and the large numbers of married women who are infected suggests that we have far to go.

This legitimization has in any case not reached Asia where gender relations have traditionally been more unequal and where the AIDS epidemic is less advanced than in Africa, so that there is not enough public support for such rights of refusal. In any case, the right can only be exercised when an infection in the husband has been identified. The meagre number of identified HIV-positive and AIDS cases in much of Asia and the actual numbers suggested by more intensive studies suggest that a large amount of unsafe sex can take place simply because partners do not know each other's infection status.

What about women in temporary or multi-partner sexual unions? While it is true that an important proportion of such women are influenced by the forces of socio-economic and cultural modernization, the poverty angle comes in when one looks at two groups of women—commercial sex workers and young girls getting into relationships with much older men because of the economic protection that they receive in return. The situation with regard to commercial sex workers has been discussed extensively in the literature and does not need detailed repetition here. We know that most commercial sex workers are motivated by their extreme poverty, the economic responsibility they frequently take for their parental families (the literature on commercial sex workers in Thailand is particularly emphatic on this score), and their lack of access to other forms of employment. We also know that very often, this same poverty makes it difficult for them to negotiate safe sexual relations with their clients.

The other group of vulnerable women, those who get into semi-stable sexual relationships with economically powerful older men deserve special mention for more than one reason. To begin with, their numbers seem to be increasing, caused at least in part by this group's growing impoverishment which some researchers attribute to new economic policies in the Third World and especially in Africa. This impoverishment often means that even expenses such as school fees need a sponsor and the 'sugar daddies' that provide such sponsorship want their pound of flesh. Second, these relationships seem to involve younger and younger girls, at least partly because older men are in fact trying to hedge their own vulnerability to HIV by seeking out much younger girls (National Academy of Sciences 1993). But there is also growing evidence that some kind of biological vulnerability may make younger girls (and post-menopausal women) more at risk of getting an HIV infection from an infected sexual partner (Reid 1993).

In the highly gender-stratified societies of Asia, while it is not clear that the position of upper-class women in the matter of demanding safe sexual relations within marriage is much better than that of poor women, it does seem to be the case that in sex outside marriage, especially in commercial sex, the poor woman is much more handicapped in this respect than is her richer counterpart. For example, Ford, Fajans, and Wirawan (1994) report in their Indonesian study that women working in low-priced brothels are less likely to know about HIV/AIDS and less likely to use condoms than women charging a higher price and operating in different locations— in the week before the survey, the former had used condoms during 19 per cent of acts of sexual intercourse compared to 71-per-cent use by those in the high-priced category. Similarly, Podhisita *et al.* (1994) describe the unwillingness of brothel owners to allow their workers access to health check-ups and treatment and their insistence that women continue to work during illness—conditions which the more expensive, self-employed commercial sex worker has much more control over.

Poor women also seem to be disproportionately handicapped in their vulnerability to transmission because of a range of reproductive tract infections which leave the genital tract of the woman bruised or damaged. The role of poverty in increasing the vulnerability of women to HIV is doubly underscored when it is such RTIs and STDs that facilitate the HIV infection (McNamara 1993). Quite apart from the cultural constraints that prevent women in many developing countries from seeking medical attention for STDs, underlying poverty and inadequate health services are undoubtedly an important factor in such negligence and consequently increased vulnerability to AIDS.

2.1. The Health Care System as Aggravator

The poverty–health care nexus is relevant to AIDS in more ways than the obvious one of poverty decreasing the access to health care in the case of an HIV infection and health care services being unwilling or unable to deal with AIDS patients. In a system of poverty, the health care system can, far from mitigating the ill effects of HIV/AIDS, in fact contribute to the spread of the infection, a factor that is as yet insufficiently incorporated into standard sexual and drug-related models of HIV transmission. The only role that the health care system is currently recognized as playing in the transmission of the HIV virus is through its use of untested or improperly tested blood and blood products.

One result of this research neglect is that we do not really know how transmissible the HIV virus is by unhygienic health care practices, although one may make some educated guesses based on the evidence of transmission by other analogous sources, such as needles among drug users. Given the paucity of data on safe health care provision practices too, much of the rest of this section relies on the information from recent studies on this subject in India, information which does not seem at all inconsistent with the expected situation in other poor countries.

Injections should not normally be a source of HIV infection in the general population (as opposed to intravenous drug users), but this situation may change as the total amount of infection in a country increases. In particular, one would expect the combination of poverty and ignorance (or powerlessness) to be highly significant in increasing the risk of infection through unsterile needles used by the health system, a situation made even more lethal by the increasingly common tendency to demand and be given injections for a range of illnesses even when they are not called for (for a discussion of the value attached to injections in Third World settings, see Wyatt 1984).

The invidious process of equating injections (even when they are only water injections) with treatment has been well brought out in several studies, which also generally conclude that the private health sector is the bigger culprit on this count and that the poor are the bigger victims. For example, one study in Maharashtra, India, found that in its sample, 72 per cent of diarrhoea incidents, 67 per cent of coughs and colds, 87 per cent of malaria cases, 61 per cent of measles cases, and 76 per cent of heart ailments were treated by the patients being given injections (Duggal and Amin 1989). In a recent Delhi study (Basu *et al* 1994), injection use was found to be as rampant and, what was even more disappointing, in only about half the cases was it definitely known that a disposable needle had been used (the fact that such 'disposable' needles often reappear in hospitals or, repackaged, in chemists' shops, is another matter which can only make things worse in current situations of poverty).

These are high levels of use and high levels of risk by any reckoning. They become even more worrying when one tries to disaggregate the population to identify the groups most at risk. All data on income differentials (for example, Basu *et al.* 1994) indicate that the poor are at much greater risk of acquiring infection through the use of unsafe needles. Even when the health care provider is the same, the private sector for example, the rich generally have access to a well-qualified and relatively responsible private health care structure, while the poor end up going to doctors who often do not have a formal medical qualification, and who usually charge a flat fee for a consultation and an injection. One study in Madhya Pradesh, India found that among cases of illness treated by the private sector, 52 per cent of the rural and 18 per cent of the urban cases had been seen by licentiates and registered medical practitioners (which is different from a formally qualified medical practitioner) (George, Shah, and Nandraj 1993). There is also evidence of the common practice of private clinics in many poor areas being manned by compounders, medical assistants, and sometimes even the spouses of doctors (see, for example, Nandraj 1994).

Not only do the poor therefore face worse health care conditions, they are usually much more likely to not even know that they are being thus undersold. This kind of finding underscores the greater exploitability of the poor when they do not even think it necessary to ask questions about matters such as the use of a safe needle. Such implicit faith in the medical system must be honoured by the state through both the public and private sectors, quite apart from efforts to increase client awareness on these issues. Even more damaging in its potential impact is the usual finding that even when the poor do know that certain services are risky and that they have the right to demand safety, they do not have the power to make such demands. Most socioeconomically depressed respondents in health studies stress that they have no way of knowing what is being done to an ill relative inside the operation or treatment room. Nor do they dare to demand either more information or the guarantee of safe medical practices. And nor are their own attitudes on such matters very encouraging, indicating the multiple fronts on which the battle against unhealthy health care must be fought. A number of respondents in the Basu *et al.* study (1994), for example, were most aggrieved when their medical bills were raised because the doctor now wanted to use a disposable needle; they were even more affronted when the doctor asked them to buy a disposable needle from the chemist—obviously the risks posed by unsterile needles are not perceived by many parts of the population.

The giving and taking of infected blood is believed to be another important source of HIV transmission. But what is not often considered is that the giving and taking of blood may have some risks associated with the needle used, apart from the risk associated with contaminated blood. By this reasoning, the blood donor is also at risk, just as the receiver of a blood transfusion is. It is revealing that once again, the ignorance about the kind of needle used in a blood transaction is so rampant— in the Delhi study (Basu *et al.* 1994), 31 per cent of donors and 65 per cent of recipients had no idea what kind of needle had been used. This is also an interesting demonstration of relative power. The giver (in this case the blood donor) is in a much better position to demand healthy conditions (that is, a sterile needle) than the taker (the blood receiver in this case) from the health care system.

Over time, as the AIDS awareness campaign reduces individual-level high-risk behaviour, the role of the health care system as an active transmitter of the infection is likely to increase (see also Ramasubban 1991). Unhygienic health care delivery practices have already been mentioned. In addition, one should probably add the role of the health care system in indirect transmission through its inability to effectively treat an important facilitating condition—sexually transmitted diseases, especially in women. According to some estimates, sexually transmitted diseases are the third major communicable disease group in India (Kapur 1982) and it bears mentioning that the literature lays the blame for the high levels of such infection in women on both the existing patriarchal structure and the low status of women in general and on a health system which is insensitive to the special needs of such women. Why do field studies find such a high level of STDs in women and clinic statistics still report such low numbers of women coming for treatment in so many parts of the Third World? Addressing the ignorance and shyness which lie behind such behaviour should be as much a part of health promotion strategy as the provision of effective curative services.

Finally, the health care system is also an abettor in the spread of AIDS through negative action. Given that a large part of the infective stage is asymptomatic, unless a mechanism exists to encourage high-risk individuals to seek diagnosis of the infection, backed up by access to services for such diagnosis, infected individuals will unwittingly spread the virus through ignorance about their own infective status. Of course there is also some evidence that in fact high risk behaviour often increases with the knowledge that a person is HIV-infected, but if this is true, it only makes the case for effective IEC (information, education, and communication) activities even stronger.

3. Poverty and the Impact of HIV/AIDS

AIDS prevention is seen as an essential and major part of any AIDS strategy today. The value of such a strategy is rightly reinforced by the fact that the disease is always fatal and is unlikely to become curable in the near future. At the same time, given the number of people already believed to be infected, a second dimension of the AIDS problem needs much greater attention than it has hitherto received. This is the need for a strategy to deal with the inevitable impact of the disease in those currently infected as well as in the new cases of infection that will undoubtedly occur even if at a slower rate (that is, if preventive strategies are effective).

This second dimension, that is, that of the impact of AIDS, is relatively tangentially considered in policy-making as yet; moreover when it is considered, it is done so more often as a justification for pumping more resources into prevention than for increasing the allocation for interventions which mitigate the adverse impact of the disease. For example, the findings of studies on the sectoral implications of an AIDS-infected workforce are more likely at the present time to be used to persuade employers in different sectors of the economy to motivate their employees to practise safe sexual behaviour than to help employers to plan to deal with the less efficient workforce which may already be on its way.

Even when there is a specific concern with the potential and actual impact of AIDS, this concern is usually limited in its scope and almost entirely concerned with two possible impacts—the psychological impact of this kind of socially debilitating disease on sufferers and their families, and the impact in terms of the high costs of medical treatment. Proposed strategies therefore centre around counselling services and an upgrading of the health sector to meet the new demands that will be made on it. While it is true that both these effects—on the psychology of the sufferer and on the payer of medical costs—are substantial and cannot be ignored, there are other economic and social costs which are equally devastating and which have not even begun to be addressed.

These costs are unique to AIDS because of the unique profile of AIDS sufferers—predominantly of working age and having a high number of economic, social, and emotional dependents. The incapacitation and death of a person in this category entails costs which go well beyond the welfare of the sufferer himself, and are not just of an emotional nature.

In recent times there have been attempts to estimate some of the economic costs of a potential epidemic of AIDS on the state and on different sectors of the economy (see, among others, Cohen 1993; Bloom and Gliend 1992; Barnett and Blaikie 1990). Many of these studies document the high economic burden that national economies or at least specific sectors of such economies will face if current trends in rising HIV/AIDS prevalence continue.

But while such modelling of macro effects is necessary, it must be noted that there are other relatively hidden costs which are potentially even more drastic. These are the costs to the *households* of AIDS sufferers, costs which the households themselves usually seek to meet to a large extent, in the developing countries at least. But if the expected rise in AIDS infection and mortality does occur, these costs will be increasingly difficult to meet by the households affected and call for an urgent review of current strategies to help individuals *and their families* to cope with the consequences of the disease.

Moreover, while the economic impact on a society or on a country of a rise in adult morbidity and mortality of the kind predicted by a rise in AIDS is a rightful matter for concern, this should be primarily because the economic wellbeing of a society or nation influences the wellbeing of its people—as individuals or households. And naturally, the wellbeing of the households directly experiencing the adult morbidity or mortality will be even more affected than the wellbeing of others who face more of the indirect fallout of the epidemic.

However, the impact on households cannot really be derived from the impact on the larger economy. The discrepancy is particularly acute in situations in which there is a labour surplus and it is the poor and the unskilled who are the primary victims of the disease. The consequent sectoral or national impact on the economy can in such cases reflect the bare tip of what happens to the economic situations of suffering households themselves. In addition, the death of an adult of productive age (which is what the typical AIDS sufferer usually is) inflicts a cost on the household which cannot be captured by any simple measures such as loss of income. The significant factor here is *adult* mortality, whether or not the immediate underlying cause is AIDS. Indeed, if HIV infection does increase as expected in poor countries, the immediate cause of death will usually be one of the several infections which currently account for only a small proportion of all mortality. But AIDS-related morbidity and mortality is also expected to have many additional ramifications which mortality from other direct causes may not have (including an economic impact generated by the possible victimization of sufferers and their families).

At the same time, just as populations are not homogeneous with respect to their vulnerability to acquiring HIV infection, nor are they homogeneous with respect to their experience of the costs of the infection once it does occur and with respect to their ability to cope with these costs. These differentials must be recognized, identified, and exploited to get the greatest benefit out of the resources allotted for impact interventions. As yet, there is a specific recognition of the differentials in risk that exist and the consequent need to tailor preventive strategies to specific risk groups, but there is much less awareness of the implications of differential impact of the disease.

One of the most obvious determinants of such impact is income. By income, one refers to several levels—the income of the individual or household faced with AIDS; the income or resource base of the larger national or regional environment in which the infection occurs; and the kind of economic system that operates—its accent on state responsibility for welfare, etc.

Very broadly, the direct household costs of an HIV/AIDS infection are incurred at two different times—during the active stages of the infection and after the patient's inevitable death and, in the first of these two periods, can be of two kinds —medical and non-medical. The non-medical costs are in turn composed of the indirect expenses associated with ill health such as special food, transport, and (very importantly) the opportunity costs of the care-givers' time; and the direct costs of the loss of the income incurred by the victim of the infection. All estimates suggest that the last of these is the most major in terms of both amount and relevance (see, for example, Bloom and Glied 1993, UNDP 1992), largely because it extends into both the time periods mentioned.

The poverty relationship with the costs of AIDS to households can be visualized at two levels. First, AIDS can result in the increased impoverishment of households. Second, the poverty level of a household to begin with can affect the household's abilities to deal with the illness and the nature of any subsequent impoverishment. This second impact becomes even more devastating if it is true, as is now being suggested in the literature, that poverty significantly reduces the length of the incubation period of the virus (see, for example, Ainsworth and Over 1994; Gilks 1993); this means that poor households face the double disadvantage of having even less time to adjust to the oncoming impact of the illness.

Besides income, other socioeconomic variables can lead to potential contradictions in the impact of AIDS as distinct from adult illness and death in general. For example because the disease can be so prolonged, there is a need for relatively long-term health care and, by extension, a care-giver; and because it is always fatal, there is always a loss of income when the victim has been an economically active person, as he is usually likely to have been, in the case of male sufferers.

The overall finding from the few existing studies—that economic status conditions the ways in which a household can handle the incapacitation or death of an adult male—is consistent with expectations. For example, there are stark economic differentials in the access to formal insurance systems to pay for health and death-related expenses. In the Delhi study (Basu *et al.* 1994) even the figure of 40 per cent of the highest income group having any kind of personal insurance seems very high when compared to the level in the lower income categories (9 per cent). Similarly, 42 per cent of respondents who were professionals had their own insurance cover, compared to 8 per cent of those in manual and unskilled populations, again a vast difference, made more vast by the fact that the poorest groups are more vulnerable to the disease and therefore have greater need for some kind of insurance cover.

The data also suggest quite naturally that it is much easier for the relatively rich to maintain the old tempo of life in the event of the breadwinner's incapacitation; their own savings are more often enough at least for a temporary tiding over of difficulties. On the other hand, the impact of illness starts telling on poor households very quickly.

Educational differences are in the same general direction as those for income and do not need separate elaboration, except to point out that education is more than a proxy for income; it also has a role to play in its own right through the modernization it confers and, more importantly, through the greater ease it affords in using formal institutions to one's benefit; there is a large literature now on the confidence associated with education which operates independently of the education–income link and which helps individuals in poor countries to deal more effectively with a range of institutions from hospitals to banks.

In addition to the role of income and economic status in mediating the household impact of AIDS, there is also, of course, the converse relationship. That is, there is the impact *on* household poverty of an illness such as HIV/AIDS. This can be substantial by any reckoning and can be expected to result, as pointed out by Bloom and Glied (1993), in widening income inequalities in a country. This is not just because the poor are disproportionately vulnerable to getting the infection; as importantly, it is because they are also more affected by the illness once it occurs.

But in addition, *all* AIDS affected households are likely to experience some pauperization as a result of the disease. This is largely because not only is there a direct cost of illness (the expenses of medical care, personal care, etc.) which are common to all illnesses, but the medical costs of AIDS in turn are likely to be much larger than those associated with other ailments, one reason being the longer duration of the disease and the other being the more costly medicines needed to temper its impact. But, as demonstrated by Bloom and Glied (1993), the non-medical costs of AIDS can be even more crippling and impoverishing. These arise directly from the loss of income associated with an AIDS victim both during ill health and after the inevitable death, given that AIDS victims are, at least at present, disproportionately from the young productive ages, as well as indirectly from the opportunity costs of care-givers' time.

Of course, this impact of HIV/AIDS on poverty is also a function of the poverty of households to begin with and the paucity of state mechanisms to cushion some of the impact. For example, in a situation of poor health services, little insurance cover and poor access to credit (a combination of circumstances not at all uncommon in much of the developing world), the usurious loans that poor families need to tide themselves over a crisis can be crippling when the crisis is as long-drawn out as in the case of AIDS.

The impoverishment of an affected household is also caused by the fact that even if another household member enters the labour force he or she can rarely earn enough to substitute for the lost income (Feachem *et al.* 1991). Such an interpretation probably explains the finding in a Bangladesh study (Pryer 1989) that dependency ratios *decreased* when the household head was incapacitated—more than one additional earner was now presumably needed to make up for the income loss (in fact this loss was rarely made up; overall poverty tended to increase in such households).

This is only natural since if an equally able potential earner already existed in the household, he/she would be likely to be already in the labour force. This partly explains the greater poverty of female-headed households; so often the women of such households have become heads only after a sudden unexpected crisis. Female-headed households also have several other characteristics that need to be better understood given the possibility that the AIDS epidemic will greatly increase their numbers. In the case of such AIDS generated households, there is also the complicating factor that the female heads themselves are also likely to be infected with the HIV virus.

These kinds of coping strategies affect general household welfare in ways which are not all linked to the direct income loss associated with AIDS. For example, if the coping strategy includes a young mother entering the labour force, there is likely to be some adverse impact on child health (see, for example, Basu and Basu 1991). When this happens, there may also be a tendency to withdraw older children from other activities such as school to take over household responsibilities—a course of action which may affect the quality of life of these older children as well as of the younger siblings under their care. There is also the income-independent impact on child health and welfare of an ill or missing parent, though admittedly this negative impact is greater for motherless than for fatherless children (see, for example, Koenig *et al.* 1988; Pryer 1989).

3.1. Women's Status

The last section assumed that the victim of an HIV/AIDS infection was always male. But of course that is not the case and as the numbers of infected women rise, it is worthwhile considering the potential impact of the death of an adult female on her household. In addition, it is worth looking at some of the ways in which the (often culturally determined) position of women affects the household impact of an illness such as AIDS in males.

There is now a growing recognition that women play an important economic role, whatever the macrostatistics on income and employment may say. In turn, this implies an economic cost to women's debilitation and death. Case studies of households in which a woman had died (Basu *et al.* 1994) underline the weaker economic position of the household after her death even when she had not been economically productive herself. In such cases, the main economic loss was attributed by her survivors to the loss of ability to control and manage the household budget.

There is also some evidence that female victims of AIDS tend to be younger than male victims; in some parts of the world this may be linked to the tendency to seek younger and younger women (as well as virgins) by men who practise multi-partner sex (for example, see Carael and Piot 1992 on the situation in sub-Saharan Africa). This means that the affected women are likely to be in more productive age groups; they are also likely to have young children on whom the impact of their illness and death is greater, and they are also likely to bear children after getting the infection, thus increasing the chances of infecting their children.

The relationship between orphanhood and child health has been mentioned earlier. Maternal orphans seem to suffer even more in this respect than paternal orphans. There is also some evidence now from Africa which suggests that extrapolating from the general female mortality cases in fact underestimates the potential impact of AIDS in women (Anderson 1994). Not only did the children of women who had lost their mothers to AIDS experience higher mortality, the children of HIV-infected mothers were actually most likely to die while their mothers were still alive. This was because the mother became too ill to care for her children some time before she died, while the community did not step in to help until she had actually died. In the present context, the possibility of similar results should also depend on the role of the larger family structure in mitigating the impact of AIDS-related morbidity and mortality, as discussed in the last section.

When the sufferer of an HIV/AIDS infection is a migrant with economic responsibility for wider kin networks in the village of origin, it is easy to see that the impact of his infection can extend geographically to affect the poverty levels of those outside his immediate household. These effects are difficult to quantify but a truly sensitive AIDS policy will have to take such things into account when it targets the families of poor sufferers of the illness. An important example of this kind involves the extremely high levels of HIV infection among commercial sex workers in the large cities of the developing world. The impact on (as opposed to the impact of) this category of female victim of HIV/AIDS has received insufficient attention in the academic literature and in the policy process. Most of these women are young, have young children, and have few other means of support. In addition, we have enough empirical evidence to conclude that many of these sex workers are the backbone of their parental family's survival in the villages that they come from and their inability to continue to send money home can have large scale negative impacts on the rural economy.

The above findings are concerned with the impact of women getting AIDS. There is another relevant aspect of the gender and AIDS question in poor households. Does the role of women have any bearing on the household's ability to meet the economic burden of AIDS in one of its members? Conversely, does AIDS-related morbidity and mortality among men affect the role of women?

When a male adult of productive age acquires a debilitating infection such as AIDS, the household impact and response should be heavily conditioned by the presence and position of its women. To begin with the illness stage, all over the world, women have traditionally been the care-givers in times of illness and in a country like India, where so much of the medical care burden is borne directly by the household rather than by the hospital, the responsibility of women is much greater. What does this additional, prolonged care-giving activity by women mean to the household?

That would depend on the position of women to begin with. One would expect that where women are economically active, their possible withdrawal from the labour force to take care of the ill, will cause some household impoverishment. At the same time, if anyone is to leave the labour force to care for the ill, it is the women, because they are traditionally believed to be better at care and also because their contributions to the household income are usually smaller than male contributions.

But there are important socioeconomic variations in female employment within a population. In particular, it is often the worst-off groups that are most likely to have working women. For example, in the Indian study (Basu *et al.* 1994) 25 per cent of the wives of illiterate men were employed (compared to 9 per cent of those with 8–12 years of schooling); 17 per cent of the lowest income respondent wives were working (compared to 7 per cent of those earning 3000–7000 rupees per month).

In such disadvantaged households, women's work is an essential part of family income compared to the relatively better-off households, in which the women have a smaller need to work, and the most well-off households, where women are again more economically active, but for reasons other than income need. If such poor women are now withdrawn from labour because their care-giving activities are needed at home, there is a resulting pauperization, because most of these women are unlikely to be in occupations which allow paid leave and because in any case, AIDS suffering is so prolonged that any employee benefits that did exist would soon cease to apply.

But even when women do not work, the additional care-giving they are required to take on can have several adverse effects on the household in general. They themselves are of course now more burdened with overall work: all studies of time-allocation by women indicate that additional jobs (within or outside the home) are taken up without existing domestic responsibilities being lessened, and the primary casualty is their time for leisure. But there is also some evidence that increased time spent on health care reduces the time available for other domestic maintenance activities, with possibly adverse effects to general household health and welfare. These costs are compounded by the nature of AIDS transmission—the wife of the AIDS victim is quite likely to be infected herself, so that there is a gradual lessening of her physical capabilities.

The time available for childcare is one such activity and its impact on child health has already been mentioned. In addition the nutritional status of the household may suffer because more has now to be bought in the market which was previously produced or at least processed in the home by the women. The supplementation of women's household work with the labour of other household members (usually daughters) also has a potential cost to these other household members themselves, as well as to the rest of the family, because of their relatively greater inefficiency. At this point, it must be added that a recognition of the woman's care-giving role is not tantamount to the policy implication that this role must therefore be exploited, and that the state can thus abdicate its own responsibility for the care of the severely ill. All that it underscores is that the family is an important location of such care and must be supported in this activity, given that non-domiciliary services for health care are unlikely to match the need for them.

When the male AIDS victim dies, there are other costs to the household which are mediated by the position of women. On the one hand there can be a rise in the proportion of women-headed households. The literature on the greater poverty and exploitation of female-headed households is large and not discussed here, but this is an important potential impact of AIDS to be considered.

Then there is the role of women in income-earning when the male breadwinner is dead. Here the hold of culture is strong. In conservative cultures, not only do women not go out to work much; they are also less likely to do so in the event of family hardship. Cultural inhibitions are a very frequently given reason for women not going out to work, so that even in the nuclear self-employed families it is often another male relative rather than the wife that is expected to take over the family enterprise. This finding has important implications for the status of women, since one form of authority replaces another in such cases.

Finally, there is one gender-linked aspect of migration with important implications for AIDS. This is the tendency for large numbers of male rural–urban to move singly or with other men, leaving their families behind in the village. In addition to the role of poverty in encouraging single migration, as already mentioned, there also seems to be a cultural element involved (Banerjee 1984; Basu, Basu, and Ray 1987), with individual male migration being more common in those regions where women are more secluded. The move to the city, and especially a move in which women are excluded, has several implications for the spread of AIDS. New sexual subcultures are generated both because of the greater freedom that the single male experiences in the city, as well as because of the greater urge to exercise this freedom, in the absence of a sexual relationship at home. The geographical spread of the infection is also larger in such cases, because the single migrant naturally retains much stronger ties with his village of origin than the family migrant (Basu, Basu, and Ray 1987).

Conclusion

This chapter has tried to outline some of the unique risks of poverty to HIV/AIDS. It has distinguished between the role of poverty in increasing the vulnerability to acquiring the infection and the role of poverty in influencing the impact of the infection once it has occurred. Several (overlapping) categories of the poor were identified as being particularly vulnerable on both these counts—those in particular geographical areas, migrants, women, children, and drug-users. This is not at all to identify AIDS intrinsically as a 'disease of poverty' (after all, it seems to have started out as a disease of affluence), but to underscore that it has become over time an increasingly common outcome of the conditions which go to make up the life of poverty—economic hardship, sexual powerlessness, poor health services, and perhaps biological vulnerability. Even worse, its prevalence has increased in precisely that group—the poor—which is least able to deal with the social and economic devastation that the infection brings in its wake.

10 Household Labour Allocation and Mobility in Times of Crisis

RENÉ WÉRY WITH CHRISTINE OPPONG

Introduction

This chapter is concerned with a variety of 'coping mechanisms' adopted to combat poverty at the household or individual level. Two related types of adaptation are dealt with: geographical mobility (temporary and permanent) and the changes in volume, types, distribution, and allocations of household labour.

A major theme is the fact that the globalization of the world's economy, has affected the international divisions of labour. Several dramatic changes have taken place in labour markets with regard to the roles played by female as well as male workers. One has been the increasing feminization of labour force and employment. Whilst recorded female labour force participation rates have been rising, in many cases those for men are on the decline. At the same time, more people than ever before are now on the move, both inside and across national borders, in search of work and less harsh living conditions. This global mobility and dispersal is affecting the residential patterns of kin, spouses, parents, and children and changing the traditional divisions of labour between the sexes and age groups. It is also profoundly altering sexual behaviour patterns and relationships, the organization of domestic groups, the relationships between family members, and the institutions of marriage and parenthood. A widely observed phenomenon is the increasing number of single mothers; in fact, the most rapidly increasing type of domestic group. Another phenomenon is the rising commoditization of sexual and domestic services.

There is general evidence that women and their children in all societies tend to form the majority of the poor, because they are less likely to have adequate access to economic and other resources: land, capital, employment, etc. The number and proportion of children in their sole charge are growing, and the number of women living in absolute poverty is increasing at a faster rate than for men.

There is, in addition, evidence that within households women bear disproportionately greater shares of the poverty burdens and that they experience poverty differently from men because of their various gender-based entitlements and responsibilities. Given their immediate and primary responsibilities for providing food for their children, they are forced to make many of the adjustments in household coping and management strategies to enable family members to survive.

The coping mechanisms which were seen in the 1960s and 1970s as cost-effective survival strategies have changed in nature with the growing extent and deepening of poverty, and particularly the rural to urban migration of relatively well-educated migrants, who succeeded in finding jobs after a time of adjustment in the labour market. Actual processes may indirectly contribute to further increase poverty. With the persistent crisis Africa has been facing for two decades now, the probability of a rural migrant successfully finding employment in an involuting labour market has decreased substantially. International migration from poverty-stricken countries or whole regions to economically fast-growing regions has become the rational alternative. However, developed countries and previously labour-importing countries also now have their own problems, including rising unemployment. Consequently, for many poor populations in the world, the range of available safe havens now look more constricted, if not increasingly hopeless. A stark example is provided by the escalating migration of women from all regions who feel compelled by poverty to enter into the 'entertainment business', despite the very high risks of HIV infection.

1. Increasing Pauperization and Inequality

A highly aggregate but significant measure of the widening poverty gap between the richest and the poorest countries is that in 1960 the income of the richest 20 per cent of world population was twenty times greater than the income of the poorest 20 per cent. In 1990 the ratio had changed to 60:1 (ILO 1995a). The overall economic performance of the Asian region as a whole has, generally, been remarkable. According to the 1992 World Development Report estimates, the proportion of the population below the World Bank's poverty line is likely to have decreased between 1985 and 1990 in South Asia from 51.8 to 49 per cent. Nevertheless, in absolute terms, half of the world's poor is concentrated in South Asia and the actual numbers of poor have, in fact, increased, staying above half a billion. Income distribution has not followed economic growth, throwing more people into poverty and exclusion. This is a demonstrable failure of growth strategies on the part of many countries. This is corroborated by the fact that progress in the UNDP's Human Development Index (HDI) has been slow in South Asia.

In sub-Saharan Africa, the proportion of the population below the poverty line has increased and, given the very high rate of population growth, this means that the number of poor has increased by more than 30 million over five years. Likewise, the proportion of the population below the poverty line has increased in the Middle East and North Africa (from 30.6 to 33.1 per cent) and Latin America and the Caribbean (from 22.4 to 25.5 per cent). However, the situation of sub-Saharan Africa is the gloomiest, since the majority of its countries feature at the bottom of the HDI.[1]

---

[1] Among the 43 countries least developed in terms of the index, thirty-two are in sub-Saharan Africa. In fact a majority of African countries are located lower down the scale of the HDI than is warranted simply in terms of GDP per capita, indicating that in terms of the socio-demographic components of the index the levels they have achieved are below average.

Moreover, when viewed in a time perspective, the situation in sub-Saharan Africa is becoming progressively worse.[2]

The composition of the impoverished population has also changed considerably over three decades of 'development'. Except for a few developing countries, the development strategy followed in the 1960s and 1970s created large imbalances between rural and urban areas, which became a cause of rural exodus. At the same time there was a low rate of labour absorption in a relatively highly capital-intensive and high-wages sector. Meanwhile, employment in the public sector grew extremely rapidly in certain countries but reputedly without creation of value, though this point is debatable if the impacts of free health and education systems on the development and sustainability of human capital are considered (Zuckerman 1989). This trend was stopped in the 1980s by the stabilization policies and structural adjustment programmes, which threw considerable numbers of civil servants onto labour markets, resulting in public sector employment decreases in all developing regions except Asia. Furthermore, the 1980s crisis was accompanied by an absolute decrease in employment opportunities in the manufacturing sector. This declined in Africa during the period at 0.5 per cent per annum. In the case of Ghana, half of its modern sector employment was apparently lost during that period (ILO 1995c).

For a time, labour surplus has been absorbed in the so-called urban informal sector, but at low levels of productivity. It is estimated that the urban informal sector employs over 60 per cent of the African urban labour force and about 20 per cent in Latin America (ILO 1995c). Meanwhile, the capacity of absorption of the informal sector is not infinite and is certainly constrained to the extent that its growth depends partly on the growth of the modern sector. Consequently, under-employment and unemployment have been rising. Urban unemployment rates approximately doubled in the worst period of the crisis in Latin America, and in Africa too, the rate of unemployment also roughly doubled during the 1980s, reaching 20 per cent of the recorded labour force (ILO 1995c). In contrast with Latin America, where the employment situation has improved in recent years, African unemployment keeps on rising, particularly affecting the skilled entrants into the labour market, who are suffering increasingly longer periods of unemployment.

Worldwide, high rates of rural to urban migration, population pressure on land and appropriation of large tracts of land by individuals and companies, have created many landless and near-landless peasants. In addition, the deterioration in the prices of agricultural commodities has, of course, hit the rural population hard, but the outcome of the crisis in Africa and Latin America, coupled with the wage-containing policies under the structural adjustment programmes, has also led to an absolute

---

[2] The 1993 UNDP World Development Report classified countries by level of improvement of the HDI between 1970 and 1990. At the bottom of the scale, more than twenty sub-Saharan countries are among those with the lowest level of improvement (even a deterioration over the period) against only ten non-sub-Saharan countries.

Table 10.1. Percentage of households female-headed and in poverty in four countries of sub-Saharan Africa

	Burkina Faso	Cameroon	Madagascar	Mali
Non-poor	4.4	12.1	11.1	5.5
Poor	14.9	24.9	14.8	10.6

Source: Lachaud 1994.

deterioration in real wages in urban areas. This has considerably reduced the rural/urban income gap.[3]

Some sub-groups of populations are clearly much more prone to poverty than others. This applies particularly to women, children, and the aged. Poor women include those women 'left behind' in the migrant labour processes, which affect large proportions of the population in certain countries (such as Southern African countries). Their survival and that of their children depend partly on the migrants' remittances, in addition to various but low incomes from farm activities, handicrafts, etc., and in the urban areas, from low-productivity, irregular, insecure, and informal activities. Irregular remittances or no remittances at all, limited access to land and other inputs, and shortage of farm labour during the agricultural work season all contribute to impoverishment. Family solidarities and even conjugal and parental supports are being whittled away by the deprivation of extreme poverty, leaving women increasingly responsible for the subsistence needs of their children.

A number of studies have indicated that the feminization of poverty is closely linked to the increase in households maintained by women and lacking support from husbands/fathers in both developed and developing countries. In a recent survey of poverty in the capital cities of African countries, the percentage of households headed by a woman and classified as poor and non-poor is shown in Table 10.1.

In Lesotho, the massive male labour migration and the dependence of many households on remittances have resulted in the incidence of poverty among households headed by a woman being 65 per cent as compared to 47 for male-headed households (Gustafsson and Makonnen 1993). However, in Latin America, urban poverty is even more concentrated than in Africa among female-headed households. In San José, Costa Rica, 20 per cent of urban households were headed by woman in the employment survey of 1971; the proportion of female headed households among the destitute and the poor was respectively 47 and 25 per cent (18 per cent among non-poor households). When a similar survey was carried out in 1982 it was found that the relative proportion of women-headed, destitute households had increased

---

[3] For a selection of six African countries on which data are available, the ratio of non-agricultural to agricultural real wages went down from 4.1 in 1975 to 3.8 in 1980 and 2.7 in 1985. In a larger sample, the wage erosion is measure by the ratio of non-agricultural wage to per capita income which went down from 4.2 in 1975 to 3.8 in 1980 and 3.0 in the mid-1980s (Vandemoortele 1991). For a global review of trends in rural/urban income gaps, see Altimir (1994) for Latin America, and Jamal and Weeks (1993) for English-speaking African countries.

somewhat, but had decreased slightly among the poor, an outcome of the functioning of Latin American labour markets during the crisis (Pollack 1989). In Venezuela in 1982, 12 per cent of households were headed by women, but among the households classified as destitute, there were 36 per cent headed by women (Lopez and Pollack 1992). In Jamaica, female headship is negatively and significantly associated with the welfare level of households (Louat *et al.* 1993).

2. Labour Trends and Labour Allocation within the Household

2.1. Poverty and Labour Market Outcomes

All studies of urban poverty show the immense role played by the functioning of the labour market in contributing to long-term poverty and exclusion of certain segments of the population.[4] Poor households are characterized by a lower and much less successful allocation of their labour force on the labour market; their active responses to market fluctuations are also limited.

Recent surveys[5] carried out in six capital cities of French-speaking African countries (Burkina Faso, Cameroon, the Ivory Coast, Guinea Conakry, Madagascar, and Mali) investigated the relationship between poverty and the labour market. Household poverty is closely associated with the status of the head of the household on the labour market. In the first four countries, 75 to 90 per cent of households whose heads are unemployed are below the poverty line and 50 per cent in the latter two. Similarly, most households whose heads are inactive are also below the poverty line, although the economic and social meaning of inactivity varies from country to country. The next type of household showing a high proportion in poverty is that with self-employed heads, usually in the informal sector; the proportion in poverty is correlated with the general level of development of the country, which is less in the Ivory Coast and Cameroon (about 30 per cent) than in the four other countries (around 75 per cent). Households with wage earning heads are on the whole better off, whether employed in the public or private sector.

The person designated head of the household is usually the main contributor to the household income, bringing 80 per cent of all resources, except in Mali and Guinea where the main contributors are usually bachelors. Other correlates of poverty are the age of the head, the education level, and sex. Poverty incidence increases among female-headed households.[6]

---

[4] For recent evidence from various sources in developing and developed countries, see Rodgers (ed. 1995), Figueiredo and Shaheed (eds. 1995) and Rodgers *et al.* (eds. 1995).

[5] These surveys were launched by the International Institute for Labour Studies (Geneva), in collaboration with national labour institutes, under the supervision of J. P. Lachaud. A comparative analysis of all surveys has been published in Lachaud (ed. 1994) and intermediate results in various publications.

[6] In these countries the latter are often widows, divorcees or spinsters, who are not economically active and who do not contribute to household income, relying entirely on other family members.

In all countries surveyed, household size is inversely correlated with income level, a noticeable gap being apparent between poor and non-poor households (see also above: Anand and Morduch, Chapter 2; Lipton, Chapter 3; and Lloyd, Chapter 6). The proportion of adults in the household is not related to income, which implies that the dependency ratio (in terms of whether or not they contribute to the household income) decreases as the level of income rises. Lachaud concludes that a worker in a poor household has twice as many dependents as a worker in a non-poor household.

Usually the level of household income is correlated with the proportion contributed by the head: that is, in poor households, survival depends on the labour supply and earnings of secondary workers—mainly wives and bachelors—particularly in the less advanced countries. The contribution of secondary workers is, on average, low (10 per cent) but is three times as important in the poor households as in the non-poor. Patterns of employment of household secondary workers follow those of the head of the household fairly faithfully, that is if active, they are in the same labour category as the head. The trend is particularly marked for the members of poor households, showing the difficulty for secondary workers of finding an entry point into the labour market and the importance of familial forms of apprenticeship training systems. Married women from poor households work as self-employed petty traders, apprentices, or family helpers, while whose from non-poor households are in the protected public or private sector, like their husbands. Male secondary workers from poor households whose level of education is higher than that of the previous generation are likely to have a salaried job but on an irregular basis with long periods of unemployment.

While the share of income contributed by active women is larger in the poor households, the average participation of women, particularly wives, is lower in poor households than in the non-poor, irrespective of the average level.[7] Moreover, the unemployment rate is almost always higher among the married women from poor households than from non-poor, although the easy entry into self-employed informal activities loosens the relationship between poverty and female unemployment.

The participation of male secondary workers varies substantially from one country to another, one factor being age, another one being possibly the 'discouraged worker' effect in view of the depressed situation of African labour markets. In the Ivory Coast, which records the highest participation of male secondary workers among the six countries, more than half from poor and intermediate households are unemployed. Those from richer households do better but their implicit unemployment rate is still about 25 per cent. This situation reflects the current overall labour

---

[7]   The average participation of married women from all households is 57 per cent in the Ivory Coast, but is only 41 per cent in poor households in contrast with 71 in the non-poor. In Cameroon, the respective percentages are 49, 37, and 67. In Mali, the average participation of married women is 20 per cent, but married women in non-poor households have a participation three times higher than in the poor (32 per cent against 11).

market situation in the Ivory Coast, which became totally incapable of absorbing new arrivals, as in other African countries.[8]

Uthoff (1990), analysing households in Central Latin America, obtained similar results. In poor households, family size and the number of children were higher than in richer ones: the percentage of active adults tends to be lower (around 50 per cent in destitute households in contrast to about two-thirds in non-poor households), even in rural Guatemala.[9] Moreover, in destitute households those economically active are twice as likely to be unemployed as those in non-poor households (except in rural areas). Furthermore, the income drawn from their activity is much less. For instance, in San José, the ratio between the per-capita income of destitute households to that of the non-poor is seven to one, and in urban Honduras nine to four, but the ratio between the income per employed person from a destitute household to that in a non-poor household is four to eight, and five to seven, respectively.

2.2. The Feminization of the Labour Force

A number of dramatic changes have taken place in labour markets with regard to the roles played by women workers (ILO 1994: PREALC 1991). In practically all developed and developing countries with sufficiently reliable data,[10] female recorded labour force participation rates rose in the 1980s while those of men fell or remained constant. A rise for both female and male participation has been recorded in only a few countries, including Chile, Thailand, Peru, and Canada (Standing 1989). The rise of female labour has been particularly impressive in Latin America, with just a few exceptions of decreasing (or stable) participation in countries with low levels of urbanization, and also where the transformation of the economy was very slow (Arriagada 1990; ECLAC 1992).

On the supply side, the increased level of women's education and the fall in fertility levels are known to be positively correlated with a higher rate of participation,

---

[8] In urban Kenya for instance, the unemployed rate in the 20–24 group was nearing 30 per cent in 1986 as against 18.5 per cent in 1978 (for the 25–29 age-groups, rates were respectively 8.6 and 4.8 per cent). People with a lower-secondary level of education had the highest unemployment rate, and in 1986, half of the unemployed had received secondary education, compared with 30 per cent in 1978. Data tend to indicate that the massive unemployment of young educated adults has become structural; 61 per cent of the employed had been jobless for more than a year (Vandemoortele 1991).

[9] In an analysis of the labour market in San José, Pollack (1989) did not, however, find a clear relationship between labour-force participation of adults and household income, or a significant positive relationship between the proportion of employed adults and income (see also Rodgers, 1989, for a sample of Asian and Latin American case studies of labour-force participation and poverty, showing various patterns). An interesting outcome of the analysis of Costa Rican data is that if the number of children in the household is negatively related with household income, the relationship disappears once income is expressed by an adult equivalent.

[10] In developing countries, there are continuing conceptual and methodological problems which hinder the estimation of female economic activities, both subsistence and market activities (see Goldschmidt Clermont 1987; Anker 1994). Methodological studies have demonstrated large variations in women's labour force, as different methods are used. For example in Africa official data sources show declines in female economic activity in countries in which a variety of sources of information show that women participate actively in food production, petty trade, and micro-enterprises.

recorded in most Latin American and Asian countries (Harper 1992). The other trend is the work provided by household secondary workers (mostly women and children), who offer their labour on the market when wages are falling and the employment of male breadwinners is declining. This situation is also characteristic of unachieved proletarianization of labour, as in India. Incomes earned by the supposedly main breadwinner are so low that they are insufficient to cover the reproduction of labour, particularly as the redistribution of income among family members is biased. Men tend to keep their income, particularly wages, for their own consumption, leaving women to provide for day-to-day family subsistence (see, for example, Mies 1986).

Structural factors also explain the increasing participation of women in the labour force. The globalization of the world economy and the delocalization of production sites of transnational enterprises create vast needs for cheap labour in countries where somewhat lenient labour legislation is in force. Female labour force participation is recorded to have substantially increased as a result of earlier developments in offshore manufacturing in electronics and garment industries, as in Korea, Malaysia, Taiwan, Mexico, and Mauritius. The labour-intensive production processes in, for example, the garment industry, require little, if any, investment, and women, especially single girls, offer a docile and cheap source of labour (Lee 1984).[11] According to Standing (1989), trends in the female labour force show a correlation between export-led industrialization and liberalization of labour markets, an example of which is provided by the free export zones in many developing countries. Jobs offered in export-led industries are semi-skilled and low-paid and women are known to have 'aspiration' and 'efficiency' wages lower than those of men.

The labour-force participation of females maintaining households is obviously far higher than that of women with husbands. In Chile, for all income classes of households headed by women, female participation was about 50 per cent in 1980 and again in 1984, except for female heads of destitute households whose participation rose slightly over the period. On the other hand, the average participation of married women was around 20 per cent, with the noticeable exception of women from non-poor households (30–34 per cent) (López and Pollack 1992). In a survey conducted in Bogotá among poor households there was a higher participation rate of female heads of households. However, many wives obtained some income from informal activities carried out at home, such as catering (García Castro 1987).

---

[11]   The development of the maquiladora system in Mexico in the 1980s was extremely rapid, and the creation of jobs in the sector compensated for the loss of jobs in the industrial sector. Most jobs were held, in the early phase, by young women. In 1981, 77 per cent of workers in maquila were women. However, in 1992, the proportion of women had fallen to 59 per cent, because of the diversification of the sector and greater importance being placed on activities traditionally associated with male workers (Gordon Rapoport *et al.* 1995).

As in other Asian countries, a survey of employment in Malaysia's free trade zones found that 83 per cent of female workers were unmarried, with an average age of 22 years (Datta-Chaudhuri 1984). The analysis of such zones in Asia concludes that in terms of employment, this source of cheap and vulnerable labour had not been tapped previously, but that the creation of the new jobs had no direct effect on male unemployment (Lee 1984).

2.3. Atypical and Precarious Employment

The 1980s saw the widespread adoption of a variety of structural adjustment programmes and stabilization policies. These have supposedly been aimed at improving economic efficiency by allowing a relatively rapid and more cost-effective adjustment to market signals. They have loosened the legally and administratively established frameworks of rules and collective agreements thought to constrain labour-market flexibility and the responsiveness of wages to market conditions. One result has been the creation of new jobs which are in atypical, often precarious, forms of work.

In Africa, most of the urban jobs created in the 1980s were in the informal sector. Vandemoortele (1991) estimates that between 1980 and 1985, the informal sector created 6 million new jobs, while the modern sector created only 0.5 million. However, there is growing evidence that the informal sector is not the sponge it was supposed to be in the 1970s and that, if it succeeds in absorbing labour, it is mostly in low-productivity activities without any prospects. For instance, women trained as nurses and teachers have been compelled through structural adjustment lay-off programmes to enter the informal sector where they are facing increasing competition from men also compelled to enter the sector (Mhone 1995).

The feminization of the service industries in Latin America during the 1980s was striking. Although the sex segregation on the labour market generally is on the decline (Gordon Rapoport 1995), women usually took precarious, low-paid jobs,[12] without managerial responsibilities, largely in the marginal informal sector, as domestics (mainly single women) or as part-time office cleaners (especially single women with responsibilities for children) (see, for example, ECLAC 1992; Villareal 1992; García Castro 1987; Gonzalez de la Rocha, cited in Roberts 1991).

In Asia, there has been a noted increase in women's involvement in micro or small-scale production activities and home-based activities, including self employment and piece-rate work. ILO labour flexibility studies in several countries, including the Philippines and Malaysia, have demonstrated a greater degree of casualization of labour. They have also demonstrated the greater vulnerability of women to exploitative conditions, such as in homework where 90 per cent of jobs are held by women (ILO 1994, 1995b).

2.4. Unemployment

Unemployment rates have been rising all over the world and women's unemployment rates tend to be higher than those of men (ILO 1994). In Africa, rates of open unemployment for females are often twice those for men and still rising. In Caribbean and Latin American countries, the differentials by sex are particularly

---

[12] Even in low-paid activities, women receive a lower wage than men; in Panama and in San José for instance, female domestic employees receive about half the wage of that earned by male domestics (Arriagada 1990).

high, in a context of high absolute levels of unemployment. Female unemployment multiplied almost fivefold in Bogotá and doubled in Caracas in the 1980s but, at the same time, the number of jobs occupied by women increased remarkably (ECLAC 1992). In most countries of Asia and the Pacific region, open unemployment rates in the recent past have been higher for women. Only in countries where labour is scarce, such as Hong Kong, Singapore, and the Republic of Korea, have female employment rates been lower than male employment rates.

An interesting trend, possibly reflecting a change in the way employers are considering women's work and the absolute need for an income, has been observed by Standing (1989). Looking at the dynamics of male and female unemployment rates in the 1970s and 1980s, he found that the ratio between male and female unemployment rates increased in three-quarters of developed countries and in about half of developing countries during the 1970s, but the trend was reversed in the 1980s, with a decreasing ratio in about 60 per cent of developed and developing countries.

2.5. Response to Crisis at the Household Level

Urban poverty increased in all Latin American countries during the 1980s (see, for instance, Contreras 1995; Altimir 1994; Rodgers 1989). The rise in unemployment appears to be the main factor explaining increased poverty. Pollack and Uthoff (1989), analysing trends in Greater Santiago (where there are comparable chronological household data) found that in 1982,[13] the unemployment rate of the heads among destitute households went up to 50 per cent, in comparison with 20 per cent in 1980. It trebled over those two years in poor and in non-poor households but remained at a much lower level in the latter (18 and 5 per cent respectively). However, the unemployment rate of wives did not follow the same trend. In 1982, it was as high as 25 per cent in destitute households, a figure comparable with the previous years and lower than in 1984. Furthermore, the unemployment rate of wives was approximately 20 per cent in poor households, but rates above 15 per cent were not exceptional in earlier years. Among non-poor households, it remained considerably less.

In 1988 Benería (1991) carried out an in-depth survey among deprived households in Mexico City to study their survival strategies in time of crisis. She distinguished two types of households according to their response to crisis. A very small proportion of sample households practically disintegrated under insurmountable problems: unemployment, inability to generate the income necessary for mere survival, domestic violence, abandonment, prostitution, drugs, criminal behaviour. The economic crisis probably intensified rather than created these problems. However, the vast majority of households had reorganized their life through three coping mechanisms: labour market adjustments, budget changes, and restructuring daily life.

---

[13]   The year 1982 was the worst year for employment and poverty. It is estimated that there were 2.1 people of working age per available job in 1969, 2.5 in 1982, and 2.2 at the end of the 1980s. Among the poorest population, the ratios are respectively 2.7 and 4.8 in 1982.

The labour market response is the increased participation of secondary workers of the household. The proportion of new household members entering the labour market was only 38 per cent for the households in extreme poverty, against 62–64 per cent for the poor and those at subsistence level. With respect to the entry of women into the labour force, it was typically that of women without children. Mothers with husbands were the last members of the household to enter the labour force. This can be explained by the role traditionally assigned to mothers within Mexican society, their heavy daily chores, the fact that taking a job would be humiliating for their husband, and also because they are the least educated persons in the household. In indigent and poor households women were mainly confined to sporadic activities in the informal sector, as street vendors, and in home-based industries. Contrary to examples in Costa Rica, for instance, in Mexico City, a response to the crisis has been an increase in the size of households, with formerly nuclear households lodging relatives without any resources.[14] The crisis has reinforced family unity and increased communication between household members, together eking out a survival existence on a daily basis, but increased tensions regarding the division of housework between members was noted. Moreover, it increased the amount of housework and, although all members took part, most of the work was still carried out by the women, even those working outside the home. The pooling of resources in a household and their intra-household distribution is known to be skewed. Usually, women's income is entirely devoted to household expenses, whereas men contribute only part of their income. Benería found that this pattern was not changed by the crisis. Even with diminished income, men were still not pooling their whole income for the household.

A general conclusion of the analysis of urban poverty, at least in Africa and in Latin America, is that poverty is much more linked to the composition of households in terms of economically active and non-active members and also in terms of individual income drawn from activity, than to the demographic structure (size and age composition). Dynamically, the labour response of household members to cyclical variations in the income of the main breadwinner, appears to be particularly marginal for the poor. The labour market is often structurally unable to absorb all the labour offered and, in times of crisis, the lowest segments of the labour force are even more excluded, passively suffering the market contraction.. Spatial international mobility becomes practically the only alternative.

3. Child Labour

In traditional agriculture, all members of the household provide labour for production activities. Caldwell and Caldwell (1992) argue that the age and sex division of labour in rural traditional societies extends to all members of the family except the

---

[14] See also Lloyd, Chapter 6 above.

very young children and the aged.[15] In pastoral societies of the Sahel, the tending of flocks of goats and sheep is common for young boys of five-to-six years of age. When they grow up, they become responsible for the larger cattle, taking the animals to the wells and drawing water (Bonnet 1993). Agricultural work, especially within the family, has often been viewed in the past as a socialization process, or looked at in a very idealistic way (see various African case studies in Rodgers and Standing 1981).

Yet, even in traditional rural societies, child labour is often less attractive. In Tanzania, the widow of a man who had died from AIDS would normally, according to the custom, be inherited, along with her children, by one of her husband's brothers. Because of the extremely poor living conditions, the practice is waning and, where it still happens, it is reported that children are often exploited and mistreated (Tibaiyuka and Kaijage 1995).

A case of open exploitation is bonded labour of children. Bondage was officially abolished in India in 1976 but is still an issue today, involving millions of children (ILO and UN Center for Human Rights 1992). The main cause of bonded labour is debt, incurred by a poor household when it is unable to meet the unexpected costs of, for example, marriage, funerals, or sickness. Children are particularly vulnerable in the bonded labour system, being mortgaged in repayment, as a substitute for their parents' compulsory services to a master, or simply because bonded labour extends to the family of a bonded man, in some sort of familial services enterprise (Dube 1981).

Besides agricultural activities, domestic services, and unpaid family work, children's work is unfortunately widespread in all regions of the world (including developed regions) in salaried activities and self-emmployment, in a range of industrial activities (Bequele and Boyden 1988).

The evidence on child labour and labour allocation within the household is very scant. The few available data would suggest that children are considered as secondary workers within the household, and that they contribute effectively to the household income. Of course, there are the famous street children in Latin American cities, considered by the authorities as abandoned, an image reinforced by the media. In fact, in a survey carried out among street children in Latin American cities, a minimum of 63 per cent of children in Asunción, 75 per cent in Lima and 81 per cent in Cochabamba, were found to be living with one or two parents. In Asunción, only 16 per cent of children had no contact with their family and 16 per cent had occasional contact (Myers 1989). Still more pronounced in the other regions of the world is the fact that street children are not generally abandoned, although the trend is rising, even in Africa (Marjuria 1994; Marguerat 1992).

The secondary-worker effect has been demonstrated in Latin America. De la Luz

---

[15] Caldwell and Caldwell (1992), reporting on a time-use survey in Bangladesh, found the average weekly inputs for adults to be about 75 hours and, for both male and female children, above 46 hours. Girls aged eleven or twelve and boys aged thirteen or fourteen are working adult hours; by the age of eight or nine, the labour input for both girls and boys is half that of an adult.

Silva (1981), in a survey in Chile, noted that parents tend not to interfere with the education of their children if they can keep them at school, but withdraw them from school if their help is needed.[16] Among the street children surveyed in Latin America, 45 per cent of children working in Asunción had started work to replace a father who had left the household, died or become unemployed (Myers 1989).

Parents also consider that children are being trained by the employer. Such importance is given to the training component that 'apprentices' in industrial activities in India (Burra 1988), in homework carpet-making (Berik 1987), and in the informal sector in African countries are either not paid or receive well below the minimum wage. Apprenticeship can provide a cheap but effective vocational training system that the African states cannot offer (Bonnet 1993).

Child labour can be associated with technological changes, including changes in production processes. For instance, in the brassware industry in India, polishing was previously done by women working at home. The demand of export markets for better quality led to the mechanization of the activity, now carried out in the factory by children because their mothers, mostly Muslim, cannot work outside the home (Burra 1989). The other trend is related to sub-contracted homework. In most cases, women are paid at a piece rate. Their children contribute to the family production process, especially as the income a woman could make daily without the help of children would be totally insufficient to ensure the reproduction of labour (see, for example, Bhatty 1980). Such familial organization of work has also been documented in the Philippines where the Muro-Ami fishing company, through a one-off payment at the end of a ten-month contract, and advances (in the form of goods from the company shops) and loans, succeeds in putting the workers in a state of revolving debt, so that child participation in collecting shellfish becomes obligatory (Rialp 1993).

4. Spatial Mobility

An obvious mechanism to escape poverty, famine and resource depletion, has always been spatial mobility. 'Classically', migration is viewed in the context of the theory of human investment as a rational choice made by an individual. Migrants do eventually tend to succeed in finding jobs and incomes in urban economies. Rural–urban migrants generally include young men from non-poor families, and with above-average education, which enables them to find jobs in the modern urban sector.[17] The

---

[16] The lack of schooling facilities and, with the cost-recovery system these days, the cost of education that parents have to meet, creates an environment in which there is a need to 'occupy' children with something productive. Many policies against child labour emphasize the need to develop educational facilities as a top priority. However, it has been shown, where those facilities exist, that children succeed in combining schooling and work (Myers 1989).

[17] Of course, there are many other types of population movements, as documented for instance by Standing (1984 and 1985), who situates labour mobility within the overall context of capitalist development and modes of production. Landless labourers and poor rural families may show a high propensity to emigrate, depending on the type of rural development taking place in their country or region. See also Oberai (1987) and Rodgers (1984).

Table 10.2. Estimates of non-nationals by region in 1993 (in millions)

Region	Economically active	Dependents	Total
Africa	5–6	11–14	16–20
America, North	7	8–10	15–17
Americas, South and Central	3–5	4–7	7–12
Asia, South, South-East and East	2–4	4–5	6–9
Asia, West (Arab States)	5	1–2	6–7
Europe (excludes ex-USSR/Yugoslavia)	1–2	12	20
Overall total	30–35	40–50	70–85

Source: ILO estimates in ILO *et al.* (1994).

consequences of migration, especially internal, in the zones of origin, have generally been perceived as positive. Migrants contribute to the diffusion of innovations and more efficient production techniques. Household members left behind are likely to receive remittances, improving their levels of consumption and investment. The effect on the production of a surplus labourer is marginal, or the loss of an economically active household member may be compensated by recruiting labour.[18]

There are currently several new trends in migration flows in the world which somewhat change the conclusions to be drawn. These include the significant increase in international migration, to which refugee numbers should be added; new forms such as contract-labour migration; the increased circularity and temporary nature of labour movements; the increasing feminization of migration flows in many regions of the world; and the growing number of unskilled migrants coming from the poorest strata of the population.

4.1. Increasing Magnitude of International Migration

Migration flows are difficult to measure. The ILO estimates that in 1993 there were about 30–35 million economically active non-nationals in the world (excluding about 25 million Russians living outside Russia), and 40–50 million dependents (Table 10.2).[19]

In terms of labour force, migrant labour amounts to 1.2 to 1.4 per cent of the total

[18] These points have also been questioned by many authors, on theoretical and factual bases. Here again, the effect of labour migration will be different in an economy 'à la Chayanov' (see House 1986, 1989), in a context of semi-capitalist developing agriculture, or in a situation where modern agriculture is practised (see for instance, Rodgers 1981, and Oberai 1987, for global reviews).

[19] The figures in Table 10.2 do not include international refugees as defined by the UNHCR, which has estimated the total number of refugees as 20 million in 1993, in contrast to 2.5 million in 1970. There are estimated to be about 8 million refugees in Africa and 6 million in Asia (ILO et al. 1994). Causes of movement may be 'genuinely' political, or economic, environmental or ethnic, or a combination of any of these. Extreme poverty or denial of access to resources is often associated with ethnicity and can degenerate into political conflicts (Rodgers et al. 1995).

world labour force. There are vast differences by country, however, both in receiving and sending labour. For example, the economically active population working abroad represents about 17 per cent of the Egyptian labour force and more than 16 and 10 per cent, respectively, of the labour forces of Swaziland and Lesotho. Another example is that of Indonesians working in Malaysia, who constitute about 12 per cent of the national labour force. In Qatar, 92 per cent of the population recorded as economically active consists of non-nationals (ILO *et al.* 1994).

Lim (1994), analysing the shape of labour movements in Asian countries, which are the most representative of current trends, distinguishes five different types of factors affecting them:

Demographic processes Not all countries are at the same stage of the demographic transition. In Asian countries, where population growth is still high, the rapid labour force growth has forced governments to look for export outlets for their labour surplus.

Economic processes These pertain to unequal levels of development and the need on the part of fast-growing economies—deeply involved in export-led growth and in the international division of labour— to keep their comparative advantages either by investing in ever-cheap labour countries, or by importing cheap labour, as Europe did 20 years ago.

Political processes Among these is the active policy of certain countries, such as Korea, to export labour some time ago, and Indonesia, where the national plan contains objectives for female emigration and remittances.

Various institutional processes Among these are the active parts played by subcontractors and transnational corporations investing—in cheap-labour countries—in off-shore production sites, through turnkey projects and their own internal labour markets.

Social processes These are numerous; among them are the networks of communities, ethnic proximity, religion (an important factor in the Middle Eastern countries), women's increased desire for economic independence, the higher job expectations of national populations even in labour surplus economies, and the selection of increasingly skilled migrants by countries of immigration (for instance in the Middle East, partly because of the changes in enterprises where migrants are employed).

4.2. Contract-labour Migration

One type of international labour flow which is fairly well documented is that of the 'contract migrant workers' from South and South East Asia to the Middle East and Asia. This type of migration is specific, to the extent that contract migrant workers

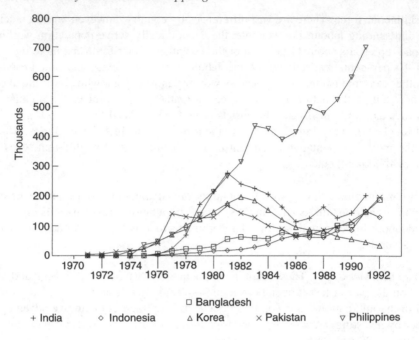

Fig. 10.1. Labour migrant flows, 1971–92, for selected Asian labour-sending countries
Source: Lim and Abella (1994).

are temporary target migrants (according to the contract, the emigrant has to return to his or her country at the end of the contract). Such workers are also recruited under precise specifications of their occupation at the destination. The nature of such important labour migration flows is well illustrated by the example of a Western construction enterprise or a public Chinese company which obtains a contract in a Middle Eastern country or in Tanzania, and recruits labour in Pakistan or nationally.

The Philippines is a major labour-sending country. At the peak of migration to the Gulf, there were more than 400,000 Filipinos migrating per year. This movement started with the oil boom in the Gulf in the 1970s, which created immense demands for unskilled and semi-skilled labour, for instance in the construction industry. This massive labour demand affected several countries in South and South East Asia (see Figure 10.1) and induced massive labour movements. In 1993, more than a million labour contracts were issued. The flow decreased with the Gulf War, the fall in oil prices, the growing indebtedness of oil-exporting countries, and the completion of large infrastructure projects.

Another fast-growing labour market, also attracting labour from new exporting countries, is that of the rapidly developing economies in South East Asia, and Japan. This labour market amounted to around 4,000 migrant workers for the Philippines in 1975. The number grew continuously to exceed 160,000 labour contracts in 1993

(Go 1995; Lim 1994; Lim and Abella 1994; Amjad 1989). In such contract-labour migrations, from the Philippines, as well from other Asian countries, the composition of the labour force working abroad has changed a lot. This has occurred with the feminization of migration flows and the fast-growing market for domestics, services and entertainers (see Section 4.3 below).

4.3. The Feminization of Migration

Migration was, in the past, demonstrably age- and sex-specific in many countries, with young males showing a higher propensity to migrate than females and old persons. The sex selectivity of migration is decreasing in many regions of the world however, with more girls and women now emigrating. The trend affects national migration processes, but there is also an increasing proportion of female international migrant workers.

Female migration is more complex than that of men. There is indeed a need to analyse how gender considerations operate at the household or family level in order to understand how female and male migrants are especially mobilized, where associational migration is involved. Among the relevant factors are the differential labour market opportunities for women and men in the societies of origin and destination. Studies from a variety of countries have demonstrated the great diversity in migration patterns and impacts according to the divisions of labour in the original and host countries (for example divisions of responsibilities in agriculture, which the migration of one sex—men for wage labour—may greatly change). While in some cases male flight from farming may leave women carrying out all the agricultural tasks, in other cases women migrate alone to improve the economic situation of their families left behind, as in the cases of Filipino and Sri Lankan women.

The evolution of rural–urban migration has been documented for instance in Mexico (ECLAC 1992). A few decades ago, education and social mobility were the main determinants of the movement of the young. While families continue to decline into poverty, parents send their children, especially girls, to look for jobs. Female migration appears to be different from that of males, being the result of a changing sexual division of labour within the household caused by poverty (Young 1982) and the lack of opportunities in the local labour markets.

Asian countries too, have witnessed marked increases of international migration flows, especially for females. Asian women and girls have entered labour markets in the Middle East, Western Europe, and Asian 'Tigers'. Filipino female migrant workers outnumber their male counterparts by twelve to one in Asian countries (three to one for all countries). Women migrants from Indonesia outnumber their male counterparts by three to one and Sri Lankan female migrant workers outnumber males by three to two. Flows of migrants from Thailand have been feminized, and women from Bangladesh are moving to Pakistan (Lim 1994; Lim and Abella 1994; Gulati 1993).

The increased proportion of female migrants in some labour-sending countries is a policy issue. Sri Lanka has no legal restrictions on women migrating to work abroad, except for nurses. Bangladesh does not allow women to work in the Gulf countries as domestics, except if accompanied by their husband. In the Philippines, the export of skilled labour (nurses, teachers) has been an active government policy for a long time. A ban on the employment of Filipino women as domestic helpers is in force for certain receiving countries (Gulati 1993).

The jobs offered to migrant girls are very limited, mainly domestic work and 'entertainment', except that the migration policy of a few receiving countries, for instance the United States, can favour more skilled labour (Weinert 1991; Anderson 1993; Gulati 1993). In spite of their qualifications (60 per cent of Filipino girls in search of jobs abroad have a college degree), more than two-thirds are domestic workers and entertainers. In Sri Lanka, where the average educational level is quite high, the majority of women who migrate abroad are recruited as domestics. This also extends to other regions of the world. In Argentina, as early as 1970, domestic servants composed 5 per cent of the female population but, of these, 63 per cent were immigrant women (Stalker 1994). The Anti-Slavery Society has estimated that there are 60,000 foreign female domestic workers in the UK (Stalker 1994). In Italy, half of the domestics workers registered with national social organizations were foreign workers (obviously this figure does not include illegal migrants; Weinert 1991).

If the jobs at the destination are socially at the bottom of the ladder, salaries may be nonetheless attractive. A Filipino migrating illegally to Italy, though severely underpaid, earns several times more as a domestic there than as a teacher in the Philippines, earning perhaps US$ 100 a month (Weinert 1991). An 'entertainer' in Japan is reputed to earn a gross income of US$ 1,500 a month (Gulati 1993).

Recruitment conditions should be noted. As in the Philippines, many Asian labour-sending countries have created government recruitment agencies and installed a system of registered agencies but, at least in Sri Lanka and the Philippines, unlicensed agencies proliferate and the vast number of illegal Filipinos in Europe normally obtain a visa through this channel (Gulati 1993). Private agencies charge exorbitant fees. The average cost of obtaining a job in the Middle East was US$ 900 in 1990 (Stalker 1994). The Anti-Slavery Society documented the case of a Filipino civil engineer who had to pay a year's salary to obtain the necessary visas (Anderson 1993).

4.4. Increased Poverty

Several surveys carried out in previous decades on the determinants of spatial mobility have shown that a relatively important proportion of rural–urban migrants and international migrants come from relatively well off families—those who can afford to pay for their children's education and who have land. A survey in Punjab for example showed that the propensity to emigrate was higher than the average among medium-sized farms and among non-agricultural, landless households. The weakest propensity to migrate was among small farmers. Whereas landless agricultural and non agricultural workers in Ecuador have a propensity to emigrate below the average, the highest propensity is shown by people on the largest farms (examples cited in Rodgers 1981).[20]

In current migration flows however, especially among international migrants, relative poverty and in many cases absolute poverty, is becoming the main driving force towards migration. Thus a survey in Tamil Nadu showed that women migrating to the Gulf come from the poorest rural households. They are ready to migrate just to get two meals a day. Usually they are heavily in debt and unemployed for a large part of the year (Anderson 1993). In Sri Lanka, half of the return migrants surveyed came from households in which income was below the national average, with 12 per cent from households with no income at all. These figures can be contrasted with the fact that the average educational level of these migrants is well above the national average. Eighty per cent of return migrants surveyed had at least completed secondary curriculum (Rodrigo and Jayatissa 1988).

Migration in the villages surveyed in the Sarakole region of Mali has become the main means of existence for almost all families. The rain-fed agricultural potential of the region is very low. Moreover, the region was severely affected by several years of drought in the 1970s and again in the beginning of the 1980s. In most 'concessions',[21] there is at least one young man who is currently abroad. He would spend a few years in France, for instance, sending remittances home regularly (once he has found a job), generally to the chief of the concession who would then redistribute them. Given the large size of the extended family, a system of rotating migrant members can perpetuate the dependency on remittances of the whole household.

The migrants, their parents, and the leaders of the villages consider migration as practically the only way for a family to survive, even just to obtain enough cash income to pay per-capita taxes, as agricultural output is not commercialized and therefore insufficient to cover such taxes. Migration is, however, somewhat selective in the sense that the larger the family and the higher the number of migrants or potential migrants, the greater the amount of remittances or the probability of some migrants being employed. Under this system, single-household concessions are at a disadvantage and especially small, female-headed households which are not part of an extended kin group.

The 'push' and 'pull' factors are not just measured in terms of aggregate income. One example is provided by the changes which have affected the urban/rural income gap in African countries. Jamal and Weeks (1993), in their analysis of a series of English-speaking African countries, record the sharp decline in the real

---

[20] Mexican internal and international migrant flows offer a similar picture. Non-migrants' households, internal migrants' households, and the households of Mexican migrants in the United States differed in terms of average sizes of landholding (respectively 4.75, 6.48, and 7.14 hectares); average numbers of adults in the family (respectively, 7.84, 8.47, 9.11); wealth (respectively, US$ 2,110, US$ 2,470 and US$ 3,470); and education levels—the highest being among internal migrants (respectively, 3.93 years of completed schooling, 6.50 and 4.06) (Stark 1991:151).

[21] A 'concession' is a very large extended family with the 'chef de la concession', the oldest man of a generation, the households of his sons, those of his brothers, those of the brothers' sons and sometimes non-relatives. It is common to find concessions with 3-4 households, 50 persons and even many more.

income of urban wage workers, and a substantial decrease in the income gap between urban wage earners and the rural population, but with much greater inequality in both (also see Vandemoortele 1991). With respect to rural–urban migration, they conclude their analysis by estimating that migration has 'hardly been abated' and urban labour markets are in greater excess supply than ever before. To explain this, the main argument is that African economies are, or at least were in the 1980s, demand-constrained and that the fall in urban wages has decreased demand for food crops and turned small producers into subsistence farmers, although still in need of cash income. Moreover, since non-farm rural activities (contributing largely to rural incomes) are linked to cash crop production, they are also another source of cash reduction. Large agricultural producers are also better equipped to adjust themselves to price fluctuations. The latter tend to create more inequalities and reinforce landlessness where population pressure is too great.

4.5. Remittances

World remittances flows were estimated at US\$ 61 billion in 1989, which seems to have been the peak year.[22] This would place migrant-worker income flows after the oil trade and before global development assistance. Lesotho is an extreme case of a country depending almost entirely on remittances for its survival. The amount of remittances accounts for more than 50 per cent of GNP. In Swaziland, another important labour-exporting country in terms of the fraction of the population working abroad, inflow of gross remittances represents 18.4 per cent of GNP. Except for these extraordinary cases, remittances represent only a small percentage of GNP, even for countries like the Philippines (3.3 per cent of GNP) and Pakistan (4.7 per cent). However, the contribution of remittances to the balance of payments is far more impressive in, for instance, Bangladesh, Burkina Faso, and Morocco (ILO *et al.* 1994). The ratio of net officially-controlled remittances to merchandise exports in 1988 amounted to 60 per cent in Bangladesh, and 46 per cent in Pakistan (about 80 per cent with unofficial flows) (Hugo 1990). Remittances are roughly equivalent to the volume of total exports in Egypt and Jordan and several times the volume in North Yemen (Abella 1994; ILO *et al.* 1994).[23]

Contract-labour migration in Asia, including remittances, is now fairly well studied, thanks to various surveys of migrants' families and return migrants.[24] The average remittances sent by Pakistani workers in the Gulf were more than 50 per cent of

[22] The actual amount of remittances is much higher than the official estimates, while remittance flows take various unofficial forms. For instance, it has been estimated that less than 60 per cent of remittances sent by Pakistani workers are been repatriated through official channels (ARTEP 1987).

[23] See Athukorola (1993) for an estimate of remittances in major Asian labour-sending countries over a period of time, in comparison with their trade balances.

[24] See in particular, two edited volumes (Amjad 1989 and Wickramasekara 1993) and the various papers produced by the Asian regional programme on international labour migration (UNDP/ARTEP-ILO, New Delhi).

their income and in addition the migrant workers were saving an extra 25 per cent, in anticipation of re-entering their home labour market (ARTEP 1987).[25]

Remittances sent by Bangladeshi migrants in the Gulf have been estimated to be four to five times the income they earned previously. In relation to the average national household income in Bangladesh, remittances from unskilled workers were three times greater, and those from professional workers eighteen times greater (Mahmud 1989). The average annual income remitted by a Filipino worker under contract labour was estimated at about US$ 2,000 (Tan and Canlas 1989).

Rural girls migrating to the cities in Thailand and in Mexico are said to be pushed into migration by their parents to help them financially, because of the need to support other children in the family and the lack of support provided by the husband, etc. However, Wolf (1992) in her study of rural Java girls working in the export sector, found daughters to be relatively independent in spending their salaries, but they would help their parents when needed and present them with radios and other prestige goods.

In Swaziland internal and mainly international emigration for wage employment has become the most common pattern for the survival of the rural Swazi 'homestead', affected by relative land scarcity and declining farm production. De Vletter (1983) found that with one-third of the adult labour force absent (including more than 20 per cent of male heads), remittances amounted to about 20 per cent of rural household income, whilst agricultural activities amounted to less than 40 per cent. About half of rural households received remittances regularly.

4.6. Impact and Use of Remittances

At the macro-level, remittances from abroad are one component of GNP and of the balance of payments. They are also a source of hard currency for some countries. For instance, remittances from Turkish workers (which at a peak in the early 1970s were equivalent to the volume of exports plus the trade deficit) make possible the import of raw material and machinery needed for the national development policy (Martin 1991), and in Asian labour-sending countries, imports of oil (Amjad 1989). Such positive macro-economic effects are self-explanatory. More interesting is the indirect macro-economic effects of remittances, which have been studied in Asian labour-sending countries (Amjad 1989; Wickramasekara 1993). The multiplier effect of remittances through their use in private construction has been recorded in Bangladesh (Mahmud 1989) and on direct employment-creation in Sri Lanka (Rodrigo and Jayatissa 1988). The creation of jobs through remittances or by the activities of return migrants has been documented in Turkey, but more important, the outflow of labour clearly relieved unemployment pressures. On the negative side, in contrast to Asian labour-sending countries, remittances from Turkish workers have

---

[25] In the survey, amounts remitted and saved are broken down by rural/urban origin of the migrants, income, and occupation. It is interesting to note that the overall percentages are fairly similar for all classes of workers.

had an inflationary effect through increasing the money supply. However, the main negative effect was, according to Martin (1991), that it allowed the government to follow a vigorous and sustained import-substitution strategy. Over the long term, this slowed down the economic take-off of the economy.

Authors who have studied the Asian contract-labour migration system agree about the positive effects of remittances on household income and poverty reduction, because of the magnitude of flows. This occurs either directly for households of migrant workers, through multiplier macro-effects, wage rises in agriculture and a few other sectors (for example, in the construction industry in Korea) because of labour shortages, or through investment, increasing labour productivity (Amjad 1989; Kazi 1989). In Sri Lanka, as most migrants are from the lowest quintile, remittances are likely to raise a substantial number of households above the poverty line (one migrant household in forty-seven).

The effects of remittances on income distribution are generally estimated to be less positive (see Rodgers 1981 and Oberai 1987, for theoretical and factual evidence). In Asian labour-sending countries, all authors agree on a deterioration in income distribution, because of the background of the majority of migrants (typically semi-skilled and skilled workers coming from a given region). Sri Lanka is a possible exception because most migrants came from the lowest income group (Amjad 1989). The trend towards a deterioration in the overall income distribution is also hypothesized in Turkey, because remittances and migrants' savings contributed to widening regional disparities by being channelled, directly and indirectly, to the most dynamic regions and sectors (Martin 1991).

There is abundant literature on the use of remittances and savings made by migrants' households because of the vested interests of governments from labour-sending countries in channelling remittances into productive activities and also through official channels (Athukorola 1993).[26]

Generally speaking, remittances are used for consumption by the migrants' households, thus improving their living conditions, which is, after all, the primary objective of migration.[27] The purchase of ostentatious imported consumption goods is recorded by some authors. In both Asia or Turkey, extensive purchase of land or properties, and investment in housing and construction, has been reported. In India, in a survey carried out in 1986, 41 per cent of remittances were used only for construction purposes (Gopinathan Nair 1993). This may be a source of inflation, as in Turkey (Martin 1991).

Another feature of remittances, documented in Bangladesh by Mahmud (1989), is that the saving propensity of households with a member abroad is much higher, both in rural and urban areas, than in non-migrant households. The surveys carried out in various Asian labour-sending countries also showed that migrants keep some

---

[26]   Tan (1987) estimated that 60 per cent of remittances from Filipino workers are going through unofficial channels, which can easily be explained by the instability of both the economy (high inflation, massive devaluation, low interest rates) and the political situation of the country during that period.

[27]   The proportion of remittances exclusively used for consumption is as high as 85 per cent in the Philippines, but less than 40 per cent in Thailand (Tan 1987).

savings in the form of financial assets abroad (Tan 1987), although with large variations from one country to another. Amjad (1989) disagrees with the idea that most remittances are used for consumption and construction. Surveys conducted in Pakistan, Sri Lanka, and Thailand, for instance, showed remittances being used for business investment (Tan 1987); also, as in Pakistan, savings made by migrants are invested on their return in small enterprises and businesses (though not very successfully because of lack of managerial skill) (Farooq-i-Azam 1987).

4.7. Impact on Labour Markets in Migrants' Country of Origin

The effect on labour migration in the country or region of origin depends on the existence of a labour surplus, the changes in the age and sex structure of the mainly rural labour force, and the type of adjustments that take place as a response to a possible labour shortage. Differences between Asian labour-sending countries and African countries are noticeable. The former have absorbed the possible negative consequences of labour shortage. In the latter case, neither the labour market nor the economy seem able to cope with a real labour shortage.[28]

In his review of contract-labour migration in Asia, Amjad (1989) concludes that, given the high level of unemployment and underemployment in the labour-sending countries, migration had no obviously unfavourable impact on their development. It acted, rather, as a safety valve, releasing pressures on local labour markets. No changes in unemployment figures have been recorded because many migrants were not looking for a job in their native country before departure. In Sri Lanka, women who were encouraged to emigrate were neither part of the employed population nor looking for a job (Rodrigo and Jayatissa 1988).

In most labour-sending countries, few sectoral labour shortages were recorded as the market was able to fill them rapidly[29] One noticeable exception is the Korean construction sector where shortages of certain skills were recorded in the late 1970s,

[28] In Latin America, the pattern of agricultural development is largely responsible for migration, where rural–urban migration predominates. As in Europe in the nineteenth century, traditional small farms tend to be absorbed into larger capitalist entities, thereby generating a labour surplus, as testified by high rates of rural unemployment. The bulk of the surplus rural workforce has to migrate to the cities.

[29] One aspect of labour-contract migration in Asia is the relatively high level of migrants' education and the waste of that investment in low-skilled jobs, such as Filipino college girls becoming maids in the Middle East (Anderson 1993; Lim 1994). In Sri Lanka, the percentage of illiterates, according to all available information, is almost nil and, of those with only primary education, perhaps around ten as an average, but the educational level of migrants is, on the whole, higher than the level of the Sri Lankan population (Rodrigo and Jayatissa 1988). Among Kerala migrant workers returning from Kuwait, less than 20 per cent had not attained matriculation (end of secondary-level education). However, 60 per cent with matriculation had only unskilled or semi-skilled production jobs (Isaac 1992).

It should also be noted that labour requirements have changed in the Gulf States due, on the one hand, to the completion of large construction projects requiring workers with only low qualifications and, on the other, to the preference shown by certain countries for recruiting educated labour.

The skill drain was perceived by some South and South-East Asian governments as a long-term threat to development. Singapore, Pakistan, and Thailand have adopted attractive policies to persuade skilled migrants to return (Lim 1994). Many governments in the region have also launched ambitious training programmes to counter the skill drained but, according to Amjad, this has been a largely ineffective and costly measure (Amjad 1989).

when the economy was in the throes of absorbing its labour surplus. It also induced a rise in wages, which 'encouraged' some workers to enter the economically active population (Hyun 1989). Similar but overall money-wage increases were recorded in Pakistan, even in rural activities, in the 1970s and early 1980s. In the Sri Lankan construction industry wages increased at a far faster pace than the cost of living index. In the Pakistan industrial sector, turnover of skilled migrants increased the cost of recruitment and training for enterprises. Lastly, one outcome of migration in Korea was to lower production quality because the skilled migrants were, at least temporarily, replaced by less skilled labour. However, no effect on the labour market or wages is detectable in large labour-surplus economies, such as the Philippines and Bangladesh (Amjad 1989).

Labour shortage arguably encourages the adoption of labour-saving techniques in certain sectors, particularly the construction industry. In countries where migration accounts for a significant percentage of labour, the labour absorption capacity of the economy could generally be reduced, but other factors are also involved and the trend does not seem to be irreversible. Such is the case in Pakistan where the mechanization of agriculture slowed down significantly after the peak of out-migration in 1978–82 (Kazi 1988).

Return migrants need opportunities for employment and many remained unemployed for long periods because of the poor economic performance of many labour-sending countries. Whilst Tan (1987) argues that Filipino return migrants opt for leisure, just waiting for another opportunity to emigrate, Amjad and others consider it a structural issue. The 'discouraged worker' effect has to be mentioned as well, evidenced in the numbers of returning migrants who remain unemployed, unable to find jobs offering wages comparable to those earned abroad. A survey carried out on Bangladeshi return migrants found a considerable deterioration in their situation in comparison with their pre-migration labour market situation (40 per cent unemployed after their return compared with 10 per cent prior to migration). According to a survey of return migrants in Pakistan, only 33 per cent were immediately reinserted into the labour market; 42 per cent were unemployed for more than six months. The same high levels of unemployment were recorded in Sri Lanka and in Thailand (Amjad 1989.).

In contrast with Asian labour-exporting countries, acute labour shortages are recorded in some African countries whose economies offer few prospects. In spite of massive out-migration, Lesotho's economy—because of severe land scarcity, little potential, and widespread deprivation—is not affected by labour shortages. On the contrary, the lack of (or misplaced) investments in agriculture, in addition to class differentiation caused by migration, causes increasing landlessness and unemployment of individuals unable to obtain wage employment either inside or outside the country (Murray 1981).

The ageing and the feminization of labour was noted by the people interviewed in Mali, although at the time the survey was carried out there was a de facto labour surplus because of the Sahelian drought. The elderly declared they would have to go on working instead of resting, since agriculture was in such a bad way. The overload was probably more critical for women, especially for married women with children, whose husbands had not sent enough money for them to hire labourers. Such a labour shortage, either because of the absence of the male labour force, or from a lack of hired labour, has immediate consequences for the production level, and more long-term consequences for land productivity, which is already declining because of population pressure on good land.

Swaziland, with a relatively diversified growing economy, is a different story. Following the migration of men there has been a shift from growing millet, which for religious reasons must be cultivated by men, to that of maize, traditionally cultivated by women. And, as elsewhere, agricultural tasks previously carried out by men are gradually being taken over by women (Standing 1987; Carloni, cited in Standing). Hybrid maize, giving higher yields per acreage, was consequently rapidly adopted by women. Hybrid maize cultivation was, however, seen by women as a way to secure a minimal level of production for self-consumption, involving little work and freeing time to engage in other work bringing in a cash income (De Vletter 1983).

In the Swazi urban areas, labour shortages have also been recorded, but they have been shown to be sectoral and, strangely enough, are not linked to wage differentials with South Africa. There have been labour shortages in Swazi agro-based industries which pay wages comparable with or higher than those in South Africa, but no labour shortages in manufacturing, where wage levels are lower (De Vletter *et al.* 1981).

4.8. Rural Production and Technologies

A review of the literature of international migration in Asian labour-sending countries and in Turkey indicates that such flows have had no obvious unfavourable impact on their development, because of the high levels of unemployment and underemployment. They have also had very positive effects on the welfare of migrants' households as well as macro multiplier effects.

At a lower level of aggregation the effects of migration flows on rural production are worth noting. Although urban poverty is increasing worldwide and a whole section of this chapter deals with the functioning and outcomes of urban labour markets, urban poverty is to a large extent a reflection of rural poverty and of rural–urban migration (Rodgers 1989). Thus, consideration of how internal and international migration affect rural output is a relevant policy issue. Its examination requires household primary data. Oberai and Singh (1983), in their survey of rural Punjab, found that both returning migrants and families with migrants were more innovative in agricultural techniques, the use of tractors, and agricultural inputs. Moreover all farms, irrespective of their size, showed the same trend. Again in India, Rosenzweig (1994) found in an analysis of national sample surveys that households using new technology had a 54 per cent higher proportion of absent sons and 61 per cent fewer co-resident married sons, controlling for age, education, and wealth.

In contrast with Asian patterns, the effects in African countries of both internal and international migration appear very negative. This is so despite some cultivation of new crops, the introduction of new production techniques by migrants, attempts to promote joint action through cooperatives, and the fact that some returning migrants have been agents of social change (see, for example, Chilivumbo 1985, on Zambia). The negative effects derive mainly from labour shortages in traditional agriculture, not compensated for by transformations such as mechanization, new labour-saving techniques in agriculture, the introduction of new crops, or higher use of agricultural inputs.

In their analysis of the urban–rural gap in Lesotho, Jamal and Weeks (1993) explain the need for private and public employers to set urban wages at an attractive level in comparison with the level in South Africa in order to retain skilled labour. However, examination of the level of remittances sent to rural households shows that the average rural income compares relatively favourably with that of semi-skilled wage earners. Lesotho agriculture does not benefit at all from such remittances. On the contrary, it suffers from the loss of rural workers who abandon agricultural activities. A critical factor is that there are no incentives for Lesotho farmers to invest in agriculture, because internal prices are kept down by fierce competition from low-cost South African products. According to Murray (1981), the increase in wages in South Africa in the 1970s only increased the opportunity cost of migration, while higher incomes permitted better investment possibilites.

In the 1970s, the effect of out-migration on Swaziland's agricultural sector seemed to be more positive, although many studies point to the workload women have to carry, practically without any help. Nor are they recognized as the main producers (having no land rights or access to credit). Surveys have shown that male migrants invested in farm equipment and agricultural inputs at higher rates than non-migrant households. They also arranged their time so that they could be on the farm for the heaviest agricultural work (ploughing). However, by the end of the 1970s, help from migrants was becoming more difficult to obtain. The majority of farms were no longer self-sufficient and only 12 per cent had a surplus to commercialize. The most innovative farms were the largest ones headed by old men, selling cash crops and maize surplus, whilst homesteads headed by women (as well as young men) were shown to be less inclined to spend on agricultural inputs, and farm productivity was on average less. Tractor-ploughing was expanding, but there is no correlation between absenteeism and tractor use (Carloni, in Standing 1987; De Vletter 1983; De Vletter *et al.* 1981).

In Cameroon, the picture is even bleaker and the authorities have been seriously worried about the food security and self-sufficiency of the country. Population pressure has been reduced by migration, but neither labour shortages nor remittances have led to the adoption of improved agricultural techniques or the purchase of equipment. Traditional labour-intensive techniques continue to be used, which means lower production in view of the depopulation and feminization of rural areas. The workforce on plantations is ageing and attempts to reorganize agricultural activities under cooperative action have failed (Timnou 1993). Wautelet (1995) is somewhat less negative, perceiving a subtle change in certain regions and agricultural sectors. However, a lasting transformation of Cameroon agriculture would require that peasants, whose social structures and means of economic reproduction have been undermined by migration flows, and who have now fallen back on subsistence agriculture, move boldly into monetarized agriculture. Wautelet, like other authors (including, for example, Requier-Desjardins 1995), argues that Cameroon institutions also need to undergo a complete transformation since in the past they have had a destabilizing and paralyzing effect on the country.

Peasants surveyed in Mali did not perceive that the migration of the productive labour force had had a negative impact on agricultural output but blamed the drought for the situation. They thought that if climatic conditions improved, it would be better for family groups and villages to work the land fully rather than migrating. With respect to the institutional transformations now widely advocated, some migrants had returned after quitting their jobs in France, and had formed cooperatives of a sort, using their limited savings on an investment in modern technology, with the intention of exploiting land in a more productive way. Their efforts had completely failed, however, because of conflict between the generations. The elderly, and the chiefs of villages and concessions, resented the innovative activities, perceiving the returning migrants as a threat to their authority and their control of land and production.

Conclusion

If poverty seemed previously to be confined to the rural areas of industrializing countries, patterns of development have succeeded in creating in urban areas and in cities all the symptoms associated with poverty: unemployment, inequality, lack of access to social infrastructures, and marginalization of population sub-groups on various grounds. Poverty allows individuals and households very few means of escape, being an outcome of macro and meso processes, especially the functioning of labour markets, which tend to exclude much of the population.

Spatial mobility, particularly across national borders, and in view of the widespread poverty within individual countries and the increasing gap between poor and rich countries, obviously offers an attractive alternative to higher participation in depressed national labour markets. We have seen that the lot of international migrants is generally a great improvement on what they can expect from staying at home, a reality indicated by the actual magnitude of international migration. However, international migration remains marginal in terms of the percentage of the population concerned in the labour-sending countries, not being larger than a few percentage points, with the exception of a few labour-reserve countries. We have sought to show the temporary and fluctuating nature of such population movements, as well as their economic impacts on the countries of origin. In the short term, the micro and macro impacts are undoubtedly positive, overall bringing money to the households and to the economy, enabling both to satisfy the most urgent needs.

There is, however, no evidence that either at the household level or at a higher one, international migration effectively contributes to long-term development. On the contrary, it seems to be harmful in countries which cannot accommodate new technologies, production methods, and institutions. When we compare the economic performance of countries which export their cheap labour with those which exploit it domestically, 'aid in place of migration' seems to be the more efficient course (Böhning and Schloeter-Paredes 1994).

11 Rapid Urbanization and the Urban Environment

DAVID SATTERTHWAITE

Introduction

This chapter reviews the range of environmental hazards present in urban areas in Africa, Asia, and Latin America and their impact on human health. It discusses the groups that are most vulnerable to environmental hazards and suggests that low-income groups (and, within such groups, women and children) bear most of the health burden arising from environmental problems. It also questions two common assumptions: that the large and often rapidly growing cities in the South have the most serious environmental problems; and that poverty necessarily contributes to environmental degradation.

1. Relationships between Population and Environment in Urban Areas

1.1. The Relationship between Population and Environmental Problems in Cities

Depending on which 'environmental problem' is considered, there can be a strong, weak or no association between the scale of the 'environmental problem' and the number of people in an urban centre. Thus, a discussion of the links between environmental problems and population in cities must specify which environmental 'problems' are being considered.

For instance, many of the cities with among the highest levels of air pollution and

This chapter draws on and develops work that has already been published, especially Satterthwaite (1994), Satterthwaite (1993), and Hardoy, Mitlin, and Satterthwaite (1992). The relationship between population and environment in urban areas has long been a particular interest of the Human Settlements Programme of the International Institute for Environment and Development in which the author works. This chapter also draws heavily on what the author learnt about health–environment linkages during work undertaken with the World Health Organization's Commission on Health and the Environment and its report *Our Planet, Our Health* (WHO 1992a) and with WHO staff and consultants who provided the specialist knowledge about health–environment linkages in urban areas. In this, special thanks are due to Wilfred Kreisel, Greg Goldstein, and Francesco Sella. However, the author remains responsible for any errors in the text.

with the most polluted waterways are also cities where there have been enormous reductions in the contributions of environment-related diseases to ill health and premature death. This is largely because a relatively high proportion of the population has access to piped water, sanitation, and health care. The life and health of urban dwellers in most small urban centres in Africa and Asia (most of which have slow population growth rates) is far more at risk from environmental hazards than those of the inhabitants of cities like Mexico City or São Paulo where problems of air pollution, water pollution. and hazardous/toxic wastes are more serious. In the small urban centres, the toll taken on human health is principally due to biological pathogens in food, carried in water or in the air, or spread by disease vectors (arising from very inadequate provision for safe and sufficient water supplies and for the disposal of excreta, inadequate provision to control disease vectors, and an inadequate health care system).

Similarly, many of the cities with the highest-quality environments are also those with the most unsustainable levels of resource use and greenhouse gas emissions. Cities that perform well in terms of air and water quality, housing quality, absence of environment-related diseases, access to open space, and protection of natural landscapes in their surrounds, are also generally those with the highest levels of non-renewable resource use per person and also the highest levels of stratospheric ozone-depleting chemical emissions and greenhouse gas emissions per person. By contrast, most urban centres in Africa and Asia and many in Latin America have levels of resource use and levels of greenhouse gas emissions per person that are one thousandth or less that of these wealthy cities and yet have life expectancies of under fifty years, infant mortality rates of 100 or more per 1,000 live births, and environment-related diseases responsible for most ill health and premature death.

The associations between 'rapid urbanization' and environmental problems also vary too much from country to country or city to city to generalize about. Certainly, there is no simple association between the most rapidly-growing cities and the most serious environmental problems—and quite often a rapidly-growing city (which is generally a prosperous city) is one where the most serious environmental problems in terms of their impact on human health are being much reduced. The city of Curitiba, which is so often held up as an example of a city in the South with a very high quality environment and a strong commitment to public transport (see Rabinovitch 1992), has also been among the world's most rapidly-growing cities over the last few decades. São Paulo, for all its huge size, very rapid growth over the last century or so, and serious environmental problems, still has piped water and electricity provided for 95 per cent of its inhabitants, and most households are also connected to public sewers and have regular solid waste collection services (Jacobi 1994).

In effect, each city, as it grows, goes through a number of stages in which the most serious environmental problems affecting the city population are addressed, but new ones also become apparent as the city's economy and size increases (see, for instance, Bartone *et al.* 1994; Satterthwaite 1997). The initial environmental problems are those caused by the concentration of people and enterprises—the environmental health problems that arise from a lack of provision for piped water supplies, sanitation and drainage, solid waste collection, and health care. Increased prosperity brings with it increased potential to reduce these environmental problems. For those with rising incomes, this also means rising capacity to pay for this provision; and if provision is efficient, most or all of the costs can be recouped. As 'environmental health problems' are addressed, and as the city's economic base grows, so chemical and physical hazards grow, many of them originating in enterprises. If growing economic prosperity is based on rapid industrialization, this can mean serious industrial air and water pollution and growing problems with hazardous wastes. In cities with rapid industrial growth, there are often strong pressures brought by industrial and commercial concerns to limit pollution control. Rapid industrial growth in the absence of pollution control can produce very unhealthy cities—of which Cubatao in Brazil is one of the best-known examples, although environmental quality in this city has improved greatly since it came to be known as 'the Valley of Death'.

As chemical and physical hazards are addressed, through much improved pollution control, waste management, and control of occupational hazards provision, they usually give way to environmental problems linked to high-consumption lifestyles and an increasing number of private automobiles. Problems of industrial pollution are often lessened too, through the deindustrialization of cities or more effective pollution control. The mix of air pollutants also changes, reflecting the increased role of automobile emissions and the reduced role of industry and power stations. And the large cities also have an increasing impact on their wider regions and eventually on global systems.

If nations are compared, there is certainly an association between economic growth, increasing levels of urbanization,[1] and increasing levels of resource use and waste generation per person. There is a strong association between increasing levels of urbanization, increasing numbers of middle- and upper-income people with high consumption lifestyles, and increasing calls made on the planet's non-renewable resources and the capacity of global systems to absorb or breakdown wastes. It is the way in which cities' environmental problems that first appear to be local in scope are transferred to the regional and the global level that the next section turns.

1.2. The Transfer of Environmental Problems from the Local to the Global

One generalization that may have widespread validity is that the more prosperous a city becomes, over time, the more the demands grow for action on the most serious local environmental problems, and the more difficult it is for those in power to ignore this. There is an association between the proportion of city populations

---

[1] At some point, the relationship between economic growth and increasing levels of urbanization weakens and stops but this is largely because the 'rural' areas have been urbanized in the sense that most rural inhabitants are not working in agriculture, forestry or fishing and many work in urban areas or in industrial, commercial or financial concerns located in 'greenfield sites' that are classified as rural.

served with piped water and provision for sanitation and the per-capita income of the country in which they are located (World Bank 1992; Bartone *et al.* 1994). As action is taken on environmental problems within the city, there is a transfer of responsibility for environmental management from the individual and household level to the neighbourhood and city level (McGranahan and Songsore 1994).

In this same process, there is also a transfer of wastes and pollutants from the city to the region and finally to the global commons. A house provided with a connection to a sewer allows the household to get rid of excreta and waste waters from the home and the residential area with great convenience, no hazard to the household, and none of the maintenance or emptying problems associated with pit latrines or even septic tanks. But initially, the sewer system may simply dump the wastes in a nearby river so the waste problem is transferred to a neighbouring area. As city-wide sewers and storm drains are developed, the problem is transferred to the region: liquid wastes are dumped untreated into the sea or estuary or other regional water bodies. Although the population in the wider region suffers—the wastes often not only contaminate the surface water used by nearby urban centres and rural settlements but also damage or destroy fisheries—the city becomes much cleaner and safer as a result. Similarly, as an efficient garbage collection system develops, it transfers city wastes to landfill sites around the city, which, if not properly managed, can contaminate groundwater. The growing demand for water in a city is usually 'solved' by drawing on ever more distant watersheds, often with damage to their ecology and sometimes with the result that water previously used by households and farmers in these localities is no longer available to them.

Air pollution is often transferred from inside the home and the city to the region. Coal- or wood-burning stoves or open fires that cause serious indoor air pollution and may contribute to high levels of air pollution in the wider city—as they do in cities such as Delhi (Centre for Science and Environment 1983) and many Chinese cities (Smil 1984)—may be replaced by electric cookers, the source of air pollution thus being transferred to the chimneys of a thermal power station. Industries or power stations may reduce their contribution to a city's air pollution by building taller chimneys that transfer the problem to more distant areas through acid precipitation.

The problems of overexploiting the ecosystems in the areas around the city to feed the city population and provide its enterprises with raw materials are solved by importing food and raw materials from ever greater distances (often increasingly from other countries) so it is distant forests and farmlands that are exploited to serve the city population. A Canadian ecologist has termed the impact that a city has on ecosystems its 'ecological footprint' and has also pointed out how international this footprint often becomes for the world's wealthiest cities (Rees 1992). A wealthy city can keep it own parks, rivers, lakes, and natural landscapes intact because the environmental damage done by the energy- and chemical-intensive food and natural-resource production that feeds its population and enterprises is now done 'overseas'. This also greatly increases the energy input into the food and raw materials—especially for food imported by air—so levels of greenhouse gas emissions per person increase very considerably.

1.3. Poverty–Environment Linkages in Urban Areas

There is surprisingly little detailed study of the relationship between the environment and poverty, despite the volumes of papers and books written on the subject. It is clear that the relationship between poverty/wealth and resource use and management is not simple. Different case studies show how both poverty and wealth can result in environmental degradation or protection depending on the range of choices open to individuals, households, and communities, and the measures (or lifestyles) they adopt. For instance, some of the world's most prosperous cities have a much lower level of resource consumption and greenhouse emissions per person than others with comparable levels of wealth (see, for instance, Newman and Kenworthy 1989).

In urban areas of the South, as later sections of this chapter will describe, people with low incomes bear most of the health burden from environmental hazards but they are not themselves a significant cause of environmental problems. Their levels of resource use and waste-generation are very low. One reason for the Third World's low use of resources is the very low incomes on which many of its urban population survive. The 600 million or so poorest urban dwellers in the Third World have too few capital goods to represent much of a drain on the world's finite non-renewable resource base. Low-income households in most cities in the South generate very little household waste and much of the metal, glass, paper, and other items in their wastes are re-used or recycled. The houses they construct make widespread use of recycled or reclaimed materials and little use of cement and other materials with a high energy input. Most poor urban dwellers rely on public transport or bicycles, or move around the city on foot, which ensures low averages for oil consumption per person. There are also many case studies of urban agriculture with very high levels of production per unit area achieved without high inputs of chemical fertilizer that reveal enormous possibilities for reducing the land area needed to feed city consumers (see Smit, Ratta, and Nasr 1996; Lee-Smith *et al.* 1987).

The poverty/environment relationship in rural areas also becomes important for cities if there is widespread environmental degradation linked to poverty. This can undermine the rural resource base on which the consumers and producers in nearby cities depend and increase migration flows to cities because many rural dwellers have livelihoods that can no longer be sustained. But here, too, it is difficult to see how poor groups can be a major source of environmental degradation since their poverty is largely a result of their being denied access to the best land, to forests, and to freshwater. How can they degrade the very resources to which they have no access?

2. Environmental Hazards and their Impact on Health

2.1. Introduction

In most urban areas in the Third World, environment-related diseases or accidents remain among the major causes of illness, injury, and premature death. In many urban areas, or in particular districts within larger cities, they are the leading causes of death and illness. Most of this health burden is preventable. Environmental hazards were also major causes of ill-health, injury, and premature death in cities in Europe and North America only a hundred or so years ago (Wohl 1983). The fact that this is no longer so reveals the extent to which human interventions can modify the urban environment and protect populations from life-threatening and health-threatening environmental hazards. Infant mortality rates provide one example of such progress. Today, in healthy, well-served cities, infant mortality rates should be less than ten per 1,000 live births and may be as low as five. In a healthy city, it is very rare for an infant or child to die from an infectious or parasitic disease. Only 100 years ago, most prosperous European cities still had infant mortality rates that exceeded 100 per 1,000 live births; in many, including Vienna, Berlin, Leipzig, Naples, St. Petersberg, and many of England's large industrial towns, the figure exceeded 200 (Wohl 1983; Bairoch 1988).

Box 11.1 lists seven kinds of health hazard that are common in urban environments. Four have a direct bearing on health: biological disease-causing agents (pathogens), chemical pollutants, a shortage of (or lack of access to) particular natural resources, and physical hazards. These are the four most pressing urban environmental problems in terms of their health impact in Africa and much of Asia and Latin America. Three others also influence health, although less directly: aspects of the built environment with negative consequences for people's health; natural-resource degradation; and national/global environmental degradation (including a rising concentration of greenhouse gases in the atmosphere and the depletion of the stratospheric ozone layer). This chapter will concentrate on the first four of these.

2.2. Biological Pathogens

Biological pathogens in the human environment—in water, food, air or soil—represent the single most serious environmental problem in terms of their impact on human health (WHO 1992a). In city environments, whether they have a negligible impact on health or are a major cause of disease and death depends above all on the quality and competence of public action to reduce or eliminate human contact with faecal matter and other life- and health-threatening biological pathogens in the air, water, food, and soil. Of paramount importance is provision for piped, treated water, sanitation, drainage, services to collect and dispose of garbage and other solid wastes, disease vector control (for instance of rats and of the *Anopheles* mosquitoes that are the vector for malaria) and preventive focused health care. Improving housing conditions is also important, so as to reduce overcrowding and to ensure that all households have adequate provision for water, sanitation, garbage collection, and health care. A prevention oriented primary health care system is essential, not only because it can rapidly treat diseases but also for its capacity to ensure that people are immunized against the many communicable diseases for which immunizations are cheap and effective. In the

1. Biological pathogens or pollutants within the human environment that impair human health—including pathogenic agents and their vectors (and reservoirs)—for instance the many pathogenic microorganisms in human excreta, airborne pathogens (for instance those responsible for acute respiratory infections and tuberculosis) and disease vectors such as malaria-carrying (Anopheline) mosquitoes

2. Chemical pollutants within the human environment—including those added to the environment by human activities (e.g. industrial wastes) and chemical agents present in the environment independent of human activities.

3. The availability, cost and quality of natural resources on which human health depends—for instance food, water and fuel.

4. Physical hazards (e.g. high risks of flooding in houses and settlements built on flood-plains or of mud slides or landslides for houses on slopes)

5. Aspects of the built environment with negative consequences on physical or psycho-social health (e.g. overcrowding, inadequate protection against noise, inadequate provision of infrastructure, services and common areas).

6. Natural resource degradation (e.g. of soil and water quality) caused by wastes from city-based producers or consumers which impacts on the health/livelihoods of some urban dwellers.

7. National/global environmental degradation with more indirect but long-term influences on human health:

   • the depletion of finite non-renewable resource bases;
   • wastes from human activities that contribute to possible threats to the functioning and stability of global cycles and systems and the increasing frequency of extreme climatic conditions (e.g. greenhouse gas emissions and gaseous emissions that contribute to the depletion of the stratospheric ozone layer).

Box 11.1 Hazards to health within the urban environment

urban areas in the South, there remain at least 600 million urban dwellers whose life and health remains continuously under threat from biological pathogens (Hardoy *et al.* 1990).

Table 11.1 lists the main water-related infections, with estimates of morbidity, mortality, and population at risk (where these are available). These are global estimates covering rural and urban areas; there are no figures which cover only urban areas. Waterborne diseases are the single-largest category of communicable diseases worldwide and account for more than 4 million infant and child deaths per year (WHO 1992a). In many Third World cities or city districts, waterborne diseases are among the major causes of infant and child death and a major cause of adult death. In contrast, very few fatal cases of waterborne diseases are now recorded in Europe or North America.

Diarrhoeal diseases account for most water-related infant and child deaths in

Table 11.1. The most serious water-related infections with estimates of the burden of morbidity and mortality they cause and the population at risk

Disease		Morbidity	Mortality (No. of deaths/year)	Population at risk
Common name	Medical name			
Water-borne and water-washed				
Cholera	Cholera*	More than 300,000	More than 6,000	
Diarrhoeal diseases	This group includes salmonellosis,* shigellosis,* Campylobacter,* E. coli, rota-virus, amoebiasis* and giardiasis*	700 million or more people infected each year, 1.8 billion episodes a year	More than 3 million	More than 2,000 million
Enteric fevers	Paratyphoid			
	Typhoid	500,000 cases; 1 million infections (1977–8)	25,000	
Infant jaundice	Hepatitis A*			
Pinworm	Enterobiasis			
Polio	Poliomyelitis	204,000	25,000	
Roundworm	Ascariasis	800–1,000 million infected; 214 million with clinical symptoms	60,000	
Leptospirosis	Leptospirosis			
Whipworm	Trichuriasis	133 million cases		
Water-washed				
Skin and eye infections				
Scabies	Scabies			
Impetigo	Impetigo			
Trachoma	Trachoma	6–9 million people blind;		500 million
Leishmaniasis	Leishmaniasis	13 million infected; 400,000 new infections/year	197,000	350 million

Other				
Relapsing fever	Relapsing fever			
Typhus	Rickettsial diseases			
Water-based				
Penetrating skin				
Bilharzia	Schistosomiasis	200 million infected	Over 200,000	500–600 million
Ingested				
Guinea worm	Dracunculiasis	Over 10 million infected		Over 100 million
Water-related insect vector				
Biting near water				
Sleeping sickness	African Trypanosomiasis	20,000 new cases/year	55,000	50 million
Breeding in water				
Filaria	Filariasis (lymphatic)	100 million people infected		900 million
Malaria	Malaria	267 million infections a year; 107 million clinical cases a year	2 million (more than half children under 5)	2,100 million
River blindness	Onchocerciasis	18 million infected (over 300,000 blind)	35,000	85–90 million
Yellow fever	Yellow fever	200,000 new cases/year	30,000	
Breakbone fever	Dengue fever	Millions of cases each year with 500,000+ people needing hospital treatment	23,000	

* Also food-borne.

Source: Adapted from WHO (1992), *Our Planet, Our Health*, Report of the World Commission on Health and Environment, Geneva. The structure of the table was drawn from Cairncross, S. and Feachem, R. G. (1983), *Environmental Health Engineering in the Tropics—An Introductory Text*, Chichester: John Wiley and Sons, and White, G. F., Bradley, D. J. and White, A. U. (1972), *Drawers of Water: Domestic Water Use in East Africa*, Chicago: University of Chicago Press. Figures for morbidity, mortality, and population at risk from WHO (1991), *Global Estimates for Health Situation Assessment and Projections 1990*, Geneva, April, with figures updated from WHO (1995), *The World Health Report 1995: Bridging the Gaps*, Geneva: World Health Organization.

urban areas, and a high proportion of illnesses. Risk factors include overcrowding, poor sanitation, contaminated water, and inadequate food hygiene (Rossi-Espagnet, Goldstein, and Tabibzadeh 1991). Many studies of poor urban districts have shown diarrhoeal diseases to be a major cause of morbidity and mortality (see, for instance, Songsore and McGranahan 1993; Misra 1990). Where water supplies and provision for sanitation are inadequate for high proportions of the entire population, they can remain one of the most serious health problems within city-wide averages.

Among the various water-related diseases listed in Table 11.1, filariasis and intestinal worms (especially ascariasis/roundworm) stand out for the millions of urban people who are debilitated by them; only a small proportion of those infected with these diseases will die as a result but they cause severe pain to hundreds of millions (WHO 1991). Various case studies in low-income settlements have shown that a high proportion of the population suffers from intestinal worms (for a summary of many of these studies, see Bradley *et al.* 1991).

Many disease vectors live, breed or feed within or around houses and settlements in urban areas (see Schofield *et al.* 1990). The diseases they carry or induce are some of the major causes of ill-health and premature death in many cities— especially malaria (*Anopheles* mosquitoes) and diarrhoeal diseases (cockroaches, blowflies, and houseflies). In many cities or poor peripheral city districts in Africa, Asia, and Latin America, malaria is one of the main causes of illness and death (Schofield *et al.* 1990; Rossi-Espagnet, Goldstein, and Tabibzadeh 1991). Many other diseases listed in Table 11.1 are also caused or carried by insects, spiders, or mites. Many of these vectors thrive when there is poor drainage and inadequate provision for garbage collection, sanitation, and piped water supply: Anopheles mosquitoes breed in standing water; the sandflies which transmit leishmaniasis can breed in piles of refuse or in pit latrines; and *Culex quinquefasciatus* mosquitoes, which are one of the vectors for bancroftian leishmaniasis, can breed in open or cracked septic tanks, flooded pit latrines, and drains (Cairncross and Feachem 1993).

Some diseases transmitted by insect vectors have long been an urban problem; for instance, reports on malaria in Freetown, Sierra Leone, date from 1926 (Blacklock and Evans 1926, quoted in Rossi-Espagnet, Goldstein, and Tabibzadeh 1991) while colonial town planning regulations in Nigeria sought to protect the colonial populations from malaria by insisting on a building-free zone between European and non-European residential areas (Aradeon, Aina, and Umo 1986). Other diseases remain concentrated in rural areas, especially those, such as schistosomiasis, which are associated with water reservoirs and irrigation canals and ditches—although even schistosomiasis is widespread in many cities (Rossi-Espagnet, Goldstein, and Tabibzadeh 1991). One reason for this is the number of infected rural inhabitants who move to urban areas. Another is that some disease vectors have adapted to urban environments or the expanding urban areas have produced changes in the local ecology that favour the emergence or multiplication of a particular disease vector; these factors help explain the rapid increase in lymphatic filariasis and malaria in urban populations (WHO 1992a). The diseases spread by the Aedes group of mosquitoes (which include dengue, dengue haemorrhagic fever, and yellow fever) are serious health problems in many cities. Pots and jars, small tanks, drums and cisterns used for storing water in houses lacking regular piped supplies can provide breeding habitats for these mosquitoes (Rossi-Espagnet, Goldstein, and Tabibzadeh 1991); so too can small pools of clean water within residential areas in, for instance, discarded tin cans and rubber tyres (Cairncross and Feachem 1993). Chagas disease, with which an estimated 18 million people in Latin America are infected, primarily affects poor rural households, as the insect vector rests and breeds in cracks in house walls. But it is increasingly an urban problem too, both through the migration of infected persons to urban areas (there is no effective treatment for the disease) and through the peri-urban informal settlements where the insect vectors are evident (Gomes Pereira 1989; Briceno-Leon 1990).

Acute respiratory infections (especially pneumonia) are a major cause of infant and child death and ill-health in urban (and rural) areas although their extent, their health impact, and the risk factors associated with them remain poorly understood. One-fifth of all infant deaths in Porto Alegre, Brazil, were found to be due to pneumonia. Mortality rates from pneumonia were six times higher in illegal settlements than in other areas, and the main cause of infant death there (Guimaraes and Fischmann 1985). Respiratory infections are also among the most common sources of ill-health among children and adults; recent studies in Jakarta (Surjadi 1993) and Accra (Songsore and McGranahan 1993) show the toll taken by these. The quality of the indoor environment has an important influence on the incidence and severity of respiratory infections—perhaps most especially through overcrowding, inadequate ventilation, dampness, and indoor air pollution from coal or biomass combustion for cooking and/or heating. A child who contracts bronchitis or pneumonia in the Third World is fifty times more likely to die than a child in Europe or North America (Pio 1986; WHO 1992a).

A combination of overcrowded conditions and a lack of health care services which can implement effective immunization programmes help ensure that the diseases spread by airborne infection or contact which are easily prevented by vaccines, such as measles and pertussis (whooping cough), remain major causes of ill health and infant and child death. Measles is a major cause of infant and child morbidity and mortality in poor urban areas (Foster 1990). Tuberculosis, another vaccine-preventable disease, is the single-largest cause of adult mortality worldwide, accounting for some 3 million deaths a year (WHO 1992a). The incidence of tuberculosis is also linked to overcrowded conditions in urban areas. The highest incidence tends to be among populations living in the poorest areas, with high levels of overcrowding and high numbers of social contacts (WHO 1992a). A combination of overcrowding and poor ventilation often means that TB infection is transmitted to more than half the family members (Cauthen, Pio, and ten Dam 1988).

2.3. Water Supply[2]

Hundreds of millions of urban dwellers still have no alternative but to use contaminated water or water whose quality is not guaranteed. Hundreds of millions more have supplies that are safer but still not sufficient to bring the health benefits that a safe and accessible water supply should bring. In 1990, around half the urban population in the South had a water supply piped into their home (WHO/UNICEF 1993) although a considerable proportion of these only had intermittent supplies (sometimes only one or two hours a day). In addition, in many piped water systems, the quality of the water is not guaranteed, especially where pipes are poorly maintained (which is often the case) and where water pressure often drops to the point where seepage into the pipe can contaminate it.

In 1990, around a quarter of the South's urban population were supplied through less convenient means—public standpipes, yard taps, protected dug wells, and boreholes/handpumps (WHO/UNICEF 1993); here, too, the quality of such water is often not fit to drink. The rest, around 300 million, did not have a safe, protected water supply and usually relied on one of two sources: water from streams or other surface sources that in urban areas are often little more than open sewers; or water purchased from vendors, the quality of which is not guaranteed, and costing per litre between four and 100 times the amount paid by richer households for publicly provided piped water (World Bank 1988). Water vendors probably serve between 20 and 30 per cent of the Third World's urban population (Briscoe 1986).

Official United Nations statistics considerably overstate the proportion of the urban population 'adequately served' with piped water. This is for two reasons. The first is the definitions used as to what is adequate; the second is the tendency of governments to greatly exaggerate, and United Nations agencies are not allowed to question the figures supplied by governments. People are considered adequately served with water if they have '. . . *access* to an *adequate amount* of *safe* drinking water located within a *convenient distance* from the user's dwelling', each of the these notions of adequacy being decided by individual countries, not by the international agencies responsible for monitoring progress (WHO/UNICEF 1993). A considerable proportion of those who are said to have 'safe' water do not have drinking water at a convenient distance. A family of five or six persons needs around 300 litres of water a day to meet all its needs, the equivalent of 30 or more full buckets. Governments often claim that if a household is within 100 metres of a public standpipe, it is adequately served. But even fetching and carrying water from a source that is twenty or thirty metres from a house is an onerous and time-consuming task, if sufficient water is to be obtained for washing, laundry, personal hygiene, and house cleaning. Eye and ear infections, skin diseases, scabies, lice, and fleas are very difficult to control without sufficient supplies of water to permit regular washing, personal hygiene, and clothes washing. The amount of water a family uses will

---

[2] Most of the statistics on global and regional coverage for water supply and sanitation are drawn from WHO/UNICEF (1993).

be much influenced by the distance that water has to be carried, so the convenience of a water source can be as important for health as its quality (Cairncross 1990).

Governments also include all those served by public standpipes or boreholes with a handpump as having safe drinking water. But it is common for there to be only one tap or pump for dozens or even hundreds of households. In low-income settlements in cities, there are often 500 or more persons per tap; a survey in one part of Dakar, Senegal, in the late 1980s found 1,513 persons to a tap (Ngom 1989). Long queues at a public tap (especially if water is only available for a few hours a day, as is often the case) and time spent making repeated trips back to the house uses up time that could be used in earning an income. In addition, many public water standpipes in urban areas are poorly maintained. It is surprising to find how many countries claim that between 80 and 99 per cent of their urban population has adequate water supplies when detailed studies from these same countries suggest much lower percentages. For instance, the official statistics for India suggest that 87 per cent of its urban population has adequate provision for safe water, while those for Pakistan claim a coverage of 80 per cent. Ghana, Ethiopia, and Burundi are among those countries claiming that more than 90 per cent of their urban population has access to safe water (WHO/UNICEF 1993).

Thus, the proportion of the world's urban population that is said to have safe water supplies is certainly much larger than the proportion that has a regular, sufficient, and convenient supply of good quality water at an affordable cost. (The same is undoubtedly true for rural areas for similar reasons.) Where data are available for a range of urban centres within a country, the proportion of the population with piped supplies is generally much lower in smaller urban centres. For instance, in Argentina, the smaller the urban centre, the higher the proportion of households lacking piped water and connection to sewers (Hardoy, Mitlin, and Satterthwaite 1992). In Bolivia, a much higher proportion of the populations of the two largest and most prosperous cities—La Paz and Santa Cruz—have safe water than in smaller, less important urban centres such as Tarija and Sucre where close to half the population lack a safe water supply (WHO/UNICEF 1993). In most countries of the South, a large proportion of the urban population lives in small and intermediate-sized urban centres where levels of provision for water supply and sanitation are usually much worse than in the larger cities.

2.4. Sanitation

Official statistics suggest that at least a third of the South's urban population is unserved by sanitation and an even greater number lacks adequate means to dispose of waste waters (Sinnatamby 1990). A much larger proportion lacks adequate provision for sanitation in the form of toilets that minimize the possibility of human contact with human excreta and are easy to keep clean; more than three-fifths of the urban population in the South are not connected to public sewer systems. Where there are sewers, typically they are located in the richer residential, governmental, and commercial areas. It is not only the smaller cities that are so badly served; many major cities with a million or more inhabitants have no sewers. Most of their inhabitants also lack connection to septic tanks or to small bore sewer systems.

Again, official statistics exaggerate the proportion of the urban population with adequate sanitation for reasons similar to those given for water supply. In reporting to United Nations agencies, governments make their own definitions with regard to what is considered an adequate sanitary facility, the distance deemed 'convenient' between the dwelling and the sanitary facility, and what constitutes 'access' (WHO/UNICEF 1993). People judged to have 'access to sanitation' often have only a communal pit latrine that has to be shared by dozens of households, where there is little or no provision for maintenance, and where there is no water source nearby to permit washing after defecation. The use of such latrines may constitute a much greater health hazard than defecation in the open. Communal toilets may be maintained to a high standard of hygiene—although it is rare for this to be achieved, without comprehensive provision for cleaning and maintenance. Thus, a considerable proportion of those judged to have provision for sanitation in government's official statistics— which then form the basis for the statistics of international agencies—do not have adequate provision. For instance, in Accra, there was a close association between the prevalence of diarrhoea in children under six and the sharing of toilets (Songsore and McGranahan 1993); officially, those who shared toilets may well have been included in the government statistics as having adequate sanitation.

Among the countries claiming in 1990 that 80 per cent of more of their urban population was provided with sanitation were Equatorial Guinea (95 per cent), Sierra Leone (92 per cent), the Sudan (88 per cent), Jamaica (100 per cent) and Cameroon (100 per cent) (WHO/UNICEF 1992). Such figures do not accord with detailed reports on levels of provision in the major cities within these countries.

2.5. Solid Waste Collection

In most cities in the South, between a third and half of the solid wastes generated within urban centres remains uncollected and such wastes generally accumulate on open spaces, wasteland and streets and bring with them serious health and environmental problems (Cointreau 1982). These wastes generally add greatly to water pollution, when it rains, as much of this waste is organic matter and ends up swept into water bodies. In many of the urban centres in the lowest-income countries, perhaps only 10–20 per cent of solid waste is collected. For instance, in a survey of thirty-four municipalities in India, more than three-fifths collected less than 40 per cent of the wastes generated daily (Nath *et al.* 1983). For Karachi, only a third of the solid waste produced in the city is being removed (Beg *et al.* 1985).

Among many municipalities in the South, solid waste collection and management often consumes as much as 20–40 per cent of municipal revenues and it often suffers more than other municipal services when budget allocations and cuts are made (Cointreau 1982). The agencies responsible for the collection and disposal of household wastes are often understaffed and underfunded—and since virtually all have to use collection trucks that are imported, there are often serious problems with collection trucks out of use because of a lack of spare parts. Too little attention to servicing and maintenance adds to this problem (see, for instance, Kulaba 1989).

The poorest areas of any city are generally the worst served by garbage collection service, or not served at all. For instance, in Dhaka, 90 per cent of the 'slum' areas are without regular garbage collection services (Momin 1992). The resulting problems are obvious—the smells, the disease vectors and pests attracted by garbage (rats, mosquitoes, flies etc.) and the overflowing drainage channels clogged with garbage. Leachates from decomposing and putrefying garbage can contaminate water sources (UNCHS 1988). Since the poorest areas of cities are also generally the ones worst served by provision for sanitation, the uncollected solid wastes usually include a significant proportion of faecal matter. The risks are obvious for children playing on open sites with faecally contaminated garbage, as also for waste-pickers sorting through the garbage, and flies and cockroaches feeding on garbage can also subsequently contaminate food (Cointreau 1982).

These problems are especially serious for the inhabitants of the larger and most densely populated informal or illegal settlements or tenement districts that have no regular garbage collection service since there is nowhere close by where wastes can be disposed of. The informal or illegal settlements on the periphery of cities, rarely receive regular waste collection services, partly because the unpaved roads are so poor that it is difficult or impossible for garbage collection trucks to enter these areas. Some municipal governments provide a less comprehensive and convenient service to such settlements in an effort to reduce costs—for instance, communal pick-up points or communal garbage skips. But the further away these are from the household, the less frequently people use them and the more garbage is dropped on the way to them (White 1993). In addition, collections from such communal points are often irregular and overflowing skips or dumps become a serious health hazard in themselves and also discourage households from using them.

2.6. Chemical Pollutants in the Urban Environment

There are several chemical pollutants, commonly found in urban areas, which affect human health or about which there is concern, even if the precise health impact remains unknown. To date, most concern regarding health effects has centred on lead (in food, water and air); indoor air pollutants from fuel combustion; toxic/hazardous wastes; and ambient air pollution.

Lead   This is a particular concern, especially as regards children, because of increasing evidence that relatively low concentrations of lead in the blood may greatly affect their mental development—and this is an effect that persists into adulthood (Needleman *et al.* 1991). Exposure to lead may also contribute significantly to higher risks of heart attacks and strokes in adults. The four major sources of lead are: exhausts from petrol-driven motor vehicles (except vehicles that use lead-free petrol); lead water piping (especially where water supplies are acidic);

industrial emissions; and lead in paint. A study of lead levels in the blood in adult volunteers in ten cities between 1979 and 1981 found the highest lead concentration in Mexico City residents; levels were above the WHO guideline—and also between two and four times higher than in cities where low-lead or lead-free gasoline was used (UNEP and WHO 1988). A study in Mexico City in 1988 found that over a quarter of the newborn infants in Mexico City had lead levels in their blood high enough to impair neurological and motor-physical development (Rothenburg *et al.* 1988). A study in Bangkok that sought to rank urban environmental problems based on their health risks suggested that lead should be ranked with airborne particulates and biological pathogens (primarily acute diarrhoea, dengue fever, dysentery, and intestinal worms) as the highest-risk environmental problems (US AID 1990).

Indoor air pollution   Emissions from coal, wood, and other biomass fuels burnt indoors certainly affect more rural than urban dwellers, since many more rural households are regularly exposed to potentially harmful emissions from open fires or poorly designed stoves with inadequate attention to venting the flue gases. Estimates suggest hundreds of millions of rural inhabitants suffer from ill-health as a result; perhaps tens of millions of urban households are similarly affected. Certainly, in many cities coal and biomass fuels are widely used, especially among poorer households. The most serious health risks are from burns and smoke inhalation (WHO 1992a). Chronic effects of smoke inhalation include inflammation of the respiratory tract caused by continued exposure to irritant gases and fumes which ' . . . reduces resistance to acute respiratory infection, and infection in turn enhances susceptibility to the inflammatory effects of smoke and fumes, establishing a vicious circle of pathological change. These processes may lead to emphysema and chronic obstructive pulmonary disease which can progress to the stage where impaired lung function reduces the circulation of blood through the lungs, causing right-side heart failure (cor pulmonale)' (Pandey *et al.* 1989, quoted in WHO 1992a). Cor pulmonale is a crippling killer disease, characterized by a prolonged period of distressing breathlessness preceding death. However, McGranahan (1991) notes that while some studies have suggested that indoor air pollution has significant effects on health, others have been unable to show a clear link.

Occupational exposure   The health impacts of occupational exposures to chemical pollutants are also an important cause of ill-health. Environmental hazards are evident in workplaces from large factories and commercial institutions down to small 'backstreet' workshops and work from the home. They include dangerous concentrations of toxic chemicals and dust, as well as other environmental hazards such as inadequate lighting, ventilation, and space, and inadequate protection of workers from machinery and noise. Many case studies show a high proportion of workers in particular industries or industrial plants whose health is affected by workplace exposures. For instance, a study of an Egyptian pesticide factory found that ' . . . about 40 per cent of the workers had problems related to pesticide poisoning, ranging from asthma to enlarged livers' (Pepall 1992: 15). In most countries, the scale of occupational injuries and diseases is almost certainly greatly underreported. For instance, the Mexican Social Security Institute reported an average of 2,000 to 3,000 cases of work-related illnesses across the country in 1988 but a study in just one large steel mill found 4,000–5,000 cases alone, with more than 80 per cent of the workers exposed to extreme heat, loud noise and toxic dust (Castonguay 1992). A paper on Bangkok's environmental problems noted that a remarkable number of Thai workers are exposed to poor working environments but that the number of workers suffering from occupational diseases is small. Phantumvanit and Liengcharernsit (1989) suggest that '. . . this may be a reflection of the difficulties of linking disease to working conditions rather than revealing a satisfactory condition' (p.38).Other studies have shown serious health impacts on workers from exposure to toxic chemicals—for instance benzene poisoning, in leather workers in Turkey (Askoy *et al.* 1976) and lead poisoning in people working in lead-acid battery repair shops in Kingston, Jamaica (Matte *et al.* 1989).

Ambient air pollution   There are also the health impacts of air pollutants outdoors. In many Third World cities, the mix and concentration of air pollutants are already high enough to cause illness in more susceptible individuals, and premature death among the elderly, especially those with respiratory problems (WHO 1992a). Current levels of air pollution may also be impairing the health of far more people but the links have not been proven. The (limited) data on air pollution in Third World cities also suggest that it is generally getting worse.

Cities have often been associated with air pollution, especially since the industrial revolution, although the burning of coal and biomass fuels in households probably made air pollution a serious problem in many cities prior to this. To what can be termed the 'traditional' pollutants that arise from the burning of coal, heavy oil, or biomass were added the pollutants that come primarily from motor vehicle traffic: the photochemical pollutants, and lead and carbon monoxide. There are also various toxic and carcinogenic chemicals that are increasingly found in urban air, although in low concentrations. These include selected heavy metals, trace organic chemicals, and fibres such as asbestos (UNEP/WHO 1992).

Although most cities have some problem with air pollution, there are large variations in the scale of air pollution and in the relative importance of the different pollutants. Pollution levels often change significantly from season to season. In many cities, they have also changed over the last 20–30 years, reflecting changes in fuel use and economic structure and, in some cases, tighter environmental regulations. In many of the larger and wealthier cities in the South, motor vehicles have become a major source of air pollution, as the number of motor vehicles in use has risen rapidly (and so too have conditions that exacerbate motor vehicle pollution such as congestion).

An extreme contrast to this is provided by some of China's major industrial centres where most ambient air pollution arises from the combustion of coal, while motor vehicles are not numerous enough to make a major contribution.

An estimated 1.4 billion urban residents worldwide are exposed to annual averages for suspended particulate matter or sulphur dioxide (or both) that are higher than the minimum recommended WHO standards (UNEP and WHO 1988). Based on exposure to suspended particulate matter alone, rough estimates indicate that if unhealthy levels of particulates were reduced to the average yearly level the World Health Organization considers safe, between 300,000 and 700,000 premature deaths a year would be avoided in the South. This is equivalent to 2–5 per cent of all deaths in those urban areas where levels of particulates are excessive (World Bank 1992). The (limited) data available for Third World cities suggest the trend is towards increasing concentrations (UNEP 1991). Comparable estimates are not possible for nitrogen oxides and carbon monoxide although studies in particular cities or city districts suggest ambient air pollution levels that can impair health. There are also concerns about the health impacts of secondary pollutants formed as a result of reactions between primary pollutants and the air—for instance, acid sulphates and ozone.

In certain industrial centres, air pollution levels can be sufficiently high to cause demonstrable health impairment. For instance, in Cubatao, Brazil, air pollution levels have been linked to reduced lung functions in children (Hofmaier 1991). Non-ferrous metal smelters are often major contributors to air pollution. Although no well-documented example was found in the Third World, a study in the Katowice district in Upper Silesia, Poland, showed how four non-ferrous metal industrial plants were responsible for a high output of lead and cadmium into the air, and this showed up as elevated lead and cadmium concentrations in the blood of 20 per cent of children. Some of those tested (especially children) were also found to exhibit the early detectable symptoms of toxic lead effects (Jarzebski 1992).

Links between health problems and air pollution levels have been suggested by comparisons between the health of people in highly polluted areas within cities and those in less polluted areas; some of these have shown a strong association between the incidence of respiratory infections and pollution levels. In addition, in cities where acute episodes of high concentrations of air pollution occur at particular times (for instance when high emissions coincide with particular weather conditions), an increased incidence of mortality among particularly vulnerable groups is common (WHO 1992a). In Latin America, recent studies suggest that air pollution levels are sufficiently high in São Paulo, Rio de Janeiro and Belo Horizonte, Bogota, Santiago, Mexico City, Monterrey and Guadalajara, Caracas, and Lima that a higher priority should be given to their control. One estimate suggests that over 2 million children suffer from chronic coughs because of urban air pollution, and that air pollution causes an extra 24,300 deaths a year in Latin America (Romieu *et al.* 1990). This same source estimated that some 65 million person-days of workers' activities were lost to respiratory related problems caused by air pollution. While the authors emphasize that these are rough estimates, the figures give an idea of the order of magnitude of the problem. Local topographical and climatic conditions can exacerbate problems, as in Mexico City where thermal inversions help trap pollutants within the valley in which the city is located.

There is also the health impact of chemical wastes dumped into water bodies or onto land sites. In most Third World cities, toxic/hazardous industrial and commercial wastes are disposed of in water bodies or land sites without special provision to treat them before disposal (to render them less damaging to human health and the local environment) or without measures to ensure that disposal itself isolates them from the environment. There is often little incentive for industry and commerce to cut down polluting emissions since few are penalized and the penalties, when finally imposed, are so small as to be little deterrent. Reports from Third World cities of severe health problems arising from human contact with toxic or hazardous wastes are increasingly common (Hardoy, Mitlin, and Satterthwaite 1992).

Consideration must also be given to the large-scale accidents where chemicals had the central role in health impacts: the accidental release of methyl iso-cyanate at Bhopal (several thousand deaths and over 50,000 seriously injured) or the natural gas explosions in Mexico City in 1984 (over 1,000 dead) or the loss of life and property resulting from explosions of gases that had accumulated in the sewers and drains in downtown Guadalajara in 1992. These and other large-scale accidents are often quoted as of major significance in terms of the health impact on urban populations. The attempts by European and North American industries to dispose of their toxic wastes in Third World nations have also received much publicity. The scale of the health impact arising from occupational exposures and from exposure to indoor and outdoor air pollution is likely to be larger and more widespread but it remains largely undocumented. The next 20–30 years may show that the health impact of chemical pollutants in the Third World—in the air and water and through direct exposure in the home or workplace—has been considerably underestimated.

2.7. The Availability, Cost, and Quality of Natural Resources

The availability to any individual or household of such natural resources as food, fuel, and freshwater is obviously central to health. The environmental dimension is prominent in that the ecosystem defines the limits for the availability of freshwater, soils, and forests but social, economic, and political factors are usually the dominant influences on who has access to them or to the land and water sources from which they can be drawn. While access to land and forests for fuel and food is normally considered a rural issue, there is increasing evidence that access to land on which food can be grown is important to poorer households in many cities, especially in poorer and less urbanized nations. For instance, a study by the Mazingira Institute pointed to the importance for most households in Nairobi (Kenya's capital and largest city) and other Kenyan urban centres of food they grow or produce themselves; under such circumstances, access to land on which crops can be grown and some livestock raised becomes of great importance to most households (Lee-Smith *et al.* 1987). Many other studies have shown the importance of urban agriculture to the livelihoods of a considerable proportion of city populations in Africa, Asia, and Latin America (Smit and Nasr 1992).

Only rarely does a shortage of freshwater explain why so many urban households lack access to safe and sufficient supplies. It is more common for these to be the result of the refusal by the government to allow them an adequate supply—for

Table 11.2. Differentials in the cost of water (ratio of price charged by water vendors to prices charged by the public utility)

City	Price ratio of water from private vendors (public utility = 1)
Abidjan	5
Dhaka	12–25
Istanbul	10
Kampala	4–9
Karachi	28–83
Lagos	4–10
Lima	17
Lomé	7–10
Nairobi	7–11
Port-au-Prince	17–100
Surabaya	20–60
Tegucigalpa	16–34

Source: World Bank, World Development Report 1988: 146.

instance, because they live in illegal settlements and are considered to have no right to public services, or because they live in a peripheral municipality within a large metropolitan centre where local authorities lack the resources to provide water supplies. Although there are cities where overall shortages inhibit improved supplies, this is not the norm. In addition, it is not necessarily poorer households' lack of capacity to pay for water which explains inadequate provision. It is common for those in squatter settlements to pay private water vendors between four and 100 times as much per litre as the middle- and upper-income groups pay for publicly provided piped water (see Table 11.2). It is generally neither a lack of water nor a lack of willingness to pay that stops piped water supplies reaching poorer areas.

2.8. Physical Hazards

The true extent of accidental injuries is often greatly underestimated in Third World cities—to the point where accident prevention and emergency services for rapid treatment receive little or no attention in environmental improvement programmes. An analysis of accidents in children in ten Third World nations found that they were the main cause of death for 5–9 year olds and 10–14 year olds (Manciaux and Romer 1986). For every accidental death, there are several hundred accidental injuries. One of the most common accidents is road accidents—responsible worldwide for over 500,000 deaths each year and many times this number of serious injuries (WHO 1992a).

Many accidental injuries are linked to poor-quality, overcrowded housing. In the predominantly low-income residential areas of cities, there is often an average of four or more persons per room and in many instances less than one square metre of floor space per person (Aina 1989, Murphy 1990). Burns, scalds, and accidental fires are common in overcrowded shelters, especially when five or more persons often live in one room and there is little chance of providing occupants (especially children) with protection from open fires, stoves, or kerosene heaters. The risk of accidental fires is further increased in most urban dwellings because of the use of flammable materials (wood, cardboard, plastic, canvas, straw). Overcrowded dwellings also make it difficult to keep medicines and dangerous household chemicals (such as bleach) out of children's reach. Here, as with many environmental problems, the level of risk is usually compounded by social factors such as a lack of adult supervision if most adults have to work. The health impact of accidents is also compounded by the lack of a health service that can rapidly provide emergency treatment, followed by longer-term treatment and care (Goldstein 1990).

There are also the physical hazards of the land sites on which housing develops. In nearly all Third World cities, there are large clusters of illegal housing on dangerous sites (for instance, steep hillsides, floodplains, or desert land) or housing built on polluted sites (for instance, around solid waste dumps, beside open drains and sewers, or in industrial areas with high levels of air pollution). Or housing develops in sites subject to high noise levels—for instance close to major highways or airports. Most cities have large areas of unused and well-located land not subject to such hazards. The problem is rarely a shortage of the resource (safe land sites) but the fact that poorer groups have no means of getting access to such sites and governments do not intervene in their favour.

2.9. Other Environment-related Hazards

Many psychosocial disorders are associated with poor-quality housing and living environments—although many non-environmental factors are also important—for instance the stress associated with inadequate income and insecure and strenuous livelihoods and insecure tenure of the shelter (for tenants or squatters), especially for those living with a constant threat of eviction. Psychosocial health problems are becoming a major cause of death and morbidity among adolescents and young adults in many urban areas of the Third World or in particular districts within urban areas. Poor-quality and overcrowded housing and living environments contribute to the stress that underlies most psychosocial disorders and these disorders may develop into particular diseases or impair the body's immune system.

Many physical characteristics of the housing and living environment can influence the incidence and severity of psychosocial disorders. These include noise, overcrowding, inappropriate design, and the stresses and difficulties caused in any house or residential area when there is inadequate or no provision for sanitation, garbage collection, and maintenance (Ekblad *et al.* 1991; Ekblad 1993). Good-quality housing and living environments can greatly reduce stress and its health consequences—

through sufficient space, location close to friends and family, easy access to desired services and facilities for safe play for children and for recreation, minimum noise, and few personal hazards. Within the wider neighbourhood in which the house is located, a sense of security, good quality physical infrastructure (roads, pavements, drains, street lights) and services (such as street cleaning), the availability of emergency services. and easy access to educational, health and social services as well as cultural and other amenities all reduce stress and contribute to good mental health. In addition to the quality of the dwelling and its neighbourhood, the subjective experience of the dweller is also important for health, that is, their level of satisfaction with the house and its neighbourhood and its location within the urban area (Ekblad *et al.* 1991; Ekblad 1993).

Many characteristics of urban neighbourhoods that are not easily identified or defined may have important influences on an individual's level of satisfaction and on the incidence of crime, vandalism and interpersonal violence. These are aspects more fully explored in cities in Europe and North America (Jacobs 1965; Newman 1972; Coleman 1990). What is probably a more important influence on health is the extent to which any individual or household has the possibility of modifying or changing their housing environment and working with others in the locality to effect change in the wider neighbourhood. Many critiques of public housing and of urban planning in Third World cities (especially 'slum' and squatter clearance and redevelopment) have centred on the loss of individual, household and community control (Turner 1976). These often document the hardships caused to households and, on occasion, the negative health consequences, although they do not examine the social pathologies that might be associated with such changes. There is also a large and varied literature on the importance for the physical and mental health of individuals and 'communities' of being able to command events which control their lives (Duhl 1990).

There are also interacting variables that can promote or prevent the process that might lead to psychosocial disorder or disease. For instance, a social support network may prevent stress from developing into stress-related disorders or diseases; '. . . strong social networks and a sense of community organization in many rundown inner city districts . . . and squatter settlements . . . might help explain the remarkably low level of psychosocial problems' (WHO 1992a: 215). The importance of such networks can also be seen in the increase in physical and mental ill-health among populations relocated from inner-city tenements or illegal settlements to 'better quality' housing, partly because such networks became disrupted (Turner 1976). However, the precise linkages between different elements of the physical environment and each psychosocial disorder or disease are difficult to ascertain—and to separate from other variables. In addition, care must be taken not to overstate the effects of environmental factors on psychosocial health when more fundamental social, economic, and political factors such as low and very unstable incomes and oppression or discrimination underlie psychosocial disorders and very poor living environments (Cohen and Swift 1993).

3. Who Bears the Health Costs of Environmental Problems?

3.1. Vulnerability to Environmental Hazards

The presence of an environmental hazard (for instance a pathogen, pollutant, or physical hazard) does not necessarily mean that it will harm someone. This depends on characteristics of the individual, household, and social group exposed to the hazard. Certain individual or group characteristics can also influence the severity of the health impact. Characteristics which influence whether ill-health or injury can be avoided, and/or the severity of the health impact include:[3]

- for biological pathogens, weak body defence (some a function of age and of nutritional status, some a function of acquired immunity);
- for physical hazards, limited mobility, strength and balance (e.g. children, older groups and people with physical disabilities facing greater risks of injury in unsafe houses built on slopes, floodplains or otherwise dangerous sites);
- for exposure to chemicals: age, activity (when exposed) and health status at the time of exposure. Certain groups are particularly susceptible to certain pollutants; for instance asthmatics are more sensitive to certain common urban air pollutants. Genetic factors may influence sensitivity to some chemicals;
- social roles that increase duration and/or severity of exposure to environmental hazards.

Factors that influence how easily the individual, household or social group can cope with environmentally induced illness or injury include:

- the extent of public, private, and community provision for health care, including emergency response to accidental injuries or acute diseases;
- the individual's or household's ability to afford health care and emergency response, to purchase medicines, and to take time off to recuperate when sick or injured;
- individual, household, or community coping mechanisms once the hazard has caused sickness or injury; for instance, knowing what to do, who to visit, and how to rearrange individual/household survival strategies.

Stephens and Harpham (1992) have pointed out that health outcomes '. . . are not only influenced by environmental conditions but also by the inputs of health services, by the characteristics of the population and by the socio-economic conditions in which people live'. Virtually all environmental health problems in urban areas have a social, economic, or political underpinning in that it is social, economic, or political factors which determine who is most at risk and who is unable to obtain the needed treatment and support, when illness or injury occurs (Hardoy, Mitlin, and Satterthwaite 1992; Douglass 1992). To give just one example,

---

[3] This list is drawn principally from Corbett 1989 and Pryer 1989; also Chambers 1989, 1994.

the high incidence of diseases associated with contaminated food and water in most poor urban communities is an environmental problem in that the disease-causing agents infect humans through the water or food they ingest—but this high incidence can also be judged to be a political problem since nearly all governments and aid agencies have the capacity to greatly reduce current levels of morbidity and mortality by improved provision of water, sanitation, and drainage. It can also be seen as a social or economic problem in that it is lower-income groups' limited means to pay for accommodation that usually underlies their poor housing conditions. This makes it difficult to isolate the impact of environmental factors on health as distinct from other factors.

The economic underpinning of environmental hazards becomes clear when we compare the hazards faced by poorer groups with those faced by richer groups. Most studies on communicable diseases and morbidity and mortality show that the most vulnerable group are predominantly the poor—be they children, adults in crowded, unhygienic conditions or workers in particular occupations (see the studies summarized in Bradley *et al.* 1991). Low-income groups are the least able to afford the homes that protect against environmental hazards, such as good-quality housing in neighbourhoods with piped water and adequate provision of sanitation, garbage collection, paved roads, and drains. In addition, higher-income groups will generally have less dangerous jobs and work in occupations where occupational hazards are minimized.

Low-income households are also more vulnerable because they lack the buffers to cope with illness or injury (see, for instance, Pryer 1993). Low-income individuals/households generally have most difficulty in getting treatment for any injury or illness—for instance, emergency services in the case of a serious accident and treatment from a health centre or hospital (Goldstein 1990). They have the least means to afford medicines and (generally) the least possibility of taking time off to allow recovery because the loss of income from doing so would press heavily on their survival, and because they are unable to afford health insurance—or obtain the jobs for which health insurance is paid by the firm.

3.2. The Geography of Inequality

If there was sufficient information available to construct a map of a city, showing the level of risk from environmental hazards in each neighbourhood, the areas with the highest risks would coincide with those with a predominance of low-income groups. In most Third World cities, the correlations between income levels and environmental hazards would be particularly strong with respect to the quality and quantity of water, the level of provision for sanitation, drainage, and solid waste collection, and the risk from floods, landslides, and other natural hazards. The reason for this is simply that poorer groups are priced out of safe, well-located, well-serviced housing and land sites. In many cities, there will be a strong correlation between indoor air quality and income because poorer groups use more polluting fuels and more inefficient stoves (or open fires) which ensure a much worse air quality indoors. The fact that poorer groups also live in more overcrowded conditions exacerbates this and the transmission of infectious diseases. A high proportion of poor groups live in shacks made of flammable material, with higher risks of accidental fires. Poorer groups will generally have the least access to playgrounds, parks and other open spaces managed for public use. The correlations between income level and level of air pollution, however, may not be so precise.

Many studies on the differentials in health status or mortality rates between city districts (or boroughs or municipalities) show conditions in poorer areas to be much worse than in the more wealthy areas or for the city average (Harpham, Vaughan, and Lusty 1988; Bradley *et al.* 1991). Infant mortality rates in poorer areas are often four or more times higher than in richer areas, with much larger differentials often apparent if the poorest district is compared to the richest district. Large differentials between rich and poor districts are also common in the incidence of many environment-related diseases—for instance tuberculosis and typhoid. Differentials in the number of people dying from certain environment-related diseases are often very large; for instance many more deaths in poorer communities are likely to come from diarrhoeal diseases and acute respiratory infections such as pneumonia and influenza. Maternal mortality rates are likely to be much higher than any city average in low-income districts where homes lack basic services, especially community-based health care with good prenatal services and emergency services. To date, the statistics showing differentials in maternal mortality have concentrated on those between rich and poor nations (among the poorest nations, maternal mortality rates can be 100 or more times that of the richest) (WHO 1992b). There are also likely to be large differentials between most low- and high-income areas in the proportion of people who are disabled or chronically ill.

3.3. What Underlies Vulnerability to Environmental Hazards?

To a large extent, capacity to pay for housing defines the scale and range of environmental hazards present in the housing and living environment, including whether or not there are safe, sufficient water supplies, sanitation, garbage collection and drainage. There is a strong association between those with inadequate incomes (or what might be termed income-poverty) and those exposed to most environmental risk in their home and workplace. In most Third World cities, low-income individuals and households have very little chance of obtaining healthy legal accommodation within a neighbourhood where environmental risks are minimized—that is, one with sufficient space, security of tenure, services and facilities, and on a site not prone to flooding, waterlogging or landslides. Many low-income groups also live in constant fear of eviction; this is a permanent worry for many tenants, temporary boarders in cheap rooming houses, those in illegal settlements, and 'land renters'.

The insecurity and the environmental hazards evident within the homes and neighbourhoods of poorer groups are in effect a combination of three factors: low-incomes; the refusal or inability of government to intervene to guarantee poorer groups access to shelters that are not so dangerous or to the resources that allow them to build these themselves; and the refusal or inability of government to provide the community-based health-care and emergency services that can do so much to prevent illness or injury and to limit its impact.

Ironically, dangerous or polluted land sites often serve poorer groups well. For these are the only sites, well-located with regard to income-earning opportunities, on which they have some possibility of living (illegally) because the environmental hazards make the sites unattractive to other potential users. It was the high concentration of low-income residents around the Union Carbide Factory in Bhopal that resulted in several thousand deaths and over 50,000 serious injuries (Centre for Science and Environment 1985).

Among those with low incomes, there will be considerable differentiation in the scale and nature of environmental hazards to which they are exposed and in the severity of the illness or injury to which these hazards contribute. Health indicators for particular poor districts are generally averages which can obscure the more serious health problems suffered by the poorer groups within that district. One study of a low-income settlement in Khulna, Bangladesh, showed the sharp differentials in work days lost to illness or injury among the inhabitants of a low-income settlement when comparing the higher-income households within the settlement to the lower-income households. It also shows how in the poorer households, such illness or injury often means growing indebtedness and undernutrition for all family members (Pryer 1993).

There are particular groups that face greater environmental risks because of their work and because of the ineffectiveness of government provision to promote occupational health and safety. There are also particularly dangerous settlements—such as those subject to landslides or flooding—where poorer groups often choose to live, because these are the only cheap (or free) urban land sites that are well-located with regard to income-earning opportunities. There are also particular groups who face most difficulty getting access to water and washing and bathing facilities—such as pavement dwellers or those who sleep in open spaces, parks, and graveyards (Patel 1990).

There is also the differentiation within low-income groups caused by demographic, health or social characteristics. Foetuses, infants, and children are at greater risk than older children or adults of dying from many environment-related diseases, such as diarrhoeal diseases, malaria, pneumonia or measles (WHO 1992a; UNICEF 1992). Women are more vulnerable than men to many environmental hazards. Sometimes this is because of their sex (that is, as a result of biological differences); for instance, women are particularly vulnerable to many environmental hazards during pregnancy and childbirth. Often it is because of gender, that is, as a result of the particular social and economic roles that women have, determined by social, economic, and political structures (Moser 1993). For instance, the fact that women take most responsibility for household management means that they suffer most from the inadequacies of water supply and sanitation provision; caring for the sick and washing soiled clothes are particularly hazardous tasks when water supplies, sanitation, and washing facilities are inadequate (Sapir 1992). Where there are high levels of indoor air pollution from coal or biomass fuels burnt on open fires or poorly vented stoves, the persons responsible for cooking and who spend most time indoors (usually women) face the greatest health burden. The nature of this vulnerability and its underlying causes constitute too broad a topic to permit a quick summary here (for more details see Moser 1987; Levy 1992; Moser 1993).

Migrants or particular migrant groups may be more vulnerable to certain environmental hazards than long-term city residents—for instance, in-migrants may lack immunity to particular diseases that are common within the urban area to which they move, whereas those who have lived there a long time have developed some immunity. Many migrants may be disadvantaged, in comparison to existing city dwellers, in terms of the quality of accommodation they can find (or the quality relative to cost). Immigrants are likely to be particularly vulnerable, especially if they are illegal immigrants, since they often face discrimination in housing and job markets and may have no protection under the law against exploitation by employers or landlords. Particular categories of migrants may be at particular risk. If women face discrimination in job and housing markets, access to education, and access to land, this will be reflected by gender differentiation in the form and scale of men's and women's population movements and in the incomes and the level of risk in jobs taken by men and women in urban areas (Chant 1992). However, existing literature on vulnerable groups in urban areas may pay too much attention to migrants and too little attention to age, gender, and income. There appears to be a tendency in the literature on health problems in cities to assume that most migrants to cities are very poor, ill-educated, ill-informed about conditions in cities, and unmotivated—which is inaccurate. It is also common to see assertions that migrants are at risk because they live in 'slums' and illegal settlements when it is low income, not length of time in the city, which is the main influence on who lives in such areas. Many illegal settlements have a predominance of city-born residents. In most instances, the scale of environmental hazards confronting any city dweller is much more likely to be related to their income level, age, and gender-defined roles than to their status as a recent migrant, well-established migrant or city-born person.

Some Conclusions

In most urban centres, poorer groups face the most serious environmental hazards and the least possibility of avoiding them or receiving treatment to limit their health impact. At least 600 million urban dwellers in Africa, Asia, and Latin America are estimated to live in 'life and health-threatening' homes and neighbourhoods because of the environmental hazards described in this chapter (Hardoy, Cairncross, and Satterthwaite 1990; WHO 1992a).

The extent of the health burden imposed by the environment on urban populations remains poorly understood. It is almost certainly underestimated, not only because of paucity of data but also because it is usually the result of the cumulative impact of a great number of environmental problems operating concurrently with many non-environmental problems.

There is great variety in the range and relative importance of environmental hazards both within and between cities and in the non-environmental factors that underlie or interact with them. For instance, in most major cities, the environmental priorities for health improvement in an inner-city tenement will differ from those in an illegal housing development. In both, environmental hazards may be major causes of ill-health, injury, and premature death. But the range of hazards and their relative importance will differ because of differences in (for instance) income level and its distribution, age structure, quality and kind of infrastructure and service provision, risk of flooding, access to health care and emergency services, and a host of other factors. What city populations need are city-specific and neighbourhood-specific understandings of the range of environmental hazards and their relative importance for health. This must be combined with an understanding of the groups most affected by them and the diverse mix of social, economic, political, and demographic factors that underlie the hazards. From this can come a city- and neighbourhood-directed programme to control environmental problems, reduce risks (especially for vulnerable groups), and ensure treatment is available where health impacts cannot be prevented. This emphasizes the need for national or international agencies to work with local groups—citizen groups and their community organizations, local doctors and other professional medical or paramedical staff, NGOs, municipal organizations, workers' unions or associations—if accurate diagnoses are to be made and effective interventions undertaken.

12 The Transition's Population Crisis: Nuptiality, Fertility, and Mortality Changes in Severely Distressed Economies

GIOVANNI ANDREA CORNIA AND RENATO PANICCIÀ

Introduction

In most of Central and Eastern Europe and the former Soviet Union (hereafter referred to in brief as 'Eastern Europe', unless explicitly specified), the economic and political reforms since 1989 have been accompanied by an unprecedented fall in output, a rapid impoverishment of large sections of society, increasing uncertainty about the future and an exceptional population crisis. For instance, between 1989 and 1994, marriage rates fell by between one-quarter and one-half in Georgia; birth rates shrank by up to 40 per cent, as in Estonia, and death rates among male adults due to cardiovascular and violent causes more than doubled, as in Russia (UNICEF 1994, 1995). To give an idea of the extent of the recent demographic crisis, it suffices to mention that by 1994 the life expectancy at birth of Russian males had fallen to the same level as that of Pakistani males, while the natural increase of the population had become negative in Bulgaria, the Czech Republic, Hungary, Romania, the three Baltic countries, Russia, Ukraine, and Belarus.

Mainstream thinking generally attributes this population crisis to factors broadly unrelated to the recent economic difficulties and social dislocations experienced during the transition. According to this thinking, the (real or apparent) causes of the phenomenon ought to be sought elsewhere.

First of all, a large part of the increase is assumed to be only recently revealed. A 'glasnost' in statistics would have revealed the exact extent of the health crisis concealed in the past by doctors and administrators eager to please the socialist authorities and fearful of being blamed for the poor performance of their hospitals (Eberstadt 1990, 1994).

We wish to thank A. K. Sen, Michael Lipton, Massimo Livi-Bacci, Michael Walton, and Stan D'Souza for commenting on an earlier draft of the paper forming the basis of this chapter. We are also indebted to Gáspár Fajth for constructing the 'public child support variable', Enrico Sborgi for assistance in data compilation and colleagues in the central statistical offices of several Eastern European countries—above all Jaroslav Novak, Juri Uljas, Zita Sniukstiene, Judit Lakatos, Andrzej Ochocki, Marious Pop, and Olga Remenets—for providing data and comments. All remaining mistakes are obviously ours. This chapter is a revised version of two previously published papers: Cornia and Paniccià (1995) and Cornia and Paniccià (1996).

Second, most of the 'real' increase in mortality is said to be due to endogenous long-term trends in cancer and diet-related mortality, that is, factors tied to the environmental degradation and poor lifestyles prevailing in and inherited from the past, and not to current economic changes (Feshback and Friendly 1992). Meanwhile, the worsening of some traditional risk factors (for instance, the increase in alcohol consumption brought about by the liberalization of alcohol sales, importation, and manufacturing) will have pushed upwards the mortality due to cirrhosis and violent causes.

As regards the contraction in the number of marriages and births and the increase in the proportion in births out of wedlock observed over the period 1989–94, the dominant viewpoint attributes them to the spread of 'individualistic' Western values and reproductive behaviours. These 'values' involve the rejection of conventional social norms, greater personal and sexual freedom and higher valuation of the opportunity cost of the consumption forgone due to the birth of a child. In particular, valuation of the opportunity cost of having a child has, according to this viewpoint, increased substantially because of the greater consumer choice brought about by trade and import liberalization. Thus, the spread of new values and opportunities has eroded the preference traditionally attached in the pre-transition society to early marriage, the restraint of sexual activities before marriage, procreation at a young age, and so on (Council of Europe 1993).

Another frequently cited explanation of the fall in fertility and nuptiality focuses on the erosion of the pro-natalist measures and incentives typical of the socialist regimes (including generous maternity leaves, childbirth and childcare grants, and other incentives to have children), changes in women's labour force participation, or, as in the case of Romania, relaxation of the norms prohibiting abortion.

These explanations are, however, unconvincing and at best partial. In addition, received overall demographic and welfare theory explains only inadequately the recent mortality, nuptiality and fertility changes observed in the Eastern European countries experiencing sudden and large shocks and mounting uncertainty. Demographic changes of the magnitude discussed in this chapter have been observed only during famines or wars; though under these circumstances large mortality increases have been most commonly caused by infectious diseases and undernutrition. Thus, while 'famine studies' (Livi-Bacci 1993; Lumey *et al.*; 1993; Lumey and Van Poppel 1994) do offer interesting insights and parallels to the analysis of 'transition' mortality and fertility, they do not refer to similar contextual situations or mortality patterns. Similarly, while extremely useful in underscoring the relationship among social structure, work organization, and health status, analyses such as 'Society, Stress and Disease' (Levi *et al.* 1981) do not deal with the impact of economic shocks and rising uncertainty on mortality and fertility. Finally, the causation process underlying the recent demographic crisis in Eastern Europe is also very different from that sketched out by standard 'demographic transition' theories. Indeed, if applied to Eastern Europe, these theories, which refer mainly to poor, mostly agrarian developing societies, would provide predictions about demographic outcomes opposed to those observed in reality since 1989.

Thus, neither current, fashionable explanations, nor the major theoretical demographic and welfare models, seem to be able to interpret the sharp demographic changes observed recently in the region. Thus, new risk factors and determinants have to be identified, new concepts developed, new theories tested and new policies devised. The past analyses which have come the closest to the approach followed in this chapter are those linking sharp and sudden changes in household incomes, unemployment, and consumer prices to demographic outcomes. These analyses are few and far between and, with the exception of those on the impact of the Great Depression (Brenner 1973; Eyer and Sterling 1977), do not refer to large, sudden, country-wide variations in aggregate demographic variables, but rather to the impact of given stress-related variables on health and various demographic outcomes at the individual level.

For instance, studies relying on microdata or fairly disaggregated data on the US, Canada, Britain, Ireland, Italy, and Finland and other Scandinavian countries, and making use of the concepts of 'psychosocial stress' have successfully tied, at the microeconomic level, changes in stress variables to mortality and fertility outcomes (Brenner 1987; Beale and Nethercott 1985, 1989; Colombino 1984; Moser *et al.* 1986, 1987; Smith 1992; Kalimo and Vuori 1993; Whelan *et al.* 1994; Bjorklund and Erikson 1995). These studies show that the most prevalent sources of stress are family instability and breakdown, job insecurity, unemployment, sudden impoverishment, high inflation, migration, and depression. Economic factors are clearly prominent in this line of analysis, as expectations are strongly influenced by current or anticipated unemployment rates, real wage drops, and high levels of inflation.

This chapter is aimed at debunking the traditional approach, at clearly stating that the large shocks in birth and death rates are compelling signs of societies in extreme distress and at testing the hypothesis that the population crisis which has been affecting most of the region for the last few years is the result of the growing economic instability and social stress evident in the region, increasingly unfavourable expectations about the future, and incomplete and inadequate policy action. Indeed, if this hypothesis about the role of economic instability and psychosocial stress is verified, the most suitable solutions to the mortality and fertility crisis of Eastern Europe would require not only stronger support measures in health and more effective family transfers, but also much more aggressive policies to enhance tax collection, to support employment, minimum wages and social safety nets, and to control inflation.

The above hypothesis is tested making use of aggregate and age-specific time-series data for 1970–89 and 1989–94 for thirteen Eastern European countries, representing 75 per cent of the population of the former Soviet Bloc. This includes countries showing considerable intercountry and interregional variation, thus allowing the risk of spurious or weak correlation and inference to be minimized. The data set covers four Central European countries (the Czech Republic, Slovakia, Hungary, and Poland), two Southeastern European countries (Romania and Bulgaria), the three Baltic nations (Estonia, Latvia, and Lithuania), the three Slavic countries of the former Soviet Union (Russia, Belarus, and Ukraine), and Moldova. The countries of the former Yugoslavia, Caucasus and Central Asia, as well as Albania and the former German Democratic Republic, have been excluded because of the influence of war on demographic outcomes, data problems or other factors.

1. A Drastic Demographic Adjustment in Relation to the Pre-transition Period

1.1. Pre-transition Trends and the 'Demographic Crisis' of the Transition

Between the end of World War II and 1989, marriage, birth and death rates in Eastern Europe evolved according to two fairly distinct patterns. Marriages and births rose, and mortality declined rapidly until the mid-to-late 1960s. In the subsequent period, these trends slowed sharply or were even reversed.

1.1.1. Crude Marriage Rate (CMR)

As in Western Europe, in the 1950s and 1960s marriage rates soared to record levels. Some 90 per cent of the people in the relevant population group married, often at a young age, and then had children fairly early, while out-of-wedlock births accounted for well below 10 per cent of total births. The age of women at first marriage and at the birth of a first child remained on average one to two years below the corresponding age in Western Europe (Table 12.1).

This pattern has changed since the mid-to-late 1960s. With the exception of Romania, between 1970 and 1989 the CMR fell markedly, though the mean age at marriage rose only very slowly. A similar though generally less pronounced trend can be observed in the total first-marriage rate, a measure of nuptiality which is independent of the age structure of the population. Compared to the Western European countries, the fall in CMR was considerably less pronounced and, with the exception of Estonia and Latvia, unaccompanied by a parallel increase in cohabitation rates (Council of Europe 1993). In addition, the mean age at first marriage increased at only one-sixth of the rate observed in Western Europe (Table 12.1).

Therefore, despite some growth in incomes and the opportunities for material consumption and the rising levels of educational attainment and employment among women, over the 1970–89 period the traditional marriage and family patterns prevailing in most of Eastern Europe were not radically altered. This stability was in part due to policy factors. Housing policy (giving precedence to young couples with children), as well as lack of financial support for cohabitation and other extra-marital arrangements, influenced the age at birth of the first child and the slow rise in cohabitation. Other, more endogenous factors, however, probably contributed to the fact that traditional family patterns in the countries of the region evolved much more slowly than they did in other countries.

The situation changed drastically, though with large variations from country to country, between 1989 and 1994 (Table 12.1). The CMR dropped by between 13 per

Table 12.1. Cumulative percentage changes in total first-marriage rate for women (TFMRW), 1970–89, and in crude marriage rate (CMR) and in mean age at first marriage of women, 1970–89 and 1989–94

	TFMRW %	CMR %		Mean age at marriage (years)		
	1970–89	1970–89	1989–94	1970	1989	1994
Belarus	–	3.2	–24.0	–	22.3	21.7
Bulgaria	–7.2	–17.1	–36.9	21.7	21.9	22.3
Czech R.	–5.4[a]	–14.8	–27.3	20.7	20.9	–
Estonia	–19.1	–11.4	–39.2	24.8	23.0	
Hungary	–20.6	–31.9	–11.5	21.1	21.4	22.0
Latvia	–	–9.8	–50.5	–	22.2	22.5[c]
Lithuania	–	–2.1	–32.3	–	–	22.5
Moldova	–	–2.1	–15.2	–	22.3	–
Poland	–5.5	–20.8	–19.8	21.9	21.8	21.7
Romania	4.7	6.9	–13.0	21.5[b]	22.1	22.4
Russia	–	–6.8	–22.5	–	22.9	22.4
Slovak R.	–	–	–23.4	–	22.9	21.3
Ukraine	–	–3.1	–18.9	–	21.5	–

[a] CSFR
[b] 1975
[c] 1993
Source: Council of Europe(1993); TransMONEE database; national statistics.

cent in Romania and 51 per cent in Estonia. On average, the decline during 1989–94 was at least twice as large as that recorded over the previous two decades. Interestingly, in six of the thirteen countries analysed, the CMR rose significantly (especially for the 20–24 age cohort) in the first reform year, often after a number of yearly drops. This phenomenon, which we called here the 'initial euphoria effect', probably reflects the exhilaration induced by political liberalization and the positive expectations about future improvements in living standards during the first year of reform.

In all countries, the decline in the CMR observed over 1989–94 was significantly greater than that expected on the basis of the 1970–89 time series data. Declines in the size of the cohorts reaching the age of most frequent marriage explain only a small part of this phenomenon. Nor can this phenomenon be attributed to a postponement of first marriages, as the *average age at marriage* did not increase meaningfully (see Table 12.1) and the drop in nuptiality affected practically all age groups (Table 12.2).

1.1.2. Crude Birth Rate (CBR) and Total Fertility Rate (TFR)

By the mid-to-late 1960s, the TFR in most of Eastern Europe had declined to 2.2–2.4: that is, levels similar to those of the countries of Western Europe. Only

Table 12.2.　Percentage changes in age-specific marriage rates, 1989–93

	15–19	20–4	25–9	30–4	35–9	40–9
Bulgaria	−58.7	−46.7	−24.6	−26.5	−27.5	−30.3
Estonia	−45.7[a]	−47.3[a]	−39.0[b]	−29.4	−26.8	−13.1
Hungary	−34.7[a]	−27.7	−17.3	−21.5	−30.4[b]	−30.6[b]
Lithuania	2.0	−32.0	−32.8	−36.5	−39.5[a]	−37.2[b]
Poland	−35.0	−20.5	−12.0	−12.0	−4.0	−35.4
Romania	−35.0[b]	−7.1	−3.3	−14.7	−16.0	−56.4[a]
Russia	0.2	−18.2	−19.4	−22.4	−27.0[a]	−25.0[b]

[a] 1989–94
[b] 1989–93.
Source: See Table 12.1.

Romania continued to have a relatively high TFR (2.9). While over the subsequent two decades the TFR and CBR in Western Europe continued to drop, in Eastern Europe the central role attributed to the family and the attendant slow decrease in marriage rates, the limited availability of or prohibition on contraception, and fairly generous pro-natalist family policies contained substantially the decline in fertility. In the mid-to-late 1980s, the TFR even recovered an upward trend in most members of the former Soviet Union, Romania, and Poland (Table 12.3). In addition, especially in Hungary, Bulgaria and Romania, the shifts from permissive to repressive abortion policy often led to sharp swings in fertility rates. Thus, only the GDR and Romania experienced over the 1970–89 period a clear fall in the TFR despite the introduction of generous social benefits, especially for unmarried mothers.

The 1989–94 period witnessed drops in the CBR and TFR similar to those observed in the case of the CMR (Table 12.3) and, in general, much larger than those projected on the basis of the pre-transition trends. The largest drops (between 35 and 41 per cent) were observed in Romania, Estonia, and Russia (where the pro-natalist or anti-abortion policies of the previous regimes were abandoned in early 1990). The CBR decreased by 15 to 28 per cent in the other countries of the former Soviet Union, Poland, and Bulgaria. In the Czech Republic, Slovakia, and Hungary the drop was delayed (until 1992) and less pronounced (about 10 per cent).

The fall in the CBR has been accompanied by an increase in the percentage of first births in the total (Table 12.3). This share has generally risen sharply, particularly in the countries with large declines in fertility, suggesting that the decrease in birth rates was mainly due to a generalized slump in fertility and not to a contraction affecting only particular groups or regions.

Similar changes have been observed for the TFR, which fell at rates considerably more rapid than those of the previous twenty years (see Table 12.3). However, in the Czech Republic, Hungary, Poland, and Slovakia, the drop in the TFR was delayed by one or two years, and in a few cases it even rose in 1990 or 1991, confirming the 'initial euphoria effect'. In the remaining countries the TFR declined by between 15

Table 12.3.   Percentage cumulative decline in crude birth rate (CBR) and total fertility rate (TFR), 1970–89 and 1989–94

	CBR		TFR		% 1st births on total births		
	1970–89	1989–94	1970–89	1989–94	1970	1989	1993–4
Belarus	−7.4	−28.4	−12.9	−25.6	43.3	48.6	–
Bulgaria	−23.3	−24.9	−12.8	−27.8	45.9	48.0	55.1[e]
Czech R.	−17.9	−16.8	−9.5	−8.5[b]	46.7[a]	45.1[a]	50.1[g]
Estonia	−2.3	−38.9	2.3	−37.7	49.4	50.0	50.1[g]
Hungary	−22.4	−0.9	−9.6	−7.3	49.3	43.8	43.6[g]
Latvia	0.2	−34.6	2.0	−32.2	52.2	46.8	49.0[f]
Lithuania	−14.2	−23.8	−17.5	−22.2	45.4	48.3	48.6[g]
Moldova	−14.9	−24.6	−3.1	−16.0[c]	37.9	40.6	46.4[f]
Poland	−11.3	−15.6	−5.5	−13.5	42.6	37.8	38.8[g]
Romania	−24.2	−41.3	−33.5	−26.6	31.6	39.2	56.0[g]
Russia	0.0	−35.6	2.0	−29.4	51.0	46.4	58.6[g]
Slovak R.	−21.8[a]	−18.6	–	−20.2	–	–	–
Ukraine	−11.2	−25.6	−8.1	−21.9	49.3	49.4	54.3[f]

[a] CSFR   [b] 1989–92   [c] 1989–93
[d] 1994   [e] 1991   [f] 1993
[g] 1988

Source: See Table 12.1.

and 30 per cent, while in Estonia it plummeted by a remarkable 37 per cent. In most countries the drop in the TFR was several times more rapid than it had been during the previous twenty years.

The drop in overall fertility (for married and unmarried women alike) affected most age groups (see Table 12.4). Only in Hungary and Poland was the contraction clearly more pronounced among younger women, thus leaving open the possibility that fertility will 'catch up' in the future. In Russia, Lithuania, and Romania, in contrast, while the natality decline involved all age groups, it appears to have been as pronounced or even more pronounced among the women in the 30–49 age group (for whom a 'catching up' in fertility is impossible) relevant to the younger women. In these countries the drop in fertility therefore appears more permanent.

As in the case of marriage, it has been suggested that the fall in the TFR may not be related to the transition, but rather to changes in lifestyles and attitudes among Eastern European women. According to this view, these women have adjusted to the values and behaviours of their Western counterparts who frequently emphasize the importance of work and career, greater individualism, and later pregnancies (Avraamova 1994). However, this is not very credible, as shown by the more rapid than average decline in fertility rates among older women (Table 12.4), by the frequent increases in the share of first births in the total, and by the results of recent surveys on factors influencing the decisions of women on childbearing. For instance, in a 1992 survey in Russia (All-Russian Centre for Public Opinion and

Table 12.4. Percentage changes in age-specific birth rates, 1989–93/4

	15–19	20–24	25–29	30–34	35–39	40–44
Bulgaria	−16.9	−32.9	−21.4	−21.2	−15.8	−55.3
Estonia[b]	−10.6	−35.1	−35.6	−43.6	−42.5	−43.1
Hungary[a]	−13.9	−16.3	−2.7	2.6	−1.8	10.0
Lithuania	1.0	−20.5	−18.9	−23.2	−13.1	16.7
Poland[b]	−12.6	−17.9	−8.7	−3.7	0.4	−4.8
Romania	−20.7	−26.3	−37.1	−51.9	−57.0	−54.9
Russia[b]	−8.8	−26.5	−37.0	−45.8	−48.2	−48.0

[a] 1989–94
[b] 1990–93
Source: See Table 12.1.

Market Research, cited in Haub 1994), three-quarters of the women interviewed cited insufficient income as a major barrier to having another child, while over half said inadequate housing was the main cause. Only 1 per cent cited interference with their educational or career aspirations as the main motivation. In addition, respectively one-fourth and one-half of these women said they might have another child if they were to receive a child allowance or if housing conditions were improved (Haub 1994).

1.1.3. *A Sharp Increase in Crude Death Rates and in Mortality Rates among Middle-aged Males*

Between the early 1950s and 1965 life expectancy at birth (LEB) improved extremely rapidly, by about eight years for men and nine years for women, mainly due to the swift decline in the number of deaths due to infectious, parasitic and respiratory diseases, injury, poisoning and 'other' causes (UN 1982). However, mortality deteriorated sharply between the mid-1960s and the mid-1980s. For the region as a whole, LEB fell by one year for men, with much larger drops in Hungary and the USSR of 2.5 and three years, respectively (UN 1982). While LEB continued to climb for women, the pace of improvement was sluggish. The deterioration was, however, particularly marked for middle-aged adults and most of all for middle-aged men (Table 12.5).

During the immediate pre-transition years, health conditions stabilized, and, with the exception of Hungary, LEB started to rise again at only a slightly slower pace than that registered in other regions. In Russia, for instance, life expectancy for males, which had touched a low of 61.5 years in 1981, recovered to 65.1 years in 1986 because of the improvement in some of the risk factors (for example, alcohol consumption) which had been responsible for the drop in life expectancy over the 1965–85 period (Tarschys 1993).

As for the CDR, between 1989 and 1994 it climbed in all but three (the Czech

Table 12.5. Cumulative percentage changes in crude death rate (CDR) and age-specific death rate (ASDR) (per 1,000 people in the corresponding age-bracket) for male adults in selected age brackets, 1970–89 and 1989–93/94

| | CDR | | Male ASDR | | | | | | | |
| | | | 35–9 | | 40–4 | | 45–9 | | 50–4 | |
	1970–89	1989–94	1970–89	1989–93/4	1970–89	1989–93/4	1970–89	1989–93/4	1970–89	1989–93/4
Belarus	32.9	24.8	n.a.	10.0[a]	n.a.	4.1[a]	n.a.	-0.7[a]	n.a.	n.a.
Bulgaria	32.3	10.5	n.a.	19.4[a]	n.a.	15.0[a]	n.a.	15.9[a]	-1.2	16.7[a]
Czech R.	-2.4	-7.3	-17.31	6.84[b]	-2.4	7.8[b]	-0.4	0.4[b]	n.a.	-1.5[b]
Estonia	5.7	25.3	n.a.	28.4[c]	n.a.	22.5[c]	n.a.	25.0[c]	78.5	30.8[c]
Hungary	17.9	5.3	58.6	29.3[d]	58.1	34.3[d]	79.0	16.8[d]	n.a.	18.0[d]
Latvia	8.4	34.4	n.a.	n.a.	n.a.	n.a.	n.a.	n.a.	n.a.	n.a.
Lithuania	15.7	21.4	n.a.	30.3[b]	n.a.	45.5[c]	n.a.	36.6[d]	n.a.	44.0[d]
Moldova	24.5	32.1	n.a.	n.a.	n.a.	n.a.	n.a.	n.a.	51.6	n.a.
Poland	22.4	-0.4	19.4	-2.7[d]	30.2	1.8[d]	45.2	-6.7[d]	32.6	-2.9[d]
Romania	12.4	9.5	30.8	18.8[d]	31.6	50.4[d]	49.1	18.7[d]	1.5	26.1[d]
Russia	23.0	45.8	-20.2	80.4[d]	-12.2	118.7[d]	2.4	41.2[d]	n.a.	51.4[d]
Slovakia	n.a.	-6.0	n.a.	3.3[c]	n.a.	-2.1[c]	n.a.	0.2[c]	n.a.	n.a.
Ukraine	32.5	26.1	n.a.	27.8[d]	n.a.	27.3[d]	n.a.	16.6[d]	n.a.	n.a.

[a] 1989–94
[b] 1989–92
[c] 1990–3
[d] 1989–93
n.a. = not available
Source: Council of Europe (1993); TransMONEE database

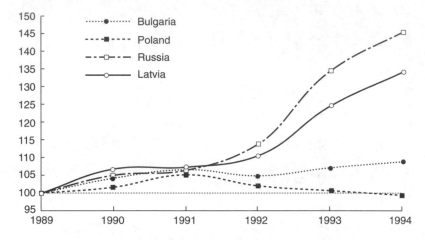

Fig. 12.1. Patterns of CDR dynamics in selected transitional economies (1989=100)
Source: UNICEF 1995.

Republic, Slovakia and Poland) of the thirteen countries covered in this chapter. The rise in mortality followed three different patterns. First, while mortality edged upward—if at times imperceptibly and temporarily—during the initial phase of the reforms in all economies in transition, this increase was swiftly reabsorbed in subsequent years in the Czech Republic, Slovakia, and Poland. In the first two countries, mortality rates, including those among at-risk middle-aged males, declined after the second or third years of transition. In a second group of countries (where the increase in the CDR during the first two transition years was clear, but still relatively contained), as in Bulgaria, the initial rise stabilized during 1992–4 at a level higher than that observed prior to the transition. The third and most worrying pattern of mortality increases was that observed in Russia, Latvia, and a few other members of the former Soviet Union, that is, countries which registered the steepest upswings in mortality. In these countries, death rates accelerated in the second and subsequent years of the transition (Figure 12.1).

A substantial part of the increasingly pervasive health crisis which has affected most of Eastern Europe is attributable to a true epidemic of heart diseases among middle-aged males. To a lesser degree, it has also been due to an upsurge of cerebrovascular diseases, lung cancer, cirrhosis of the liver, and suicide among the same population group. Smaller yet significant increases in female mortality due to heart diseases and cirrhosis of the liver have contributed to a worsening of the overall health picture. Only for respiratory diseases, in some cases, has there been some decline (Tables 12.6 and 12.7).

The current mortality crisis affecting Eastern Europe is far more pronounced and widespread than the crises recorded in the region over the 1965–85 period or during the Great Depression in the Western industrialized countries. During 1929–33, for instance, the CDR in the US continued a downward trend, and mortality among

Table 12.6. Contribution of causes of death to CDR changes, 1989–94

	Absolute change in CDR	% of total change in CDR due to						
		Infectious diseases	Cancer	Health & circulatory diseases	Respiratory diseases	Digestive diseases	External causes	Other causes
Belarus	2.5	–0.1	6.1	25.4	–5.6	1.2	16.7	56.3
Bulgaria	1.2	4.2	16.7	54.5	–32.3	2.6	7.6	46.8
Hungary	0.9	–1.1	38.8	30.4	2.4	26.3	2.3	0.9
Lithuania	2.2	2.7	10.0	29.2	0.2	2.1	28.2	27.5
Romania	1	1.0	15.5	66.8	–34.3	10.7	–3.8	45.1
Russia	3.8	1.0	4.4	45.1	4.0	2.9	35.7	7.0
Slovakia	–0.6	–3.7	–32.3	–25.5	52.7	27.8	10.9	70.1
Ukraine	2.6	1.1	3.2	47.2		15.0	1.0	32.5

Source: See Table 12.1.

Table 12.7. Suicides and homicides among males aged 20–59: 1994 as percentage of rates in 1989

	Suicides	Homicides
Belarus	141.70	171.43
Bulgaria	102.09	193.98
Estonia*	169.26	261.74
Hungary	84.70	159.29
Latvia*	191.71	277.54
Lithuania	176.52	268.14
Poland	126.63	160.33
Romania	123.86	114.29
Russia*	157.39	236.61
Slovakia*	87.08	191.18
Ukraine*	116.64	

* 1993 as percentage of 1989 rate.
Source: See Table 12.1

males due to homicide, suicide, and ulcers surged only for those age, sex and professional groups most adversely affected by the increase in unemployment and other negative events (Eyer and Sterling 1977; UNICEF 1994).

The increases in mortality have been much more pronounced among men than among women (Ukraine is the only exception.) In Russia, for instance, the CDR rose twice as quickly among men as among women. In addition, 'transition mortality' hit most severely not the traditionally vulnerable groups, namely, children, pregnant and lactating mothers and the elderly, but rather the working-age male population. The greatest *relative* jump in death rates occurred among the 35–39 or 40–44 age groups. (For the Russian men in these age groups the risk of death has almost doubled over the past four years.) The largest absolute climb occurred among men in the 50–59 age group (UNICEF 1994). In general, age-specific death rates among women varied in remarkably similar ways to those among males, though the upswings were much more gentle or even negative and had a lower starting point.

These large rises in mortality rates among male adults and the widening of life expectancy differentials between the sexes are cause for serious concern, since they bear witness to a large and unexpected increase in the number of premature and preventable deaths and provide a clear indication of the extreme stress to which these societies are being subjected. From a population perspective they are also worrying because they have further exacerbated the imbalance in the sex ratio and the dependency ratio, raised the number of incomplete families, increased widowhood, and caused considerable economic losses: all of which reduce the nuptiality and reproductive potential of the population and therefore tend to 'endogenize' the marriage and fertility crisis.

1.2. Significance of Recent Changes in Demographic Behaviour

This section tests the significance of the changes in demographic behaviour occurring between the pre-transition (1970–89) and the transition (1989–94) periods for the CMR, TFR, and CDR. For each of these variables, a *test of predictive failure* has been carried out for the nine of the thirteen countries covered by this chapter for which it has been possible to extend backwards to 1970 the time series for these three variables (Table 12.9). The 1970–94 data have been interpolated by means of one of the following two functions:

$$y = a + b \cdot \log (\text{Time}) + [d_1 \cdot \text{dummy90} + d_2 \cdot \text{dummy91} + d_3 \text{dummy92} + d_4 \cdot \text{dummy93} + d_5 \cdot \text{dummy94}] \tag{1}$$

$$y = a + b \cdot \log (\text{Time}) + c \cdot (\log^2 (\text{Time})) + [d_1 \cdot \text{dummy90} + d_2 \cdot \text{dummy91} + d_3 \cdot \text{dummy92} + d_4 \cdot \text{dummy93} + d_5 \cdot \text{dummy94}] \tag{2}$$

The parts of the equations outside the brackets represent the proper functional form of the model. The variables within the brackets are dummies, they are equal to '1' for the relevant year and '0' for the other years, so that their parameters indicate the deviation from the pre-1989 period. For the TFR, data availability problems have required that the estimation period be narrowed to 1975–94, except for Russia, Romania and Lithuania, for which the estimation period is 1970–94. All estimates of the above equations have statistically significant 'a', 'b' and 'c' parameters and show a good 'fit', except for Poland in the case of the CMR.

If the t-statistics of d_1, d_2, d_3, d_4 and d_5—expressed in absolute terms—are above the established absolute threshold determined both by a certain level of probability (90–95 per cent) and by the degrees of freedom of the estimate, then the actual value is significantly different from that predicted on the basis of the time trend up to 1989. In addition, if the F-statistic—expressed in absolute terms—is above the

Table 12.8. *T*-statistics of variations from the expected trend and overall *F*-statistic of predictive failure, 1990–4

(a) *Crude marriage rate*

Functional form	Bulgaria Model 1	Czech R. Model 1	Estonia Model 1	Hungary Model 2	Latvia Model 1	Lithuania Model 1	Poland Model 1	Romania Model 1	Russia Model 1
1990	-1.252**	4.546	-2.582	1.188**	-2.089*	2.087*	1.336**	2.077*	-1.239**
1991	-7.793	-4.453	-4.742	-1.241**	-2.944	-0.277**	0.570**	-0.443**	-1.645*
1992	-8.393	-2.979	-5.968	-2.974	-5.149	-3.831	0.237**	-1.889*	-4.457
1993	-9.246	-5.263	-6.402	-4.272	-7.683	-8.064	0.204**	-3.805	-2.956
1994	-8.698	-6.585	-5.903	-1.463**	-8.741	-6.663	0.460**	-4.840	-2.755
Overall predictive Failure (F-stat)	25.611	35.833	9.832	6.072	40.400	24.930	0.524**	5.104	16.70

(b) *Total fertility rate*

Functional form	Bulgaria Model 1	Czech R. Model 1	Estonia Model 1	Hungary Model 2	Latvia Model 1	Lithuania Model 1	Poland Model 1	Romania Model 1	Russia Model 1
1990	-2.607	-0.560**	-4.889	0.422**	-1.783	-1.651**	0.650**	-1.570**	-3.309
1991	-5.641	-0.871**	-9.757	0.489**	-3.217	-2.182	1.990*	-2.696	-5.053
1992	-7.580	-2.813	-11.396	-1.112**	-4.213	-3.271	0.251**	-2.738	-6.759
1993	-8.780	–	-14.552	-2.519	-5.701	-5.861	0.418**	-2.948	-8.049
1994	-9.594	–	-15.115	-2.972	-6.290	-7.129	0.492**	-2.938	-7.555
Overall predictive Failure (F-stat)	24.343	2.690*	59.472	4.159	9.868	12.813	2.400**	3.008	16.879

Table 12.8 *continued*

(c) *Crude death rate*

Functional form	Bulgaria Model 1	Czech R. Model 1	Estonia Model 1	Hungary Model 2	Latvia Model 1	Lithuania Model 1	Poland Model 1	Romania Model 1	Russia Model 1
1990	1.618*	0.889**	2.320	1.339**	2.112*	1.496**	-0.128**	-1.358**	1.624**
1991	2.630	0.339**	2.818	1.195**	2.266	2.358	0.888**	-0.734**	2.224
1992	1.747*	1.636**	4.117	2.260	3.113	2.618	-0.305**	2.197	4.082
1993	2.522	2.124*	6.682	2.659	6.286	5.650	-0.745**	2.179	9.028
1994	3.723	2.233	8.383	2.139	8.090	5.661	-1.396**	2.195	10.889
Overall predictive Failure (F–stat)	3.917	2.465*	16.781	1.726**	16.611	9.193	0.773**	2.987	33.630

* = Not significant at 5% but significant at 10%.

** = Not significant at 10%.

Note: Models selected by using the Amemiya selection criterion.

Source: See Table 12.1.

Table 12.9. Summary statistics of the test of predictive failure for the CMR, TFR, and CDR, 1990–4

Country	CMR		TFR		CDR		Overall score t-test
	Overall F-Test	t-test	Overall F-Test	t-test	Overall F-Test	t-test	
Bulgaria	Yes	4	Yes	5	Yes	4	13/15
Czech Rep.	Yes	5	No	1	No	3	9/13
Estonia	Yes	5	Yes	5	Yes	5	15/15
Hungary	Yes	2	Yes	2	No	3	7/15
Latvia	Yes	5	Yes	4	Yes	5	14/15
Lithuania	Yes	4	Yes	4	Yes	4	12/15
Poland	No	0	No	0	No	0	0/15
Romania	Yes	3	Yes	4	Yes	3	10/15
Russia	Yes	3	Yes	5	Yes	4	12/15
Total of significant cases	8	31	7	30	6	31	
No. of significant over total cases	8/9	31/45	7/9	30/43	6/9	31/45	

Source: Authors' calculations.

threshold established as above, then the model fails to predict the correct value of the variable over the entire 1990–4 transition period (Table 12.8).

In the case of the CMR the coefficients of the dummy variables are significant at the 5 per cent level of probability in about two-thirds of the cases. In five cases the *t*-statistics are significant at between the 10 and 5 per cent level, while in 12 cases it is not significant at the 10 per cent level (Table 12.9). It is interesting to note that the statistical significance of the dummies generally increases over time, indicating that the deviation from past nuptiality trends is generally intensifying. As expected, the parameters of the dummies are generally negative. The only exceptions are those of the 1990 dummies for Romania, the Czech Republic, and Lithuania, which indicate positive and statistically significant deviations from long-term trends, thus corroborating the hypothesis of an 'initial matrimonial euphoria' in the first year of reform in some countries.

The overall *F*-test of predictive failure (which verifies if the post-transition observations taken as a whole have been correctly predicted by the 1970–89 time trend) is confirmed in all countries except Poland, where even the 10 per cent drop in the CMR in relation to 1989 does not appear to be significantly different from that projected on the basis of the long-term trend. In Poland, in other words, the decline in nuptiality does not appear to be related to the transition, but to longer-term trends in family-formation behaviour.

The test of predictive failure produces slightly stronger results for the TFR than it does in the case of the CMR (Table 12.8a). Out of forty-three t-statistics for the coefficients of the dummy variables measuring the variation from the expected trend for the TFR, only eleven are not significant at the 10 per cent probability level, while two others are significant between the 10 and the 5 per cent levels. These results confirm that radical departures from previous reproductive behaviours have taken place in all nine countries studied, with the exception of Poland and the Czech Republic, in which the deviations from the long-term trend are generally small and insignificant and in which the overall test of predictive failure is rejected. However, also in these two countries, the changes in the size and the sign of the t-statistics in 1992–4 indicate that the behaviour of the TFR might gradually be approaching the general pattern.

Finally, the test of predictive failure has been applied to the CDR (Table 12.8c). The results are only marginally weaker than those in the other two cases. The values of the dummy coefficients are positive (indicating an increase in the CDR greater than that suggested by the long-term trend) and significantly different from zero in twenty-seven cases, while in four cases the deviation is significant between the 10 and 5 per cent levels of probability. Also in this case the value of the coefficients tends to rise over time, thus pointing to an aggravation of the mortality crisis. Poland and the Czech Republic appear almost completely unaffected by the recent mortality crisis. In Hungary the overall predictive failure test is rejected, though the data suggest that it would have been verified had the test been applied not to the 1990–4 period but to the 1992–4 period. In Hungary, in other words, the mortality crisis started taking effect two years after the beginning of the reforms.

In summary, in the twenty-seven possible cases, the test of predictive failure suggests there has been a break-up of the pre-89 trends, except in Poland for the CMR and TFR, the Czech Republic for the TFR, and in these two countries—and with the qualifications mentioned above—for the CDR (Table 12.9).

Though often showing sizeable variations in relation to the 1989 levels, in Poland and to a lesser degree in the Czech Republic the main demographic indicators have been basically unaffected by the (comparatively smaller) negative shocks of the last five years. The deviations observed reflect, in other words, the continuation of a long-term trend and cannot be attributed to the problems triggered by the transition. By and large, this outcome has been expected in the case of the Czech Republic, which contained and immediately reversed the 1991 surge in poverty, drastically limited the spread of unemployment, and moved relatively smoothly towards the market.

In contrast, these results are somewhat puzzling in the case of Poland. In that country, the sharp 1990 rise in poverty was not reversed, and registered unemployment stabilized at a high level (about 16 per cent), despite a recovery of GDP in 1992–4. These results may therefore signal that the transition crisis is less severe than revealed by poverty, wage and unemployment data (which would tend to over-estimate the extent of the economic crisis). But these results may also signal that the demographic crisis began before 1989, or that positive expectations about the over-all outcome of the transition (favourably influenced by the 1992–4 recovery of GDP) prevailed over the negative influences of spreading poverty and high unemployment.

In contrast, in the other seven countries the test of predictive failure is accepted for all three variables, thus confirming that the transition has brought about drastic and sudden changes in family-formation behaviour, fertility, and mortality. The countries in which the deviations appear most marked are Latvia, Estonia, and Russia.

The results arrived at on the basis of the data on these nine countries can easily be extended to the remaining four included in this chapter. Indeed, changes over 1989–94 in Slovakia are similar to those observed in the Czech Republic, while those in Ukraine, Belarus and Moldova are comparable to those in the other countries of the former Soviet Union.

In conclusion, in ten of the thirteen countries included in this chapter, the economic shocks caused by the transition have induced large and statistically significant deviations from the long-term trend in the main demographic variables. While the impact is important—though limited to nuptiality and fertility—in the Czech Republic and Slovakia, only Poland seems to have been generally unaffected by the population crisis of the transition.

2. Causes of the Break-up of Trends

This chapter now examines the causes of the large deviations in the demo-graphic variables. It focuses, in particular, on the causal relationship among current economic and social dislocations, social stress, and demographic adjust-ment.

In spite of the hopes placed on a rapid move to a market economy, it is now evident that the transition has met with formidable and unexpected difficulties. All countries have been affected, though in various degrees, by a large fall in GDP, an inflationary outburst, a collapse in employment, a steep drop in household incomes, a large surge in income inequality, and a sizeable reduction in social expenditure. Table 12.10 details the general depth of the economic and distributive crisis and the considerable degree of variance with which these phenomena have occurred within the region.

2.1. Determinants of the Fall in the Crude Marriage Rate

The discussion in Section 1 suggests that the recent decline in nuptiality is the result neither of a contraction in the size of the cohorts reaching the age of most frequent

Table 12.10. Selected economic indicators: 1989–94 overall variation

	Registered Unemployment rate (absolute variation)	Unemployment rate ILO stand. (absolute variation)	Employment rate (absolute variation)	Real income per capita (1989=100)	Real average wage (1989=100)	Gini coefficient (absolute variation)	CPI (% cumulative increase)	New housing units (% cumulative decline)	GDP (% cumulative decline)	Industrial prod (% cumulative decline)
Belarus	2.1	n.a.	-8.4	n.a.	65.4	n.a.	838849.6	46.1	-37.3	-37.1
Bulgaria	14.1	20.5	-26.1	55.5	62.4	12.0	2842.1	72.4	-27.8	-63.3
Czech Rep.	3.3	4.0	-6.0	82.2[b]	85.8	2.5	254.3	67.0	-20.1	-43.6
Estonia	1.5	n.a.	-4.2[d]	n.a.	n.a.	10.9	10852.0	79.4	-35.1[e]	-79.7
Hungary	11.3	10.8	-19.0	90.0	88.3	1.6	311.5	59.2	-17.0	-20.2
Latvia	6.4	n.a.	-8.5	n.a.	52.5	n.a.	8989.6	78.1	-50.5	-80.6
Lithuania	3.8	n.a.	-10.9	n.a.	32.8	9.5	33991.6	76.4	-65.8	-95.5
Moldova	1.0	n.a.	-1.7	30.3	29.0	13.3	188955.0	72.8	-61.7	-78.1
Poland	16.0	14.4	-7.8	91.0	72.5	5.1	2926.2	52.3	-7.5	-11.9
Romania	11.0	8.5	-6.0[d]	80.7	52.5	4.9	7563.1	39.2	-24.5	-59.1
Russia	1.7	8.0	-7.0[a]	79.0	63.8	15.2	164117.7	56.8[a]	-48.3	-61.1
Slovakia	14.4	13.7	-16.8	77.1	71.6	3.0	273.5	73.8	-19.1	-39.9
Ukraine	0.4	n.a.	-6.4	96.3[f]	28.5	3.4[c]	122330.4	55.3	-49.1	-61.4

[a] 1989–93
[b] 1990–4
[c] 1993
[d] 1992
[e] 1989–92

n.a. = not available
Source: TransMONEE Database.

marriage, nor (except for Poland) of factors already at work prior to the transition. In addition, the stability of the mean age at marriage of women, the fact that the decline in marriage rates has concerned all age groups (see Table 12.2) and the limited evidence for increases in cohabitation suggest that the present drop in nuptiality is not, as suggested by some, the result of a shift towards a 'Western' marriage pattern. Other factors could be responsible for these changes, including the following.

2.1.1. Unfavourable Changes in the Sex Ratio

The surge in mortality among young and middle-aged males may have worsened the sex ratio in the age bracket in which people are most likely to marry (20–49) and thus reduced the chances of first marriage or remarriage among women. The empirical evidence (TransMONEE Database, November 1995), however, indicates that only modest variations have occurred so far in this regard. While this might be due to problems in the yearly computation of population structure by cohorts and sex (which often relies on theoretical models and not on an updating based on the civil register), it is likely also that it is too soon to observe statistically significant changes in the sex ratio.

2.1.2. Variables Measuring Current Economic Difficulties of the Marriageable Population

The establishment of a new household involves considerable start-up costs (for the ceremony itself, the purchase or rental of a new house, furniture, household equipment, and so on), while the maintenance (or reproduction) cost of the new family is, at least in the early phases of the marriage, higher than those borne by the two families of origin (because of the new fixed costs to be paid for rent, utilities, and so on). At the same time, even under normal circumstances, life-cycle theory suggests that earnings, savings and access to credit are all generally lower at a younger age.

To start with, except for the Czech Republic, *registered unemployment* rose sharply in 1991 and 1992 in all countries of Central and Southeastern Europe, though it rose only marginally in the former Soviet Union. However, if we account for persons involuntarily working part-time, on leave without pay or with only partial wages, this rate would increase to around 12 per cent (UNECE 1994). So far, registered unemployment has started to decline only in Hungary and to stabilize in Poland.

In view of these and other measurement problems, it might be preferable to measure the extent of the shock borne by the labour market by means of *changes in the employment rate*. This variable captures not only the surge in unemployment, but also the increase in the number of discouraged workers, early retirements, and childcare leaves. If this measure of labour market change is adopted, the differences among countries are narrowed, but not eliminated.

While employment rates have declined sharply for the entire active population, economic recession and an increasingly difficult transition from school to work have caused proportionately greater difficulties for the new entrants in the labour force. While there are no available data on the employment rate by age, the registered unemployment rate (from both the unemployment register and labour force survey) has generally risen more rapidly among workers in the 15–24 age bracket. The share of unemployment in this age group within the total varies between 29 and 45 per cent, while this group's share in the entire working-age population is around 20–30 per cent.

The economic difficulties of the marriageable population have also been influenced by the sharp decline in *real wages and incomes per capita*. Real wages fell sharply in all countries of the region during the first two reform years, though the fall was most pronounced in the countries where the drop in employment was less marked. In most cases, real wages continued their slide in the third, fourth and fifth years of transition, though at a slower pace and despite the rise in real wages in Central Europe since 1994. With the single exceptions of Hungary and the Czech Republic, by the end of 1994 the fall had reached or exceeded the 30 per cent mark (UNICEF 1995). Even in the countries (such as Poland and Romania) which experienced a recovery in 1993–4, real wages have either stagnated, or further contracted. Only in Central Europe, therefore, has the five-year decline in real wages ended.

Another factor which has rendered marriage more problematic is the increasingly difficult access to and greater cost of *housing* and related charges (for heating, electricity, water, maintenance, and so on). To start with, the severe recession in the first half of the 1990s seriously affected the construction sector (particularly the building of public flats, see Cornia and Sipos 1991), thus causing a sharp and generalized decline in the number of new housing units completed per year (Table 12.10). Thus, although housing shortages and forced cohabitation were common during the socialist period, the phenomena have worsened in recent years. Between 1989 and 1994, the number of new housing units dropped by over 70 per cent in Bulgaria, Latvia, Lithuania, Estonia, and Moldova, by 67 per cent in the Czech Republic, and by 52 per cent in Poland. In addition, the liberalization of the rental market and, in some countries such as Russia, the repatriation of workers and military personnel from other countries have drastically reduced the chances of securing even minimum housing for new couples (UNICEF 1995). While privatization in housing has favoured the old tenants, the supply of subsidized housing for young couples has basically dried up, and many new couples have now to pay open market prices for housing (UNICEF 1995).

2.1.3. Variables Measuring the Expectations Concerning Future Living Conditions

Marriage rates have also been affected by worsening expectations about future living standards. By using the hypothesis of 'adaptive expectations' it is possible to proxy the expectation term by combining the 'lagged' value of a few variables, such as the unemployment rate, the employment rate and the wage rate, inflation and relative prices. In the model here, expectations at the time 't' ('EXP_t') about living standards are proxied by the employment level (ER) lagged one year and by the *current* rate of inflation ('CPI_h'). Thus:[1]

$$EXP_t = f(ER_{t-1}, CPI\_h_t) \tag{1}$$

The reason for the introduction of the *current* values of CPI_h is that, as amply demonstrated by the literature on Latin America (see, for instance, Cardoso 1992), in countries experiencing very high rates of inflation, expectations are greatly influenced by *current* changes in the price level. Though part of this information is included in the computation of wages in real terms (lagged one year), high inflation *per se* is perceived as a serious source of instability by most economic agents.

In this regard, the transition has been characterized by sharp increases in the price level following the puncturing of the inflationary 'bubble' inherited from the socialist era, the price 'overshootings' induced by the macroeconomic approaches adopted, and the implementation of structural reforms (such as price liberalization, the elimination of subsidies, and the introduction of value-added tax) which always generate sizeable price shocks.

After these initial outbursts, inflation was brought down to more tolerable but still significant levels in most countries of Central Europe and the Baltics and in Moldova (UNICEF 1995). Inflation remains very high in Russia, Belarus, and Ukraine (where in 1994 alone the consumer price index rose respectively by 411, 2321, and 140 per cent) and other countries which followed lax or inconsistent fiscal and monetary policies.

Under conditions of high inflation, wages, pensions, and child allowances are thus bound to trail permanently behind the price level, as no indexation system can work meaningfully under circumstances of hyper- or very high inflation. In addition, inflation imposes a highly regressive tax on the population (Gil-Diaz 1987), rapidly erodes real government resources, prevents even well-meaning governments from establishing adequate social safety nets, offers the opportunity for considerable shifts in wage, income, and asset distribution and in relative prices (see Table 12.10), destroys the financial savings of households, and leads to a more than proportional increase in the prices of those goods and services (such as housing rental, heating charges, and goods for children) that, by pushing up disproportionately the cost of marriage and of the birth and raising of a child, influences the decisions of young couples to marry and have children. Finally, inflation generates expectations of additional social dislocations due to the introduction of the harsh stabilization measures normally used to control it.

The results of the econometric analysis in which the above determinants of nuptiality have been explicitly considered are now presented.

In the theoretical model employed in this chapter, the CMR is dependent on three

---

[1] Actually, both variables have been standardized (that is, divided by that country's standard deviation), so as to improve comparability.

Table 12.11. Result of the regression analysis on the determinants of the crude marriage rate (CMR)

Model estimate	Coefficient	Estimation by FGLS	
		Standard error	t-statistics
Constant	−0.7999	0.3097	−2.5828
ΔlnEXP	0.1798	0.0460	3.9043
ΔlnAWI	0.2034	0.0466	4.3664
lnNHU(t–1)	0.1913	0.1048	1.8268

Notes:

dependent variable	= ΔlnCMR	First differences of CMR in log
explanatory variables	= ΔlnEXP	First differences of the log of the Expectation Index
	ΔlnAWI	First differences of the log Real Average Wage Index
	ΔlnNHU	First differences of the log New Housing Units Index
R-square adj.	= 0.5504	
Durbin-Watson	= 1.7499	
Hausman test	= 1.4073	

sets of variables: a demographic factor (the sex ratio in the 20–49 age group), the current economic difficulties of the marriageable population (measured by the wage rate, ARW, and the availability of housing, which is proxied by the number of new housing units completed every year, (NHU)), and the expectations about future living standards, EXP, defined above. Thus:

$$CMR_t = f(ARW_t, NHU_t, EXP_t) \qquad (2)$$

The equation has been applied to pooled cross-country and time series data over 1989–4 by means of the FGLS (Feasible Generalized Least Squares) procedure (Greene 1990). To avoid the spurious causality due to the similar trends in the series (expressed in absolute figures)—and therefore also the first-order correlation of the residuals—and heteroscedasticity problems, the regression has been carried out in first differences of log. The results are reported in Table 12.11.

The results are satisfactory from an econometric perspective. All parameters are significatively different from zero; the Durbin-Watson statistic indicates a low correlation of the residuals, and the fit is more than acceptable considering that the regression is carried out in first differences and on pooled data, as the Hausman test accepts the hypothesis of random effects.

All parameters have the expected sign, including the constant, which would indicate a natural tendency towards a gentle decline in nuptiality. (This parameter is, however, not significant.) Interestingly, it appears that the sum of the elasticities is considerably smaller than 1, suggesting a less than proportional decline in marriage rates in relation to changes in the rate determinants. It also appears that the variables measuring the current economic problems faced by the potential brides and grooms (that is, changes in real wages and housing availability) dominate in broadly equal manner in the decision to marry. Indeed, the elasticities of these two variables explain about 65 per cent of the total variation of the CMR.

2.2. Determinants of the Fall in the Total Fertility Rate

The discussion in Section 1 suggests that the contraction in the TFR observed over 1989–94 was not mainly due either to a shrinkage of the cohorts of women in the fertile age group, or to a shift towards Western reproductive behaviours. The drop, which affected women of all ages, is to be attributed largely to the current economic difficulties, the weakening of family support policies, negative expectations about the future and, in Romania, changes in anti-abortion legislation. These factors are discussed in greater detail hereafter.

2.2.1. *Variables Measuring the Cumulative Effect of the Decline in Marriage Rates on Natality*

As noted, declining nuptiality, higher outmigration of young males and greater mortality among middle-aged males may have contributed to a drop in birth rates by *reducing the share of married women in the most fertile age group and, ceteris paribus, matrimonial fertility* The impact of these changes was probably imperceptible in the first year or two, but ought in principle to have intensified over time with the persistent changes in nuptiality, male mortality, and migration.

2.2.2. *Variables Measuring the Current Economic Difficulties of the Population of Reproductive Age*

In the theoretical model here (see Equation 3 below), the decision to have a child depends on current family income of couples of reproductive age.[2] This in turn depends on changes in the employment rate, the average wage (ARW) and other incomes.

Over the last five years, these three variables have evolved negatively in most of the region. The cost of raising a child has skyrocketed because of the more than proportional increase in the prices of the goods and services consumed by children (milk, children's clothes, kindergartens, education, and medical services). In view of the large subsidies linked with these goods and services in the past, the prices of these goods and services have often risen much more quickly than has the average consumer price index. As for the changes in real wages and incomes, the same arguments developed in 2.1.2. apply.

2.2.3. *Variables Measuring Changes in Family Support Policies*

Traditionally, most of the literature on reproductive behaviour has emphasized the role of 'family-support' policies in the decision to have children (Kamerman and

---

[2] This is, of course, an oversimplification: unfortunately, other potentially relevant data are difficult to measure or estimate.

Khan 1995). In Eastern Europe this support was generally provided in two ways (Zimakova 1994): through child allowances aiming at offsetting an important part of the cost of raising a child and through the provision of highly subsidized child-care services which were meant to support parents, and particularly women, in the workforce in their task of raising and socializing children. To capture these various effects, an ordinal variable, the 'public child support variable' (PCSV), is used here. It combines three factors: the current real value and coverage of child allowances, the current percentage of 0-to-2 year-olds with a parent on parental leave *or* enrolled in crèches (for a discussion on this variable see Cornia-Paniccià 1995; Fajth 1994; UNICEF 1993), and the current availability of places in public kindergartens, prox-ied here by the kindergarten enrolment rate.

Because of cuts in public expenditure on defence, general administration, and production and consumption subsidies, the share of child allowances in total public expenditure and, less frequently, GDP has generally increased. In most cases, however, the real value of child allowances has declined, often sharply and often more quickly than average wages and pensions (UNICEF 1995). The moderating effect of these allowances on the fall of household incomes has therefore been far less positive than intended. The fall has been particularly sharp in Latvia and Russia, where child allowances had dropped almost to zero by the end of 1993, thus aggra-vating more than proportionately the economic circumstances of families with children.

2.2.4. Variables Measuring Expectations about Future Living standards

In conclusion, the theoretical model presented here to explain the changes in the TFR can be expressed as follows:

$$\text{TFR}_t = f[(\text{CMR}_t - \text{CMR}_{89})_{t-1}, \text{ARW}_t, \text{PCSV}_t, \text{EXP}_t] \tag{3}$$

As in the previous case, all variables have been expressed in first differences of log. The results of the regression are reported in Table 12.12. They are generally satis-factory from an econometric viewpoint. All parameters are significatively different from zero at a fairly high level of probability (except for PCSV, which is significant only at a 90 per cent level); the Durbin-Watson statistic and the Hausman test are in the acceptance region of their hypotheses.

All parameters have the expected sign and are of a plausible order of magnitude. Also in this case the sum of the elasticities is considerably lower than unity, suggesting a less than proportional variation of the TFR in relation to the TFR determinants. It is interesting to note that there is a clear and highly significant impact of lower nuptiality on natality. The lagged cumulated variation in the former explains about one-third of the overall variation of the latter. This conclu-sion contributes further to the rejection of the view that the decline in birth is due to the adoption of a Western model of reproductive behaviour (which would involve a much more tenuous relationship between these two variables because of the large share of births out of wedlock). These results tend also to confirm that

Table 12.12. Result of the regression analysis on the determinants of the total fertility rate (TFR)

Model estimate	Coefficient	Estimation by FGLS	
		Standard error	*t*-statistics
Constant	1.1237	0.7857	1.4301
ΔlnEXP	0.1139	0.0371	3.0684
ΔlnAWI	0.1522	0.0463	3.2837
ΔlnCMR89(*t*-1)	0.1670	0.0602	2.7765
ΔlnPCSV	0.0950	0.0577	1.6459

Notes:

dependent variable	= ΔlnTFR	First differences of TFR in log
explanatory variables	= ΔlnEXP	First differences of the log of the Expectation Index
	ΔlnAWI	First differences of the log Real Average Wage Index
	ΔlnCMR89	First differences of the log Cumulated CMR from 1989
	ΔlnPCSV	First differences of the log Public Child Support Index
R-square adj.	= 0.7014	
Durbin-Watson	= 1.8699	
Hausman test	= 1.8216	

family support policies have a positive but modest impact (that is, with an elasticity explaining only about 16 per cent of the overall variation over the entire sample) on the decision to have a child.

Contrary to the case of nuptiality, expectations about the future do not seem to play a dominant role in the decision to have a child. However, this impact is probably more marked in the case of the countries which suffer from a generally 'gloomy' situation, reflecting an overall erosion in post-Soviet society and greater lack of confidence in the national economy and civil society.

Thus, in a context such as that in Russia, a sharp stabilization in the rate of inflation and an increase in employment rates (which explain expectations about the future) would have an impact on natality that would be seven times greater than the impact of a proportionate improvement in family support policies and twice as large as the impact of a similar improvement in the average real wage (that is, the variable which in this model measures the current economic problems faced by the potential brides and grooms). More generally, except for family support, all other variables have far greater elasticities for the countries of the former Soviet Union than they do for the other countries.

2.3. Factors Explaining the Increase in Mortality

As is customary in the analysis of mortality (Mosley and Chen 1984), this chapter attempts to separate the causes of the higher mortality rates into changes in risk factors and disease control.

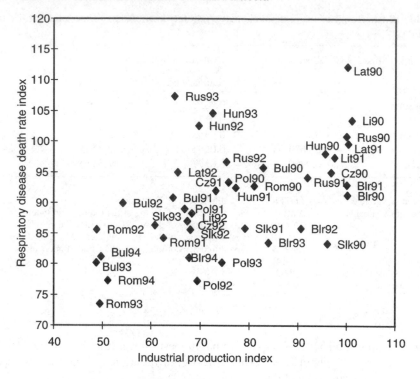

Fig. 12.2. Respiratory disease death rate versus industrial production, 1990–4
Source: Council of Europe (1993), TransMONEE database, national statistics.

2.3.1. Variables Measuring Changes in Risk Factors

Five factors commonly discussed in the literature have been identified. These are analysed separately below in relation to changes in cause-specific mortality rates.

Environmental pollution   While Eastern Europe has long been suffering from severe environmental contamination, there is no evidence that this factor has contributed to the surge in mortality observed over recent years. Industrial emissions (IE) have generally been dropping in line with the recession-induced fall in industrial production (Table 12.10). In Russia, for instance, the emission of harmful substances into the air fell by 17 per cent between 1990 and 1992 (Nell and Stewart 1994). In addition, the introduction of sectoral and pricing reforms for energy and raw materials has contributed to the reduction of emissions per unit of output. Finally, political freedom has led to stricter restrictions on emissions and other forms of pollution. These conclusions are reinforced by the decline in mortality due to respiratory diseases observed during the past five years (Figure 12.2), suggesting that industrial emissions are associated with respiratory mortality. This variable is therefore included in the regression analysis below.

Table 12.13. Number of litres of pure alcohol consumed per person.

Countries	1989	1990	1991	1992	1993	1994
Czech R.	8.2	8.9	9.1	9.4	9.2	
Estonia	n.a.	n.a.	n.a.	8.3	7.4	7.9
Hungary	11.3	11.1	10.7	10.5	10.6	
Latvia	5.7	5.3	5.3	5.2	6.4	7.8
Lithuania	6.0	5.0	5.6	3.6	2.5	
Poland	5.5	4.6	5.5	5.2	5.8	5.2
Romania	3.9	3.8	4.1	4.8	4.0	
Russia	5.3	5.6	5.6	5.0	6.0	
Slovakia	3.4	3.4	2.8	2.9	2.2	2.4
Ukraine	3.8	4.1	4.1	2.5	n.a.	n.a.

n.a. = not available
Source: See Table 12.1.

Diet and alcohol consumption   The massive belt-tightening imposed on most households by the 1989–94 recession should have entailed an important drop in the consumption of food and, in particular, of alcoholic beverages (which are generally considered 'superior' goods). The drop in food consumption has concerned in particular animal proteins and involved most of the population. However, in view of the high calorie and fat consumption in the past and of the substitution of expensive with cheap sources of nutrients, the drop in food expenditure has not exacerbated the risk of death due to insufficient calorie and protein intake.

As for alcohol consumption, it should be noted that the depressionary effect of the fall in incomes was offset by the decline in the relative price of alcohol, thus leaving broadly unchanged the alcohol-purchasing power of wages, and by the liberalization of alcohol import and consumption. Alcohol intake therefore probably decreased less than expected on the basis of changes in wages and incomes (UNICEF 1994). This argument is apparently confirmed by official data which show no radical changes in consumption except in the Czech Republic and Estonia, where there was an increase, and of Ukraine and Lithuania, where there was a sharp decrease (Table 12.13). These data, however, are biased downwards, since they do not adequately reflect the increase in alcohol imports, production by an increasingly unregulated private sector, illicit production, and home-distillation by consumers. Indeed, alcohol is generally perceived as a stress-reliever, and people resort to it more frequently in times of painful social adjustments. Furthermore, controls on the trade, consumption, and even production of alcohol have become less stringent.

In short, diet and alcohol consumption are only poorly documented, or not at all. Moreover, the data we have suggest that these variables have probably not greatly influenced the mortality increase of the early 1990s in the region; they are therefore omitted from the estimate.

Smoking   This is a main risk factor in premature deaths due to various types of cancers and all types of cardiovascular diseases, cirrhosis of the liver, and other non-medical fatalities due to fire, suicide and so on. Over 1989–93, cigarette consumption does appear to have slightly declined throughout the region, as incomes dropped and prices—particularly of imported goods—soared, though these data do not include information on the consumption of smuggled cigarettes (WHO-HFA 1994). Its relation to changes in the CDR indeed suggests almost complete independence between the two phenomena. In addition, the impact of more smoking on lung cancer and cardiovascular mortality would require protracted exposure to this additional risk for a significant number of years. The variable is therefore omitted from the formal regression analysis.

Psychosocial stress   Social stress is increasingly recognized as a main factor in deaths due to heart diseases, ulcers, cirrhosis, alcohol psychosis, and suicide. Stress arises in situations where individuals are called upon to react to new and unexpected situations for which they do not know the appropriate coping behaviours. This leads to physiological and psychological arousal, provoking sudden changes in heart rate, blood pressure and viscosity, and in the ability to maintain coherent behaviour. Stress-related mortality is particularly associated with family breakdown, poverty, job insecurity, unemployment, migration, and difficult emotional states such as anger, depression, and hopelessness (Eyer and Sterling 1977; Smith 1992; Beale and Nethercott 1985, 1989; Moser *et al.* 1986, 1987). For instance, the death rates due to heart diseases, suicide, and other causes among divorced men, widowers, and migrants are up to two to four times higher than they are among married men or men who remain in a stable community (Eyer and Sterling 1977). Higher suicide, stroke, and ulcer prevalence has also been found among the unemployed, as shown, for instance, by data on the US, Canada and Britain (Eyer and Sterling 1977). In addition, a recent study has determined that myocardial infarction was more prevalent by a factor of 1.5–1.6 among adults suffering from depression, anger, or inability to cope than it was in a control group (Anda *et al.* 1993).

Stress has been found to be most frequent and pronounced among young and middle-aged male adults. Interestingly, women seem to be less susceptible than men to stress-induced mortality, possibly suggesting that women have been exposed to risks of lower intensity, that social conventions shelter them from stress more than they do males, or that specific physiological factors give them greater protection.

All the stress factors mentioned above—poverty, unemployment, uncertainty, migration, divorce, separation, hopelessness, and so on—have intensified during the 1990s. Poverty rates have risen sharply, particularly among the working-age population and their children. For instance, in Hungary in 1992 the incidence of poverty among households with two unemployed persons was close to 50 per cent (Lakatos 1993, cited in UNICEF 1995). Unemployment has shot up throughout the region (see Table 12.10). Large domestic and international migrations—often occurring under very unfavourable conditions, entailing the redefinition of survival strategies and greater stress—have been reported in practically all of these countries following the breakdown of states, the return of troops posted abroad, and large flows of refugees fleeing ethnic strife. At the same time, family conflicts, domestic violence, loss of self-esteem, and alcoholism have risen. Divorce rates have, in contrast, remained broadly constant, except in Russia and Ukraine, where a sharp escalation in this indicator has compounded the risk of a higher incidence of stress-related ailments among adults.

Economic hardship and greater psychosocial stress have created the conditions for violent or irrational reactions, non-compliance with regulations, and illegal behaviours. Yet, rises in 'external' mortality as large as those described in this chapter could not have taken place, particularly in the countries of the former Soviet Union, without a major collapse of the regulatory, inspection, and repressive apparatuses of the state.

Though intellectually stimulating, the variable 'social stress' is not easy to proxy quantitatively. Poverty rates can in principle provide a good measure of stress. They encompass the effect of many of the factors responsible for social stress (and in particular the loss of employment, the fall in incomes, the surge in inflation and, indirectly, the economic losses caused by divorce, widowhood, and family conflicts), while are likely to correlate closely with hopelessness and loss of self-esteem. Indeed, the largest increases in poverty have generally been recorded in those countries (such as Russia, Latvia, Lithuania, Bulgaria, and Moldova) which have recorded large increases in mortality. In addition, poverty appears to have struck most severely the population groups (working-age people and their dependents rather than the elderly) affected by large rises in stress-related mortality.

However, poverty rates can be computed only for those countries and years for which household budget surveys are available, that is, only for 51 per cent of the countries and years included in this analysis. Furthermore, substantial differences in the quality of the poverty rates to be used (even when these have been obtained using identical methodologies) and their average lower reliability in relation to mortality or other data would introduce a large but unknown bias in the estimates here.

For all these reasons, psychosocial stress is proxied here by means of an 'economic stress index' (ESI) reflecting the joint impact of other variables on which information is available for a greater number of countries and years, for example, the average real wage index (ARW), the employment rate (ER), and the rate of inflation (CPI_h).

The use of a 'synthetic' variable (ESI) summarizing the impact of these three variables, rather than the use of any single one of them, is dictated by the fact that the economic impact of the transition has been quite different from one country to another. Employment rates, for instance, have contracted significantly in Central Europe, but not in the countries of the former Soviet Union. The latter, in turn, have experienced average falls in real wages that are far more pronounced than those in the other countries. In general, inflation has been much higher in the latter than it has in the former group of countries. Here, the economic stress index (ESI_t) is calculated as the first principal component extracted, for each country, from the following variables: ERz_t, $ARWz_t$ and $(CPIz_t)^{-1}$, where, as in the case of the CMR, the suffix 'z' indicates that the variables have been standardized by the relevant country- and variable-specific standard deviation.

2.3.2. Variables Measuring Changes in Disease Control

Detailed analyses of the health sector and of the mortality rates of the hospitalized population (Davis 1993) indicate that in several transitional economies, the recent increase in mortality may also be due to the contraction of already low health expenditures and the subsequent decline in access to health care, the unavailability of inputs, and the diminishing effectiveness of the fragile health system inherited from the socialist era in the face of sharp increases in risk factors. Real public-health expenditures dwindled, except for those in the Czech Republic, Poland and Hungary. Past achievements have been maintained or improved upon in Central Europe, but appear to have deteriorated in Romania, Bulgaria, Russia, Ukraine, and most countries of the former Soviet Union.

In addition, public health expenditure declined more rapidly than revealed by the data, owing to the transition-induced fall in the outlays of trade unions, the military and large enterprises which, in the past, assigned considerable resources to health care. With the incipient 'marketization' of medical care, more resources are now being assigned by households to health care. While these expenditures can sustain the care of more well-off people, they have only modest effects on the health care of the majority.

The decline in health expenditure has generally led not so much to staff dismissals, as to sharp cuts in expenditure on wages, infrastructure, the purchase of new equipment, and the maintenance of outdated diagnostic and surgical equipment. In a period of rapid increases in morbidity due to diseases that require intensive care, this trend has exacerbated the traditional gap between the 'extensive' health approach and the mature mortality pattern of the region (Eberstadt 1990). The sharpest disruption in the functioning of health services, however, has been caused by a growing shortage of inputs that is due to multiple supply, price, and budgetary shocks and the chaotic privatization of pharmacies.

In view of the above discussion, the theoretical model presented here should be specified as follows:

$$CDR_t = f(IE_t, ESI_{t-1}, HE_t) \tag{4}$$

where the explanatory variables include industrial emissions (IE_t) proxied by production, the index of real health expenditure per capita (HE), and the 'economic stress index' (ESI) lagged one year. A one-year lag has been introduced because ESI could have an impact on the CDR that is distributed over time. The lagged effect of the ESI should therefore be taken into consideration. Nonetheless, there were two factors to keep in mind in our specification search:

(i) the limited time-horizon of the estimate that drastically truncates the possible usable lags;
(ii) the presence of autocorrelation in the series ESI, as well as in first differences.

Table 12.14a. Result of the regression analysis on the determinants of the crude death rate (CDR)

Model estimate	Coefficient	Estimation by FGLS	
		Standard error	*t*-statistics
Constant	–0.1442	0.0823	–1.7529
ΔlnIX	0.0188	0.0287	0.6714
ΔlnESI	0.2022	0.0748	2.7032
ΔlnHE	–0.1115	0.0305	–3.6581

Notes:
R-square adj.	=	0.4926	
Durbin-Watson	=	2.8356	
Hausman test	=	2.7145	
dependent variable	=	ΔlnCDR	First differences of CDR in log
explanatory variables	=	ΔlnESI	First differences of the log of the Economic Stress Index
		ΔlnHE	First differences of the real per-capita Public Health Expenditure in log
		ΔlnIX	First differences of the Industrial Production Index in log

As a consequence of these factors, and after various tests on the appropriateness of specification, we have introduced the ESI in the specification with only one lag, omitting the current value and other lags.

As in the case of the estimates of the CMR and TFR, the three variables are expressed in first differences of logarithms in order to eliminate spurious causality and heteroscedasticity. The results of the regression—carried out on pooled cross-country and time series data over 1989–94 by means of the FGLS procedure—are reported hereafter in Table 12.14a. The results of the regression model (equation 4) are somewhat unsatisfactory. The Durbin-Watson statistic lies in the not-decision bounds; the adjusted *r*-square is acceptable, but the Hausman test allows to accept the hypothesis of random effects at a very low probability (between 10 and 5 per cent). The parameters of ESI_t and HE_t have the expected sign and are significantly different from zero. However, the parameter of IE is not statistically significant. It has therefore been omitted and the regression repeated (Table 12.14b), leading to a somewhat better fit, more significant parameters, and a decisive improvement in the DW test and especially in the Hausman one where the hypothesis of random effects is accepted at a very high-probability level. The size and elasticities of the parameters clearly indicate that ESI_{t-1} explains a greater share of the observed variation in mortality. Indeed, the elasticity of health expenditure per capita is about 50 per cent of that of the economic stress index.

Tentative Conclusions

The above analysis has attempted to document the extent and causes of the population crisis observed in thirteen Eastern European countries during the recent transition to

Table 12.14b. Result of the regression analysis on the determinants of the crude death rate (CDR)

Model estimate	Coefficient	Estimation by FGLS	
		Standard error	*t*-statistics
Constant	0.2728	0.4052	0.6732
ΔlnESI	0.1893	0.0396	4.7801
ΔlnHE	−0.1047	0.0334	−3.1343

Notes:
R-square adj.	= 0.5167	
Durbin-Watson	= 1.7853	
Hausman test	= 0.9612	
dependent variable	= ΔlnCDR	First differences of CDR in log
explanatory variables	= ΔlnESI	First differences of the log of the Economic Stress Index
	ΔlnHE	First differences of the real per-capita Public Health Expenditure in log

the market economy. Although data and estimation problems suggest considerable caution and call for further work in this area, some conclusions seem to appear from this chapter.

While a number of important demographic changes occurred in the 1970s and 1980s, in about three-quarters of the cases examined the recent shifts in nuptiality, fertility, and mortality show large, growing, and statistically significant variations from past trends. Only Poland and, to a lesser extent, the Czech Republic appear to be little affected by the demographic crisis of the 1989–94 period.

There is little or no evidence that these drastic variations in natality and fertility are the result of shifts towards Western models of marriage or reproductive behaviour. Instead, they appear to be due to negative shifts in the economic circumstances of the marriageable population and the families already formed and, in particular, to the fall in real wages, growing shortages, and the rising cost of housing and of other goods needed to establish and maintain a family. They are also due to the deterioration in and the modest impact of family policies on reproductive behaviours.

Overall, expectations about the economic and social outcomes of the current crisis appear to exert a very important influence on the decision to marry and, particularly, to have a child.

The analysis suggests that none of the traditional risk factors (environmental degradation, smoking, diet, and alcohol consumption) explains much of the recent increase in mortality, either because there is sufficient evidence that the variable in question moved in a favourable direction (as in the case of industrial emissions and smoking), or because the existing information is ambiguous or apparently unrelated with the observed mortality outcomes. In this area, however, considerable data availability and reliability problems blur the picture and require major efforts in the proper surveying and analysis of this phenomenon.

The transition has clearly been accompanied by a number of unexpected effects which reflect initial favourable perceptions of the transition (as in the case of the initial 'marriage euphoria effect') and/or significant regional differences in impact for the variables discussed above. The countries of the former Soviet Union appear, in particular, to have been affected by more than proportional variations in demographic outcomes, suggesting more negative expectations about the future or a greater erosion of the state. These factors—untested in this chapter—possibly explain the much larger variations in natality and mortality (in relation to unitary changes in the independent variables) relative to the countries of Eastern and Central Europe.

The above changes have led in all the countries analysed, except Poland, to a net natural decrease in populations and to a series of undesirable demographic developments which, unless they are reversed in the immediate future, are bound to affect welfare levels and economic growth negatively in the medium and even the long term. Indeed, over time, the downward spiral in nuptiality, fertility, and mortality tends to become self-reinforcing.

The close connection established in this chapter between economic events, public policies, and demographic outcomes implies that the current population prospects of the region will not improve if the ongoing process of impoverishment continues and if public policy is either aloof (in the belief that these trends reflect physiological decisions of freer and more mature societies gradually adopting Western lifestyles), or continues to be focused on narrowly-defined sectoral responses in the areas of lifestyles, targeted health intervention and, at best, some family support measures. This chapter has underscored the importance of inflation control, support for minimum wages, and family and housing allowances (all measures entailing adequate tax collection and regulatory measures, among others), as well as interventions to reduce psychosocial stress in order to stabilize and reverse the recent negative changes in nuptiality, fertility, and mortality.

This chapter has also shown the weight expectations represent in decisions about marriage and natality. This suggests that, *ceteris paribus*, a fairly rapid turn-around in these two areas could take place if the economic climate were to improve, however modestly. In this regard, prospects for poverty alleviation appear not entirely negative, and a broad-based, equitable recovery could reabsorb much of the existing poverty and psychosocial stress relatively rapidly. Indeed, the present 'poverty gap' is smaller than it is in other regions of the world, and the considerable 'human capital' existing in the region should permit a rapid boost of the economy and the lifting of many people out of poverty. While a continuation of the present population crisis is plausible or even likely in those countries where the transition has met the greatest difficulties, the introduction of broad-based and proactive policy measures along the lines sketched in this chapter could lead to fairly rapid demographic stabilization and recovery in a number of the countries of Central Europe.

References

Chapter 1

Anand, S. and Harris, C. J. (1990), 'Food and Standard of Living: An Analysis Based on Sri Lankan Data', in J. P. Drèze and A. K. Sen (eds), *The Political Economy of Hunger*, 297–350. Oxford: Clarendon Press.

Basu, A. M. (1992), 'The Status of Women and the Quality of Life among the Poor', *Cambridge Journal of Economics*, 16: 249–67.

Citro, C. and Michael, R. T. (eds) (1995), *Measuring Poverty. A New Approach*. Washington: National Academy Press.

Clark, G. L. and Whiteman, J. (1983), 'Why Poor People Do Not Move: Job Search Behavior and Disequilibrium amongst Local Labor Markets', *Environment and Planning*, A15, 85–104. Also published in D. J. Bogue, E. E. Arriaga, and D. L. Anderton (eds), *Readings in Population Research Methodology* (1993), 4, ch. 14: 191–206.

Dasgupta, P. S. (1993), *An Inquiry into Well being and Destitution*. Oxford: Clarendon Press.

Drèze, J. P. and Sen, A. K. (1989), *Hunger and Public Action*. Oxford: Clarendon Press.

Galbraith, J. K. (1980), *The Nature of Mass Poverty*. New York: Penguin Books.

Hagenaars, A. J. M. (1986), *The Perception of Poverty*. Amsterdam: Elsevier.

Lanjouw, P. and Ravallion, M. (1995), 'Poverty and Household Size', *The Economic Journal*, 105 (November): 1415–34.

Livi Bacci, M. (1994), *Population and Poverty*, 'Distinguished Lecture Series in Population and Development', Cairo: IUSSP.

Sen, A. K. (1976), 'Poverty: An Ordinal Approach to Measurement', *Econometrica*, 44/2: 219–31.

—— (1992), *Inequality Re-examined*. Oxford: Clarendon Press.

—— (1995), *Mortality as an Indicator of Economic Success and Failure*, Innocenti Lectures. Florence: UNICEF.

UNDP (United Nations Development Programme) (1997), *Human Development Report*. New York: Oxford University Press

—— (1990), *Human Development Report. Poverty*. New York: Oxford University Press.

World Bank (1996), *Poverty Reduction and the World Bank: Progress and Challenges in the 1990s*. Washington, DC: World Bank.

—— (1997a), *World Development Indicators*. Washington, DC: World Bank.

—— (1997b), *World Bank Atlas*. Washington, DC: World Bank.

Chapter 2

Ahlburg, D. A. (1994), 'Population Growth and Poverty', in Cassen (ed.), (1994).

Anand, S. (1983), *Inequality and Poverty in Malaysia: Measurement and Decomposition*. New York: Oxford University Press.

Anand, S. (1994), 'Population, Well-being, and Freedom', in G. Sen, A. Germain, and L. C. Chen (eds), *Population Policies Reconsidered*. Cambridge, MA: Harvard University Press.

—— and Harris, C. J. (1990), 'Food and Standard of Living: An Analysis Based on Sri Lankan Data', in J. P. Drèze and A. K. Sen, *The Political Economy of Hunger*, 1. Oxford: Clarendon Press.

—— and Linton, O. B. (1993), 'On the Concept of Ultrapoverty', Center for Population and Development Studies, Working Paper 93/02 (June). Cambridge, MA: Harvard University.

Atkinson, A. B. and Micklewright, J. (1992), *Economic Tranformation in Eastern Europe and the Distribution of Income*. Cambridge and New York: Cambridge University Press.

Bangladesh Bureau of Statistics (1991), *Report on the Household Expenditure Survey 1988–89*. Dhaka: Ministry of Planning.

—— (1992), *Statistical Pocket Book of Bangladesh*. Dhaka: Bureau of Statistics/Ministry of Planning.

Becker, G. S. (1981), *A Treatise on the Family*. Cambridge, MA: Harvard University Press.

—— and Tomes, N. (1976), 'Child Endowments and the Quantity and Quality of Children', *Journal of Political Economy* (supplement), 84.

Behrman, J. R. (1993), 'The Contribution of Human Capital to Economic Development: Some Selected Issues', World Employment Programme Research Working Paper 36, November. Geneva: International Labour Office.

Ben-Porath, Y. and Welch, F. (1976), 'Do Sex Preferences *Really* Matter?', *Quarterly Journal of Economics*, 90/2: 285–307.

Berlin, I. (1969), *Four Essays on Liberty*. Oxford: Oxford University Press.

Birdsall, N. (1988), 'Economic Approaches to Population Growth', in H. B. Chenery and T. N. Srinivasan (eds), *Handbook of Development Economics*, 1. Amsterdam: North-Holland.

Birdsall, N. (1994), 'Government, Population, and Poverty: A Win-Win Tale', in Cassen (ed.) (1994).

Bongaarts, J. (1994), 'The Impact of Population Policies: Comment', *Population and Development Review*, 20/3 (September): 616–20.

Boserup, E. (1965), *The Conditions of Agricultural Progress*. Chicago, IL: Aldine Publishing Co.

Bourguignon, F. and Chiappori, P.-A. (1992), 'Collective Models of Household Behavior: An Introduction', *European Economic Review*, 36: 355–64.

Cain, M. (1983), 'Fertility as an Adjustment to Risk', *Population and Development Review*, 9/4 (December): 688–702.

Caldwell, J. C. (1982), *Theory of Fertility Decline*. London: Academic Press.

Cassen, R. (ed.) (1994), *Population and Development: Old Debates, New Conclusions*, ODC Policy Perspectives 19. New Brunswick: Transaction Publishers.

Chen, M. and Drèze, J. P. (1992), 'Widows and Well-Being in Rural North India', London School of Economics (Suntory-Toyota International Centre for Economics and Related Disciplines) Working Paper DEP/40 (September).

Dasgupta, P. S. (1993), *An Inquiry into Well-Being and Destitution*. Oxford: Clarendon Press.

—— (1994), 'The Population Problem', in Sir F. Graham-Smith (ed.), *Population: The Complex Reality*. London: The Royal Society.

—— (1995), 'Population, Poverty and the Local Environment', *Scientific American*, 272/2 (February): 26–31.

—— and Mäler, K.-G. (1995), 'Poverty, Institutions, and the Environmental Resource Base', in J. R. Behrman and T. N. Srinivasan (eds), *Handbook of Development Economics*, 3. Amsterdam: North-Holland, forthcoming.

Deaton, A. S. (1997), *The Analysis of Household Surveys: A Microeconometric Approach to Development Policy*. Baltimore: Johns Hopkins/ World Bank.

—— and Muellbauer, J. N. J. (1980), *Economics and Consumer Behavior*. Cambridge: Cambridge University Press.

Drèze, J. P. (1990), 'Widows in Rural India', Development Economics Research Programme, Discussion Paper 26, London School of Economics (August).

—— and Sen, A. K. (1989), *Hunger and Public Action*. Oxford: Clarendon Press.

Ehrlich, P. and Ehrlich, A. H. (1990), *The Population Explosion*. New York: Simon and Schuster.

Gertler, P. J. and Molyneaux, J. W. (1994), 'How Economic Development and Family Planning Programs Combined to Reduce Indonesian Fertility', *Demography*, 31/1 (February): 33–63.

Haddad, L., Hoddinott, J., and Alderman, H. (1994), 'Intrahousehold Resource Allocation: An Overview', World Bank Policy Research Paper 1255 (February).

Hoddinott, J. (1992), 'Rotten Kids or Manipulative Parents: Are Children Old Age Security in Western Kenya?', *Economic Development and Cultural Change*, 40/3 (April): 545–65.

Klibanoff, P. and Morduch, J. (1995), 'Decentralization, Externalities, and Efficiency', *Review of Economic Studies*, 62: 223–47.

Knowles, J. C., Akin, J. S., and Guilkey, D. K. (1994), 'The Impact of Population Policies: Comment', *Population and Development Review*, 20/3 (September): 611–15.

Lanjouw, P. and Ravallion, M. (1995), 'Poverty and Household Size', *The Economic Journal*, 105 (November): 1415–34.

Lee, R. D. and Miller, T. (1991), 'Population Growth, Externalities to Childbearing, and Fertility Policy in Developing Countries', *Proceedings of the World Bank Annual Conference on Development Economics 1990*: 275–304.

Leung, S. F. (1988), 'On Tests for Sex Preferences', *Journal of Population Economics*, 1: 95–114.

—— (1991), 'A Stochastic Dynamic Analysis of Parental Sex Preferences and Fertility', *Quarterly Journal of Economics*, 106: 1063–88.

Lipton, M. (1983), 'Demography and Poverty', World Bank Staff Working Paper 623, Washington, DC (November).

—— and Ravallion, M. (1995), 'Poverty and Policy', in J. R. Behrman and T. N. Srinivasan (eds), *Handbook of Development Economics*, 3. Amsterdam: North-Holland.

Livi-Bacci, M. (1994), *Poverty and Population*, Distinguished Lecture Series on Population and Development, International Union for the Scientific Study of Population; presented at International Conference on Population and Development, Cairo (September).

Malthus, T. (1914 [1803]), *An Essay on Population* (second edition). London: J. M. Dent and Sons.

Morduch, J. (1994), 'Poverty and Vulnerability', *American Economic Review* (Papers and Proceedings), 84/2 (May): 221–5.

—— and Ahmad, A. (1996), 'Identifying Sex Bias in Bangladesh: Evidence from Linked Household Surveys' (revised), mimeo. Cambridge, MA: Harvard University.

—— and Stern, H. (1996), 'Using Mixture Models to Detect Sex Bias in Health Outcomes in Bangladesh', *Journal of Econometrics*.

Nag, M. (1992), 'Family Planning Success Stories in Bangladesh and India', Policy Research Working Paper 1041, Population and Human Resources Department, World Bank, Washington, DC (November).

Nugent, J. B. (1985), 'The Old Age Security Motive for Fertility', *Population and Development Review*, 11/1 (March): 75–97.

Pritchett, L. H. (1994a), 'Desired Fertility and the Impact of Population Policies', *Population and Development Review*, 20/1 (March): 1–55.

—— (1994b), 'The Impact of Population Policies: Reply', *Population and Development Review*, 20/3 (September): 621–30.

Rosenzweig, M. R. (1988), 'Risk, Implicit Contracts and the Family in Rural Areas of Low-Income Countries', *Economic Journal*, 98 (December): 1148–70.

—— and Schultz, T. P. (1982), 'Genetic Endowments and the Intrafamily Distribution of Resources: Child Survival in Rural India', *American Economic Review*, 72/4: 802–15.

Schultz, T. P. (1981), *Economics of Population*. Reading, MA: Addison-Wesley.

—— (1988), 'Economic Demography and Development', in G. Ranis and T. P. Schultz (eds), *The State of Development Economics*. Oxford: Basil Blackwell.

—— (1994), 'Human Capital, Family Planning, and Their Effects on Population Growth', *American Economic Review* (Papers and Proceedings), (May).

Schultz, T. W. (ed.) (1974), *Economics of the Family*. Chicago: University of Chicago Press.

Sen, A. K. (1983), 'Economics and the Family', *Asian Development Review*, 1: 14–26, Manila, Philippines.

—— (1985a), *Commodities and Capabilities*. Amsterdam: North-Holland.

—— (1985b), 'Well-being, Agency and Freedom: The Dewey Lectures 1984', *Journal of Philosophy*, 82/4: 169–221.

—— (1987), *The Standard of Living*, The Tanner Lectures. Cambridge: Cambridge University Press.

—— (1990), 'Gender and Cooperative Conflicts', in I. Tinker (ed.), *Persistent Inequalities: Women and World Development*. New York: Oxford University Press.

—— (1992), 'Missing Women', *British Medical Journal*, 304 (No. 6827): 587–8.

—— (1994), 'Population: Delusion and Reality', *The New York Review of Books*, 41/15 (22 September): 62–71.

Simon, J. (1977), *The Economics of Population Growth*. Princeton: Princeton University Press.

Smith, A. (1925 [1776]), *An Inquiry into the Nature and Causes of the Wealth of Nations*, (ed. E. Cannan). London: Methuen and Co.

Solow, R. M. (1956), 'A Contribution to the Theory of Economic Growth', *Quarterly Journal of Economics*, 70/1 (February): 65–94.

Strauss, J. and Thomas, D. (1995), 'Human Resources: Empirical Modeling of Household and Family Decisions', in J. R. Behrman and T. N. Srinivasan (eds), *Handbook of Development Economics*, 3A. Amsterdam: Elsevier.

Thomas, D. (1990), 'Intrahousehold Resource Allocation: An Inferential Approach', *Journal of Human Resources*, 25: 635–64.

Timmer, C. P. (1994), 'Population, Poverty, and Policies', *American Economic Review* (Papers and Proceedings) (May).

United Nations Development Programme (1995), *Human Development Report 1995*. New York: Oxford University Press.

World Bank (1990), *World Development Report 1990-Poverty*. New York: Oxford University Press.

Yamaguchi, K. and Ferguson, L. R. (1995), 'The Stopping and Spacing of Childbirths and their Birth-History Predictors: Rational-Choice Theory and Event-History Analysis', *American Sociological Review*, 60 (April): 272–98.

Chapter 3

Allison, C., Cheong, K. C., and Yap, L. (1989), *Rapid Population Growth in Pakistan: Causes and Consequences*, Report 7522-PAK (EMENA). Washington, DC: World Bank.

Anand, S. and Ravallion, M. (1993), 'Human Development in Poor Countries: On the Role of Private Incomes and Public Services', *Journal of Economic Perspectives*, 7/1.

Barro, R. (1991), 'Economic Growth in a Cross-section of Countries', *Quarterly Journal of Economics*, 106/2.

Bauer, J. and Mason, A. (1993), 'Equivalence Scales, Costs of Children and Poverty in the Philippines and Thailand', in Lloyd (ed.).

Benefo, K. and Schultz, T. P. (1994), 'Determinants of Fertility and Child Mortality in Côte d'Ivoire and Ghana', Working Paper 103, Living Standards Measurement Study. Washington, DC: World Bank.

Becker, G. and Lewis, H. (1973), 'On the Interaction between the Quantity and Quality of Children', *Journal of Political Economy*, 81/2.

Birdsall, N. (1979), *Siblings and Schooling in Urban Colombia*, Ph.D. (unpub.). New Haven: Yale University.

—— and Griffin C. (1993), 'Population Growth, Externalities, and Poverty', in Lipton and van der Gaag (eds).

—— and James E. (1993), 'Efficiency and Equity in Social Spending: How and Why Governments Misbehave', in Lipton and van der Gaag (eds).

—— Ross, D. and Sabot, R. (1994), 'Inequality and Growth Reconsidered', mimeo. Oxford: St. Anthony's College.

Boserup, E. (1965), *The Conditions of Agricultural Progress*. Bombay: Asia.

Cain, M. (1985), 'Consequences of Reproductive Failure: Dependence, Morbidity, and Mortality Among the Elderly in Rural South Asia', Working Paper 119, Center for Policy Studies. New York: Population Council.

Chen, S., Datt, G., and Ravallion, M. (1995), 'Is Poverty Increasing in the Developing World?', *Review of Income and Wealth*.

Clarke, G. (1995), 'More Evidence on Income Distribution and Growth', *Journal of Development Economics*, 47/2.

Coulombe, H. and McKay, A. (1994), 'The Causes of Poverty: A Study Based on the Mauritania Living Standards Survey 1989–90', in T. Lloyd and O. Morrissey (eds) (1994), *Poverty, Inequality and Rural Development*. Basingstoke: Macmillan.

Daly, H. (1985), 'Marx and Malthus in North-East Brazil: A Note on the World's Largest Class Difference in Fertility and its Recent Trends', *Population Studies*, 39/2.

Datt, G. and Ravallion, M. (1992), 'Growth and Redistribution Components of Changes in Poverty Measures: A Decomposition with Applications to Brazil and India in the 1980s', *Journal of Development Economics*, 38.

Datta, G. and Meerman, J. (1980), 'Household Income or Household Income Per Capita in Welfare Comparisons?', Staff Working Paper 378. Washington, DC: World Bank.

DeGraaff, D., Bilsborrow, R., and Herrin, A. (1993), 'The Implications of High Fertility for Children's Time Use in the Philippines', in Lloyd (ed.).

Desai, S. (1993), 'The Impact of Family Size on Children's Nutritional Status: Insights from a Comparative Perspective', in Lloyd (ed.).

Drèze, J. (1990), 'Widows in Rural India', DEP 26, London: London School of Economics, Development Economics Research Programme.

Easterlin, R. and Crimmins, E. (1985), *The Fertility Revolution: a Supply–Demand Analysis.* Chicago: University of Chicago.

Eastwood, R. and Lipton, M. (1997), 'The Impact of Changes in Human Fertility on Poverty', Economics Working Papers (mimeo), Brighton: University of Sussex.

Evenson, R. (1993), 'India: Population Pressure, Technology, Infrastructure, Capital Formation, and Rural Incomes', in Jolly and Torrey (eds).

Flegg, A. (1979), 'The Role of Inequality in the Determination of Birth Rates', *Population Studies*, 33.

Gaiha, R. and Kazmi, N., 'Aspects of Poverty in Rural India' (mimeo), Delhi: University of Delhi, Faculty of Management Studies.

Glewwe, P. 'Investigating the Determinants of Household Welfare in Côte d'Ivoire', Working Paper 71, Living Standards Measurement Study. Washington, DC: World Bank.

Goody, J. (1972), 'The Evolution of the Family', in Laslett and Wall (eds).

Greenhalgh, S. (1985), 'Sexual Stratification: The Other Side of "Growth with Equity" in East Asia', *Population and Development Review*, 11/2.

Hayami, Y. and Ruttan, V. (1971, 1985), *Agricultural Development: An International Perspective.* Baltimore: Johns Hopkins.

Hajnal, J. (1982), 'Two Kinds of Pre-industrial Household Formation System', *Population and Development Review*, 8/3.

Hoddinott, J. (1993), 'Family Size and Support to the Elderly in Western Kenya', in Lloyd (ed.).

Johnson, D. G. and Lee, R. D. (eds) (1987), *Population Growth and Economic Development: Issues and Evidence.* Madison: University of Wisconsin Press.

Jolly, C. and Torrey, B. (1993), *Population and Land Use in Developing Countries.* Washington, DC: National Academy Press (for National Research Council).

Kakwani, N. (1993), 'Measuring Poverty: Definitions and Significance Tests With Application to Côte d'Ivoire', in Lipton and van der Gaag (eds).

Kelley, A. and Schmidt, R. (1994), 'Population and Income Change: Recent Evidence', Discussion Paper 249. Washington, DC: World Bank.

King, E. (1987), 'The Effect of Family Size on Family Welfare: What Do We Know?', in Johnson and Lee (eds).

Knodel, J. (1993), 'Fertility Decline and Children's Education in Thailand: Some Macro and Micro Effects', in Lloyd (ed.).

Klapisch, C. (1972), 'Household and Family in Tuscany in 1427', in Laslett and Wall (eds).

Krishnaji, N. (1984), 'Family Size, Levels of Living and Differential Mortality in Rural India: Some Paradoxes', *Economic and Political Weekly*, 9/6.

Ladurie, E. le Roy (1979), *Carnival in Romans* (tr. M. Feeney). New York: Braziller.

Lalou, R. and Mbacké, C. (1993), 'The Micro-consequences of High Fertility on Child Malnutrition in Mali', in Lloyd (ed.).

Lanjouw, P. and Ravallion, M. (1995), 'Are Larger Households Really Poorer?', *Economic Journal*, forthcoming.

Lam, D. (1987), 'Distribution Issues in the Relationship between Population Growth and Economic Development', in Johnson and Lee (eds).

Laslett, P. (1971), *The World We Have Lost* (2nd ed.). New York: Scribners.

—— and Wall, R. (1972), *Household and Family in Past Time*. Cambridge: Cambridge University Press.

—— (1978), 'The Stem-family Hypothesis and Its Privileged Position', in K. Wachter,

E. Hammell, and P. Laslett (eds), *Statistical Studies of Historical Social Structure*. New York: Academic Press.

Lazear, E. and Michael. R. (1980), 'Family Size and the Distribution of Per Capita Income', *American Economic Review*, 70/1.

Levine, R. and Renelt, D. (1992), 'A Sensitivity Analysis of Cross-country Growth Regressions', *American Economic Review*, 75.

Lipton, M. (1983), 'Demography and Poverty', Staff Working Paper 623. Washington, DC: World Bank.

—— (1990), 'Responses to Rural Population Growth: Malthus and the Moderns', in G. McNicoll and M. Cain (eds), *Rural Development and Population: Institutions and Policy*. New York: Oxford University Press.

—— (1991), 'Accelerated Resource Degradation by Third World Agriculture: Created in the Commons, in the West, or in bed?', in S. Vosti, T. Reardon, W. von Urff, and J. Witcover (eds), *Agricultural Sustainability, Growth and Poverty Alleviation: Issues and Policies*. Feldafing: DSE/IFPRI.

—— (1994a), 'Growing Points in Poverty Research: Labour Issues', Discussion Paper 66. Geneva: International Institute of Labour Studies.

—— (1994b), 'An Escape from the Malthus Rectangle? Poverty and Conversion Efficiency', *Pakistan Development Review*, forthcoming.

—— (1995), '*Successes in Anti-Poverty*', Issues in Development, 8. Geneva: International Institute of Labour Studies.

—— and van der Gaag, J. (eds) (1993), *Including the Poor*. Washington, DC: World Bank.

—— and Ravallion, M. (1995), 'Poverty and Policy', in J. Behrman and T. N. Srinivasan, *Handbook of Development Economics*, 3. Amsterdam: North Holland.

Lloyd, C. B. (ed.) (1993), *Fertility, Family Size, and Structure*. New York: Population Council.

—— (1994), 'Investing in the Next Generation: The Implications of High Fertility at the Level of the Family', Working Paper 63. New York: Population Council.

—— and Gage-Brandon, A. (1993), 'Does Sibsize Matter? The Implications of Family Size for Children's Education in Ghana', in Lloyd (ed.).

Lutz, W. and Holm, E. (1993), 'Mauritius: Population and Land Use', in Jolly and Torrey (eds).

Mahmud, S. and McIntosh, J., 'Returns to Scale from Family Size - Who Gains from High Fertility?', *Population Studies*, 34/3.

Malthus, T. R. (1798, 1803), 'An Essay on the Principle of Population', in T. R. Malthus, *On Population* (ed. G. Himmelfarb, 1960). New York: Modern Library.

—— (1824), 'Population'. London (1830): Encyclopaedia Britannica, in F. Osborn (ed.) (1960), *Three Essays on Population*. New York: Mentor.

Mortimore, M. and Tiffen, M. (1994), *More People, Less Erosion: Population and Land Use in Machakos District, Kenya*. London: Overseas Development Institute.

Mueller, E. (1984), 'Income, Aspirations and Fertility in Rural Areas of Less Developed Countries', in W. Schutjer and C. S. Stokes (eds), *Rural Development and Human Fertility*. New York: Macmillan.

Payne, P. and Lipton, M. (1994), *How Third World Households Adapt to Dietary Energy Stress*. Food Policy Studies 2. Washington, DC: International Food Policy Research Institute.

Persson, T. and Tabellini, G. (1994), 'Is Inequality Harmful for Growth?' *American Economic Review*, 84/3.

Repetto, R. (1974), 'The Relationship of the Size Distribution of Income to Fertility and the Implications for Development Policy', in World Bank, *Population Policies and Economic Development*. Baltimore: Johns Hopkins.

—— (1977), 'Income Distribution and Fertility Change', *Population and Development Review*, 3/4.

—— (1979), *Economic Equity and Fertility in Developing Countries*. Baltimore: Johns Hopkins.

Ruttan, V. (1993), 'Population Growth, Environmental Change, and Innovation: Implications for Sustainable Growth in Agriculture', in Jolly and Torrey (eds).

Ryan, J. and Walker, R. (1990), *Village and Household Economies in India's Semi-arid Tropics*. Baltimore: Johns Hopkins.

Schultz, T. P. (1981), *Economics of Population*. Reading, MA: Addison-Wesley.

Sen, A. K. (1967), 'Isolation, Assurance and the Social Rate of Discount', *Quarterly Journal of Economics*, 81/2.

—— (1981), *Poverty and Famines*. Oxford: Oxford University Press.

—— (1985), 'Poor, Relatively Speaking', *Oxford Economic Papers*, 35.

Shah, A. (1968), 'Changes in the Indian Family', *Economic and Political Weekly*, 3: 1–2.

—— (1973), *Household Dimensions of the Family in India*. Berkeley: University of California Press.

Shreeniwas, S. (1993), 'Family Size, Structure, and Children's Education: Ethnic Differentials Over Time in Peninsular Malaysia', in Lloyd (ed.).

Simon, J. (1986), *Theory of Population and Economic Growth*. Oxford: Blackwell.

United Nations (1993), *World Population Prospects: The 1992 Revision*. New York: United Nations.

—— and Gobin, R. (1980), 'The Relationship Between Population and Economic Growth in LDCs', *Research in Population Economics*: 215–35.

Stokes, C. S. and Schutjer, W. (1984), 'Access to Land and Fertility in Developing Countries', in W. Schutjer and C. S. Stokes, *Rural Development and Human Fertility*. New York: Macmillan.

Summers, R. and Heston, A. (1991), 'The Penn World Tables (Mark 5): An Expanded Set of International Comparisons, 1950–1988', *Quarterly Journal of Economics*, 106/2.

UNDP (1997), *Human Development Report*. New York: Oxford University Press.

Vosti, S., Witcover, J., and Lipton, M. (forthcoming), 'Effect of the Green Revolution on Cross-district Differences in the Decline of Human Fertility in India'.

Wall, R., Robin, J., and Laslett, P.(eds) (1983), *Family Forms in Historic Europe*. Cambridge: Cambridge University Press.

World Bank (1990), *World Development Report*. New York: Oxford University Press.

—— (1994), *Population and Development: Issues for the World Bank*. Washington, DC: World Bank.

Chapter 4

ACC/SCN (1992), *Second Report on the World Nutrition Situation*. Geneva: United Nations.

Barac-Nieto, M., Spurr, G. B., Maksud, M. G., and Lotero, H. (1978), 'Aerobic Work Capacity In Chronically Undernourished Adult Males', *Journal of Applied Physiology*, 44: 209–15.

Branca, F., Pastore, G., Demissie, T. and Ferro-Luzzi, A. (1993), 'The Nutritional Impact of Seasonality in Children and Adults of Rural Ethiopia'. *European Journal of Clinical Nutrition*, 47: 840–50.

Brooke, O. G. and Cocks, T. (1974), 'Resting Metabolic Rate in Malnourished Babies in Relation to Total Body Potassium', *Acta Pediatrica Scandinavica*, 63: 817–25.

Chavez, A., Martinez, C., and Bourges, H. (1972), 'Nutrition and Development of Infants from Poor Rural Areas: 2. Nutritional Level and Physical Activity'. *Nutrition Reports International*, 5: 139–44.

—— —— (1979), 'Nutricion y Desarrollo Infantil', *Nueva* Editorial Interamericana, Mexico.

Chen, L. C., Chowdhury, A. K. M. A., and Huffman, S. L. (1980), 'Anthropometric Assessment of Energy-Protein Malnutrition and Subsequent Risk of Mortality among Preschool Aged Children', *The American Journal of Clinical Nutrition*, 33: 1836–45.

Davies, C. T. M. (1973), 'Relationship of Maximum Aerobic Power Output to Productivity and Absenteeism of East African Sugar Cane Workers', *British Journal of Industrial Medicine*, 30: 146–54.

De Onis, M., Monteiro, C., Akré, J., and Clugston, G. (1993), 'The Worldwide Magnitude of Protein-Energy Malnutrition: An Overview from the WHO Global Database on Child Growth', *Bulletin of the World Health Organization*, 71: 703–12.

De Vasconcellos, M. (1994), 'Body Mass Index: Its Relationship with Food Consumption and Socioeconomic Variables in Brazil', *European Journal of Clinical Nutrition*, 48(Suppl.3): S115–23.

FAO/WHO. (1992), *International Conference on Nutrition. Nutrition and Development: a Global Assessment*

Ferro-Luzzi, A. (1988), 'Marginal Energy Malnutrition: Some Speculations on Energy Sparing Mechanisms'. in K.J. Collins and D.F. Roberts (eds), *Capacity for Work in the Tropics*, 141–64. Cambridge: University Press.

——, Pastore, G., and Sette, S (1988), 'Seasonality in Energy Metabolism'. in B. Schurch, and N. S. Scrimshaw (eds), *Chronic Energy Deficiency: Consequences and Related Issues*, 37–8. Lausanne: IDECG.

—— (1990), 'Social and Public Health Issues in Adaptation to Low Energy Intakes', *American Journal of Clinical Nutrition*, 51: 309–15.

——, Sette, S., Franklin, M., and James, W. P. T. (1992), 'A Simplified Approach to Assessing Adult Chronic Energy Deficiency', *European Journal of Clinical Nutrition*, 46: 173–86.

——, Branca, F., and Pastore, G. (1994), 'Body Mass Index Defines The Risk of Seasonal Energy Stress in the Third World'. *European Journal of Clinical Nutrition*, 48(Suppl.3), S165–78.

Forbes, G. B. (1987), 'Lean Body Mass-Body Fat Interrelationships in Humans', *Nutrition Reviews*, 45: 225–31.

Grantham-McGregor, S., Gardner, J. M. M., Walker, S., and Powell, C. (1990), 'The Relationship Between Undernutrition, Activity Levels and Development in Young Children', in B. Schürch and N. S. Scrimshaw (eds), *Activity, Energy Expenditure and Energy Requirements of Infants and Children*, 361–83. Lausanne: IDECG.

James, W. P. T., Ferro-Luzzi, A., and Waterlow, J. C. (1989), 'Definition of Chronic Energy Deficiency in Adults. Report of Working Party of IDECG', *European Journal of Clinical Nutrition*, 42: 969–81.

Keys, A., Brozek, J., Henschel, A., Mickelson, O. and Taylor, H. L. (1950), *The Biology of Human Starvation*. Minneapolis: University of Minnesota Press.

Kielmann, A. A. and McCord, C. (1978), 'Weight-For-Age as an Index of Risk of Death in Children', *The Lancet*, 1: 1247–50.

Kusin, J. A., Kardjati, S. R. L., and Renqvist, U. H. (1993), 'Chronic Undernutrition in Pregnancy and Lactation', *Proceedings of the Nutrition Society*, 52: 19–28.

Longhurst, R. (1984), 'The Energy Trap: Work, Nutrition and Child Malnutrition in Northern Nigeria', *Cornell International Nutrition Monograph* Series 13, Ithaca.

Martorell, R., Kettel Khan, L., and Schroeder, D. G. (1994), 'Reversibility of Stunting: Epidemiological Findings in Children from Developing Countries', *European Journal of Clinical Nutrition*, 48(Suppl.1): S45–57.

Maxwell, S. and Frankenberger, T. R. (1992), *Household Food Security: Concepts, Indicators, Measurements. A Technical Review*. Rome: UNICEF/IFAD.

Naidu, A. N. and Rao, N. P. (1994), 'Body Mass Index: A Measure of the Nutritional Status in Indian Populations', *European Journal of Clinical Nutrition*, 48(Suppl.3): S131–40.

Parra, A., Garza, C., Garza, Y., Saravia, J. L., Hazlewood, C. F., and Nichols, B. L. (1973), 'Changes in Growth Hormone, Insulin and Thyroxin Values and in Energy Metabolism of Marasmic Infants', *Journal of Pediatrics*, 82: 133–42.

Payne, P. and Lipton, M. (1994), *How Third World Rural Households Adapt to Dietary Energy Stress*. Washington: IFPRI,.

Pelletier, D. L. (1994), 'The Relationship between Child Anthropometry and Mortality in Developing Countries: Implications for Policy, Programs and Future Research, *American Journal of Clinical Nutrition*, 124: 2047-81 (Supplement).

Pryer, J. (1993), 'Body Mass Index and Work-Disabling Morbidity: Results from a Bangladeshi Case Study', *European Journal of Clinical Nutrition*, 47: 653–57.

Rutishauser, I. H. E. and Whitehead, R. G. (1972), 'Energy Intake and Expenditure in 1-3-Year-Old Ugandan Children Living in a Rural Environment', *British Journal of Nutrition*, 28: 145–52.

Shetty, P. S. and Kurpad, A. V. (1990), 'Role of the Sympathetic Nervous System in Adaptation to Seasonal Energy Deficiency', *European Journal of Clinical Nutrition* 44(Suppl.1): 47–53.

—— and W. P. T. James (1994), *Body Mass Index. A Measure of Chronic Energy Deficiency in Adults*. Rome: FAO.

Spurr, G. B., Barac-Nieto, M., and Maksud, M. G. (1977), 'Productivity and Maximal Oxygen Consumption in Sugar Cane Cutters', *American Journal of Clinical Nutrition* 30: 316–21.

——, Reina, J. C., Dahne, H. W., and Barac-Nieto, M. (1983), 'Marginal Malnutrition in School-Aged Colombian Boys: Functional Consequences in Maximum Exercise', *American Journal of Clinical Nutrition*, 37: 834–47.

—— (1984), 'Physical activity, Nutritional Status and Physical Work Capacity in Relation to Agricultural Productivity', in E. Pollitt, P. Amante (eds), *Energy Intake and Activity*, 207–61. New York: Alan Liss.

—— (1988), 'Body Size, Physical Work Capacity, and Productivity in Hard Work: is Bigger Better?', in J.C. Waterlow (ed.), *Linear Growth Retardation in Less Developed Countries*. New York: Raven Press, 215–39.

Stein, J. and Fenigstein, H. (1946), 'Anatomie Pathologique de la Maladie De Famine', in E. Apfelbaum (ed.), *Maladie de Famine. Recherches Cliniques sur la Famine Exécutées dans le Ghetto de Varsovie en 1942*, 21–77. Warsaw: American Joint Distribution Committee.

Sukhatme, P. V. and Margen, S. (1982), 'Auto-Regulatory Homeostatic Nature of Energy Balance', in P. V. Sukhatme (ed.), *Newer Concepts in Nutrition and their Implications for Policy*, 101–11. Pune (India): Maharastra Association for the Cultivation of Science.

Torun, B. and Viteri, F. E. (1981), 'Energy Requirements of Pre-School Children and Effects of Varying Energy Intakes on Protein Metabolism', *Food and Nutrition Bulletin*, 3/5: 229–41.

United Nations. (1990) 'Nutrition Relevant Actions in the Eighties: Some Experience and Lessons from Developing Countries'. Background paper for the ACC/SCN Ad Hoc Group Meeting on Policies to Alleviate Underconsumption and Malnutrition in Deprived Areas, 12–14 November 1990, London.

Waterlow, J. C. (1990), 'Energy-Sparing Mechanisms: Reductions in Body Mass, BMR and Activity: Their Relative Importance and Priority in Undernourished Infants and Children', in B. Schürch, N. S. Scrimshaw (eds), *Activity, Energy Expenditure and Energy Requirements of Infants and Children*, 239–50. Lausanne: IDECG.

——, Golden, M. H. N., and Patrick, J. (1978), 'Protein Energy Malnutrition Treatment', in J. W. T. Dickerson and H. A. Lee (eds), *Nutrition in the Clinical Management of Disease*, 49–71. London: Edward Arnold.

WIIO (1983), *Measuring Change in Nutritional Status*. Geneva: World Health Organization.

Chapter 5

Alamgir, M. (1980), *Famine in South Asia*. Cambridge, MA: Oelgeschlager, Gunn and Hain.

Antonov, A. (1975), 'Children Born During the Siege of Leningrad in 1942', *Journal of Paediatrics*, 30: 750–9.

Beilik, R. J. and Henderson, P. L. (1980), 'Mortality, Nutritional Status and Diet During the Famine in Karamoja, Uganda', *Lancet*, 2: 1330–3.

Bongaarts, J. and Cain M. (1982), 'Demographic Responses to Famine', in K. M. Cahill (ed.), *Famine*. New York: Orbis Books.

Boyle, P. P. and O'Grada, C. (1986), 'Fertility Trends, Excess Mortality, and the Great Irish Famine', *Demography*, 23/4: 543–9.

Cain, M. (1981), 'Risk and Insurance: Perspectives on Fertility and Agrarian Change in India and Bangladesh', *Population and Development Review*, 7/3: 435–74.

Caldwell, J. C. (1975), 'The Sahelian Drought and Its Demographic Implications', Overseas Liaison Committee Paper 8, Washington, DC: American Council of Education.

—— (1976), 'Toward a Restatement of the Demographic Transition Theory', *Population and Development Review*, 2/3, 4: 321–66.

—— (1977), 'Demographic Aspects of Drought, An Examination of the African Drought of 1970–74', in D. Dalby, R. J. H. Church and F. Bezzaz (eds), *Drought in Africa 2*. London: International African Institute.

—— (1982), *The Theory of Fertility Decline*. London: Academic Press.

—— (1983), 'Direct Economic Costs and Benefits of Children', in R. A. Bulatao and R. D. Lee (eds), *Determinants of Fertility in Developing Countries, 1: Supply and Demand for Children*. London: Academic Press.

Campbell, D. J. (1990), 'Strategies for Coping with Severe Food Deficits in Rural Africa: Review of the Literature', *Food and Foodways*, 4/2: 143–62.

Chen, L. C. and Chowdhury, A. A. K. (1977), 'The Dynamics of Contemporary Famine', Mexico International Population Conference, 1, Liège: International Union for the Scientific Study of Population.

Connell, K. H. (1955), 'Marriage in Ireland After the Famine: The Diffusion of the Match', *Journal of Statistical and Social Inquiry*, 19: 82–103.

Corbett, J. (1988), 'Famine and Household Coping Strategies', *World Development*, 16/9, 1099–112.

Crotty, R. (1966), *Irish Agricultural Production: Its Volume and Structure*. Cork: Cork University Press.

Cullen, L. (1987), *An Economic History of Ireland since 1660*. Second edition. London: Batsford.

Dasgupta, P. and Ray, D. (1990), 'Adapting to Undernourishment: The Biological Evidence and Its Implications', in J. Drèze, and Sen (eds), *The Political Economy of Hunger, 1*. WIDER Studies in Development Economics. Oxford: Clarendon Press.

Davies, S. (1993), 'Are Coping Strategies a Cop Out?', *IDS Bulletin*, 24/4: 60–72.

de Waal, A. (1989), *Famine that Kills: Darfur, Sudan, 1984–85*. Oxford: Clarendon Press.

Dyson, T. (1991a), 'On the Demography of South Asian Famines: Part I', *Population Studies*, 25/1.

—— (1991b), 'On the Demography of South Asian Famines: Part II', *Population Studies*, 25/2.

—— (1993), 'Demographic Responses to Famine in South Asia', *IDS Bulletin*, 24/4: 17–26.

—— and Maharatna, A. (1991), 'Excess Mortality During the Bengal Famine', *Indian Economic and Social History Review*, 28/3.

—— —— (1992), 'On the Demographic Consequences of the Bihar Famine of 1966–67 and the Maharashtra Drought of 1970–73', *Economic and Political Weekly*, 27/26.

Faulkingham, R. H. and Thorbahn, P. F. (1975), 'Population Dynamics and Drought: A Village in Niger', *Population Studies*, 29/3: 463–477.

Flinn, M. W. (1970), *British Population Growth, 1700–1850*. London: Macmillan.

—— (1974), 'The Stabilization of Mortality in Pre-Industrial Western Europe', *Journal of European Economic History*, 3.

Fogel, R. W. (1992), 'Second Thoughts on the European Escape from Hunger: Famines, Chronic Malnutrition, and Mortality Rates', in S. R. Osmani (ed.), *Nutrition and Poverty*. WIDER Studies in Development Economics. Oxford: Clarendon Press.

—— (1994), 'Economic Growth, Population Theory, and Physiology: The Bearing of Long-Term Processes on the Making of Economic Policy', *American Economic Review*, 84/3, 369–95.

Gopalan, C. (1992), 'Undernutrition: Measurement and Implications', in S. R. Osmani (ed.), *Nutrition and Poverty*. WIDER Studies in Development Economics. Oxford: Clarendon Press.

Heer, D. M. and Smith, D. O. (1967), 'Mortality Level and Desired Family Size', Proceedings of the 1967 Conference of the International Union for the Scientific Study of Population. Canberra: IUSSP.

Helleiner, K. F. (1967), 'The Population of Europe from the Black Death to the Eve of the Vital Revolution', in E. E. Rich and C. H. Wilson (eds), *The Cambridge Economic History of Europe, Vol. IV: The Economy of Expanding Europe in the Sixteenth and Seventeenth Centuries*. Cambridge: Cambridge University Press.

Hill, A. (1989), 'Demographic Responses to Food Shortages in the Sahel', *Population and Development Review*, 15 (supplement, G. McNicoll and M. T. Cain (eds), *Rural Development and Population: Institutions and Policy*), 168–92.

Hugo, G. J. (1984), 'The Demographic Impact of Famine: A Review', in B. Currey, and G. Hugo (eds), *Famine as a Geographical Phenomenon*. Dordecht (Holland): Reidel.

Iliffe, J. (1987), *The African Poor*, African Studies Series 58, Cambridge: Cambridge University Press.

James, W. P. T. and Shetty, P. S. (1994), *Body Mass Index: A Measure of Chronic Energy Deficiency in Adults,* Food and Nutrition Paper 56, Rome: FAO.

Jones, E. L. (1988), *Growth Recurring: Economic Change in World History.* Oxford: Clarendon Press.

Khan, A. R. (1977), 'Poverty and Landlessness in Rural Bangladesh', in, *Poverty and Landlessness in Rural Asia.* Geneva: ILO.

—— (1988), 'Population Growth and Access to Land', in R. D. Lee, W. B. Arthur, A. C. Kelly, G. Rodgers, and T. N. Srinivasan (eds), *Population, Food and Rural Development.* New York: Oxford University Press.

Knodel, J. (1975), 'Influence of Child Mortality on Fertility in European Populations in the Past: Results from Individual Data', in *Seminar on Infant Mortality in Relation to the Level of Fertility.* Paris: Committee for International Co-ordination of National Research in Demography.

Ladurie, E. L. R. (1974), *The Peasants of Languedoc.* Urbana: University of Illinois Press.

Lee, R. D. (1980), 'A Historical Perspective on Economic Aspects of the Population Explosion: The Case of Preindustrial England', in R. A. Easterlin (ed.), *Population and Economic Change in Developing Countries.* Chicago: University of Chicago Press.

Livi-Bacci, M. (1983), 'The Nutrition-Mortality Link in Past Times: A Comment', in R. I. Rotberg and T. K. Rabb (eds), *Hunger and History: The Impact of Changing Food Production and Consumption Patterns on Society.* Cambridge: Cambridge University Press.

Maharatna, A. (1992), 'The Demography of Indian Famines: A Historical Perspective', unpublished PhD thesis. London: University of London.

Malthus, T. R. (1798), *An Essay on the Principle of Population as It Affects the Future Improvement of Society,* 1st edition, London.

McAlpin, M. B. (1983a), *Subject to Famine: Food Crises and Economic Change in Western India, 1860–1920.* Princeton: Princeton University Press.

—— (1983b), 'Famines, Epidemics, and Population Growth: The Case of India', in R. I. Rotberg and T. K. Rabb (eds), *Hunger and History: The Impact of Changing Food Production and Consumption Patterns on Society.* Cambridge: Cambridge University Press.

McKeown, T. (1983), 'Food, Infection and Population', in R. I. Rotberg and T. K. Rabb (eds), *Hunger and History: The Impact of Changing Food Production and Consumption Patterns on Society.* Cambridge: Cambridge University Press.

Meuvret, J. (1965), 'Demographic Crisis in France from the Sixteenth to the Eighteenth Century', in D. V. Glass and D. E. C. Eversely (eds), *Population in History: Essays in Historical Demography.* London: Edward Arnold.

Notestein, F. W. (1945), 'Population: The Long View', in T. W. Schultz (ed.), *Food for the World.* Chicago: University of Chicago Press.

O'Brien, G. (1921), *The Economic History of Ireland from the Union to the Famine.* London: Maunsel.

O'Rourke, K. (1991), 'Did the Irish Famine Matter?', *Journal of Economic History,* 51/1: 1–22.

Osmani, S. R. (1992), 'On Some Controversies in the Measurement of Undernutrition', in S. R. Osmani (ed.), *Nutrition and Poverty.* WIDER Studies in Development Economics. Oxford: Clarendon Press.

Sandberg, L. and R. Steckel (1987), 'Heights and Economic History: The Swedish Case', *Annals of Human Biology,* 14: 101–10.

Schofield, R. (1983), 'The Impact of Scarcity and Plenty on Population Change in England, in R. I. Rotberg and T. K. Rabb (eds), *Hunger and History: The Impact of Changing Food Production and Consumption Patterns on Society*. Cambridge: Cambridge University Press.

Seaman, J. (1993), 'Famine Mortality in Africa', *IDS Bulletin*, 24/4: 27–32.

Sen, A. (1981), *Poverty and Famines: An Essay on Entitlement and Deprivation*. Oxford: Clarendon Press.

Srinivasan, T. N. (1983), 'Malnutrition in Developing Countries: the State of Knowledge of the Extent of its Prevalence, its Causes and its Consequences', background paper prepared for FAO's Fifth World Food Survey (mimeo.),. Economic Growth Center, Yale University.

Steckel, R. H. (1995), 'Stature and the Standard of Living', *Journal of Economic Literature*, 33/4, December.

Stein, Z., Susser, M., Saenger, G., and Marolla, F. (1975*), Famine and Human Development: The Dutch Hunger Winter of 1944/45*. New York: Oxford University Press.

Toulmin, C. (1986), 'Access to Food, Dry Season Strategies and Household Size amongst the Bambara of Central Mali', *IDS Bulletin*, 17/3: 58–66.

Watkins, S. C. and Menken, J. (1985), 'Famine in Historical Perspective', *Population and Development Review*, 11/4: 647–75.

White, C. (1987), 'Changing Animal Ownership and Access to Land among the Woodabe (Fulani) of Central Niger', paper presented at the workshop on Changing Rights in Property and Pastoral Development, University of Manchester, 23–5 April.

Wrigley, E. A. (1969), *Population and History*. London: Widenfield and Nicholson.

—— and Schofield, R. S. (1981), *The Population History of England, 1541–1871: A Reconstruction*. Cambridge, MA: Harvard University Press.

Chapter 6

Agarwal, B. (1994), 'Gender and Command over Property: A Critical Gap in Economic Analysis and Policy in South Asia', *World Development*, 22/10: 1455–78.

Ayad, M. *et al.* (1994), *Demographic Characteristics of Households*, DHS Comparative Studies 14, Macro International Inc., Calverton, MD.

Bauer, J. and Mason A. (1993), 'Equivalence Scales, Costs of Children, and Poverty in the Philippines and Thailand', in C. B. Lloyd (ed.), *Fertility, Family Size, and Structure: Consequences for Families and Children*. New York: The Population Council.

Becker, G. S. (1991), *A Treatise on the Family, Enlarged Edition*. Cambridge: Harvard University Press.

Ben-Porath, Y. (1980), 'The F-Connection: Families, Friends, and Firms and the Organization of Exchange', *Population and Development Review*, 6/1: 1–30.

Blackwood, D. L. and Lynch, R. G. (1994), 'The Measurement of Inequality and Poverty: A Policy Maker's Guide to the Literature', *World Development*, 22/4: 567–78.

Blanc, A. K. and Lloyd C. B. (1994), 'Future Data Needs on Women', in *Review of the Availability and Quality of Global Demographic Data*, Hearings Before the Subcommittee on Census, Statistics and Postal Personnel of the Committee on Post Office and Civil Service, House of Representatives, 103rd Congress, Second Session, 2 August 1994, Washington, DC.

Boserup, E. (1970), *Woman's Role in Economic Development*. New York: St. Martin's Press.

Browning, M., Bourguignon, F., Chiappori, P., and Lechene, V. (1994), 'Income and Outcomes: A Structural Model of Intrahousehold Allocation', *Journal of Political Economy*, 102/6: 1067–96.

Bruce, J. and C. B. Lloyd (1997) 'Finding the Ties that Bind: Beyond Headship and Household', in J. Hoddinott and H. Alderman (eds), *Intrahousehold Resource Allocation in Developing Countries: Models, Methods, and Policies*, Baltimore: Johns Hopkins Press.

——, ——, and Leonard, A. (1995), *Families in Focus: New Perspectives on Mothers, Fathers, and Children*. New York: The Population Council.

Burch, T. K. (1982), 'Household and Family Demography', in John A. Ross (ed.), *International Encyclopedia of Population*, 1. New York: The Free Press.

—— and Matthews, B. J. (1987), 'Household Formation in Developed Societies' *Population and Development Review*, 13/3: 495–511.

Butz, W. P. and Stan, P. J. E. (1982), 'Interhousehold Transfers and Household Structure in Malaysia', *Population and Development Review*, 8: 92 115.

Buvini, C. M. and Gupta, G. R. (1994), *Targeting Poor Woman-Headed Households and Woman-Maintained Families in Developing Countries: Views on a Policy Dilemma*, Population Council/International Center for Research on Women Working Paper. New York: The Population Council.

Caces, F., Arnold, F., Fawcett, J. T., and Gardner, R. W. (1985), 'Shadow Households and Competing Auspices', *Journal of Development Economics*, 17/12: 5–25.

Casper, L. M., McLanahan, S. S., and Garfinkel, I. (1994) 'The Gender-Poverty Gap: What We Can Learn from Other Countries', *American Sociological Review*, 59: 594–605.

DeGraff, D. S. and Bilsborrow, R. E. (1993), 'Female-Headed Households and Family Welfare in Rural Ecuador', *Journal of Population Economics*, 6: 317–36.

De Vos, S. (1987), 'Latin American Households in Comparative Perspective', *Population Studies*, 41: 501–17.

Eggebeen, D. J. and Lichter, D. T. (1991), 'Race, Family Structure and Changing Poverty Among American Children', *American Sociological Review*, 56/6, 801–17.

Ermisch, J. F. and Overton, E. (1985), 'Minimal Household Units: A New Approach to the Analysis of Household Formation', *Population Studies*, 39: 33–54.

—— and Wright, R. E. (1994), 'Entry to Lone Parenthood: An Analysis of Marital Dissolution in Great Britain', *Genus*, 50/3–4: 75–95.

Fields, G. S (1994), 'Poverty and Income Distribution: Data for Measuring Poverty and Inequality Changes in the Developing Countries', *Journal of Development Economics*, 44: 87–102.

Folbre, N. (1994), 'Children As Public Goods'. American Economics Association Papers and Proceedings: The Economic Support of Child-Raising, 84/2: 86–90.

Foster, A. D. (1993), 'Household Partition in Rural Bangladesh', *Population Studies*, 47: 97–114.

Gage, A. J., Sommerfelt, A. E., and Piani, A. L. (1995), 'Family Structure and Child Health in Sub-Saharan Africa', paper presented at the Annual Meeting of the Population Association of America, 6–8 April, San Francisco.

Greeley, M. (1994), 'Measurement of Poverty and Poverty of Measurement', *IDS Bulletin*, 25/2: 50–8.

Greenhalgh, S. (1982), 'Income Units: The Ethnographic Alternative to Standardization', *Population and Development Review*, 8 (Supplement): 70–91.

Haddad, L. and Kanbur, R.(1990), 'How Serious Is the Neglect of Intra-Household Inequality?', *The Economic Journal*, 100/402: 866–81.

Hajnal, J. (1982), 'Two Kinds of Preindustrial Household Formation System', *Population and Development Review*, 8/3: 449–94

Hammel, E. A. (1980), 'Household Structure in Fourteenth-Century Macedonia', *Journal of Family History*, 5: 242–73.

Handa, S. (1994), 'Gender, Headship and Intrahousehold Resource Allocation', *World Development*, 22/10: 1535–47.

Hirschman, C. (1994), 'Family and Household Structure in Vietnam', paper presented at the Annual Meeting of the Association for Asian Studies, March 1994, Boston.

Hoddinott, J. (1993), 'Family Size and Support to the Elderly in Western Kenya', in C. B. Lloyd (ed.), *Fertility, Family Size, and Structure: Consequences for Families and Children*. New York: The Population Council.

Horton, S. and Miller, B. D. (1989), 'The Effect of Gender of Household Head on Food Expenditures: Evidence from Low-Income Households in Jamaica', paper presented at the Conference on Family, Gender Differences, and Development, 4–6 September 1989, Yale University, New Haven.

Kennedy, E. and Peters, P. (1992), 'Household Food Security and Child Nutrition: The Interaction of Income and Gender of Household Head', *World Development*, 20/8: 1077–85.

Kossoudji, S. and Mueller. E. (1983), 'The Economic and Demographic Status of Female-Headed Households in Rural Botswana', *Economic Development and Cultural Change*, 31/4: 831–59.

Knodel, J., Chayovan, N., and Siriboon, S. (1992), 'The Impact of Fertility Decline on Familial Support for the Elderly: An Illustration from Thailand', *Population and Development Review*, 18/1: 79–103.

Kuznets, S. (1978), 'Size and Age Structure of Family Households: Exploratory Comparisons', *Population and Development Review*, 4/2: 187–223.

Lesthaeghe, R. (1992), 'The Second Demographic Transition in Western Countries: An Interpretation', paper presented at the IUSSP Seminar on Gender and Family Change in Industrialized Countries, 26–30 January 1992, Rome.

Livi-Bacci, M. (1994), 'Poverty and Population', IUSSP Distinguished Lecture Series on Population and Development, International Conference on Population and Development, September 1994, Cairo, 17.

Lloyd, C. B. (1994), 'Investing in the Next Generation: The Consequences of High Fertility at the Level of the Family', in R. Cassen (ed.), *Population and Development: Old Debates, New Conclusions*. Washington, DC: Overseas Development Council.

—— and Desai, S. (1992), 'Children's Living Arrangements in Developing Countries', *Population Research and Policy Review*, 11: 193–216.

—— and Gage-Brandon, A. (1993), 'Women's Role in Maintaining Households: Family Welfare and Sexual Inequality in Ghana', *Population Studies*, 47: 115–31.

—— and Blanc, A. K. (1996), 'Children's Schooling in Sub-Saharan Africa: The Role of Fathers, Mothers, and Others', *Population and Development Review*, 22/2: 265–98.

Louat, F., van der Gaag, J., and Grosh, M. (1992), 'Welfare Implications of Female Headship in Jamaican Households', paper presented at the IFPRI-World Bank Conference on Intrahousehold Resource Allocation. Washington, DC: Policy Issues and Research Methods.

Massey, D. S. (1990), 'Social Structure, Household Strategies, and the Cumulative Causation of Migration', *Population Index*, 56/1: 3–26.

—— and Parrado, E. (1994), 'Migradollars: The Remittances and Savings of Mexican Migrants to the USA', *Population Research and Policy Review*, 13/1: 3–30.

Neupert, R. F. (1992), 'Extended Households: A Survival Strategy in Poverty', in C. Goldscheider (ed.), *Fertility Transitions, Family Structure and Population Policy*, Boulder, CO: Westview Press.

Parsons, D. O. (1984), 'On the Economics of Intergenerational Control', *Population and Development Review*, 10/1: 41–54.

Quisumbing, A, Haddad, L., and Pena, C. (1995), 'Gender and Poverty: New Evidence from Ten Developing Countries', Food Consumption and Nutrition Division Discussion Paper 9, International Food Policy Research Institute: Washington, DC.

Sanjek, R. (1982), 'The Organization of Households in Adabraka: Towards a Wider Comparative Perspective', *Comparative Studies in Society and History*, 24/1: 57–103.

Sawhill, I. V. (1988), 'Poverty in the U.S.: Why Is It So Persistent?', *Journal of Economic Literature*, 26: 1073–119.

Sen, A. K. (1981), *Poverty and Famines: An Essay on Entitlement and Deprivation*. Oxford: Clarendon Press.

—— (1983), 'Development: Which Way Now?', *The Economic Journal*, 93/372: 745–62.

—— (1990), 'Gender and Cooperative Conflicts', in I. Tinker (ed.), *Persistent Inequalities: Women and World Development*. New York: Oxford University Press.

Shapiro, D. (1990), 'Farm Size, Household Size and Composition, and Women's Contribution to Agricultural Production: Evidence from Zaire', *The Journal of Development Studies*, 27/1: 1–21.

Stark, O. and Lucas, R. E. B. (1988), 'Migration, Remittances and the Family', *Economic Development and Cultural Change*, 36/3: 465–82.

Stark, O. and Taylor, J. E. (1989), 'Relative Deprivation and International Migration', *Demography*, 26/1: 1–14.

United Nations (1973), *The Determinants and Consequences of Population Trends: New Summary of Findings on Interaction of Demographic, Economic and Social Factors, 1*. New York: United Nations.

—— (1995), *Living Arrangements of Women and Their Children in the Third World: A Demographic Profile*. New York: United Nations.

United Nations Development Programme (1994), *Human Development Report*. New York: United Nations.

World Bank (1990), *World Development Report 1990*. New York: Oxford University Press.

Chapter 7

Aaby, P. (1988), 'Malnutrition and Overcrowding/Intensive Exposure in Severe Measles Infection: Review of Community Studies', *Review of Infectious Diseases*, 10/2: 478–91.

—— (1992), 'Overcrowding and Intensive Exposure: Major Determinants of Variations in Measles Mortality in Africa', in van de Walle, Pison and Sala-Diakanda (eds), *Mortality and Society in sub-Saharan Africa*, 319–48. Oxford: Clarendon Press.

——, Andersen, M., and Knudsen, K. (1993), 'Excess Mortality After Early Exposure to Measles' *International J. Epidemiology*, 22/1: 156–62.

Ahlburg, D. (1994), 'Population Growth and Poverty', in R. Cassen (ed.), *Population and Development: Old Debates, New Conclusions*, 127–48, New Brunswick (USA) and Oxford (UK). Washington, DC: Transaction Publishers for Overseas Development Council.

Anand, S. (1994), 'Population, Well-Being and Freedom' in G. Sen, A. Germain and L. C. Chen (eds), *Population Policies Reconsidered*, 75–88. Boston: Harvard University Press:

Axinn, W. (1993), 'The Effects of Children's Schooling on Fertility Limitation', *Population Studies*, 47/3: 481–94.

Bakketieg, L. S., Bjerkedal, T., and Hoffman, H. (1986), 'Small-For-Gestational Age Births in Successive Pregnancy Outcomes: Results from a Longitudinal Study of Births in Norway', *Early Human Development*, 14: 187–200.

Basu, A. (1993), 'Family Size and Child Welfare in an Urban Slum: Some Disadvantages of Being Poor But "Modern"', in C. Lloyd (ed.) (1993).

Bauer, J. and Mason, A. (1993), 'Equivalence Scales, Costs of Children, and Poverty in the Philippines and Thailand', in C. Lloyd (ed.).

Behrman, J. R. and Wolfe, B. L. (1987), 'How Does Mother's Schooling Affect Family Health, Nutrition Medical Care Usage, and Household Sanitation?', *Journal of Econometrics*, 36: 185–204.

Bledsoe, C., Hill, A., D'Alessandro, U., and Langerock, P. (1994), 'Constructing Natural Fertility: The Use of Western Contraceptive Technologies in Rural Gambia', *Population and Development Review*, 20 /1: 81–114.

Boerma, J. T. and Bicego, G. T. (1992), 'Preceding Birth Intervals and Child Survival: Searching for Pathways of Influence', *Studies in Family Planning*, 23/4: 243–56.

Bongaarts, J. (1987), 'Does Family Planning Reduce Infant and Child Mortality Rates?', *Population and Development Review*, 13/2: 323–34.

Buvinic, M. L. and McGreevey, W. P.(eds) (1983), *Women's Work, Poverty and the Third World*: 35–61. Baltimore, MD: Johns Hopkins University Press.

——, Potter, J., and Trussell, J. (1988), 'Does Family Planning Reduce Infant Mortality? An Exchange', *Population. and Development Review*, 14/1: 171–90.

Cain, M. (1986), 'Consequences of Reproductive Failure: Dependence, Mobility and Mortality among the Elderly of Rural South Asia', *Population Studies*, 40/3: 375–88.

Cebu Study Team (1991), 'Underlying and Proximate Determinants of Child Health: The Cebu Longitudinal Health and Nutrition Study', *American Journal of Epidemiology*, 133/2: 185–201.

—— (1992), 'A Child Health Production Function Estimated from Longitudinal Data', *Journal of Development Economies*, 38: 323–51.

Chambers, R. (ed.) (1989), *Vulnerability: How the Poor Cope*. Brighton: IDS Publications.

Cochrane, S., Kozel, V., and Alderman, H. (1990), 'Household Consequences of High Fertility in Pakistan', *World Bank Discussion Paper*. Washington: World Bank.

Curtis, S. L., Diamond, I., and McDonald, J. W. (1993), 'Birth Interval and Family Effects on Postneonatal Mortality in Brazil', *Demography*, 30/1: 33–44.

David, P. H. (1994), 'Pace of Childbearing and the Concentration of Risk', paper presented at the Annual Meeting of the Population Association of America, Miami.

DeGraff, D., Bilsborrow, R., and Herrin, A. (1993), 'The Implications of High Fertility for Children's Time Use in the Philippines', in C. Lloyd (ed.) (1993).

DeLancey, V. (1990), 'Socioeconomic Consequences of High Fertility for the Family', in Ascadi, G. Johnson-Ascadi and R. Bulatao (eds), *Population Growth and Reproduction in Sub-Saharan Africa: Technical Analyses of Fertility and its Consequences*. Washington, DC: World Bank.

Desai, S. (1993), 'The Impact of Family Size on Children's Nutritional Status: Insights from a Comparative Perspective', 155–92, in C. Lloyd (ed.) (1993).

Echeverria, *et al*, (1986), 'The Mother-Child Relationship in the Etiology of Severe Under-Nutrition', *Nutrition Reports International*, 33/3: 517–25.

Eloundou-Enyegue, P. (1994), 'Why Trade Quantity for Child Quality? A "Family Mobility" Thesis', *Population Research Institute Working Paper 94–15*, University Park, Pennsylvania State University.

Erickson, J. and Bjerkedal, T. (1978), 'Interpregnancy Interval: Association with Birth Weight, Stillbirth, and Neonatal Death', *Journal of Epidemics and Common Health*, 32: 124–30.

Evans, T. (1989), 'The Impact of Permanent Disability on Rural Households: River Blindness in Guinea', in R. Chambers (ed.) (1989).

Ferguson, A. (1978), 'Prolonged Impairment of Cellular Immunity in Children with Intrauterine Growth Retardation', *Journal of Pediatrics*, 93/1: 52–6.

Ferraz, E. M., Gray, R. H., Fleming, P. L., and Maia, T. M. (1988), 'Interpregnancy Interval and Low Birth Weight: Findings from a Case-Control Study', *American Journal of Epidemics*, 128/5: 1111–16.

Folbre, N. (1994), *Who Pays for the Kids? Gender and the Structures of Constraint*. London and New York: Routledge.

Gardiner, E. and Yerushalmy, J. (1939) 'Familial Susceptibility to Stillbirths and Neo-natal Deaths', *American Journal of Hygiene*, 30:11–31.

Geronimus, A. and Korenman, S. (1993), 'Maternal Youth or Family Background? On the Health Disadvantages of Infants with Teenage Mothers', *American Journal of Epidemics*, 137/2: 213–25.

Gomes, M. (1984), 'Family Size and Educational Attainment in Kenya', *Population and Development Review*, 10/4: 647–60.

Guilkey, D., Popkin, B., Akin J., and Wong, E. (1989), 'Prenatal Care and Pregnancy Outcome in Cebu, Philippines', *Journal of Development Economics*, 30: 241–72.

——, ——, ——, Rindfuss, R. R., and Paqueo, V. (1988), 'Child Spacing in the Philippines: The Effect of Current Characteristics and Rural Development', *Population Studies*, 42/2; 259–73.

Guo, G. (1993), 'Use of Sibling Data to Estimate Family Mortality Effects in Guatemala', *Demography*, 30/1: 15–32.

Haaga, J. (1989), 'Mechanisms for the Association of Maternal Age, Parity and Birth Spacing with Infant Health', in A. M. Parnell (ed.), *Contraceptive Use and Controlled Fertility: Health Issues for Women and Children*. Washington DC: National Academy Press.

Hobcraft, J. (1987), *Does Family Planning Save Lives?*, Technical background paper, International Conference on Better Health for Women and Children through Family Planning, The Population Council, Nairobi.

—— (1991), 'Child Spacing and Child Mortality', Proceedings of the Demographic and Health Surveys World Conference, 2, Columbia, MD: IRD/Macro International.

——, McDonald, J. W., and Rutstein, S. O. (1983), 'Child-spacing Effects on Infant and Early Child Mortality', *Population Index*, 49/4: 585–618.

House, J., Landis, K. R., and Umberson, D. (1988), 'Social Relationships and Health', *Science*, 241 /29 (July): 540–5.

—— and Mortimer, J. (1990), 'Social Structure and the Individual: Emerging Themes and New Directions', *Social Psychology Quarterly*, 53/2: 71–80.

Institute of Medicine (1992), *Nutrition Issues in Developing Countries*. Washington, DC: National Academy Press.

Jeejebhoy, S. (1993), 'Family Size, Outcomes for Children and Gender Disparities: The Case of Rural Maharashtra', in C. Lloyd, (ed.) (1993).

Johnson, D. G. and Lee R. D. (eds) (1987), *Population Growth and Economic Development: Issues and Evidence*. Madison: University of Wisconsin Press.

Joshi, H. (1990), 'The Cash Opportunity Costs of Childbearing: An Approach Using British Data', *Population Studies*, 44/1: 41–60.

King, E. M. (1987), 'The Effect of Family Size on Family Welfare: What Do We Know?', in D. G. Johnson and R. D. Lee (eds) (1987).

—— and Evenson, R. E.(1983), 'Time Allocation and Home Production in Philippine Rural Households', in M. L. Buvinic and W. P. McGreevey (eds) (1983).

Klebanoff, M. A. (1988), 'Short Interpregnancy Interval and the Risk Of Low Birthweight', *American Journal of Public Health*, 78/6: 667–70.

Knodel, J. and Hermalin, A. I. (1984), 'Effects of Birth Rank, Maternal Age, Birth Interval and Sibship Size on Infant and Child Mortality: Evidence from 18th and 19th Century Reproductive Histories', *American Journal of Public Health*, 74/10: 1098–106.

Koenig, M. A., Mozumder, A. K., Korshed, M., Cleland, J., Rahman, M., and Rahman, F. (1991), 'Birth Intervals, Prematurity, and Childhood Mortality: Further Evidence From Rural Bangladesh', unpublished manuscript.

Kramer, M. S. (1987), 'Intrauterine Growth Retardation and Gestational Duration Determinants', *Pediatrics*, 80/4: 502–11.

Levison, D. (1989), 'Family Composition and Child Labor: Survival Strategies of the Brazilian Poor', presented at the annual meeting of the Population Association of America, Baltimore, cited in Lloyd (1994).

Lloyd, C. (1993), *Fertility, Family Size and Structure: Consequences for Families and Children*. New York: The Population Council.

Lloyd, C. (1994), 'Investing in the Next Generation: The Implications of High Fertility at the Family Level', *Population Council Working Paper No. 63*. New York: The Population Council.

Lunn, P. G. (1985), 'Maternal Nutrition and Lactational Infertility: The Baby in the Driving Seat', J. Dobbing (ed.), *Maternal Nutrition and Lactational Infertility*, Nestlé Nutrition, 9: 41–64. New York: Vevey/Raven Press.

Lynch, K. A. and Greenhouse J. B. (1994), 'Risk Factors for Infant Mortality in Ninteenth-Century Sweden', *Population Studies*, 48/1: 117–35.

Magnus, B. B. (1986), 'Reply', *Early Human Development*, 13: 340–1.

Magaud and Henry (1968), 'Le Rang de Naissance dans les Phénomènes Démographiques', *Population*, 23: 879–920.

Mahmud, S. and MacIntosh, J. P. (1980), 'Returns to Scale to Family Size - Who Gains from High Fertility?', *Population Studies* 34/3: 500–6.

Maine, D. and MacNamara, R.(1985), *Birth spacing and Child Survival*. NY: Center for Population and Family Health, Columbia University.

Mason, K. O. and Palin, V. T. (1981), 'Female Employment and Fertility in Peninsular Malaysia: The Maternal Role Incompatibility Hypothesis Reconsidered', *Demography*, 18/4: 549–75.

Mavalankar, D. V., Gray, R. H., Tivedi, C. R., and Parikh V. C. (1994), 'Risk Factors for Small for Gestational Age Births in Ahmedabad, India', *Journal of Tropical Pediatrics*, 40: 285–90.

Merchant, K. and Martorell, R. (1989), 'Frequent Reproductive Cycling: Does it Lead to Nutritional Depletion of Mothers?', *Progress in Food and Nutrition*.

Miller, J. E. (1989a), 'Is the Relationship Between Birth Intervals and Perinatal Mortality Spurious? Evidence from Hungary and Sweden', *Population Studies*, 43/3: 479–96.

—— (1989b), 'Determinants of Intrauterine Growth Retardation: Evidence Against Maternal Depletion', *Journal of Biosocial Science*, 21: 235–43.

——, Trussell, J., Pebley, A., and Vaughan B. (1992), 'Birth Spacing and Child Mortality in Bangladesh and the Philippines', *Demography* 29/2: 305–18.

Moser, C. and Sollis, P. (1991), 'A Methodological Framework for Analysing the Social Costs Of Adjustment at the Micro-Level: The Case of Guayaquil, Ecuador', in S. Joekes and N Kabeer (eds), *Researching the Household: Methodological and Empirical Issues*. Brighton, UK: IDS Publications

Mueller, E. and Short, K. (1983), 'Effects of Income and Wealth on the Demand for Children', 590–42, R. Bulatao and R. Lee, (1983), *Determinants of Fertility in Developing Countries*, 1 and 2. New York: Academic Press.

Myntti, C. M. (1993), 'The Social Determinants of Child Morbidity and Mortality in Yemen: Insights from Social Science Theory', Paper presented at the IUSSP 22nd General Population Conference, Montreal, Canada, 24 August–1 September.

Nault, F., Desjardins, B., and Legaré, J. (1990), 'Effects of Reproductive Behaviour on Infant Mortality of French Canadians During the Seventeenth and Eighteenth Centuries', *Population Studies*, 44/2: 273–86.

Ounsted, M. (1986), 'Transmission Through the Female Line of Foetal Growth Constraint', *Early Human Development*, 13: 339–40.

Panter-Brick, C. (1993), 'Seasonality of Reproductive Function and Weight Loss in Rural Nepali Women', *Human Reproduction*, 8 /5: 684–90.

Popkin, B. M., Guilkey, D., Flieger, W., and Schwartz, J. B. (1993b), 'Survival in the Perinatal Period: A Prospective Analysis', *Journal of Biosocial Science*, 25: 359–70.

——, ——, ——, Guilkey, D., Akin, J., Adair, L., and Udry, J. R. (1993a), 'Nutrition, Lactation and Birth Spacing in Filipino Women', *Demography*, 30/3: 333–52.

Pryer J. (1989), 'When Breadwinners Fall Ill: Preliminary Findings From a Case Study in Bangladesh', in R. Chambers' (ed.), *Vulnerability: How the Poor Cope*. Brighton: IDS Publications.

—— (1993), 'Nutritionally Vulnerable Households in the Urban Slum Economy: A Case Study from Khulna, Banlgadesh', in *Urban Ecology and Health in the Third World*: 61–74. Cambridge: Cambridge Univ. Press,

Rahman, M. and Davanzo, J. (1993), 'Gender Preference and Birth Spacing in Matlab, Bangladesh', *Demography*, 30/3: 315–32.

Rainwater, L. (1960), *And the Poor Get Children*. Chicago: Quadrangle Books.

Read, J. S., Clemens, J. D., and Klebanoff, M. (1994), 'Moderate Low Birthweight and Infectious Disease Mortality During Infancy and Childhood', *American Journal of Epidemiology*, 140/8: 721–33.

Reves, R. (1985), 'Declining Fertility in England and Wales as a Major Cause of the Twentieth Century Decline in Mortality', *American Journal of Epidemiology*, 122/1: 112–25.

Rindfuss, R., Palmore, J., and Bumpass, L. (1989), 'Analyzing Birth Intervals: Implications for Demographic Theory and Data Collection', in M. Stycos (ed.) (1989), *Demography as an Interdiscipline*. New Brunswick, N J: Transaction Publishers.

Rodriguez, G., Hobcraft, J., McDonald, J., Menken, J., and Trussell, J. (1984), 'A Comparative Analysis of Determinants of Birth Intervals', *World Fertility Survey Comparative Studies*, No. 30. Voorburg, Netherlands: International Statistical Institute.

Rodgers, G. (1984), *Poverty and Population, Approaches and Evidence*. Geneva: International Labour Office.

Roman, E. (1984), 'Foetal Loss Rates and their Relation to Pregnancy Order', *Journal of Epidemic and Community Health*, March, 38/1: 29–35.

Santow, G. and Bracher, M. (1989), 'Do Gravidity and Age Affect Pregnancy Outcome? *Social Biology*, 36/1–2: 9–22.

Scheper-Hughes, N. (1987), 'Introduction: the Cultural Politics of Child Survival', in Scheper-Hughes (ed.), *Child Survival: Anthropological Perspectives on the Treatment and Maltreatment of Children*, 1–32. Dordrecht: D. Reidel Publishing Co.

Schultz, T. P. (1984), 'Studying the Impact of Household Economic and Community Variables on Child Mortality', in W. H. Mosley and L. C. Chen (eds), *Child Survival: Strategies for Research, Population and Development Review, Suppl.10*. New York: Population Council.

Scrimshaw, S. and Scrimshaw, M. (1990), 'Maternal Management Strategies on a Guatemalan Coastal Plantation: Differential Success in Maintaining Child Health', unpublished manuscript.

—— (1978), 'Infant Mortality and Behavior in the Regulation of Family Size', *Population and Development Review*, 4/3: 383–402.

Sen, A. (1995), 'Mortality as an Indicator of Economic Success and Failure', First Innocenti Lecture, UNICEF-IUSSP Conference on Demography and Poverty, Florence, 3 March.

Sommerfelt, A. E. and Stewart, M. K. (1994), Children's Nutritional Status', *DHS Comparative Studies 12*. Calverton, MD: Macro International Inc.

Syme, S. L. and Berkman, L. (1978), 'Social Class, Susceptiblity and Sickness', *American Journal of Epidemiology*, 104/7: 1–8.

Tekçe, B. (1990), 'Households, Resources and Child Health in a Self-Help Settlement in Cairo, Egypt', *Sociology, Science and Medicine*, 30/8: 929–40.

Trussell, J., Martin, L. G., Feldman, R., Palmore, J. A., Concepcion, M., and Dato' Abu Bakar, D. N. (1985), 'Determinants of Birth-Interval Length in the Philippines, Malaysia, and Indonesia: A Hazard-Model Analysis', *Demography*, 22/2: 145–68.

UNICEF (1992), *The State of the World's Children*. Oxford: Oxford University Press.

Victora, C. G., Smith, P. G., Vaughn, J. P., Nobre, J. C., and Lombardi, C. *et al* (1988), 'Influence of Birth Weight on Mortality from Infectious Diseases: A Case-Control Study', *Pediatrics*, 91: 807–11.

Williams, D. (1990), 'Socioeconomic Differentials in Health', *Social Psychology Quarterly*, 53/2: 81–99.

Winkvist, A., Rasmussen, K., and Habicht, J. P. (1992), 'A New Definition of Maternal Depletion Syndrome', *American Journal of Public Health*, 82/5: 691–93.

Winikoff, B. (1987), 'Technical Background Paper', International Conference on Better Health for Women and Children through Family Planning. Nairobi: The Population Council.

Wolfe, B. and Behrman, J. (1982), 'Determinants of Child Mortality, Health and Nutrition in a Developing Country', *Journal of Development Economics*, 11: 163–93.

World Bank (1990), *Poverty: World Development Report 1990*. New York: Oxford University Press.

—— (1993), *Investing in Health: World Development Report 1993*. New York: Oxford University Press.

Zenger, E. (1992), 'Infant Mortality, Birth Order and Sibship Size: The Role of Heterogenous

Risk and the Previous-Death Effect', *Office of Population Research Working Paper* 92–4, July, Princeton.

—— (1993), 'Siblings' Neonatal Mortality Risks and Birth Spacing in Bangladesh', *Demography*, 30/3: 477–88.

Chapter 8

AbouZahr, C. and Royston, E. (1991), *Maternal Mortality: A Global Fact Book*. Geneva: World Health Organization.

Abrahamse, A. F., Morrison, P.A., and Waite, L. J. (1988*), Beyond Stereotypes: Who Becomes a Single Teenage Mother?* Santa Monica: RAND Corporation.

Adedoyin, M. A. and Adetoro, O. O. (1989), 'Pregnancy and its Outcome Among Teenage Mothers in Ilorin, Nigeria', *East African Medical Journal*, 66: 448–52.

Adegbola, O. (1987), 'A Comparative Study of Mortality of Children of Formal and Informal Unions'. Paper presented at the IUSSP Seminar on Mortality and Society in Sub-Saharan Africa, 19–23 October 1987, Yaoundé, Cameroon.

Adewunmi, O. A. (1986), 'Maternal Mortality in Ibadan City', *West African Journal of Medicine*, 5: 121–27.

Agyei, W. K., Epema, E. J., and Lubega, M. (1992), 'Contraception and Prevalence of Sexually Transmitted Diseases among Adolescents and Young Adults in Uganda', *International Journal of Epidemiology*, 21: 981–98.

Ajayi, A. A., Marangu, L. T., Miller, J., and Paxman, J. M. (1991), 'Adolescent Sexuality and Fertility in Kenya: A Survey of Knowledge, Perceptions and Practices', *Studies in Family Planning*, 22: 205–16.

Akuffo, F. O. (1987), 'Teenage Pregnancies and School Dropouts: The Relevance of Family Life Education and Vocational Training to Girls' Employment Opportunities', in C. Oppong (ed.), *Sex Roles, Population and Development in West Africa*, 154–64. James Currey.

Armstrong, A. K. (1987), 'Access to Health Care and Family Planning in Swaziland: Law and Practice', *Studies in Family Planning*, 18: 371–82.

—— (1992a), 'Maintenance Payments for Child Support in Southern Africa: Using Law to Promote Family Planning', *Studies in Family Planning*, 23: 217–28.

—— (1992b), 'Struggling over Scarce Resources: Women and Maintenance in Southern Africa', Regional Report: Phase One. Harare: University of Zimbabwe Publications.

Barbosa, R. M. and Ariltio, M. (1993), 'The Brazilian Experience with Cytotec', *Studies in Family Planning*, 24: 236–40.

Barker, G., Knaul and Rich, S. (1992), 'Influences on Adolescent Sexuality in Nigeria and Kenya: Findings from Recent Focus Group Discussions', *Studies in Family Planning*, 23: 199–210.

Barreto, T., Campbell, O. M. R., Davies, L. J., Fauveau, V., Filippi, V. G. A., Graham, W. J., Mamdani, M., Rooney, C. I. F., and Toubia, N. F. (1992), 'Investigating Induced Abortion in Developing Countries: Methods and Problems', *Studies in Family Planning*, 23: 159–70.

Barron, S. L. (1986), 'Sexual Activity in Girls under 16 Years of Age', *British Journal of Obstetrics and Gynaecology*, 93: 787.

Becker, G., Landes, E., and Michael, R. (1977), 'An Economic Analysis of Marital Stability', *Journal of Political Economy*, 85: 1141–87.

Billy, J., Landale, N. S., and McLaughlin, S. D. (1986), 'The Effect of Marital Status at First Birth on Marital Dissolution among Adolescent Mothers', *Demography*, 23: 329–50.

Blanchet, T. (1988), 'Maternal Mortality in Bangladesh: Anthropological Assessment Report', unpublished report prepared for NORAD (WHE 2032).

Bledsoe, C. (1990), 'School Fees and the Marriage Process for Mende Girls in Sierra Leone', in P. Reeves Sanday and R. Gallagher Goodenough (eds), *Beyond the Second Sex: New Directions in the Anthropology of Gender,* 283–309. Philadelphia: University of Pennsylvania Press.

—— (1994), 'Children are Like Young Bamboo Trees': Potentiality and Reproduction in Sub-Saharan Africa', in K. Lindahl-Kiessling and H. Landberg (eds), *Population, Economic Development, and the Environment*, 105–38. Oxford: Oxford University Press.

—— and Isuigo-Abanihe, U. (1989), 'Strategies of Child-Fosterage among Mende Grannies in Sierra Leone', in R. J. Lesthaeghe (ed.), *Reproduction and Social Organization in Sub-Saharan Africa*, 442–74. Berkeley: University of California Press.

—— and Barney Cohen (eds) (1993), *Social Dynamics of Adolescent Fertility in Sub-Saharan Africa*. Washington, DC: National Academy Press

Boohene, E., Tsodzai, J., Hardee-Cleaveland, K., Weir, S., and Janowitz, B. (1991), 'Fertility and Contraceptive Use among Young Adults in Harare, Zimbabwe', *Studies in Family Planning*, 22: 264–71.

Brandon, A. J. (1990), 'Marriage Dissolution, Remarriage and Childbearing in West Africa: A Comparative Study of Côte d'Ivoire, Ghana and Nigeria'. Unpublished PhD Dissertation, University of Pennsylvania.

Brooks-Gunn, J., and Furstenberg Jr., F. F. (1986), 'The Children of Adolescent Mothers: Physical, Academic and Psychological Outcomes', *Developmental Review*, 6: 224–51.

Burton, L. M. (1990), 'Teenage Childbearing as an Alternative Life-Course Strategy in Multigeneration Black Families', *Human Nature*, 1: 123–43.

Caldwell, J. C., Caldwell, P., and Quiggin, P. (1989), 'The Social Context of AIDS in Sub-Saharan Africa', *Population and Development Review*, 15: 185–234.

Card, J. J., and Wise, L. L. (1981), 'Teenage Mothers and Teenage Fathers: The Impact of Early Childbearing on the Parents' Personal and Professional Lives', in Frank F. Furstenberg, Jr., Richard Lincoln, and Jane Menken (eds), *Teenage Sexuality, Pregnancy, and Childbearing*, 167–83. Philadelphia: University of Pennsylvania Press.

Carloni, A. S. (1981), 'Sex Disparities in the Distribution of Food Within Rural Households', *Food and Nutrition*, 7: 3–12.

Castle, M. A., Likwa, R., and Whittaker, M. (1990), 'Observations on Abortion in Zambia', *Studies in Family Planning*, 21: 231–35.

Costa, S. H. and Vessey, M. P. (1993), 'Misoprostol and Illegal Abortion in Rio de Janeiro, Brazil', *Lancet*, 341: 1258–61.

Craig, A. P. and Richter S. L. (1983), 'Unplanned Pregnancies Among Urban Zulu Schoolchildren: A Summary of the Salient Results from a Preliminary Investigation', *Journal of Social Psychology*, 121: 239–46.

David, H. P. (1992), 'Abortion in Europe 1920–91: A Public Health Perspective', *Studies in Family Planning*, 23: 1–22.

—— and Pick de Weiss, S. (1992), 'Abortion in the Americas', *Reproductive Health in the Americas*. Washington, DC: Pan American Health Organization.

Demographic and Health Surveys (1990), 'Adolescent Fertility in Sub-Saharan Africa'. Paper Presented at the International Forum on Adolescent Fertility, Washington, DC, 22–24 September.

Du Toit, B. M. (1987), 'Menarche and Sexuality Among a Sample of Black South African Schoolgirls', *Social Science and Medicine*, 24: 561–71.

Dynowski-Smith M. (1989), 'Profile of Youth in Botswana', Intersectoral Committee on Family Life Education, Gaborone, Botswana.

Dixon-Mueller, R. (1993), 'The Sexuality Connection in Reproductive Health', *Studies in Family Planning*, 24: 269–82.

Dryfoos, J. G. (1990), *Adolescents at Risk: Prevalence and Prevention*. New York: Oxford University Press.

Eshiwani, G. S. (1985), 'Women's Access to Higher Education in Kenya: A Study of Opportunities and Attainment in Science and Mathematics Education', *Journal of East African Resource Development*, 15: 91–110.

Ferguson, A., Gitonga, J., and Kabira, D. (1988), *Family Planning Needs in Colleges of Education: Report of a Study of 20 Colleges in Kenya*. Nairobi, Kenya: Ministry of Health, Division of Family Health.

Feyisitan, B., and Pebley, A. R. (1989), 'Premarital Sexuality in Urban Nigeria', *Studies in Family Planning*, 20: 343–54.

Fortes, M. (1959), *Oedipus and Job in West African Religion*. Cambridge: Cambridge University Press.

Friedman, H. L. (1989), 'The Health of Adolescents: Beliefs and Behaviour', *Social Science and Medicine*, 9: 309–15.

Furstenberg, F. F. (1990), 'Coming of Age in a Changing Family System', in S. Feldman, and G. R. Elliott (eds), *At the Threshold: The Developing Adolescent*, 147–70. Cambridge, Massachusetts, and London, England: Harvard University Press.

Furstenberg, Frank F., Jr. (1981), 'The Social Consequences of Teenage Parenthood', in F. F. Furstenberg, Jr., R. Lincoln, and J. Menken (eds), *Teenage Sexuality, Pregnancy, and Childbearing*, 184–210. Philadelphia: University of Pennsylvania Press.

—— and Brooks-Gunn, J. (1985), 'Causes, Consequences, and Remedies', in L. Aiken and D. Mechanic (eds), *Applications of Social Science to Clinical Medicine and Health Policy*. New Brunswick, New Jersey: Rutgers University Press.

——, ——, and Chase-Lansdale, J. (1989), 'Teenage Pregnancy and Childbearing', *American Psychologist*, 44: 313–20.

——, ——, and Hughes, M. E. (1992), 'The Next Generation: The Children of Teenage Mothers Grow Up', in Margaret K. Rosenheim, and Mark F. Testa (eds), *Early Parenthood and Coming of Age in the 1990s*, New Brunswick, New Jersey: Rutgers University Press,113–35.

——, ——, and Levine, J. A. (1990), 'The Children of Teenage Mothers: Patterns of Early Childbearing in Two Generations', *Family Planning Perspectives*, 22: 54–61.

Gage, A. J. (1993), 'The Formation and Stability of Informal Unions in Côte d'Ivoire', *Journal of Comparative Family Studies*, 24: 219–33.

—— and Bledsoe, C. (1994), 'The Effects of Education and Social Stratification On Marriage and the Transition to Parenthood in Freetown, Sierra Leone', in C. Bledsoe and G. Pison (eds), *Nuptiality in Sub-Saharan Africa: Contemporary Anthropological and Demographic Perspectives*. Oxford: Clarendon Press, 148–64.

—— and Meekers, D. (1994a), 'Sexual Activity Before Marriage in Sub-Saharan Africa', *Social Biology*, 41: 44–60.

——, Brandon, A. J., and Meekers, D. (1994b), 'The Social Supports for Unmarried Mothers'. Paper presented at the 1994 Annual Meeting of the Population Association of America, 5–7 May, Miami, Florida.

Gage, A. J., Brandon, A. J., and Meekers, D. (1993), 'Sex, Contraception and Childbearing Before Marriage in Sub-Saharan Africa', *International Family Planning Perspectives*, 19: 14–18, 33.

Garey, A. I. (1992), 'Residence and Support of Children in Botswana: Implications for Fertility', unpublished research proposal.

Geronimus, A. T. (1987), 'On Teenage Childbearing and Neonatal Mortality in the United States', *Population and Development Review*, 13: 245–79.

—— (1992), 'Teenage Childbearing and Social Disadvantage: Unprotected Discourse', *Family Relations*, 41: 244–48.

—— and Korenman, S. (1993), 'Maternal Youth or Family Background? On the Health Disadvantages of Infants with Teenage Mothers', *American Journal of Epidemiology*, 137: 213–25.

——, ——, and Hillemeier, M. M. (1994), 'Does Young Maternal Age Adversely Affect Child Development? Evidence from Cousin Comparisons in the United States', *Population and Development Review*, 20: 585–609.

Görgen, R., Maier, B., and Diesfeld, H. J. (1993), 'Problems Related To Schoolgirl Pregnancies in Burkina Faso', *Studies in Family Planning*, 24: 283–94.

Gould, J. B. and LeRoy, S. (1988), 'Socio-economic Status and Low Birth Weight: A Racial Comparison', *Pediatrics*, 82: 896–904.

Guèye, M. and van de Walle, E. (1988), 'Some Joint Determinants of Fertility and Infant and Child Mortality in Sub-Saharan Africa'. Paper presented at the IUSSP African Population Conference, Dakar, Senegal, 7–12 November.

Harrell-Bond, B. (1975), *Modern Marriages in Sierra Leone*. The Hague: Mouton Publishers.

Harrison, K. A. (1989) 'Obstetric Fistulae'. Unpublished paper prepared for a Technical Working Group. Geneva: WHO.

Hayes, Cheryl (ed.) (1987), *Risking the Future: Adolescent Sexuality, Pregnancy and Childbearing*, 1. Washington, DC: National Academy Press.

Hofferth, S. L. and Hayes, C. D. (eds) (1987), 'Risking the Future: Adolescent Sexuality, Pregnancy, and Childbearing', National Academy of Sciences. Washington, DC: National Academy Press.

Hoffman, S. D., Foster, E. M., and Furstenberg, Jr., Frank F. (1993), 'Reevaluating the Costs of Teenage Childbearing', *Demography*, 30: 1–13.

Hull, T. H., Sarwano, S. W., and Widyanatoro, N. (1993), 'Induced Abortion in Indonesia', *Studies in Family Planning*, 24: 241–51.

Huntington, D., Lettenmaier, C., and Obeng-Quaidoo, I. (1990), 'User's Perspective of Counseling Training in Ghana: the "Mystery Client" trial', *Studies in Family Planning*, 21: 171–77.

Jacobson, J. (1990), 'The Global Politics of Abortion', *World Watch Paper 97*, Washington, DC: World Watch Institute.

Jessor, R. and Jessor, S. (1977), *Problem Behaviour and Psychosocial Development: A Longitudinal Study of Youth*. New York: Academic Press.

Kane, T.T., De Buysscher, R., Taylor-Thomas, T., Smith, T., and Jeng, M. (1993), 'Sexual Activity, Family Life Education, and Contraceptive Practice among Young Adults in Banjul, The Gambia', *Studies in Family Planning*, 24: 50–61.

Karanja, W. (1987), ' "Outside Wives" and "Inside Wives" in Nigeria: A Study of Changing Perceptions of Marriage', in D. Parkin, and D. Nyamwaya (eds), *Transformations of African Marriage*, 247–61. Manchester, England: Manchester University Press for the International African Institute.

Keonig, M. A., Fauveau, V., Chowdhury, A. I., Chakraborty, J., and Khan, M. A. (1988), 'Maternal Mortality in Matlab, Bangladesh: 1976–85', *Studies in Family Planning*, 19: 69–80.

Kershaw, G. (1973), 'The Kikuyu of Central Kenya', in A. Molnos (ed.), *Cultural Source Material for Population Planning in East Africa*, 1. Nairobi: East African Publishing House.

Khasiani, S. (1985), A*dolescent Fertility in Kenya with Special Reference to High School Teenage Pregnancy and Childbearing*. Nairobi, Kenya: Population Studies and Research Institute, University of Nairobi.

Konje, J. C., Obisesan, K. A., and Ladipo, O. A. (1992), 'Health and Economic Consequences of Septic Induced Abortion', *International Journal of Gynecology and Obstetrics*, 37: 193–97.

Kwast, B. E., Rochat, R. W., and Kidane-Mariam, W. (1986), 'Maternal Mortality in Addis Ababa, Ethiopia', *Studies in Family Planning*, 17: 288–301.

Ladner, Joyce (1971), *Tomorrow's Tomorrow: The Black Woman*. New York: Doubleday.

LeGrand, T. K. and Mbacké, C. S. M. (1993), 'Teenage Pregnancy and Child Health in the Urban Sahel', *Studies in Family Planning*, 24: 137–49.

Lema, V. M. (1990), 'Sexual Behaviour, Contraceptive Practice and Knowledge of Reproductive Biology among Adolescent Secondary School Girls in Nairobi, Kenya', *East African Medical Journal*, 67: 86–94.

Lesthaeghe, R., Kaufmann, G., and Meekers, D. (1989), 'The Nuptiality Regimes in Sub-Saharan Africa', in R. J. Lesthaeghe (ed.), *Reproduction and Social Organization in Sub-Saharan Africa*, 238–337. Berkeley, California: University of California Press.

Lister, U. G. (1984), 'Vesico-Vaginal Fistulae', *Postgraduate Doctor*, October, 321–23.

Lovel, H. (1988), 'Wasted Pregnancies', *People*, 15.

Makinson, C. (1985), 'The Health Consequences of Teenage Fertility', *Family Planning Perspectives*, 17: 132–9.

Mafany, N. M., Mati, J. K., and Nasha, B. T. (1990), 'Knowledge of and Attitudes Towards Sexually Transmitted Diseases among Secondary School Students in Fako District Cameroon', *East African Medical Journal*, 67: 706–11.

Mahomed, K., Ismail, A., and Masona, D. (1989), 'The Young Pregnant Teenager—Why the Poor Outcome?', *Central African Journal of Medicine*, 35: 403–6.

Makinwa-Adebusoye, P. (1991), 'Pregnancy and Abortion Among Urban Youth in Nigeria', *Africa Population Studies*, 6: 40–57.

Manning, W. D. and Landale, N. S. (1994), *One Parent or Two? Entry into Premarital Motherhood among Cohabiting and Single Women*. Population Research Institute Working Paper Series, 94–10. The Pennsylvania State University.

Marsiglio, W. (1986), 'Teenage Fatherhood: High School Accreditation and Educational Attainment', in A. B. Elster, and M. E. Lamb (eds), *Adolescent Fatherhood*. New Jersey: Erlbaum, Hillsdale.

Martinez, G. and Krieger, F.W. (1984), 'Milk-Feeding Patterns in the United States', *Pediatrics*, 1985, 1004–8.

Meekers, D. (1994), 'The Implications of Premarital Childbearing for Infant Mortality: The Case of Côte d'Ivoire', in C.Bledsoe and G. Pison (eds), *Nuptiality in Sub-Saharan Africa: Contemporary Anthropological and Demographic Perspectives*, 296–312. Oxford: Clarendon Press.

Menken, J. (1981), 'The Health and Social Consequences of Teenage Childbearing', in F. F. Furstenberg, Jr., R. Lincoln, and J. Menken (eds), *Teenage Sexuality, Pregnancy, and Childbearing*. 167–83. Philadelphia: University of Pennsylvania Press.

Molokomme, A. (1990), 'Women's Law in Botswana: Law and Research Needs,' in Julie Stewart and Alice Armstrong (eds), *The Legal Situation of Women in Southern Africa*, 7–46. Harare: University of Zimbabwe Publications.

—— (1991), *Children of the Fence: The Maintenance of Extramarital Children Under Law and Practice in Botswana*. Research Reports 46, African Studies Centre, Leiden.

Moore, K. A. and Burt, M. R., (1982*), Private Crisis, Public Cost: Policy Perspectives on Teenage Childbearing*. Washington DC: Urban Institute.

—— and Snyder, N. O. (1991), 'Cognitive Attainment among Firstborn Children of Adolescent Mothers', *American Sociological Review*, 56: 612–24.

Morgan S. P. and Rindfuss, R. R. (1985), 'Marital Disruption: Structural and Temporal Dimensions', *American Journal of Sociology*, 90: 1055–77.

National Institute of Development, Research, and Documentation (1988), Report on Teenage Pregnancies in Botswana, Gaborone: University of Botswana.

Ngubane, H. (1977), *Body and Mind in Zulu Medicine: An Ethnography of Health and Disease in Nyuswa-Zulu Thought and Practice*. London: Academic Press.

Nichols, D., Woods, E. T., Gates, D. S., and Sherman, J. (1987), 'Sexual Behavior, Contraceptive Practice, and Reproductive Health among Liberian Adolescents', *Studies in Family Planning*, 18: 169–76.

Nortman, D. (1974*), Parental Age as a Factor in Pregnancy Outcome and Child Development*. Reports on Population/Family Planning, 16. New York: The Population Council.

Obbo, C. (1987), *African Women: Their Struggle for Economic Independence*. London: Zed Press.

O'Connel, R. M. and Rogers, C. (1984), 'Out of Wedlock Premarital Pregnancies and their Effect on Family Formation and Dissolution', *Family Planning Perspectives*, 16: 157–62.

Odujinrin, O. M. T. (1991), 'Sexual Activity, Contraceptive Practice and Abortion among Adolescents in Lagos, Nigeria', *International Journal of Gynaecology and Obstetrics*, 34: 361–66.

Okagbue, I. (1990), 'Pregnancy Termination and the Law in Nigeria', *Studies in Family Planning*, 21: 197–208.

Orubuloye, I. O., Caldwell, J. C., and Caldwell, P. (1992), 'Diffusion and Focus in Sexual Networking: Identifying Partners and Partners' Partners', *Studies in Family Planning*, 23: 343–51.

Paxman, J., Rizo, A., Brown, L., and Benson, J. (1993), 'The Clandestine Epidemic: The Practice of Unsafe Abortion in Latin America', *Studies in Family Planning*, 24: 205–26.

Pilon, M. (1994), 'Types of Marriage and Marital Stability: The Case of the Moba-Gurma of North Togo', in C.Bledsoe and G. Pison (eds), *Nuptiality in Sub-Saharan Africa: Contemporary Anthropological and Demographic Perspectives*, 130–47. Oxford: Clarendon Press.

Plotnick, R. D. (1992), 'The Effects of Attitudes on Teenage Premarital Pregnancy and its Resolution', *American Sociological Review*, 57: 800–11.

Prada, E., Singh, S., and Wulf, D. (1988), *Adolescentes de Hoy, Padres del Manana: Colombia*. New York: Alan Guttmacher Institute.

Rosenberg, M. (1990), 'The Self-concept: Social Product and Social Force', in M. Rosenberg and R. Turner (eds), *Social Psychology: Sociological Perspectives*. New Brunswick, New Jersey: Transaction Publishers.

Schapera, I. (1941), *Married Life in An African Tribe*. New York: Sheridan House.

Schoepf, Brooke Brundfest (1988), 'Women, AIDS, and Economic Crisis in Central Africa', *Canadian Journal of African Studies*, 22: 625–44.

Schonhofer, P. S. (1991), 'Misuse of Misoprostol as an Abortifacient May Induce Malformations', *Lancet*, 337: 1, 534–35.

Singh, S., and Wulf, D. (1990), *Today's Adolescents, Tomorrow's Parents: A Portrait of the Americas*. New York: The Alan Guttmacher Institute.

Soskolne, V., Aral, S. O., Magder, L. S., Reed, D. S., and Bowen, G. S. (1991), 'Condom Use with Regular and Casual Partners among Women Attending Family Planning Clinics', *Family Planning Perspectives*, 23: 222–25.

Stack, C. (1974), *All Our Kin*. New York: Harper and Row.

—— and Burton, L. M. (1993), 'Kinscripts', *Journal of Comparative Family Studies*, 24: 157–70.

Strobino, D. M. (1987), 'The Health and Medical Consequences of Adolescent Sexuality and Pregnancy: A Review of the Literature', in S. L. Hofferth and C. D. Hayes (eds), *Risking the Future: Adolescent Sexuality, Pregnancy, and Childbearing*, 93–122. Washington, DC: National Academy Press, National Academy of Sciences.

Sullivan, J. M., Rutstein, S. O., and Bicego, G. T. (1994), 'Infant and Child Mortality'. *Demographic and Health Surveys Comparative Studies 15*. Calverton, Maryland: Macro International, Inc.

Taffel, S. (1989), 'Trends in Low Birth Weight: United States 1975–85'. Vital and Health Statistics, 21/48, *DHHS Publication 89–1926*. Rockville, Maryland: National Center for Health Statistics.

Teachman, J. D. (1983), 'Early Marriage, Premarital Fertility and Marital Dissolution', *Journal of Family Issues*, 4: 105–26.

Tietze, C. and Henshaw, S. K. (1986) *Induced Abortion: A World View 1986, 6th Edition*. New York: The Alan Guttmacher Institute.

Ulin, P. R. (1992), 'African Women and AIDS: Negotiating Behavioral Change', *Social Science and Medicine*, 34: 63–73.

Uniugbe, J. A., Oronsaye, A. U., and Orhue, A. A. E. (1988), 'Abortion-Related Morbidity and Mortality in Benin City, Nigeria: 1973–1985', *International Journal of Gynecology and Obstetrics*, 26: 435–39.

United Nations (1989), *Adolescent Reproductive Behaviour*. Population Studies 109/1, ST/ESA/SER.A/109/ADD.1. New York: United Nations.

United States Bureau of the Census (1991), *Fertility of American Women: June 1990*. Current Population Reports P-20/436. Washington, DC: US Government Printing Office.

Van de Walle, E., and Meekers, D. (1994), 'Marriage Drinks and Kola Nuts', in C. Bledsoe and G. Pison (eds), *Nuptiality in Sub-Saharan Africa: Contemporary Anthropological and Demographic Perspectives*, 57–73. Oxford: Clarendon Press.

Ventura, S. J. (1984), 'Trends in Teenage Childbearing, United States 1970–1981', *Vital and Health Statistics*, 21/41, DHHS Publication (PHS) 84–1919. Rockville, Maryland: National Center for Health Statistics.

Vieira Matos, *et al.* (1985), 'Mortalidade Materna Hospitalar nas Unidades Mistas da Fundação SESP 1979–1981', *Revista da Fundação*, SESP, 30: 33–40.

Weissman, C., Plichta, S., Nathanson, C., Ensminger, M., and Courtland R. J. (1991), 'Consistency of Condom Use for Disease Prevention among Adolescent Users of Oral Contraceptives', *Family Planning Perspectives*, 23: 71–4.

World Health Organization (1977), *Health Needs of Adolescents: Report of a WHO Expert Committee*. Technical report 609. Geneva: World Health Organization.

Worth, D. (1989), 'Sexual Decision-Making and AIDS: Why Condom Promotion among Vulnerable Women is Likely to Fail', *Studies in Family Planning*, 20: 297–307.

Wu, L. L. and Martinson, B. C. (1993), 'Family Structure and the Risk of a Premarital Birth', *American Sociological Review*, 58: 210–32.

Zabin, L. S., Hirsch, M. B., and Emerson, M. R. (1989), 'When Urban Adolescents Choose Abortion: Effects on Education, Psychological Status and Subsequent Pregnancy', *Family Planning Perspectives*, 21: 258–65.

Chapter 9

Ainsworth, M. and Over A. M. (1994), 'The Economic Impact of AIDS on Africa', in M. Essex *et al.* (eds), *AIDS in Africa*. New York: Raven Press Ltd.

Anderson, D. (1994), 'Towards a More Effective Policy Response to AIDS', Liège, Belgium, International Union for the Scientific Study of Population.

Awusabo-Asare, K., Anarfi, J. K., and Agyeman, D. K. (1993), 'Women's Control Over Their Sexuality and the Spread of STDs and HIV/AIDS in Ghana', *Health Transition Review*, 3.

Banerjee, B. (1984), 'Rural to Urban Migration and Conjugal Separation: An Indian Case Study', *Economic Development and Cultural Change*, 32.

Barnett, T. and Blaikie P. (1990), *AIDS in Africa; Its present and future impact*. London: Guilford Press.

Basu, A. M., Basu, K., and Ray R. (1987), 'Migrants and the Native Bond: An Analysis of Microlevel Data from Delhi', *Economic and Political Weekly*, Annual Number, 22.

—— —— (1991), 'Women;s Economic Roles and Child Survival: The Case of India', *Health Transition Review*, 1.

——, D. B. Gupta and G. Krishna (1994), *The Household Impact of Adult Morbidity and Mortality*. New Delhi: Institute of Economic Growth.

Bloom, D. E. and Glied, S. (1993), 'Who is Bearing the Cost of the AIDS Epidemic in Asia?', in D. E. Bloom and J. V. Lyons (eds), *Economic Implications of AIDS in Asia*. New Delhi: United Nations Development Programme.

Carael, M. and Piot, P. (1992), 'The AIDS Epidemic in Sub-Saharan Africa', in E. van de Walle, G. Pison, and M. Sala-Diakanda (eds), *Mortality and Society in Sub-Saharan Africa*. Oxford: Clarendon Press.

Cleland, J. and Way, P. (1994), 'Introduction', *Health Transition Review*, 4.

Cohen, D. (1993), *Economic Impact of the HIV Epidemic*. New York: UNDP, HIV and Development Programme.

Connolly, M. and Franchet, C. N. (1993), 'Manila Street Children Face Many Risks', *Network*, 14.

Duggal, R. and Amin, S. (1989), 'Cost of Health Care; Survey of an Indian District', Bombay: Foundation for Research in Community Health.

Feachem, G. A. *et al.* (1991), *'The Health of Adults in the Developing World'*. Washington, DC: World Bank.

Ford, K., Fajans, P. and Wirawan, D.N. (1994), 'AIDS Risk Behaviours and Sexual Networks of Male and Female Sex Workers and Clients in Bali, Indonesia', *Health Transition Review*, 4.

Ford, N. and S. Koetsawang (1991), 'The Socio-Cultural Context of the Transmission of HIV in Thailand', *Social Science and Medicine*, 33.

George, A., Shah, I., and Nandraj, S. (1993), 'A Study of Household Health Expenditure in Madhya Pradesh'. Bombay: Foundation for Research in Community Health.

Gilks, C. F. (1993), 'The Clinical Challenge of the HIV Epidemic in the Developing World', *The Lancet*, 342.

Kapur, T. R. (1982), 'Patterns of Sexually Transmitted Diseases in India', *Indian Journal of Dermatology, Venerology and Leperology*, 53.

Koenig, M. A. *et al.* (1988), 'Maternal Mortality in Matlab, Bangladesh', *Studies in Family Planning*, 19.

Latham, M. C. (1993), 'AIDS in Africa: A Perspective on the Epidemic', *Africa Today*, 40.

McKenna, N. (1993), 'A Disaster Waiting to Happen', WorldAIDS, 27 May.

McNamara, R. (1993), *Female Genital Health and the Risk of HIV Transmission*. New York: UNDP, HIV and Development Programme.

Miguez-Burbaro, M. J. *et al.* (1993), 'Risk of HIV-1 Infection in Runaway Children in Columbia' (letter), *Lancet*, 342.

Nandraj, S. (1994), 'Beyond the Law and the Lord: Quality of Private Health Care', *Economic and Political Weekly*, 29.

National Academy of Sciences (1993), *Social Dynamics of Adolescent Fertility in Sub-Saharan Africa*. Washington, DC: National Academy Press.

Orubuloye, I. O., Caldwell, J. C., and Caldwell, P. (1993), 'African Women's Control Over their Sexuality in an Era of AIDS: A Study of the Yoruba in Nigeria', *Social Science and Medicine*, 37.

Podhisita, C. *et al.* (1994), 'Sociocultural Context of Commercial Sex Workers in Thailand: An Analysis of their Family, Employer and Client Relations', *Health Transition Review*, 4.

Pryer, J. (1989), 'When Breadwinners Fall Ill: Preliminary Findings from a Case Study in Bangladesh', *IDS Bulletin*, 20.

Ramasubban, R. (1991), 'Sexual Behaviour and the Conditions of Health Care: Potential Risks for HIV Transmission in India', in T. Dyson (ed.), *Sexual Behaviour and Networking: Anthropological and Sociocultural Studies on the Transmission of HIV*. Belgium: Ordina Press.

Reid. E. (1993), *Placing Women at the Centre of the Analysis*. New York: UNDP, HIV and Development Programme.

United Nations Development Programme (1992), *AIDS and Asia: A Development Crisis*. New Delhi: UNDP.

World Bank (1993), *World Development Report 1993*. Washington, DC: The World Bank

World Health Organization (1992), *Global Health Situation and Projections-Estimates*. Geneva: WHO.

Wyatt, H. V. (1984), 'The Popularity of Injections in the Third World: Origins and Consequences for Poliomyelitis', *Social Science and Medicine*, 19.

Chapter 10

Abella, M. (1994), 'International Labour Migration in the Middle East: Patterns and Implications on Sending Countries', in M. Macura and D. Coleman (eds), *International Migration: Regional Processes and Responses*. New York and Geneva: United Nations.

Adepoju, A. and Oppong, C. (eds) (1994), *Gender, Work and Population in Sub-Saharan Africa*. London: James Currey and Heinemann.

Altimir, O. (1994), 'Cambios de la Desigualdad y la Probreza en la América Latina', *El Tziminestre Económico*, LXI, 241.

Amjad, R. (ed.) (1989), *To the Gulf and Back. Studies of the Eonomic Impact of Asian Labour Migration*. New Delhi: ILO-ARTEP.

Anderson, B. (1993), *Britain's Secret Slaves. An Investigation Into the Plight of Overseas Workers*. London: Anti-Slavery International and Kalayaan.

Anker, R. (1994), 'Measuring Women's Participation in the African Labour Force', in A. Adepoju and C. Oppong (eds).

Arriagada, I. (1990), 'Unequal Participation by Women in the Working World'. *CEPAL Review*, 40.

ARTEP, (1991), *Statistical Report 1990. Asian Regional Programme on International Labour Migration*. Bangkok: ILO-ROAP.

—— (1987), *Impact of Out And Return Migration on Domestic Employment in Pakistan*. New Delhi: ILO-ARTEP.

Athukorola, P. (1993), *Enhancing Developmental Impact of Migrant Remittances: A Review of Asian Experiences*. New Delhi: ILO-ARTEP.

Benería, L. (1991), 'Structural Adjustment, the Labour Market, and the Household: The Case of Mexico', in G. Standing and V. Tokman (eds).

Bequele, A. and Boyden, J. (1988), 'Working Children: Current Trends and Policy Responses', *International Labour Review*, 127: 2.

—— —— (eds) (1988), *Combating Child Labour*. Geneva: ILO.

Berik, G. (1987), *Women Carpet Weavers in Rural Turkey: Patterns of Employment, Earnings and Status*. Geneva: ILO.

Bhatti, Z. (1980), *Economic Role and Status of Women. A Case Study of Women in the Beedi Industry in Allahabad*. World Employment Programme Working Papers, Geneva: ILO.

Bhöning, W. R. and Schloeter-Paredes, M. L. (eds) (1994), *Aid in Place of Migration*. Geneva: ILO.

Bonnet, M. (1993), 'Child Labour in Africa', *International Labour Review*, 132: 3.

Burra, N. (1989), *Child Labour in the Brass-Ware Industry of Moradabad, India*. New Delhi: ILO-ARTEP.

—— (1988), *The Informalisation of Employment: Child Labour in Urban Industries of India*, World Employment Programme Working Papers, Geneva: ILO.

Caldwell, J. C. and Caldwell, P. (1992), 'Family Systems: Their Viability and Vulnerability', in E. Berquo and P. Xenos (eds), *Family Systems and Cultural Change*. Oxford: Clarendon Press.

Chilivumbo, A. (1985), *Migration and Uneven Rural Development in Africa: The Case Of Zambia*. New York: Lanham.

Contreras, V. (1995), *América Latina: Indicadores Económicos, Laborales y Sociales*. Santiago: ILO-PREALC.

Date-Bah, E. (1986), 'Sex Segregation and Discrimination in Accra-Tema: Causes and Consequences', in R. Anker and C. Hein (eds), *Sex Inequalitities in Urban Employment in the Third World*. London: MacMillan.

Datta-Chaudhury, M. (1984), 'The Role of Free Trade Zones in Employment Creation and Industrial Growth in Malaysia', in E. Lee (ed.).

De la Luz Silva, M. (1981), 'Urban Poverty and Child Work: Elements for the Analysis of Child Work in Chile', in G. Rodgers and G. Standing (eds).

De Vletter, F. (1983), 'A Socio-Economic Profile of Rural Swazi Homesteads: A Summary Of Findings from the Swaziland Rural Homestead Survey', in F. De Vletter (ed.), *The Swazi Rural Homestead*. University of Swaziland.

De Vletter, F. *et al.* (1981), 'Labour Migration in Swaziland', in W.R. Böhning (ed.), *Black Migration to South Africa*. Geneva: ILO.

Dube, L. (1981), 'The Economic Role of Children in India: Methodological Issues', in G. Rodgers and G. Standing (eds).

ECLAC, (1992), *Major Changes and Crisis: The Impact on Women in the Latin America and the Caribbean*. Santiago: ECLAC-UN.

Farooq-i-Azam, (1987), *Re-Integration of Return Migrants in Asia: A Review and Proposals'*. New Delhi: ILO-ARTEP.

Figueiredo, J. B. and Shaheed, Z. (eds) (1995), *Reducing Poverty Through Labour Market Policies*. Geneva: IILS-ILO.

García Castro, M. (1987), *Mujeres Pobres Como Jefes de Hogar y Como Esposas en el Proceso de Reproducción en Bogotá: Identidad y Heterogeneidades*, World Employment Programme Working Papers. Geneva: ILO.

Go, S. (1995), 'Emigration Pressures and Export of Labour from the Philippines'. Paper presented at Migration and the labour market in Asia in the year 2000, Tokyo, 19-20 January 1995, Government of Japan, OECD, Japan Institute of Labour.

Goldschmidt-Clermont, L. (1987), *Economic Evaluations of Unpaid Household Work: Africa, Asia, Latin America and Oceania*. Geneva: ILO.

Gopinathan Nair, P. R. (1993), *International Labour Migration Statistics in India*. New Delhi: ILO-ARTEP.

Gordon, F. (1981), 'Easing the Plight of Migrant Workers' Families in Lesotho', in W.R. Böhning (ed.), *Black migration to South Africa*. Geneva: ILO.

Gordon Rapoport, S. *et al.* (1995), 'Economic Restructuring and Social Exclusion in Mexico', in G. Rodgers *et al.* (eds).

Gulati, L. (1993), *Women Migrant Workers in Asia: A Review*. New Delhi: ILO-ARTEP.

Gunn, S. E. and Ostos, Z. (1992), 'Le Multiple Dilemne du Travail des Enfants: le Cas des Petits Trieurs d'Ordures aux Philippines'. *International Labour Review*, 131: 6.

Gustafsson, B. and Makonnen, N. (1993), 'Poverty and Remittances in Lesotho'. *Journal of African Economies*, 2: 1.

Harper, C. (1992), 'La Fecundidad y la Participación Feminina en la Fuerza de Trabajo', in C. M. López *et al.* (eds), *Genero y Mercado de Trabajo in América Latina*. Santiago: ILO-PREALC.

House, W. J. (1989), 'Population, Poverty, and Underdevelopment in the Southern Sudan'. *Journal of Modern African Studies*, 27/2.

—— (1986), *Population, Poverty and Deprivation in Southern Sudan: A Review*, World Employment Programme Working Papers. Geneva: ILO.

Hugo, G. (1990), 'Recent International Migration Trends in Asia. Some Implications for Australia'. Paper presented to the 5th Conference of the Australian Population Association, Melbourne.

Hyun, Oh-Seok, (1989), 'The Impact of Overseas Migration on National Development: The Case of the Republic of Korea', in R. Amjad (ed.).

ILO, (1995a), 'Quand le Tissu Social se Déchire', *Travail*, 11 March.

—— (1995b), 'Home Work'. International Labour Conference, 82nd session, report 5(1), Geneva: ILO.

—— (1995c), *World Employment 1995. An ILO Report*. Geneva: ILO.

—— (1994), 'The Changing Role of Women in the Economy: Employment and Social Issues'. Second item on the agenda Committee on Employment and Social Policy, Governing Body, 261st Session. Geneva: ILO.

ILO and UN Center for Human Rights, (1992), *Children in Bondage. A Call for Action.* Geneva: ILO.

——, IOM, and UNHCR, (1994), 'Migrants, Refugees and International Cooperation. A Joint Contribution to the International Conference on Population and Development'. Geneva: ICPD (1994).

Isaac, T. M. T. (1992), *Economic Consequences of the Gulf Crisis: A Study of India with Special Reference to Kerala.* New Delhi: ILO-ARTEP.

Jamal, V. and Weeks, J. (1993), *Africa Misunderstood or What Happened to the Rural-Urban Gap'.* Basingstoke: Macmillan.

Kazi, S. (1989), 'Domestic Impact of Overseas Migration: Pakistan', in R. Amjad (ed.).

Lachaud, J.-P. (ed.), (1994), *Pauvreté et Marché du Travail Urbain an Afrique Subsaharienne* Analyse comparative. Geneva: IILS-ILO.

Lee, E. (ed.), (1984), *Export Processing Zones and Industrial Employment in Asia.* Bangkok: ILO-ARTEP.

Lim, L. L. (1994), 'International Labour Migration in Asia: Patterns, Implications and Policies', in M. Macura and D. Coleman (eds), *International Migration: Regional Processes and Responses.* New York and Geneva: United Nations.

—— (1993), 'Growing Economic Interdependence and its Implications for International Migration'. Paper presented at the ICPD Expert Group meeting on population distribution and migration, Santa Cruz, January 1993.

—— and Abella, M. (1994), 'The Movement of People in Asia: Internal, Intra-Regional and International Migration', *Asian and Pacific Migration Journal,* 3: 2-3.

López, C. M. and Pollack, M. (1992), 'La Incorporación de la Mujer en las Politicas de Desarrollo', in C.M. López *et al.* (eds), *Genero y mercado de trabajo in América latina.* Santiago: ILO-PREALC.

Louat, F. *et al.* (1993), *Welfare Implications of Female Headship in Jamaican Households.* LSMS Working Paper 96, Washington DC: World Bank.

Mahieu, F. R. (1995), 'Les Stratégies Individuelles face à la Pauvreté: Côte d'Ivoire Versus Burundi', in Ph. Hugon *et al. L'Afrique des Incertitudes.* Paris: IEDES-PUF.

Mahmud, W. (1989), 'The Impact of Overseas Labour Migration on the Bangladesh Economy', in R. Amjad (ed.).

Marguerat, Y. (1992), 'Histoire de la Marginalité Juvénile à Lomé', in *Les Jeunes en Afrique.* Paris: L'harmattan.

Marjuvia (collective), (1994), *A l'Écoute des Enfants de la Rue en Afrique Noire.* Fayard, Paris.

Martin, Ph. L. (1991), *The Unfinished Story: Turkish Labour Migration to Western Europe.* Geneva: ILO.

Mhone, G. (1995), *African Women Workers, Economic Reform, Globalization, AIDS and Civil Conflict.* Equality for Women in Employment working paper, Geneva: ILO.

Mies, M. (1986), *Indian Women in Subsistence and Agricultural Labour.* Geneva: ILO.

Murray, C. (1981), *Families Divided. The Impact of Migrant Labour Migration in Lesotho.* Cambridge: Cambridge University Press.

Myers, W. E. (1989), 'Urban Working Children: A Comparison from South America'. *International Labour Review,* 128: 3.

Oberai, A. S. (1987), 'Migration, Urbanization and Development'. Background papers for training in population, human resources and development, 5, ILO, Geneva.

—— and Singh, H. K. M. (1983), *Causes and Consequences of Internal Migration. A Study in the Indian Punjab.* New Delhi: Oxford University Press.

Oppong, C. (1995), 'A High Price to Pay for Education, Subsistence or a Place in the Job Market'. Paper presented at the John Caldwell seminar 'The Continuing Demographic Transition', Canberra.

—— (1992), 'Traditional Family Systems in Rural Settings in Africa', in E. Berquo and P. Xenos (eds) *Family Systems and Cultural Change*. Oxford: Clarendon Press.

Oppong, C. and Wéry, R. (1994), *Women, Population and Development in Sub-Saharan Africa*. Liège: IUSSP.

Palmer, I. (1991), *Gender and Population in the Adjustment of African Economies: Planning for Change*. Geneva: ILO.

Phongpaichit, P. (1982), *From Peasant Girls to Bangkok Masseuses*. Geneva: ILO.

Pollack, M. (1989), 'Poverty and the Labour Market in Costa-Rica', in G. Rodgers (ed.).

—— and Uthoff, A. (1989), 'Poverty and the Labour Market: Greater Santiago, 1969-85', in G. Rodgers (ed.).

PREALC (1991), *Insercion Laboral y Estratificacion Socio-Economica de la Mujer en el Area Andina*. PREALC Documentos de trabajo 358, Santiago: ILO-PREALC.

—— (1988), *Sobrevivir en la Calle. El Commercio Ambulante en Santiago*. Santiago: ILO-PREALC.

Requier-Desjardins, D. (1995), 'Impact des Instabilités et Gestion du Risque et de l'Incertitude Alimentaire en Afrique Sub-Saharienne', in Ph. Hugon *et al*. L'Afrique des Incertitudes. Paris: IEDES-PUF.

—— (1994), 'L'Économie des Organisations' et l'analyse du Comportement des Unités Domestiques Africaines', *Economie Appliquée*, 46: 4.

Rialp, V. (1993), *Children and Hazardous Work in the Philippines*. Geneva: ILO.

Roberts, B. (1991), 'The Changing Nature of Informal Exployment: The Case of Mexico', in G. Standing and V. Tokman (eds), *Towards Social Adjustment. Labour Market Issues in Structural Adjustment*. Geneva: ILO.

Rodgers, G. (1981), *Migration and Income Distribution*. World employment programme working papers, Geneva: ILO.

—— (1984), *Poverty and Population: Approaches and Evidence*. Geneva: ILO.

—— (ed.), (1989), *Urban Poverty and the Labour Market. Access to Jobs and Incomes in Asian and Latin American Cities*. Geneva: IILS-ILO.

—— (ed.), (1995), *The Poverty Agenda and the ILO. Issues for Research and Action*. Geneva: IILS-ILO.

—— and Standing, G. (eds), (1981), *Child Work, Poverty and Underdevelopment*. Geneva: ILO.

—— *et al*. (eds), (1995), *Social Exclusion: Rhetoric, Reality, Responses*. Geneva: IILS-ILO.

Rodrigo, C. and Jayatissa, R. A. (1988), *Maximising Benefits from Labour Migration: Sri Lanka*. New Delhi: ILO-ARTEP.

Rosenzweig, M. R. (1994), 'Transfers from Parents to their Adult Children in the Developed and the Developing Countries', in United Nations, *Ageing and the family*. New York.

Stalker, P. (1994), *The Work of Strangers: A Survey of International Labour Migration*. Geneva: ILO.

Standing, G. (1989), *Global Feminisation through Flexible Labour*, World Employment Programme Working Papers. Geneva: ILO.

—— (ed.), (1985), *Labour Circulation and the Labour Process*. London: Croom Helm.

—— (1984), *Population Mobility and Productive Relations. Demographic Links and Policy Evolution*, World Bank Staff Working Papers 695. Washington DC: World Bank.

Standing, H. (1987), 'Gender Relations and Social Transformation in Swaziland. Some

Comments on Future Research Possibilities', in M. Neocosmos (ed.) *Social Relations in Rural Swaziland. Critical Analyses*. University of Swaziland.

Stark, O. (1991), *The Migration of Labor*. Cambridge: Basil Blackwell.

Tan, E. (1987), *Migrants' Savings, Remittances and Labour Supply Behaviour: A Comparative Experience of Asian Countries*. New Delhi: ILO-ARTEP.

—— and Canlas, D. B. (1989), 'Migrant's Saving Remittance and Labour Supply Behaviour: The Philippines Case', in R. Amjad (ed.).

Tibaijuka, A. and Kaijage, F. (1995), 'Patterns and Processes of Social Exclusion in Tanzania', in G. Rodgers *et al.* (eds).

Timnou, J-P. (1993), 'Migration, Urbanisation et Développement au Cameroun', *Les Cahiers de l'IFORD*, 4, IFORD-CEPED.

United Nations, (1990), *Summary Report of the UN Expert Group Meeting on International Migration Policies and the Status of Female Migrants*, San Miniato, Department of International Economic and Social Affairs, ESA/P/WP.111, New York.

UNDP (various years), *Rapport sur le Développement Humain*. Economica, Paris.

Uthoff, A. (1990), 'Population and Development in the Central American Isthmus'. *CEPAL Review*, 40.

Vandemoortele, J. (1991), 'Labour Market Informalisation in Sub-Saharan Africa', in G. Standing and V. Tokman (eds), *Towards Social Adjustment: Labour Market Issues in Structural Adjustment*. Geneva: ILO.

Villareal, M. (1992), 'Sector Informal, Pobreza y Mujer. El caso de Bolivia', in M.C. López *et al.* (eds), *Genero y Mercado de Trabajo in América Latina*. Santiago: ILO-PREALC.

Wautelet, J.-M. (1995), 'Disparités Régionales et Différentiations des Paysanneries au Cameroun', *Revue Tiers-Monde*, 36, 141.

Weinert, P. (1991), *Foreign Female Domestic Workers: Help Wanted!*, World Employment Programme Working Papers. Geneva: ILO.

Wéry, R. (1987), 'Women in Bamako: Activities and Relations', in C. Oppong (ed.), *Sex Roles, Population and Development in West Africa*. London: JamesCurrey.

Wickramasekara, P. (ed.), (1993), *The Gulf Crisis and South Asia. Studies on the Economic Impact*. New Delhi: ILO-ARTEP.

Wolf, D. L. (1992), *Factory Daughters. Gender, Household Dynamics, and Rural Industrialization in Java*. Berkeley: University of California Press.

World Bank (various years), *World Development Report*. Oxford: Oxford University Press.

Young, K. (1982), 'Formas de Apropriación y la División Sexual del Trabajo: Un Estudio de Caso en Oaxaca, México', in M. León (ed.), *Las Trabajadoras del Agro*. Bogotá: ACEP.

Zuckerman, E. (1989), *Adjustment Programs and Social Welfare*, World Bank Discussion Papers. Washington DC: World Bank.

Chapter 11

Aina, T.A. (1989), *Health, Habitat and Underdevelopment-with Special Reference to a Low-Income Settlement in Metropolitan Lagos*, IIED Technical Report, London.

Aradeon, D., Aina, T. A., and Umo, J. (1986), 'South-West Nigeria', in J. E. Hardoy and D. Satterthwaite (eds), *Small and Intermediate Urban Centres: Their Role in Regional and National Development in the Third World*, Hodder and Stoughton (UK) and Westview (USA). 228–78.

Arrossi, S., Bombarolo, F., Hardoy, J. E., Mitlin, D., Coso, L. P., and Satterthwaite, D. (1994), *Funding Community Initiatives*. London: Earthscan Publications.

Askoy, M. *et al.* (1976), 'Types of leukaemia in a chronic benzene poisoning', *Acta Haematologica,* 55: 67–72.

Bairoch, P. (1988), *Cities and Economic Development: From the Dawn of History to the Present.* London: Mansell.

Bartone, C., Bernstein, J., Leitmann, J., and Eigen, J. (1994), *Towards Environmental Strategies for Cities; Policy Considerations for Urban Environmental Management in Developing Countries,* UNDP/UNCHS/World Bank Urban Management Program, 18, Washington DC: World Bank.

Beg, M., Ali, A., Mahmood, S. N., and Naeem, S. (1985) 'Environmental Problems of Pakistan (1): Composition of Solid Wastes of Karachi', *Pakistan Journal of Science, Industry and Resources,* 28/3 (June): 157–62.

Blacklock, D. B. and Evans, A. M. (1926), 'Breeding places of Anopheline mosquitoes in and around Freetown, Sierra Leone', *Annals of Tropical Medicine and Parasitology,* 20/59–86, quoted in Rossi-Espagnet, A., Goldstein, G. B., and Tabibzadeh, I. (1991), 'Urbanisation and Health in Developing Countries: A Challenge for Health for All', *World Health Statistical Quarterly,* 44/4: 186–244.

Bradley, D., Stephens, C., Cairncross, S., and Harpham, T. (1991), *A Review of Environmental Health Impacts in Developing Country Cities,* Urban Management Program Discussion Paper 6, Washington DC: World Bank, UNDP, and UNCHS (Habitat).

Briceno Leon, R. (1990), *La Casa Enferma: Sociologia de la Enfermedad de Chagas,* Capriles C.A. Caracas, Consorcio de Ediciones.

Briscoe, J. (1986), 'Selected primary health care revisited', in J. S. Tulchin (ed.), *Health, Habitat and Development.* Boulder: Lynne Reinner.

Cairncross, S. (1990), 'Water Supply and the Urban Poor', in J. E. Hardoy *et al.* (eds), *The Poor Die Young: Housing and Health in Third World Cities,* London: Earthscan Publications.

—— and Feachem, R. G. (1993), *Environmental Health Engineering in the Tropics: An Introductory Text.* Chichester: John Wiley and Sons (2nd edition).

Castonguay, G. (1992) 'Steeling Themselves with Knowledge', report on the work of Cristina Laurell, *IDRC Reports,* 20/1 (April): 10–12.

Cauthen, G. M., Pio, A., and ten Dam, H.G.(1988), *Annual Risk of Tuberculosis Infection.* Geneva: World Health Organization.

Centre for Science and Environment (1983), *The State of India's Environment: A Citizen's Report.* Delhi: Centre for Science and Development.

—— (1985), *The State of India's Environment: A Second Citizens' Report.* Delhi: Centre for Science and Development.

Chambers, R. (1989), 'Editorial Introduction: Vulnerability, Coping and Policy', in *Vulnerability: How the Poor Cope,* IDS Bulletin, 20/2 (April): 1–7.

—— (1994), 'Poverty and Livelihoods: Whose Reality Counts?', An overview paper prepared for the Stockholm Roundtable on Global Change, 22–24 July.

Chant, S. (1992), 'Conclusion: Towards a Framework for the Analysis of Gender-Selective Migration', in S. Chant (ed.), *Gender and Migration in Developing Countries.* London: Belhaven Press.

Cohen, L. and S. Swift (1993), 'A Public Health Approach to the Violence Epidemic in the United States', *Environment and Urbanization,* 5/2 (October): 50–66.

Cointreau, S. (1982), *Environmental Management of Urban Solid Waste in Developing Countries,* Urban Development Technical Paper 5, Washington DC: World Bank.

Coleman, A. (1990), *Utopia on Trial: Vision and Reality in Planned Housing*, London: Hilary Shipman Ltd.

Corbett, J. (1989), 'Poverty and Sickness: The High Costs of Ill-Health', in *Vulnerability: How the Poor Cope*, IDS Bulletin, 20/2 (April).

Douglass, M. (1992), 'The Political Economy of Urban Poverty and Environmental Management in Asia: Access, Empowerment and Community-based Alternatives', *Environment and Urbanization*, 4/2 (October): 9–32.

Duhl, Leonard J. (1990), *The Social Entrepreneurship of Change*, New York: Pace University Press.

Ekblad, S. (1993), 'Stressful Environments and their Effects on Quality of Life in Third World Cities', *Environment and Urbanization*, 5/2 (October): 125–34.

—— et al. (1991), *Stressors, Chinese City Dwellings and Quality of Life*. Stockholm: Swedish Council for Building Research.

Esrey, S. A. and Feachem, R. G.(1989), *Interventions for the Control of Diarrhoeal Disease: Promotion of Food Hygiene*, WHO/CDD/89.30, Geneva: World Health Organization.

Foster, S.O. (1990), 'Measles, the Ultimate Challenge in Urban Immunization', in *Universal Child Immunization-Reaching the Urban Poor*, Urban Examples 16, New York: UNICEF.

Fox, J. P., Hall, C. E., and Elveback, L. R. (1970), *Epidemiology, Man and Disease*, London: Macmillan.

Germain, A. and Ordway, J. (1989), *Population Control and Women's Health: Balancing the Scale,* International Women's Health Coalition in cooperation with the Overseas Development Council, New York.

Goldstein, G. (1990) 'Access to Life-saving Services in Urban Areas', in J. E. Hardoy *et al.* (eds), *The Poor Die Young: Housing and Health in Third World Cities.* London: Earthscan Publications, 213–27.

Gomes Pereira, M. (1989), 'Characteristics of Urban Mortality from Chagas' Disease in Brazil's Federal District', *Bulletin of the Pan American Health Organization,* 18/1.

Guimaraes, J. J. and Fischmann, A. (1985), 'Inequalities in 1980 Infant Mortality among Shantytown Residents and Non-shantytown Residents in the Municipality of Porto Alegre, Rio Grande do Sul, Brazil', *Bulletin of the Pan American Health Organization,*19: 235–51.

Hardoy, J. E. *et al.* (eds), (1990) *The Poor Die Young: Housing and Health in Third World Cities.* London: Earthscan Publications.

Hardoy, J. E., Mitlin, D., and Satterthwaite, D. (1992), *Environmental Problems in Third World Cities.* London: Earthscan Publications.

Harpham, T., Vaughan, P. and Lusty. T. (1988), *In the Shadow of the City: Community Health and the Urban Poor.* Oxford: Oxford University Press.

Hofmaier, V. A. (1991), *Efeitos de Poluicao do ar sobre a Funcao Pulmonar: un Estodo de Cohorte em criancas de Cubatao*, São Paulo School of Public Health.

Jacobs, J. (1965), *The Death and Life of Great American Cities*. London: Pelican.

Jacobi, P. R. (1994), 'Household and Environment in the City of Sao Paulo: Problems, Perceptions and Solutions, *Environment and Urbanization*, 6/1 (April).

Jarzebski, L. S. (1992), *Case Study of the Environmental Impact of the Non-ferrous Metals Industry in the Upper Silesian Area*, Paper prepared for the WHO Commission on Health and the Environment.

Kulaba, S. (1989), 'Local Government and the Management of Urban Services in Tanzania', in R. E Stren. and R. R. White (eds), *African Cities in Crisis*. USA: Westview Press, 203–45.

Lee Smith, D., Matundu, M. Lamba, D., and Gathuru, P. K. (1987), *Urban Food and Fuel Study*. Nairobi: Mazingira Institute.

Levy, C. (1992) 'Gender and the Environment: The Challenge of Cross-cutting Issues in Development Policy and Planning', *Environment and Urbanization*, 4/1 (April): 120–35.

Manciaux, M. and Romer, C. J. (1986), 'Accidents in Children, Adolescents and Young Adults: A Major Public Health Problem', *World Health Statistical Quarterly*, 39/3: 227–31.

Manciaux, M. (1988), 'Urban Slum and Squatter Settlements: Implications for Child Health', in *Child Abuse and Urban Slum Environments*, WHO/ISPCAN, Pre-Congress Workshop, WHO/MCH/86.15, Geneva: WHO, 20–30.

Matte, T. D., Figueroa, J. P., Ostrowski, S., Burr, G. *et al.* (1989), 'Lead Poisoning Among Household Members Exposed to Lead-acid Battery Repair Shops in Kingston, Jamaica (West Indies)', *International Journal of Epidemiology*, 18: 874–81.

McGranahan, G. (1991), *Environmental Problems and the Urban Household in Third World Countries*. Stockholm: Stockholm Environment Institute.

—— and Songsore, J. (1994), 'Wealth, Health and the Urban Household; Weighing Environmental Burdens in Accra, Jakarta and Sao Paulo', *Environment*, 36/6 (July/August): 4–11 and 40–45.

Misra, H. (1990), 'Housing and Health Problems in Three Squatter Settlements in Allahabad, India' in J. E. Hardoy *et al.* (eds), *The Poor Die Young: Housing and Health in Third World Cities*. London: Earthscan Publications.

Momin, M. A. (1992), 'Housing in Bangladesh', *The Bangladesh Observer*, February 12, quoted in ESCAP, *State of Urbanization in Asia and the Pacific 1993*, Economic and Social Commission for Asia and the Pacific, ST/ESCAP/1300, New York: United Nations.

Moser, C. O. N. (1987), 'Women, Human Settlements and Housing: A Conceptual Framework for Analysis and Policy-making', in C. O. N. Moser and L. Peake (eds), *Women, Housing and Human Settlements*, London and New York: Tavistock Publications.

—— (1993), *Gender Planning and Development; Theory, Practice and Training*. London and New York: Routledge.

Murphy, D. (1990), *A Decent Place to Live-Urban Poor in Asia*. Bangkok: Asian Coalition for Housing Rights.

Nath, K. J. *et al.* (1983) 'Urban Solid Waste: Appropriate Technology', Proceedings of the 9th Water and Waste Engineering for Developing Countries Conference, Loughborough University of Technology, England 1983, quoted in UNCHS (1988), *Refuse Collection Vehicles for Developing Countries*, HS/138/88E, Nairobi: UNCHS (Habitat).

Needleman, H. L., Schell, A., Bellinger, D. Leviton, A., and Allred, E. N. (1991), 'The Long-term Effects of Exposure to Low Doses of Lead in Childhood: An Eleven Year Follow-up Report', *New England Journal of Medicine*, 322/2 (January): 83–8.

Newman, P. W. G. and Kenworthy, J. R. (1989), *Cities and Automobile Dependence: An International Sourcebook*. Aldershot: Gower Technical.

Newman, O. (1972), *Defensible Space: Crime Prevention through Urban Design*. New York: Macmillan.

Ngom, T. (1989) 'Appropriate Standards for Infrastructure in Dakar', in, R. E. Stren and R. R. White (eds), *African Cities in Crisis*. USA: Westview Press, 176–202.

Pandey, M. R., Basnayat, B., and Neupane, R. P. (1989), 'Indoor Air Pollution in Developing Countries and Acute Respiratory Infection', *Lancet*, 1: 427–9.

Patel, S. (1990), 'Street Children, Hotels Boys and Children of Pavement Dwellers and Construction Workers in Bombay: How They Meet Their Daily Needs', *Environment and Urbanization*, 2/2 (October): 9–26.

Pepall, J. (1992), 'Occupational Poisoning', Report on the work of Mohamad M. Amr, in *IDRC Reports,* 20/1, Ottawa, 15.

Phantumvanit, D. and Liengcharernsit, W. (1989), 'Coming to Terms with Bangkok's Environmental Problems', *Environment and Urbanization,* 1/1 (April): 31–9.

Pio, A. (1986), 'Acute Respiratory Infections in Children in Developing Countries: An International Point of View', *Pediatric Infectious Disease Journal,* 5/2: 179–83.

Pryer, J. (1989), 'When Breadwinners Fall Ill: Preliminary Findings from a Case Study in Bangladesh', in *Vulnerability: How the Poor Cope,* IDS Bulletin, 20/2 (April): 58–62.

—— (1993), 'The Impact of Adult Ill-health on Household Income and Nutrition in Khulna, Bangladesh', *Environment and Urbanization,* 5/2 (October): 35–49.

Rabinouitch, J. (1992), 'Curitiba: Towards Sustainable Urban Development', *Environment and Urbanization,* 4/2: 62–73.

Rees, W. E. (1992) 'Ecological Footprints and Appropriated Carrying Capacity: What Urban Economics Leaves Out', *Environment and Urbanization,* 4/2 (October).

Robotham, D. (1994), 'Redefining Urban Health Policy: The Jamaica Case', Paper presented at the Urban Health Conference, London School of Hygiene and Tropical Medicine, 6–8 December.

Romieu, Isabelle *et al.* (1990), 'Urban Air Pollution in Latin America and the Caribbean: Health Perspectives', *World Health Statistics Quarterly,* 23/2: 153–67.

Rossi-Espagnet, A., Goldstein, G. B., and Tabibzadeh, I. (1991), 'Urbanization and Health in Developing Countries: A Challenge for Health for All', *World Health Statistical Quarterly,* 44/4: 186–244.

Rothenburg, S. J., Schnaas-Arrieta, L., Perez-Guerrero. I. A. *et al.* (1989), 'Evaluacion del Riesgo Potencial de la Exposition Perinatal al Plombo en el Valle de Mexico', *Perinatologia y Reproduccion Humana,* 3/1: 49–56.

RRA Notes (1989–95), Sustainable Agriculture Programme, London: IIED.

Sapir, D. (1990), *Infectious Disease Epidemics and Urbanization: A Critical Review of the Issues,* Paper prepared for the WHO Commission on Health and Environment, Division of Environmental Health, Geneva: WHO.

Satterthwaite, D. (1993), 'The Impact on Health of Urban Environments', *Environment and Urbanization,* 5/2 (October): 87–111.

—— (1994) 'Health and Environmental Problems in the Cities of Developing Countries', in United Nations, *Population Distribution and Migration,* Proceedings of the United Nations Expert Meeting on Population Distribution and Migration, Department of Economic and Social Information and Policy Analysis, ST/ESA/SER.R/133, New York: United Nations.

Satterthwaite, D. (1997), 'Environmental Transformations in Cities As They Get Larger, Wealthier and Better Managed', *The Geographical Journal,* 163/2,: 216–24.

Schofield, C. J., Briceno-Leon, R., Kolstrup, N., Webb, D. J. T., and White, G. B. (1990), 'The Role of House Design in Limiting Vector-borne Disease', in J. E. Hardoy *et al.* (eds), *The Poor Die Young: Housing and Health in Third World Cities.* London: Earthscan Publications, 189–212.

Sinnatamby, G. (1990) 'Low-cost Sanitation' in J. E. Hardoy *et al.* (eds), *The Poor Die Young: Housing and Health in Third World Cities.* London: Earthscan.

Smil, V. (1984), *The Bad Earth: Environmental Degradation in China.* New York: M. E. Sharpe and London: Zed Press.

Smit, J. and Nasr, J. (1992), 'Urban Agriculture for Sustainable Cities: Using Wastes and Idle Land and Water Bodies as Resources', *Environment and Urbanization,* 4/2 (October): 141–52.

Smit, J., Ratta, A. and Nasr, J. (1996), *Urban Agriculture: Food, Jobs and Sustainable Cities*, Publication Series for Habitat II, 1, New York: UNDP.

Songsore, J. and McGranahan, G. (1993), 'Environment, Wealth and Health: Towards an Analysis of Intra-urban Differentials Within Greater Accra Metropolitan Area, Ghana', *Environment und Urbanization*, 5/2 (October): 10–24.

Stephens, C. and Harpham. T. (1992), 'The Measurement of Health in Household Environmental Studies in Urban Areas of Developing Countries: Factors to be Considered in the Design of Surveys', Urban Health Programme, London School of Hygiene and Tropical Medicine, London

Surjadi, C. (1993), 'Respiratory Diseases of Mothers and Children and Environmental Factors among Households in Jakarta', *Environment and Urbanization*, 5/2 (October): 78–86.

Tiffen, M. and Mortimore, M. (1992) 'Environment, Population Growth and Productivity in Kenya: A Case Study of Machakos District', *Development Policy Review*, 10: 359–87.

Turner, J. F. C. (1976), *Housing By People-Towards Autonomy in Building Environments*, Ideas in Progress, London: Marion Boyars.

UNCHS (1988), *Refuse Collection Vehicles for Developing Countries*, HS/138/88E, Nairobi: UNCHS (Habitat).

UNEP (1991), *Environmental Data Report, 1991–2*, GEMS Monitoring and Assessment Research Centre, Blackwell, Oxford and Massachusetts.

—— and WHO (1987), *Global Pollution and Health* - results of health-related environmental monitoring, Global Environment Monitoring Service.

—— —— (1988), *Assessment of Urban Air Quality*, Global Environment Monitoring Service, United Nations Environment Programme and World Health Organization.

—— —— (1992) *Urban Air Pollution in Megacities of the World*, Published on behalf of the World Health Organization and the UN Environment Programme. Oxford: Blackwell.

UNICEF (1992), *Environment, Development and the Child*, Environment Section, Programme Division, New York.

USAID (1990), *Ranking Environmental Health Risks in Bangkok*, Office of Housing and Urban Programs, Washington DC.

White, R. R. (1993), *North, South and the Environmental Crisis*, Toronto: University Press.

WHO (1991), *Global Estimates for Health Situation Assessments and Projections 1990*, Division of Epidemiological Surveillance and Health Situation and Trend Analysis, World Health Organization, WHO/HST/90.2, Geneva.

—— (1992a), *Our Planet, Our Health*, WHO Commission on Health and Environment, World Health Organization, Geneva, April.

—— (1992b), *Reproductive Health: a Key to a Brighter Future*, WHO Special Programme of Research Development and Research Training in Human Reproduction, Geneva.

—— and UNICEF (1992) Water Supply and Sanitation Sector Monitoring Report 1990 (Baseline Year), WHO/UNICEF Joint Monitoring Programme, Geneva.

—— —— (1993), *Water Supply and Sanitation Sector Monitoring Report 1993*, Water Supply and Sanitation Collaborative Council, World Health Organization and UNICEF.

Wohl, Anthony S. (1983), *Endangered Lives: Public Health in Victorian Britain*. London: Methuen.

World Bank (1988), *World Development Report 1988*. Oxford: Oxford University Press.

—— (1992), *World Development Report 1992*. Oxford: Oxford University Press.

Chapter 12

Anda, R., Williamson, D., Jones, D., Macera, C., Eaker, E., Classman A., and Marks J. (1993), 'Depressed Effect, Hopelessness and the Risk of Ischemic Heart Disease in a Cohort of US Adults', *Epidemiology,* 4/4.

Avraamova, E. (1994), 'Social and Demographic Dimensions of the Economic Transition: Impact on Families with Children'; presented at the 'International Symposium on Social Policies during Economic Transition: Child Health, Basic Education and Social Protection', Beijing, 18–21 July 1994.

Beale and Nethercott (1985), 'Job Loss and Family Morbidity: A Study of a Factory Closure', *Journal of the Royal College of General Practioners,* 35: 510–14.

—— (1989), 'The Nature of Unemployment Morbidity', *Journal of the Royal College of General Practioners,* 38: 200–2.

Brenner, H. M. (1973), 'Foetal, Infant and Maternal Mortality during Periods of Economic Instability', *International Journal of Health Services,* 3, 2: 145-59.

—— (1987), 'Economic Instability, Unemployment Rates, Behavioural Risks and Mortality Rates in Scotland, 1952-1983', *International Journal of Health Services,* 17/3: 75–87.

Cardoso, E. (1992), 'Inflation and Poverty', Working Paper 4,006. Cambridge, MA: National Bureau of Economic Research.

Cornia, G. A. (1994), 'Poverty, Food Consumption and Nutrition during the Transition to the Market Economy in Eastern Europe', AEA Papers and Proceedings, 84/2 (May).

—— and Sandor, S. (eds) (1991), *Children and the Transition to the Market Economy: Safety Nets and Social Policies in Central and Eastern Europe.* Aldershot, UK: Avebury.

—— and Paniccia, R. (1995), 'The Demographic Impact of Sudden Impoverishment: Eastern Europe during 1989–94', Innocenti Occasional Papers, Economic Policy Series, 49 (July), Florence: UNICEF International Child Development Centre.

—— —— (1996), *The Transition's Population Crisis: An Econometric Investigation of Nuptiality, Fertility and Mortality in Severely Distressed Economies.* MOCT-MOST, 6, Kluwer Academic Publishers.

Council of Europe (1993), *Recent Demographic Developments in Europe and North America, 1992.* Strasburg: Council of Europe Press.

Davis, C. (1993a), 'The Health Sector in the Soviet and Russian Economies: From Reform to Fragmentation to Transition', US Congress (1993), *The Former Soviet Union in Transition,* 2: 852–73. Washington, DC: US Congress.

—— (1993b), 'Is Economic Transition a Prescription for Bad Health?: The Case of the Russian Federation'. Paper presented at a workshop at the Institute of Economics and Statistics, University of Oxford, 11, November 1993.

Eberstadt, N. (1990), 'Health and Mortality in Eastern Europe 1965–85', *Communist Economies,* 2/3.

—— (1994), 'A Demographic Crisis After Communism'. Mimeo.

Eyer, J. and Sterling, P. (1977), 'Stress-related Mortality and Social Organization', *The Reviezv of Radical Political Economics,* 9/1 (Spring).

Fajth, G. (1994), 'Family Support Policies in Transistional Economies: Challenges and Constraints', *Innocenti Occasional Papers,* Economic Policy Series, 43 (August). Florence: UNICEF International Child Development Centre.

Feshback, M. and Friendly Jr., A. (1992), *Ecocide in the USSR.* New York: Basic Books.

Francisco, G. D. (1987), 'Some Lessons from Mexico's Tax Reform', in David Newbery and

Nicholas Stern (eds) (1987), *The Theory of Taxation for Developing Countries:* 333–59. New York: Oxford University Press.

Greene, W. H. (1990), *Econometric Analysis.* New York: Macmillan.

Haub, C. (1994), 'Population Change in the Former Soviet Republics', *Population Bulletin,* 19/4 (December), Washington, DC: Population Reference Bureau, Inc.

Kamerman, S. B. and Khan, A. J. (1997), 'Investing in Children: Government Expenditures for Children and Their Families in Western Industrialized Countries', in G. A. Cornia and S. Danziger (1997), *Child Poverty and Deprivation in the Industrialized Countries, 1945-1995: Golden Age, Stagnation, Transition.*

Levi, L. (ed.) (1981), *Society, Stress and Disease.* New York: Oxford University Press.

Livi-Bacci, M. (1993), 'On the Human Costs of Collectivization in the Soviet Union', *Population and Development Review,* 19/4 (December).

Lumey, L. H., Ravelli, A. C., Wiessing, L. G., Kopper, J. G., Treffers, P. E., and Stein, Z. A. (1993), 'The Dutch Famine Birth Cohort Study: Design, Validation of Exposure and Selected Characteristics of Subjects after 42-year Follow-up', *Pediatric and Perinatal Epidemiology,* 7: 354–67.

—— and Van Poppel, F. W. A (1994), 'The Dutch Famine of 1944-45: Mortality and Morbidity in Past and Present Generations', *The Society for the Social History of Medicine,* 07/02: 229–46.

Mosley, W. H. and Chen, L. C. (1984), 'An Analytical Framework for the Study of Child Survival in Developing Countries', *Population and Development Review,* 10/25-45.

Nell, J. and Stewart, K. (1994), 'Death in Transition: The Rise in the Death Rate in Russia Since 1992'. *Innocenti Occasional Papers,* Economic Policy Series, 45 (December). Florence: UNICEF International Child Development Centre.

Smith, R. (1992), 'Without Work, All Life Goes Rotten', *British Medical Journal,* 305/24 (October): 972.

Tarschys, D. (1993), 'The Success of a Failure: Gorbachev's Alcohol Policy, 1985–88', *Europe-Asia Studies,* 45/1.

UN (1982), *Levels and Trends of Mortality since 1950.* New York: United Nations.

UNECE (1994), *Economic Bulletin for Europe,* 46. Geneva: UN Economic Commission for Europe.

UNICEF (1993), 'Public Policy and Social Conditions', *Economies in Transition Studies,* Regional Monitoring Report, I (November). Florence: UNICEF International Child Development Centre.

—— (1994), 'Crisis in Mortality, Health and Nutrition', *Economies in Transition Studies,* Regional Monitoring Report, 2 (August). Florence: UNICEF International Child Development Centre.

—— (1995), 'Poverty, Children and Policy: Responses for a Brighter Future', *Economies in Transition Studies,* Regional Monitoring Report, 3. Florence: UNICEF International Child Development Centre.

Whelan, C. T., Hannan, D. F., and Creighton, S. (1991), 'Unemployment, Poverty and Psychological Distress', *General Research Series Papers,* 150. Dublin: Economic and Social Research Institute.

WHO (1994), *Health for All Database.* Copenhagen: Regional Office for Europe, World Health Organization.

Zimakova, T. (1994), 'A Fragile Inheritance: Family Policy in a Changing Eastern Europe', *Research Report,* 94–311 (May). Ann Arbor, MI: Population Studies Centre, University of Michigan.

Index